LAWYERS, LITIGATION AND
ENGLISH SOCIETY SINCE 1450

Lawyers, Litigation and English Society Since 1450

Christopher W. Brooks

THE HAMBLEDON PRESS

LONDON AND RIO GRANDE

Published by The Hambledon Press 1998
102 Gloucester Avenue, London NW1 8HX (UK)
PO Box 162, Rio Grande, Ohio 45674 (USA)

ISBN 1 85285 156 2

A description of this book is available from
the British Library and from the Library of Congress

Typeset by Carnegie Publishing Ltd, Chatsworth Road, Lancaster

Printed on acid-free paper and bound in Great Britain by
Cambridge University Press

Contents

Figures

Preface

The essays gathered together in this book are best explained in terms of a personal course of study which began, in the early 1970s, with an interest in the role of lawyers and legal ideas in parliamentary debates during the early seventeenth century, the age of Sir Edward Coke. Only two of the essays here take up such questions in any detail. This is because I soon became convinced that the kind of understanding I wanted of the political history of the period could only be achieved by trying to gain a better appreciation of what social life, more broadly defined, was like. Since I was interested in the political ideas expressed by lawyers, an examination of lawyers and what lawyers did seemed a logical place to start. What began as a digression became an ongoing preoccupation.

Although the book is unorthodox in that it consists of a series of studies more or less evenly divided between work which has been published elsewhere and that which has not hitherto appeared in print, there is, I hope, an evident unity of themes and concerns. The idea of publishing in this form arose from a growing awareness that, as much by chance as by design, I had gradually accumulated material which constituted a version of the history of court usage and the legal profession from the later middle ages to the twentieth century, an account that, whatever its flaws, was not readily available elsewhere and which might, therefore, be useful to others.

I am grateful to Martin Sheppard, of the Hambledon Press, for undertaking publication; I have valued his editorial advice, his patience and the care he has taken in preparing the text for the press. The previously unpublished papers have been extensively revised, but nothing of substance has been altered in those which have appeared elsewhere.

Nearly three decades ago, Professor John Baker accurately described the post-medieval period as the 'Dark Age of English Legal History'. While much still remains to be done, a number of scholars have during the intervening years produced illuminating work on many aspects of the sixteenth, seventeenth, eighteenth and nineteenth centuries. My debt to the writings of others will be clear from the footnotes, but I also warmly thank those friends who have helped me more directly either by reading one or more chapters or by passing on references: Paul Brand, James Cockburn, Henry Horwitz, David Lemmings, Wilfrid Prest, Tim Stretton and David Sugarman. In addition, it is a pleasure to acknowledge the recent work of Bill Champion and Craig Muldrew: their own studies of early modern litigation have done a great deal to encourage me to persist with my own.

Closer to home, grants made from staff travel funds by the History Department and the University of Durham have enabled me to carry out research in London and in archives in other parts of the country. As always, I owe an immeasurable debt to Sharyn Brooks, both for her forbearance in putting up with my obsessions and for her help with many different aspects of the research and writing. Finally, I feel particularly lucky that, during the period in which much of the work was done, I was able to benefit from the advice and quiet encouragement of my friend, and former colleague, Michael Lobban. Although I wish the book itself was more worthy, I will always associate it with an enjoyable and fruitful collaboration during what was in most other respects a bleak epoch in British academic life.

Durham   Christopher Brooks

January 1998

Acknowledgements

1   This appears here for the first time.

2   Published originally in *Legal Records and the Historian*, ed. J.H. Baker (Royal Historical Society, London, 1978).

3   Reprinted with permission from *The First Modern Society: Essays in English History in Honour of Lawrence Stone*, eds A.L. Beier, David Cannadine and James M. Rosenheim (Cambridge University Press, Cambridge, 1989). The World Copyright is held by the Past and Present Society, 175 Banbury Road, Oxford, England.

4   This appears here for the first time.

5   This appears here for the first time in English.

6   This appears here for the first time.

7   This appears here for the first time.

8   First published in *The Roots of Liberty: Magna Carta, Ancient Constitution and the Anglo-American Tradition of Rule of Law*, ed. Ellis Sandoz (University of Missouri Press, Columbia, MO, 1993).

9   First published in *The Middling Sort of People: Culture, Society and Politics in England, 1550–1800*, eds Jonathan Barry and C.W. Brooks (Macmillan Press, Ltd., Basingstoke and St Martin's Press, New York, NY, 1994).

Abbreviations

Add.   Additional Manuscripts, Department of Manuscripts, British Library, London

BL   British Library, London, Department of Manuscripts

PRO   Public Record Office, London

Citations to printed law reports are made either to the original editions or to the works of named reporters reprinted in *The English Reports* (London, 1900–32), a multi-volume collection of the principal reports from the mid sixteenth to the nineteenth centuries.

1

Introduction

There are a number of ways to approach to the study of legal history. While one of the most familiar of these is of course the examination of the evolution of legal doctrine, that which is pursued in this book is by contrast based on an attempt to reconstruct the social history of lawyers; to look at the work they did in court for the people they served as clients; and to investigate the impact of legal culture on the more general social and political life of the country.

The first half of the book has grown out of the discovery of an unexpected solution to a methodological problem that arose during the early stages of research towards a mass-biographical account of the 'lower-branch' of the legal profession in the period 1550–1650.[1] As is well-known, since its earliest days in the thirteenth century, the English legal profession has been divided into two groups.[2] The first of these, 'the upper branch', was composed of serjeants at law and barristers, the lawyers who enjoyed a monopoly over advocacy in civil cases heard before the high courts in London. The second, the attorneys and solicitors (or 'lower branch'), were by contrast concerned primarily with organising cases, handling the procedural aspects of litigious work and providing other miscellaneous legal services such as conveyancing. The task of finding out who was qualified to act as an advocate in the early modern period is relatively easy because the call to the bar, or right of audience, was granted by one of the four inns of court in London, societies which kept registers of admissions.[3] The attorneys, on the other hand, present more difficult problems. Although many of them were members of legal inns, the records of the inns to which they belonged, the inns of chancery, have mostly been lost.[4] The key to identifying such practitioners therefore turned out to be two series of records kept by the major royal courts, King's Bench and Common Pleas: the docket rolls and the rolls of warrants of attorney. As it happens, since one function of the attorneys was

[1] Now published as C. W. Brooks, *Pettyfoggers and Vipers of the Commonwealth: The 'Lower Branch' of the Legal Profession in Early Modern England* (Cambridge, 1986).

[2] For the most recent authoritative account see P. Brand, *The Origins of the English Legal Profession* (Oxford, 1992).

[3] For an excellent study which makes use of such materials, see Wilfrid R. Prest, *The Rise of the Barristers: A Social History of the English Bar, 1590–1640* (Oxford, 1986).

[4] C. W. Brooks, The *Admissions Registers of Barnard's Inn, 1620–1869*, Selden Society supplementary series, 12 (London, 1995), pp. 1–2.

to act in the name of the people who employed them, these same records also provide information about the identity, social status and place of residence of the litigants, as well as a very brief indication of the nature of the case which had brought them into court.[5]

For a post-graduate student who grew up in the United States during the civil rights campaigns of the 1950s and 1960s, and who was working, in the early 1970s, at a time when scholars were beginning to investigate criminal legal records,[6] the idea of combining a study of the legal profession with an investigation of court usage appeared a potentially useful approach to take to the task of studying the relationship between law and society. While the technical pitfalls involved in using court records to trace patterns of litigation seemed formidable, the risky nature of what then seemed a novel historical approach was to a degree offset by the discovery that, since the early nineteenth century, parliament has been encouraging court officials to undertake precisely the same task.[7] Although the results may still seem problematical to some, the mere fact that they involve the interpretation of sources and quantification does not necessarily mean that they are any more (or less) open to question than more conventional legal historical analyses.

The earliest fruits of this approach, as Chapter 2 indicates, suggested two conclusions. The first was that during the second half of the sixteenth century there was an increase in the size of the legal profession that far outstripped increases in population, a result to some degree anticipated but none the less unexpected in its scale. The second, much more surprising, finding was that there was also a massive growth in the amount of litigation that came before the courts, the greater proportion of it consisting of actions of debt which were brought by people of ordinary, middling status. Although these observations pointed to several different lines of further inquiry, problems raised by some of the existing secondary literature indicated that it would be difficult to understand the Tudor and Stuart developments without looking back to the fifteenth century, when the volume of central court business was low.[8] A subsequent investigation of the late seventeenth and eighteenth centuries (Chapter 3) produced yet another surprise: a period which is noted for the consolidation of the state and for commercial, even industrial, expansion was evidently also one in which litigation in all the courts of the realm declined from a high point in the seventeenth century to reach a nadir in 1750.[9] Gradually, as the interpretative puzzles became more complex, and as students of the contemporary legal scene became increasingly interested in both 'hyperlexis' and the problem of access to the courts, it emerged that there was sufficient source material available for the

[5] See Chapter 2, pp. 9–10.
[6] For some of the relevant literature, see Chapter 7, pp. 179–80.
[7] See below, pp. 11, 28ff and 108.
[8] See Chapter 4, pp. 66.
[9] See Chapter 3, pp. 29ff.

study of civil litigation over very long periods of English history.[10] The potential advantage of such an approach was that a comparative treatment would add perspective to how we see the role of lawyers and the courts in the present as well as how we see them in the past.

Chapter 4 outlines a chronology of the changes in the relationship between the civil (as opposed to the criminal) law and society over the course of English history since 1200, one which may be of use to others either as a signpost or a target. It argues against any kind of linear, or progressive, evolution over time, showing that there have been ebbs and flows, changes as well as continuities in the nature of court usage over some eight centuries. Perhaps surprisingly, the continuities involve the composition of the litigants and the nature of their business. More predictably, the changes have been caused by the impact of demographic and economic trends, as well as alterations in the legal profession and in the relationships between jurisdictions. It suggests, for example, that the late fourteenth and early fifteenth centuries constituted a surprisingly important phase in the history of the profession, while arguing that the eighteenth century may have been one during which professional lawyers and courts, on the local as well as the national level, became to a degree disconnected from society. Nineteenth-century reforms, most notably the creation of new county courts, did little to remedy this. Access by ordinary people to justice has probably been more problematic in the twentieth century (despite the British experiment with state-funded legal aid) than it was at any time before 1700.

These observations are the starting points for the remainder of the book. Chapter 5 puts together insights from work on the legal professions of the sixteenth and seventeenth centuries, barristers as well as attorneys, with what has been learned more recently about their state in the eighteenth. The argument is that the decline in legal business from about 1700 onwards was accompanied by a decline in many of the institutional features, such as the legal inns, which had characterised the profession in the earlier period. Whether this might better be labelled a transformation than deprofessionalisation (as it is characterised here) is probably a matter for debate. The point is that the commonly held view that the eighteenth century was a time of advancement for lawyers is open to doubt. Contracting in size, the profession was not so popular as a career choice as it is often imagined to have been. Lawyers were probably less readily available in the provinces than they had been a century earlier, while eighteenth-century governments were in general more successful in finding new ways to tax legal practitioners

---

[10] 'Hyperlexis', or excessive litigiousness, is discussed in Marc Galanter, 'Reading the Landscape of Disputes: What We Know and Don't Know (and Think We Know) about our Allegedly Contentious and Litigious Society', *UCLA Law Review*, 31 (1983), pp. 6–11. While Galenter suggests that anxiety about excessive litigiousness is a new concern of the later twentieth century, the phenomenon was also much discussed in the late sixteenth and early seventeenth centuries. See below, pp. 13–14, 22–25 and 86–87.

than in guaranteeing the quality of their training. Chapter 5 suggests, for example, that attacks on the unreformed attorneys, which have dominated so much writing about them in the nineteenth and twentieth centuries, appear to have taken on their modern form for the first time in the 1790s.[11] They are reflections on the state of the profession as it was after 1750, not as it was before 1700.

Nevertheless, as Chapter 6 shows, during the eighteenth century, various forms of apprenticeship, including those inherited from the period before 1700, provided continuity in the ways in which lawyers were trained, and served as the basis for many of the reforms in legal education which took place in the nineteenth century, when the numbers of lawsuits and the numbers of lawyers began to grow once again. While campaigns to improve legal education in the late Georgian and early Victorian periods were not the dismal failures they have sometimes been portrayed as, the persistence of apprenticeship as the primary method of training for both branches of the profession did inhibit plans for the introduction of more academic methods and the creation of an effective professoriate. Based on the examples found in Germany and the United States, this more ambitious reform agenda was promoted by those who wanted to raise English law onto a more juris-prudential and intellectual plane, where it could be learned more effectively by students and more readily appreciated by the wider public. Whether their failure was due primarily to the strength of the vocational tradition, or merely a manifestation of what Donald Kelley has described as a more general displacement of legal science from the European intellectual firmament, is a question that requires further research.[12] Whatever the answer, legal culture was arguably less significant in eighteenth- and nineteenth-century England than it had been before 1700, when the intellectual life of the law was on firmer institutional foundations and legalistic approaches to political and social issues were not only common, but quite often paramount.

The general thrust of several of the chapters in this book is that there is a need for constant review and revaluation of our perception of the role of law in the present because this inevitably influences our view of the past. To make such a statement is of course merely to retail a variation on a commonplace of the historian's craft, but there are good grounds for pleading the particular case, especially since the state of legal history as a subject of study is one of the issues at stake. The teaching of English law and the teaching of history were introduced at the same time (and briefly in the same faculties) in the reformed Victorian universities, which of course already taught divinity.[13]

---

[11] See Chapter 5, pp. 136, 141.

[12] D. R. Kelley, *The Human Measure: Social Though in the Western Legal Tradition* (Cambridge, MA, 1990).

[13] R. N. Soffer, *Discipline and Power: The University, History and the Making of an English Elite, 1870–1930* (Stanford, CA, 1994), pp. 54–55, 64–67; J. P. Kenyon, *The History Men* (London, 1983).

The contribution to medieval history made by the turn-of-the-century gener-ation of legal historians led by F. W. Maitland is well known. In the mid and later twentieth century, in contrast, while that other 'pillar' of pre-modern English society, religion, has been widely and illuminatingly studied, legal history has been considerably less fashionable.

One reason for the more limited contribution of legal history to general history has undoubtedly been the preoccupation of university law depart-ments with purely vocational subjects. But the attitudes and assumptions of academic historians may also be significant. The lack of interest in legal institutions and ideas, which until recently seems to have characterised the approach of many early modern social historians, arguably owes much to the particularly twentieth-century sense of disjunction between law and society. At the same time, the inaccessibility of modern courts, and the view that law is nothing other than legislative fiat, fits well with another important concern of recent historiography, the distinction between elite and popular culture.[14] The result is that some of the most compelling accounts of early modern social history have been written without exploring the legal dimen-sion in detail, largely because it has been taken for granted that the law, especially the civil as opposed to the criminal law, was of little consequence for, or offered little in the way of agency to, the vast majority of the population.[15] In a book published as recently as 1996, one of the most important mid twentieth-century British historians of the seventeenth cen-tury, Christopher Hill, has restated the case for seeing English law merely as the tool of the ruling elite, a weapon useful only for the protection of property and the oppression by the gentry of the rest of the population.[16] Dr Hill's principal argument in support of this proposition is the observation that the 'law' was made in parliament, and enforced in the localities, by a social elite who were looking out primarily for themselves. While this view is certainly not to be dismissed lightly, he does not bother to complicate the issue by confronting any of the recent works which have argued that there was a surprisingly large degree of participation in early modern legal pro-cesses by social groups apart from the gentry. Since for Dr Hill the role of

[14] The seminal work on this subject was of course P. Burke, *Popular Culture in Early Modern Europe* (London, 1978). For thoughts on some of the problems involved, see G. Strauss, 'The Dilemma of Popular History', *Past and Present*, 132 (1991), pp. 130–49.

[15] See below, Chapter 7, pp. 189–90. For examples of newer work in which legal processes do figure significantly see P. Griffiths, A. Fox and S. Hindle, eds, *The Experience of Authority in Early Modern England* (London, 1996). In addition, it is notable that some of the most interesting work on law and agency has been done in connection with women. See, for example, Jenny Kermode and Garthine Walker, eds, *Women, Crime and the Courts in Early Modern England* (London 1994).

[16] C. Hill, *Liberty against the Law: Some Seventeenth-Century Controversies* (London, 1996). Revealingly, Hill (p. 338) is evidently uncomfortable with the more favourable picture of law as a cultural resource that is found in the final chapter of Edward Thompson, *Whigs and Hunters: The Origins of the Black Act* (London, 1975), a characterisation which I have always found particularly thought-provoking.

law is predetermined, legal history is evidently irrelevant to his study of social and political relationships.

By contrast, Chapter 7 in this book was written to make exactly the opposite case. Arguing that the modern concept of professionalisation has done much to distort our view of the past, it claims that law and legal discourse should be taken seriously precisely because they were accessible in the period before 1700 to a wide cross-section of the population. While attempting to suggest some lines for further research, it also indicates work which has already borne fruit. Others will have to judge (and investigate further) these alternative characterisations of the role of the law in the past, but the question at stake has much to do with how we characterise English society before 1700 at the most general level. Was the great mass of the population living in an illiterate, hierarchical, patriarchal and deferential society in which the only form of protest was to break the law? Or did they inhabit instead a litigious, even quarrelsome, world where self-interest had a good deal to do with the acceptance of political authority and where individuals knew something about what they were entitled to and how to go about getting it by utilising legal processes?

The final two chapters turn to detailed studies of the contribution of law and lawyers to political thought and action during the Tudor and early Stuart periods, a subject which has remained of perennial interest,[17] even though general historians have expressed doubts about the ultimate influence of ideas such as 'law and liberty' on political reality.[18] The immediate aim of Chapter 8, on the place of Magna Carta and the 'ancient constitution' in sixteenth century legal thought, was to investigate the Tudor characteristics of what Professor Pocock long ago dubbed the 'common law mind'.[19] While it suggests that values surrounding the idea of the rule of law were important, the overall thrust of the chapter is to cast English legal thought during this period more in terms of the jurisprudential values of European humanism than in terms of an insular historical view that sought the solution to current problems by reference to past precedents. Although the conclusion indicates some of the reasons why Sir Edward Coke's particular brand of ancient constitutionalism may have achieved a wider currency during the seventeenth century, the implications of the argument are that it is unlikely that 'the common law mind' can be properly understood without taking into account the influence of the complex tradition of European jurisprudence, or indeed that of the Protestant Reformation. At a more general level, the

[17] See for example, J. P. Sommerville, *Politics and Ideology in England, 1603–1640* (London, 1986); G. Burgess, *The Politics of the Ancient Constitution* (Basingstoke, 1992); Paul Christianson, *Discourse on History, Law, and Governance in the Public Career of John Selden, 1610–1635* (Toronto, 1996).

[18] The twentieth-century historiography is briefly and well summarised in D. Underdown, *A Freeborn People: Politics and the Nation in Seventeenth-Century England* (Oxford, 1996), pp. 1–4.

[19] For the historiography, see Chapter 8, pp. 199–200.

piece is part of an (as yet incomplete) inquiry into the evolution of English legal discourse over a long period from the early sixteenth century through to the end of the Civil War period, a study designed to trace changes and to seek out the ways in which legal ideas were expressed in different forums. If the chapter has any claim to a degree of methodological innovation it is that, rather than concentrating on parliamentary debates or state trials, it draws some of its principal source material from professional works, including lectures (or 'readings') given by lawyers within the legal inns, and speeches made to grand jurors and magistrates assembled at quarter sessions and assizes.

Just as historians of religion nowadays are interested in the content of sermons and the beliefs of parishioners, as well as formal theology, so too the student of legal thought needs to supplement an understanding of the content and genealogy of legal ideas with an investigation of how, and with what result, they were exchanged with the public. Working within the broad context of a general evaluation of the relationship between the three learned discourses — religion, medicine and law — and the middling sections of early modern society, Chapter 9 was written with this goal in mind. A consideration of the social origins of most early modern 'professional' men, as well as a look at the social composition of those who used their services, suggests that we should expect there to be a relationship between professional ideologies and the values of that 70 per cent of the population between the extremes of poverty, on the one hand, and great wealth on the other. Indeed, during much of the period, professional men evidently thought it so important to propagandise for their particular way of seeing the world that there is a good case for seeing this as amounting in effect to an educative process. It is also significant that the clergy and the lawyers competed with each other in expressing the unique, or paramount, importance of their own disciplines, while at the same time frequently borrowing ideas from one another. Like most other recent examinations of the subject, the essay sees the accession of Charles I in 1625 as a point of significant divergence between some brands of clerical political thought and that expressed by the lawyers,[20] but one of its broader implications is that it is probably dangerous to ignore the possibilities for the interaction between religion and law at any point in the sixteenth and seventeenth centuries.[21] Furthermore, there were amongst the lawyers, just as there were amongst the clergy, a number of different lines of thought about the power of princes and the place of 'the people' in the political processes of the day. As has often been pointed out, religion and law provided the terms of the debate during a period of unprecedented

[20] For example, Burgess, *Politics of the Ancient Constitution*.
[21] For a good illustration of this point compare Burgess, *Politics of the Ancient Constitution*, ch. 4, with Alan Cromartie, *Sir Matthew Hale, 1609–1676: Law, Religion and Natural Philosophy* (Cambridge, 1995)

national turmoil. It is ultimately not surprising therefore that law, like religion, became contested territory in the 1640s and 1650s.

Although legal thought certainly continued to figure significantly in the political life of the nation after the Restoration,[22] the logic of Chapters 2–6 is that, after 1700, the reach of the central courts never again penetrated so deeply into the localities, and legal culture rarely if ever again attained the same general importance. Like so much else in the following pages, this hypothesis will no doubt be greatly refined by further research.

---

[22] Starting points on this subject include J. G. A. Pocock, *Virtue, Commerce, and History: Essays on Political Thought and History, Chiefly in the Eighteenth Century* (Cambridge, 1985); David Lieberman, *The Province of Legislation Determined: Legal Theory in Eighteenth-Century Britain* (Cambridge, 1989); J. C. D. Clark, *The Language of Liberty, 1660–1832: Political Discourse and Social Dynamics in the Anglo-American World* (Cambridge, 1994).

2

Litigants and Attorneys in the King's Bench and Common Pleas, 1560–1640

The late sixteenth and early seventeenth centuries were a great age for lawyers. The most famous members of the profession, Egerton, Coke, Noy, Hakewell, Dodderidge, Whitelocke, played an active role in early Stuart political controversy.[1] King Charles I relied so heavily on the advice of his judiciary that the members of the Long Parliament were as anxious to impeach judges as they were Archbishop Laud. Yet, while we can appreciate the importance of these lawyer politicians, we know all too little about the structure of the legal profession, its aims, or the way in which the judicial system it operated touched on the lives of those who used it. In any society, the administration of justice is made up of so many different components – the litigants, the lawyers, the courts, the bureaucracy, procedural and substantive law – that it is difficult to say very much about any one part without looking at the others. None the less, in the history of English law during the sixteenth and seventeenth centuries, two particular features stand out. The first is that between 1560 and 1640 there was a great, and probably unprecedented, increase in the amount of litigation entertained by the two main common law courts at Westminster, the King's Bench and Common Pleas. The second is that the increase in litigation was accompanied by an increase in the number of lawyers. Both of these points have been recognised for a long time but, because the plea rolls are such intractable sources,[2] the exact dimensions of the increase – who the clients were, how many lawyers practised – have never been fully explored. The purpose of this chapter is to say something about the number of cases entering the two courts, about the social status of the litigants and, finally, about the lawyers (particularly the attorneys) who served them.

The study is based mainly on two sets of documents from the King's Bench and Common Pleas, the docket rolls and the rolls of warrants of

---

[1] Many of the issues first raised in this chapter are developed further in C. W. Brooks, *Pettyfoggers and Vipers of the Commonwealth: The 'Lower Branch of the Legal Profession in Early Modern England* (Cambridge, 1986)

[2] J. H. Baker, 'The Dark Age of Legal History', *Legal History Studies 1972: Papers Presented to the Legal History Conference at Aberystwyth, 18–21 July 1992*, ed. Dafydd Jenkins (Cardiff, 1975), p. 2, quotes Maitland's comment that the plea rolls are so unwieldy 'that we can hardly hope that much will ever be known about them'.

attorney. There is no good source from which the number of actions commenced in the two courts can be derived, but the docket rolls are a satisfactory source from which to discover the number of cases in advanced stages which were in progress during any particular year. Counts of docket roll entries have yielded statistics on the number of cases in the King's Bench and Common Pleas for the years 1560, 1580, 1606 and 1640.[3] At the same time, information about the social status and geographical origins of the litigants, along with the forms of action on which they were suing, has been collected from the rolls of warrants, which are found at the end of the plea rolls of each court. An analysis has been made of litigants in sample terms in 1560, 1606 and 1640.[4] It should be emphasised that both the docket rolls and the rolls of warrants are short cuts to the plea rolls, which are of course the only authoritative source.[5] Because they are short cuts, worries about their completeness and accuracy inevitably arise and should be kept in mind. But all major problems can be satisfactorily resolved, and on some crucial points – such as the identification of all litigants who claimed the social rank of gentleman or above – there is every reason to believe that the rolls of warrants are more accurate than most other early modern documents.

Studies by Drs Blatcher, Hastings and Ives show that at the end of the fifteenth century about 2000 cases in advanced stages were making their way through the King's Bench and Common Pleas each year.[6] Following

[3] The docket rolls used for the Common Pleas are PRO, IND 54–56, 157–65, 353–58; for the King's Bench, IND 1336, 1339, 1347, 1356, 1370. The docket rolls of both courts relate only to cases enrolled by the prothonotaries and therefore in advanced stages: either cases in which both parties were in court or in which the plaintiff was about to outlaw a defendant for failing to appear. They do not provide a guide to the actual number of suits commenced.

[4] The rolls of warrants used are in PRO, CP 40/1187, 1753, 2476; and KB 27/1194, 1395, 1649.

[5] The use of these documents has required a detailed study of their history, and the procedures which produced them. The most important point is that, since during this period each King's Bench case received only one entry in the plea rolls (and hence in the docket rolls), there is no chance that the numbers of cases have been inflated by counting the same case twice. However, Common Pleas docket rolls could contain more than one reference to the same case in any one year or term. Studies of sample case loads of various attorneys suggest that about 80 per cent of the total docket roll entries represent individual cases, so total counts of Common Pleas entries have been reduced by 20 per cent to allow for duplication.

[6] M. Blatcher, 'Touching the Writ of Latitat', *Elizabethan Government and Society*, ed. S. T. Bindoff et al. (London, 1961), p. 201 n. 1; E. W. Ives, 'Common Lawyers in Pre-Reformation England', *Transactions of the Royal Historical Society*, 5th series, 18 (1968), p. 167; M. Hastings, *The Court of Common Pleas in Fifteenth-Century England* (Ithaca, NY, 1947), p. 183. The work of Blatcher and Ives suggests that an average of about 400–500 cases a year in the King's Bench is likely for the early 1490s; these figures, which are based on the docket rolls, are comparable with mine. The Common Pleas presents difficulties, mainly because there are no docket rolls for that period. For Michaelmas 1483, Hastings counted 6000 plea-roll entries but, since about 5100 of these were related to mesne process, this figure is not comparable with the King's Bench

this period came a decline in the fortunes of the common law, which Dr Ives associates with the transfer of property litigation to Chancery. By the opening years of the reign of Elizabeth I, however, the King's Bench had recovered its position, with 914 suits in 1560. Because there is no complete series of docket rolls for the Common Pleas before 1580, exact estimates of its business in 1560 are difficult, though it is probable that the court had surpassed its late fifteenth-century volume of about 1500 suits each year. From 1560 litigation in both courts clearly began to soar. By 1580 King's Bench litigation had increased by four times to just over 4000 suits a year. The 9300 cases in the Common Pleas at the same date represent an equally remarkable increase. Taken together, the two courts were hearing about six times more cases than they had been at the end of the fifteenth century. The increase continued, though at a slower pace, between 1580 and 1606. Business in the Common Pleas doubled; that of the King's Bench went up by more than 50 per cent. From 1606 there was a steady but much less rapid growth, so that by 1640 a total of just over 29,000 cases were making their way through the courts: 8500 in the King's Bench and 20,625 in the Common Pleas. By 1640 there was three times more litigation than in 1580, perhaps fifteen times more than there had been in the 1490s.

Figure 2.1

Cases in Advanced Stages in the King's Bench and Common Pleas,
1490–1640[a]

	1490	*1560*	*1580*	*1606*	*1640*
King's Bench	500	914	4000	6945	8537
Common Pleas	1600	[not known]	9300	15,508	20,625
Total	2100		13,300	23,453	29,162

[a] See also C. W. Brooks, *Pettyfoggers and Vipers of the Commonwealth: The 'Lower Branch' of the Legal Profession in Early Modern England* (Cambridge, 1986), p. 51.

These estimates of the volume of early modern litigation can be compared with those for England just before the great law reforms, when figures were compiled by the Parliamentary Committee on Courts of Justice and reported in 1829. According to this source, between 1823 and 1827 an average of 72,224 actions were commenced in the King's Bench and Common Pleas during each year.[7] In 1606 the same two courts were handling a combined

figures; if we multiply the remaining 900 entries by twenty and divide by eight (the ratio of return-days in Michaelmas term to the total number in the year: D. Sutherland, *The Assize of Novel Disseisin* (Oxford, 1973), p. 178) we obtain a total of 2100 cases a year in advanced stages; if we then make the same 20 per cent allowance for duplication as for the Common Pleas figures, a total estimate of 1680 emerges.

[7] *Parliamentary Papers, 1829*, v, *First Report of His Majesty's Commissioners [on the] Common Law* (London, 1829), p. 11.

total of about 23,500 cases at stages in which both parties had come into court or in which the plaintiff was about to outlaw the defendant for failing to appear. Thus, if a threefold increase in population between 1606 and the 1820s is allowed for, the raw statistics suggest that the rate of litigation was about the same during the two periods.

Suits commenced and suits in advanced stages are not comparable. In any age many more suits are commenced than reach the stage at which both parties are about to appear in court. For example, figures compiled by a contemporary about the numbers of original writs sued out in Chancery between 1569 and 1584 suggest that up to twice as many suits may have been commenced as reached advanced stages in the Common Pleas.[8] This information implies that there was in fact more litigation per head of population under Elizabeth I and the early Stuarts than there was in the early nineteenth century, and this conclusion is supported by what is known about the volume of litigation in other courts. Perhaps surprisingly, the number of suits commenced in Chancery was much the same during the two periods. It averaged about 1000 in the late sixteenth century and 1500 in the ten years from 1800 to 1809.[9] On the other hand, common law actions started in the Exchequer between 1823 and 1827 averaged about 7400 a year,[10] probably considerably more than were entertained by that court in the early seventeenth century. Against this must be set the existence, as a thriving early-modern jurisdiction, of the Star Chamber (abolished in 1641) and the fact that in this period justice was less confined to the central courts than it was during the reign of George IV. In the late sixteenth and early seventeenth centuries town courts, and even manorial courts, were still active, whereas they had fallen into disuse by the beginning of the nineteenth century It is therefore very likely that the late sixteenth and early seventeenth centuries were the most litigious periods in English history. If England in the mid twentieth century seems less litigious, it is (at least, according to Abel-Smith and Stevens) not because there are fewer disputes to settle but because arbitration boards and special tribunals have provided a way to take them out of court. This has meant a corresponding decline in the general influence of lawyers in political life and social planning.[11]

Comparisons with distant future ages would have meant little to Elizabethan Englishmen, however, because for them the most striking feature of the administration of justice was the rapidity with which the number of lawsuits increased between 1560 and 1640. During the reign of Henry VIII, common

---

[8] 'Mr Jones Plan to Farm the Seals for Original Writs', BL, MS Lansdowne 47, fol. 122.

[9] For the late Elizabethan estimate, see W. J. Jones, *The Elizabethan Court of Chancery* (Oxford, 1967), p. 304 n. 1. Early nineteenth-century figures for bills in Chancery are given in *Parliamentary Papers 1811: Report from the Committee Appointed to Enquire into the Causes that Retard the Decisions of Suits in the High Court of Chancery* (London, 1811), p. 956.

[10] *First Report on the Common Law*, p. 11.

[11] B. Abel-Smith and R. Stevens, *Lawyers and the Courts* (London, 1967), pp. 1–2.

lawyers had been worried that empty courts would put them out of business.[12] From the reign of Elizabeth I the concern was rather that there were too many suits. No one welcomed this new 'multiplicity of suits', and explanations of it, along with proposals for remedies, began to proliferate. With a few not entirely insignificant exceptions, the reforms on which everyone agreed in principle failed to amount to anything. But contemporary analyses of the causes of the increase were realistic and can help us to understand something about how laymen and lawyers conceived the relationship between law and society. Some explained the increase in litigation in terms of failings within the law itself, in particular its uncertainty.[13] Others talked about changes in society or about failings in human nature.[14] In the late sixteenth century, criticisms of the obscurity and inadequacy of the common law seem to have had their widest currency – it is in this context that Francis Bacon's celebrated proposals for reform and even codification should be seen. His ideas were not exceptional, but only the clearest expression of the flexible outlook of Elizabethan lawyers.[15] With the reign of James I, however, the use of precedents and legal arguments in constitutional disputes brought more partisan defences of the common law. In a political atmosphere where law was looked to as a constitutional guide, the notion that it was uncertain about men's property could not be entertained.[16] As Elizabethan reliance on reason and natural law gave way to the more certain – but in the long run more inhibiting – historical myths of Sir Edward Coke, sociological interpretations of the increase in litigation became more popular.

In terms of general explanations of the sudden increase in common law litigation, it is difficult to add to the views of Egerton, Bacon, Davies and Coke. What we can do is follow the leads they give us. There is, for example, evidence that some aspects of the substantive law were as uncertain as contemporaries claimed. The rules about important concepts such as the equity of redemption or perpetuities were undergoing change throughout the period. But knowledge of substantive law during this period is all too limited, so we must leave this aspect of the problem to those better able to deal with it.[17]

---

[12] F. W. Maitland, *English Law and the Renaissance* (Cambridge, 1901), pp. 22, 82–83.

[13] There are many examples. The Lansdowne MSS in the BL contain a number of projects for law reform. PRO, SP 12/107/95 is a draft parliamentary bill (dated 1576) proposing a code of law and decentralisation of justice. For more see C. Brooks and K. Sharpe, 'Debate: History, English Law and the Renaissance', *Past and Present*, 72 (1976), p. 135.

[14] These are usually the products of the early seventeenth century. See the works of Coke and Davies, cited below.

[15] Brooks and Sharpe, 'History, English Law and the Renaissance', pp. 134–35. Bacon's scheme to reform the statutes was supported by some of the most important lawyers of the day: William Hakewell, Thomas Hedley, Henry Hobart, Henry Finch, William Noy and James Whitelocke.

[16] Ibid., p. 141.

[17] See Baker, 'The Dark Age of Legal History', p. 2.

The idea that the influx of litigation was caused by social change has found wide acceptance among social historians in the twentieth century. In the seventeenth century, two very concise statements of this point of view came from Sir John Davies and Sir Edward Coke. Davies claimed that there were more suits, not because the law was imperfect, but because, 'the commodities of the earth being more improved, there is more wealth and consequently there are more contracts real and personal in the world, which breedeth unthrifts, banckruptes, and bad debtors, more covetousness, and more malice ...'[18] To this Coke added that the general causes of litigation were the advent of peace and plenty, and the dissolution of the monasteries into many hands.[19] With these views in mind we can now turn to the people who were bringing this vastly increased volume of litigation into the King's Bench and Common Pleas.

The social composition of litigants changed relatively little between 1560, the starting-point of the influx of suits, and 1640. Throughout the period, men styled either 'gentleman' or above made up about 30 per cent of all Common Pleas and 20 per cent of all King's Bench litigants. Therefore between 70 and 80 per cent (a considerable majority) of those who utilised these courts were not members of what, for the sake of convenience, is generally called the landed gentry. The non-gentry litigants included in roughly equal proportions men who owned land and those who did not. One-third of all Common Pleas cases arose from the yeomanry, while in the King's Bench these small landowners accounted for about 15 or 20 per cent of all litigants. But another 25 per cent of the litigants in the Common Pleas, and 35 to 40 per cent of those in the King's Bench, were from the commercial and other classes who either owned no land or for whom it did not serve as a principal source of income. This group of litigants represents a wide range of wealth and occupations. Most were merchants, provincial tailors, grocers, chapmen, bakers or innkeepers; but carpenters, bricklayers, miners and labourers, as well as a few university dons, are also included. The remainder of the litigants in both courts (about 10 per cent) were lawyers (mainly attorneys), clergymen and widows who were involved in suits relating to the estates of deceased husbands.[20]

The distribution of litigation in the Common Pleas, and to a lesser extent in the King's Bench, appears to reflect fairly accurately the distribution of wealth in the nation as a whole. It has been estimated that the gentry classes probably owned about 30 per cent of the national wealth; as we have seen,

---

[18] J. Davies, 'A Discourse of Law and Lawyers' (1615), in *The Complete Works of Sir John Davies*, ed. A. B. Grosart (3 vols, London, 1869–76), iii, p. 266.

[19] Bodleian Library, Oxford, MS Ashmole 1159, fol. 78.

[20] In the rolls of warrants all litigants above the rank of gentleman are styled. Below the rank of gentleman, defendants are described more precisely than plaintiffs, so the detailed statistics for those below that rank are based on the status of defendants only.

they appear as about the same percentage of all litigants in the courts.[21] As in most legal tribunals, wealth was the most important factor in determining how much any particular group used the courts. On the other hand, although it must be true that very few of the litigants below the rank of gentleman came from that part of the population (perhaps 33 per cent) which lived on or below the edge of subsistence, it is clear that provincial farmers, merchants, tailors, miners, and occasionally even labourers, could find legal representation and use the courts. These groups were certainly better represented in the King's Bench and Common Pleas than they were at the inns of court, where comparable statistics indicate that only about 10 per cent of the entrants were below the rank of gentleman.[22] Moreover, though the gentry made up about 25 to 30 per cent of the litigants in both courts, the King's Bench attracted an even lower percentage of clients from this group. In the Common Pleas, if there was any trend at all during these years, it was towards the commercial and lower agricultural classes. If we consider only the status of plaintiffs, the gentry presence in the Common Pleas declined between 1560 and 1640 from 30 per cent to 26 per cent. Indeed, the change may be more substantial than the raw data suggests, since about 5 per cent of those plaintiffs listed in the commercial grouping in 1560 were large London merchants, some of whom were of, or above, the rank of gentleman and many of whom were undoubtedly quite wealthy. On this point exact quantitative evidence is not available, but it appears from the plea rolls that these large merchants made up a much more significant proportion of total litigants in 1560 than they did in later years. There is therefore reason to believe that the status of plaintiffs was undergoing a slight decline. This was complemented by an increase in the number of defendants who were from the groups of gentleman and above. In the Common Pleas between 1560 and 1640 the number of gentry defendants increases by 14 per cent, in the King's Bench by about 7 per cent. The implication of these changes must be that a larger percentage of men above the rank of gentleman were being sued by their social inferiors.

How does this picture of King's Bench and Common Pleas litigants compare with what little we know about social change during the period? It is likely that the reigns of Elizabeth I and the early Stuarts saw an increase in the national wealth. For those with some wealth, even if it were that of the village yeoman, it seems to have been a time of inflation and greater material prosperity.[23] Sir John Davies's explanation of the increase in litigation on this basis seems plausible, but whether or not the national wealth was being redistributed in any meaningful way is more difficult to say. In one case, that of the attorneys, where we can be reasonably sure that there

[21] G. E. Aylmer, *The King's Servants* (2nd edn, London, 1974), pp. 326–31.
[22] W. R. Prest, *The Inns of Court under Elizabeth I and the Early Stuarts, 1590–1640* (London, 1972), p. 30.
[23] W. G. Hoskins, *Essays in Leicestershire History* (Liverpool, 1950), p. 135.

was an increase in the size and wealth of the group, this seems to be reflected in their presence in the courts. The number of Common Pleas attorneys grew at least threefold during the period, and they appear as litigants just about that much more often in 1640 than in 1560. Seen from the vantage point of the Common Pleas, if it is true that the non-landed classes gained an increased share of the national pie, it appears to have made relatively little impact. These groups may have been slightly more liable to sue in 1640 than in 1560, but their overall presence in the courts stayed more or less the same. In the King's Bench the status of litigants was even lower than in the Common Pleas; but, once more, there was very little real change over the period. The evidence of both courts suggests that in general we need to be cautious when talking about changes in the status of litigants as a major factor in the legal development of the period.

It is impossible to know exactly how wealthy the non-gentry litigants in the King's Bench and Common Pleas were, but some estimate of the possible range of their wealth can be hazarded. The average Exeter merchant may have earned around £100 a year in the early seventeenth century. In medium- and smaller-sized towns, merchant income was probably (on a liberal estimate) no more than £50 a year, and this is also about the right figure for the average yeoman farmer.[24] Husbandmen and artisans were worth even less. If these figures are right, the implication is that litigation was not nearly so expensive as has usually been thought, an observation supported by the evidence which remains about the costs of suits. The account book of the Hitchin attorney George Draper contains the charges for hundreds of cases. Very few seem to have cost more than £5, almost none more than £10.[25] My own calculations of the cost of a suit for a £100 debt in the King's Bench and Common Pleas come to between £6 and £8. Indeed, the very large number of litigants from the less wealthy classes suggests that the early modern courts were surprisingly accessible. It was in the eighteenth and especially the late nineteenth centuries that complaints were heard that high costs were driving clients out of court.[26]

The reasons why men went to law varied from case to case, but some general idea of the issues involved can be gathered from the forms of action on which they sued.

[24] For some estimates of merchant wealth, see R. Grassby, 'The Personal Wealth of the Business Community in Seventeenth-Century England', *Economic History Review*, 2nd series, 23 (1970), pp. 231–32.

[25] 'The Account Book of George Draper'. I am grateful to Messrs Hawkins and Co., Portmill Lane, Hitchin, Hertfordshire, for allowing me to consult this manuscript in their possession.

[26] R. Boote, *Historical Treatise of an Action or Suit at Law* (2nd edn, London 1781), p. iii; Abel-Smith and Stevens, *Lawyers and the Courts*, p. 87.

Figure 2.2

Forms of Action in King's Bench and Common Pleas, 1560–1640[a]

	1560		1606		1640	
	CP[b]	KB	CP	KB	CP	KB
	Percentage		Percentage		Percentage	
Debt	67	19	80	46	88	80
Trespass	16	55	6	23	3	5
Actions on the Case	2	19	2	19	5	13
Ejectment	1	—	2	8	1	2.5
Miscellaneous[c]	14	7	10	5	3	—
Total	100	100	100	100	100	100

[a] Based on the rolls of warrants cited in note 2 above. The total numbers of cases in each year for each court are: Common Pleas, 923; 1934; 1229. King's Bench, 82; 1411; 979.

[b] Common recoveries – collusive actions for the breaking of entails – which accounted for seventy-nine (or 9 per cent) of Common Pleas actions in the 1560 sample, have not been included in these figures. After 25 Elizabeth I, recoveries were moved from the plea rolls to a new series of recovery rolls (CP 43), so they do not figure elsewhere in the table. From sample recovery rolls in later years (CP 43/3 and CP 43/91), it is clear that recoveries continued to be an important source of business.

[c] The miscellaneous actions include detinue, covenant, breaches of statutes, waste (Common Pleas only) and writs of error (King's Bench only).

By 1560 the old real actions at common law had virtually disappeared.[27] In their place, as ways of trying rights to land, came first various types of actions of trespass and then *ejectio firmae*, which by the early seventeenth century covered disputes about title to both freehold and copyhold land. Some of the actions of trespass in Figure 2.2 involved questions about land, but some also involved chasing cattle, knocking down hedges, breaking a close and mowing grass, breaking doors and windows, and digging in another man's mine.[28] These cases, like those brought in the court of Chancery to determine manorial customs, often involved long-standing disputes of considerable personal or social consequence. They also reflect an agrarian society where force and violence still played a large part in men's affairs. For example, disputes over enclosures could result in actions of trespass; the great chronicler of lawsuits, John Smith of Nibley, explained how the breaking of closes and forcible entry were commonplace tactics in the property

[27] Sutherland, *Assize of Novel Disseisin*, ch. 5; J. H. Baker, *An Introduction to English Legal History* (London, 1971), p. 167.

[28] Anon., *The Practick Part of the Law: Shewing the Office of a Complete Attorney* (London, 1658), pp. 102–4; A. Fitzherbert, *La Nouvelle Natura Brevium* (London, 1635 ed.), pp. 85–92.

disputes of his master, Lord Berkeley.[29] Throughout the period under discussion, actions of trespass and ejectment continued to make up an important part of the business of the courts; but, as Figure 2.2 shows, the percentage of litigation they constituted (though probably not their absolute numbers) had declined dramatically by 1640. In both the King's Bench and Common Pleas, the forms of action which grew most in frequency during this period were debt and actions on the case. In 1560, 67 per cent of cases in the Common Pleas and 19 per cent of those in the King's Bench were based on debt. By 1640 over 80 per cent of all the cases in both courts involved actions of debt, mostly debt on contracts. The second most prevalent kinds of suit were actions on the case, which in 1640 made up 13 per cent of King's Bench litigation and 5 per cent of that in the Common Pleas.

Jurisdictional changes may have been partly responsible for the relative growth of actions of debt in the King's Bench and Common Pleas. The spectacular increase in the percentage of debt cases in the King's Bench is certainly a product of the steady rise in popularity of bill procedure, which gave the court competence to hear such cases. Moreover, the relative decline of trespass may reflect a movement of cases in that category away from the common law courts into Star Chamber or Chancery, or even their reincarnation as actions on the case. Yet if we allow for changes in jurisdiction, we have also to allow for the fact that, even in 1640, Star Chamber and Chancery handled many times less business than the King's Bench and Common Pleas. On balance, it appears that the increase in the amount of litigation in the central courts was accompanied by a significant change in its nature.

The extent to which these changes in the frequency of the various forms of action may reflect changes in society is difficult to assess. There can be little doubt that the legal disputes of the sixteenth and seventeenth centuries often involved more than a man seeking a remedy for a simple wrong done to him. England in these times was a close-knit society and, as in some primitive cultures, lawsuits probably involved long-standing animosity between neighbours more frequently than they do today.[30] The vexatious litigant, the man who sued on the slightest chance for gain or merely to annoy an old rival, was a familiar player on the Elizabethan and early Stuart stage.[31] The local connections of rival litigants made the fear of partisan juries widespread.[32] Violence could erupt as a consequence of a long-standing dispute. John Smith writes of how two of Lord Berkeley's followers became overheated and 'multiplied suits against Sir Thomas like the heads of Hidra,

[29] John Smith [of Nibley], *The Lives of the Berkeleys* (3 vols, Gloucester, 1883–95), ii, pp. 296, 302–3.

[30] M. Gluckman, 'The Judicial Process among the Barotse of Northern Rhodesia', in *The Sociology of Law*, ed. V. Aubert (London, 1969), p. 167.

[31] Jones, *Elizabethan Court of Chancery*, p. 315.

[32] A. H. Smith, *County and Court: Government and Politics in Norfolk, 1558–1603* (Oxford, 1974), p. 150.

soe farr forth suffering their passions to transport them that instead of rakes and sheafpikes to gather tithe to harvest ... they carried their workfolks out of Berkeley town armed with swords and bucklers, halberds and such like weapons'.[33] Professor Barnes's work on Star Chamber suggests that the court was the ideal place for the rich man who was willing to try anything in order to win a feud. Barnes also suggests that since so many of the gentry of the age went to the inns of court, many of them must have been able to direct their own suits.[34] Knowledge of the law rather than of martial arms was the Elizabethan way to vanquish an enemy.[35]

Although the vexatious and learned litigant may have been notorious, the status of the people who sued in the King's Bench and Common Pleas suggests, nevertheless, that he was far from typical. It is clear that between 1560 and 1640 the majority of litigants (70 per cent) were not necessarily very rich. Nor could they have been very learned in the law. As we have seen, most were from social groups below those which can be associated with the inns of court. These were by any definition the typical litigants, though they were not the spectacular ones. They were dependent on the legal profession for advice, and in turn the legal profession (especially the attorneys) were dependent on them for the bulk of their business. As Figure 2.2 indicates, by 1640 the vast majority of these litigants were in court on actions of debt or actions on the case. With the important exception of some kinds of action on the case (such as slander), these suits were more likely to have been the result of business dealings than of vindictiveness or ancient disputes between neighbours. On the other hand, actions of trespass – at least, according to seventeenth-century writers – arose from wrongs accompanied by 'a kinde, or at least with a colour of violence'.[36] Although the level of violence represented by these actions can be exaggerated, they do clearly indicate incidents in which men acted first and only afterwards went to law. As cases of debt grew, and those of trespass declined, it is possible to see a society in which the rule of law was replacing individual action. The courts were becoming more important as sources of particular remedies than as arenas for personal feuds.

Consideration of the increase in litigation and of the kinds of people involved in it leads to a number of other problems. Questions about the relationship between the King's Bench and Common Pleas, and their relationship with other courts, are obvious. For example, how important were the costs of

[33] Smith, *Lives of the Berkeleys*, ii, p. 313.

[34] Thomas G. Barnes, 'Star Chamber Litigants and their Counsel, 1596–1641', in *Legal Records and the Historian*, ed. Baker, pp. 7–28. For the 'learned lay clients' see also his review of Prest, *Inns of Court, 1560–1640, American Historical Review*, 78 (1973), p. 1055.

[35] L. Stone, *The Crisis of the Aristocracy* (Oxford, 1966), pp. 240–42.

[36] W. Sheppard, *The Faithful Councellor: or The Marrow of the Law in English* (London, 1653), p. 280.

various courts in determining their availability? From the point of view of professional legal assistance, and perhaps of procedure in general, I suspect that the two common law courts were cheaper than either Star Chamber or Chancery.[37] At this date many suits could go a long way in the King's Bench and Common Pleas without much assistance from barristers or serjeants, who were more expensive than attorneys.[38] One of the most important consequences of the increase in litigation was the changes it brought in the judicial bureaucracy. It is significant that the most severe attacks on the Chancery and Common Pleas during the investigations of Charles I's commissions on fees came from the attorneys.[39]

To conclude, I would like to look at yet another contemporary opinion about the causes of the increase in litigation: the notion that swarms of attorneys were creating a multitude of suits. Initially, we can turn for help to some facts about numbers. In 1560 there were about 150 attorneys acting in both the King's Bench and Common Pleas; in 1606 there were 1000; and in 1640 a minimum of 1400.[40] This verifies contemporary notions about the numbers of attorneys, but until 1606 their rise followed closely that of the number of suits. In general, this trend continued until 1640, but at that date there is some evidence of overcrowding. In Warwickshire, there were forty-five attorneys in 1640. There were still forty-five Common Pleas men in 1732 when the increase in population and the prosperity of Birmingham must have made for more work.[41] More important, although the possibilities of death or financial disaster as the result of the Civil War need to be taken into account, it seems that many of the Warwickshire attorneys who were not well established in 1640 failed to flourish thereafter. The number of attorneys increased so quickly during the reign of Elizabeth I that it is difficult to see where they all came from, how they were trained or whether they were trained at all. The answers to these questions probably lie in the inns of court and inns of chancery. Dr Prest's figures for inns of court admissions suggest that there was a steep rise in the number of entrants between 1550 and 1570.[42] This was the critical period in terms of the increase in litigation; and it is likely that some of the non-legal factors operative in the growing interest in higher education during the English Renaissance

---

[37] Chancery and Star Chamber suits may have been more costly simply because the procedure of taking evidence in written depositions required much time and effort. Certainly Archbishop Williams, lord keeper 1621–25, believed that poor men praised the common law because it was cheaper than equity: G. W. Thomas, 'Archbishop John Williams: Politics and Prerogative Law' (unpublished D. Phil. thesis, University of Oxford, 1974), p. 37.

[38] A short tract in the Bedford County Record Office, L28/47 ('A Problem whence it comes to passe that the Courte of Chancery of late ... is so frequented'), suggests that barristers were rarely needed in the Common Pleas or King's Bench except in difficult cases.

[39] The commissioners' papers are in PRO, E 215.

[40] The sources for the numbers of attorneys are those cited in nn. 2 and 3 above.

[41] 'Roll of Attorneys 1732', PRO, CP 11/2.

[42] For inns of court admissions, see Prest, *Inns of Court, 1590–1640*, pp. 5–7.

produced lawyers and attorneys who made litigation more available than it ever had been before. The close relationship between the increase in the size of the profession and the increase in litigation makes it difficult to break into the circle of cause and effect.

There are a few other pieces of information which shed more light on the problem. First, contemporary opinion should not be ignored. Secondly, as we have seen, the sorts of people who used the King's Bench and Common Pleas were the sorts of people who must have depended heavily on legal advice. Lastly, we must try to see what the raw figures for numbers of attorneys at various dates really meant in the context of specific communities within the population. In 1560 there were very few attorneys in England; there were, of course, even fewer barristers, but the lower branch is the main concern here. In 1560 there was one attorney for every 20,000 people (taking the population as 3,500,000). In 1606 there was one for every 4000; in 1640 one for every 2500; and in 1732 one for every 1500 people in the country.[43] In 1560 this meant that, in some parts of England, access to legal services can hardly have been easy. There were only three attorneys handling cases for Warwickshire at that date, and it seems unlikely that more than one of these lived in the county. Similarly, in Berkshire and Oxfordshire an attorney named John Grove handled most cases, but his practice was spread over both the vast Western and the Oxford circuits; probate evidence suggests that he lived in Somerset. Naturally, the more prosperous counties had more attorneys. There were five or six reasonably busy members of the lower branch in Gloucestershire at the beginning of the reign. Norfolk, long known for the litigiousness of its population, and accounting for 13 per cent of all Common Pleas litigation in 1560, had fifteen Common Pleas attorneys.[44] Further research is needed on the legal profession of this litigious county, but fifteen attorneys probably meant that the legal profession was beginning to be important in the various administrative posts which existed in town and county government. In Warwickshire, however, and presumably in other less litigious counties, it was not until the seventeenth century that attorneys moved into posts such as town clerk or took over as manorial stewards. By the reign of James I the profession was beginning to make a significant impact on local government. More important, by 1580, and certainly by 1600, there were enough attorneys in most parts of England to be readily available to litigants who wanted them. It must be true that the increased availability of lawyers made litigation possible for more members of the population, even if it did not directly cause it.

An illustration of this point is the slowness with which the King's Bench came to rival the Common Pleas in volume of litigation. Even in 1640, in spite of its evident procedural advantages, the King's Bench handled only about one-third as many cases as the Common Pleas. The best explanation

---

43 For revisions of these figures in the light of subsequent research, see Chapter 7, pp. 182–85.

44 Percentage of cases from the rolls of warrants of attorney, cited in n. 3 above.

of why this was so is simply that the King's Bench had fewer attorneys. From about 1570 the attorneys, once operative in both courts, became segregated into one or the other of them. In the King's Bench this process went even further, so that by 1606 the vast majority of the 240 attorneys in the court were also clerks of the chief clerk (prothonotary), an innovation which evidently kept down the number of attorneys. In 1640 the Common Pleas had over 1000 attorneys, but the King's Bench only 300. Since there were fewer attorneys in the latter, it was more difficult for cases to reach it.

The increase in the amount of litigation in the central courts, the trend for the courts to become more open to non-gentry elements in society and the increase in the number of lawyers may therefore have been seen in a positive light, as the spread of valuable remedies to greater numbers of people. Most contemporaries did not, however, think of it that way. To them the multiplicity of suits was a disaster, and the attorneys who brought the cases into the courts a group of dishonest tricksters who were a cancer in the body of the commonwealth. Allegations that the attorneys stirred up suits were accompanied by charges of corruption, a picture of the profession that has come down into the writings of recent historians. Yet, while dishonest attorneys did of course exist, it is easy to show that these were no more typical of the profession as a whole then than they are in the second half of the twentieth century. For example, relative to the number of practitioners there were very few cases in the papers of the early Stuart commissioners of fees against the attorneys.[45] More lawyers certainly meant more who were corrupt; more lawyers also made regulation of them a more important issue. But, in general, the quality and nature of the lower branch of the legal profession have changed less between 1600 and the present than the attitudes of society towards them.

There were several reasons for the distrust and dislike of attorneys. They were almost always of lower social status than their critics; and the economic thinking of the day held that lawyers, instead of adding to the national wealth, siphoned their income from those farmers, merchants and tradesmen who did. The author of *Britannia languens* thought that, as men's estates crumbled, the lawyers made profits just as 'doubtless did some bricklayers get estates by the burning of the city'.[46] These social and economic views of the profession were combined in the caricatures of lawyers which found their way onto the Jacobean stage, in plays such as Jonson's *Staple of the News*.

What men thought about lawyers was also closely connected with what they thought about lawsuits, and, ultimately, with what they thought about the functions of law. In modern capitalist societies, law is often described as

---

[45] PRO, E 215.

[46] '*Britannia Languens*: or A Discourse of Trade' (1680), in *A Select Collection of Early English Tracts on Commerce*, ed. J. R. McCullock (Cambridge, 1970), pp. 302, 375.

a means of resolving conflicts between individuals.[47] In the sixteenth and seventeenth centuries, its role was much more comprehensive. Writers from Sir John Fortescue in the late fifteenth century to Sir Henry Finch in the early seventeenth century thought that the law was the means by which society was held together. Fortescue wrote that the laws were the sinews which extended through the kingdom and held together the body of the people. Finch described law as a means of well ordering civil society. His contemporary William Fulbecke believed that without law, 'which I interpret to be an order established by authority, neither house, nor city, nor nation, nor mankind, nor nature, nor world can be'.[48] The idea that law functioned as a remedy, or that increased wealth and trade made more suits inevitable, did exist; but in theory, and in the minds of laymen, law was more than a mere arbiter; it was a reflection of God's will about the way the world should be, a set of precepts which enabled men to tell right from wrong.

These notions about the functions of law implied that lawsuits were a potential breach of the social order, more the product of the ill will of men than the result of business dealings or personal accident. An Elizabethan parliamentary bill for law reform mentions 'the multitude of contentions which for lack of charity rise upon the smallest occasions betwene neighbours'.[49] The Jesuit Robert Parsons thought that covetousness caused the multitude of suits.[50] Another author compared vain men who spent money on lawsuits with those who spent it on extravagant clothing.[51] The lawyers, too, were ambivalent about the reasons for going to law. An early seventeenth-century Recorder of London, Sir Anthony Benn, thought that suits were connected mostly with the fact that men said to themselves 'what is thine is mine' as well as 'what is mine is mine'.[52] Sir John Davies cynically observed that if only all men lived according to the law of nature there would be no need for litigation.[53]

Since lawsuits were seen as a social evil, it was only natural that, in an age when their number was increasing rapidly, lawyers should have been discredited. The ideal lawyer ought to have been an agent of reconciliation; instead, the multiplicity of suits seemed to reflect a legal profession which

[47] See, e.g., H. G. Bredemeier, 'Law as an Integrative Mechanism', in *Sociology of Law*, ed. Aubert, p. 53.

[48] Sir John Fortescue, *De laudibus legum Anglie*, ed. S. B. Chrimes (Cambridge, 1942), p. 31; H. Finch, *Law or a Discourse Thereof in Foure Bookes* (London, 1627), p. 1; W. Fulbecke, *A Direction or Preparative to the Study of Law* (London, 1603), p. 2.

[49] 'Reformacyons Proposed in Parliament' (1576): PRO, SP 12/107/96.

[50] R. Parsons, 'A Memorial of the Reformation of England', in *The Jesuits' Memorial*, ed. E. Gee (London, 1690), p. 244.

[51] *Opinion Diefied: Discovering the Ingins, Traps, and Traynes that are Set in this Age, Whereby to Catch Opinion. By B[read] R[yce] Gent., Servant to the King* (London, 1613), p. 21.

[52] 'Essayes Written by Anthony Benn, Knight, Recorder of London', Bedford County Record Office, Bedford, L28/46, fol. 17v.

[53] Davies, 'A Discourse of Law and Lawyers', p. 267.

encouraged contention between neighbours. Consequently, many men appear to have agreed with the lesson which Robert Burton learned from Plato: that it was a 'great sign of an intemperete and corrupt common wealth where lawyers and physicians did abound'.[54]

Attitudes towards litigation and hence towards lawyers may also have contained a political element. In 1640 one in every eighty Englishmen was using the king's courts, and using these courts implied recognition of the king's rule, often at the expense of the powerful local magnate or lord of the manor. During the late sixteenth century, the common lawyers completely undermined the authority of manorial jurisdictions by recognising the right of copyholders to sue in the central courts.[55] Most lawyers probably agreed with Roger Wilbraham that 'it is every subject's natural birthright to enjoy the benefit of the prince's lawes'.[56] Coke claimed in public that if 'Justice [was] withheld, only the poorer sort are those that smart for it', presumably because they would then be swamped by their richer neighbours.[57]

That some of the better sort objected to the increase in litigation, because it implied giving ordinary people more access to remedies through law, is suggested by one of the few contemporary comments which argued in favour of the increase in litigation and which spoke sympathetically of the attorneys. Its author was a lawyer (probably an attorney) named William Barlee. While something of a crank, Barlee was thoughtful, and the attorneys have their say too rarely for his evidence not to be useful. During the 1570s he was writing a 'concordance of all written lawes concerning lords of manors', the aim of which was to make the law known to lords of manors and their tenants.[58] But, because the 'concordance' was designed to disseminate legal knowledge, Barlee feared that the judges might oppose it on the grounds that:

> Many suits have arisen in the comen courts, amongst subjects ... since our statute lawes were published in the English tongue to the common sort of people. And for this only cause, some ... would have the knowledge of our common laws obscurely hid from the common sort of people, as they are now.

Against this position, Barlee argued that the same reasons had been set forth for the withholding of English scriptures, but had been defeated by natural reason and the express word of God. He concluded by mentioning

---

[54] R. Burton, *The Anatomy of Melancholy* (2 vols, London, 1813), ii, p. 86.

[55] See, generally, C. Calthrope, *The Relation between the Lord of a Manor and the Copy-Holder his Tenant* (London, 1635).

[56] 'Sir Roger Wilbraham's Diary and Commonplace Books (1593–1646)', Folger Shakespeare Library, Washington, DC. MS Mb. 42 (microfilm of typescript copy).

[57] *The Lord Coke His Speech and Charge* (London, 1607), sig. Civ.

[58] W. Barlee, *A Concordance of All Written Lawes Concerning Lords of Mannours, theire Free Tenentes, and Copieholders*, Manorial Society, 6 (London, 1911).

that counsellors were often helped by learned attorneys, and chastised 'those lawyers who forgett how by juste suits wrongfull dealings are quietly suppressed'.[59] Standing alone, the views of Barlee may not have strength enough to carry convincingly an argument in favour of the increase in litigation. But it must be remembered that the arguments against the increase, and against the attorneys, came largely from the legal and social establishment. Barlee's ideas suggest how an alternative position could be formulated; their existence should cause us to wonder why the increase in litigation and lawyers was usually deplored.

The point to be made here is not that, as a group, the attorneys can be seen as in any way especially committed to upholding the rights of the common sort of people. Lawyers are always likely to be found on both sides of a dispute. Barlee himself was concerned that his work, which touched on the thorny question of the rights of copyholders, should not get into the hands of 'rash headed fellows, lest they tare you or your friends in pieces. I mean lest they vexe [lords of manors]'.[60] He did appreciate, nevertheless, that the poor as well as the rich could benefit from litigation; and attorneys, whether or not they intended it, made it possible for more of the lower sort to sue. Despite perpetual complaints about increased fees, law in the seventeenth century was not prohibitively expensive, and the courts opened relatively quickly to a large section of the population. In an age of rising prices, the rights of landholders became crucial: enough examples of the struggles between landlords and tenants exist to make it clear that recourse to the law was important to both sides. Legality also came into the relationship between urban corporations and the central government. In both cases men who were unlearned in the law could benefit from the increased availability of lawyers. The fact that there were more lawyers than ever before may have forced the law into the position of arbiter. What is evident is the fact that the existence of more lawyers made the law a weapon which could be put into the hands of ordinary men. An example of the exaggerated reaction this development brought from some of the ruling classes in the sixteenth and seventeenth centuries is contained in a petition to the House of Commons just after the Restoration. It accused the attorneys of stirring up suits, and attacked them for using the style of 'gentleman'. But it went on to say that 'they are bold impudent fellows that scarce allow any priviledges, noe not to the very best of his Majestie's subjects'. One of them, claimed the petitioner, had been instrumental in drawing up the indictment of the late martyr, King Charles I.[61]

[59] Letter from Barlee to William Lord Burghley, dated November 1578, BL, MS Lansdowne 99, fol. 134.

[60] Barlee, *Concordance*, p. 1.

[61] 'Attorneys in Parte Anatomized: By a Christian Hand', Bodleian Library, MS Ashmole 15371, fos 2–12.

3

Interpersonal Conflict and Social Tension: Civil Litigation in England, 1640–1830

Since the mid 1970s there has been lively debate about the role of law in the seventeenth and eighteenth centuries. Work by Douglas Hay, E. P. Thompson, J. A. Sharpe, J. M. Beattie and many others has been full of insights which have extended the horizons of social and political as well as legal history.[1] One curious fact about the vast majority of these studies, however, is that they have focused almost exclusively on the criminal law. With the notable exception of some perceptive comments by Lawrence Stone (an historian who has always had time for the litigious),[2] the civil law, or the rules and legal processes by which people made and enforced agreements about property rights, contracts and debts, or sued for remedies in actions of slander or negligence, has been largely ignored. Yet it is arguable that the civil law is even more important than the criminal law in maintaining the social and economic relationships in any society. It is certainly the case that many more people of all ranks of society in early modern England came into contact with the legal system through the civil rather than the criminal courts. To take but one example, in 1776 more than half of the prison population of England and Wales was composed of insolvent debtors rather than criminals.[3]

Lawsuits are, therefore, an important part of the story of the administration of justice. This chapter undertakes a preliminary investigation of the subject by reconstructing the volume and nature of civil litigation in the main royal courts at Westminster in the period between 1640 and 1830, from the English Civil War to the point at which major law reforms began to transform the old common law system. The study is based partly on data collected by

[1] For example, Douglas Hay et al., *Albion's Fatal Tree: Crime and Society in Eighteenth-Century England* (London, 1975); J. A. Sharpe, *Crime in Early Modern England, 1550–1750* (London, 1984); J. M. Beattie, *Crime and the Courts in England, 1660–1800* (Oxford, 1986). I would like to thank David Lemmings, Joanna Innes, and Henry Horwitz for their helpful comments on an earlier draft of this chapter.

[2] Lawrence Stone, *The Crisis of the Aristocracy, 1558–1641* (Oxford, 1965), pp. 240–42; idem, 'Interpersonal Violence in English Society, 1300–1980', *Past and Present*, 101 (1983), pp. 22–33; J. A. Sharpe, 'Debate: The History of Violence in England. Some Observations', ibid., 108 (1985), pp. 206–15; Lawrence Stone, 'A Rejoinder', ibid., pp. 216–24.

[3] John Howard, *The State of Prisons* (first published 1777; London, 1929), p. 17. There were 2437 debtors out of a total population of 4084.

parliamentary inquiries in the 1820s, but mostly on figures obtained from the records of the courts of King's Bench, Chancery and Common Pleas.

Quantifiable information about litigation can be extracted from certain groups of records which were generated within the courts for the purposes of providing easier access to the main series, collecting fees or complying with technical formalities. First, alphabetical indexes of all of the bills filed in the court of Chancery, which survive from 1673 to 1859, are an excellent guide to the numbers of causes commenced in the court, although they tell little about the litigants or their troubles.[4] Secondly, the docket rolls and docket books of the King's Bench and Common Pleas were formalised notes, compiled in the offices of the prothonotaries, which provide a key to the contents of the plea rolls of the two courts. The entries in them have been counted in order to obtain figures on the numbers of cases which had reached 'advanced stages': the point at which the defendant had come to court in order to answer the plea of the plaintiff and either put himself on the country or confess the action.[5] Thirdly, in order to be sure of collecting their fees, the prothonotaries of the Common Pleas made notes of the number of *nisi prius* records, or cases being sent to trial in the country, which they issued each term. These provide easily collectable material on the number of lawsuits in the court which had surpassed the procedural stages and were about to be argued before a jury.[6] Fourthly, the rolls of warrants of attorney, which survive for the entire period in Common Pleas but not in King's Bench, were an enrolment of the certificates which verified the appointment by litigants of their lawyers. They give brief details about the social status of the litigants and their business, both of which have been subjected to quantitative analysis.[7]

The statistical profile of court usage which these sources reveal is hardly perfect. The different types of document tell us different things about each court, but provide incomplete data. For example, it would ideally be desirable to compare the number of causes started in each court at as many dates as possible across the entire period but, until commissions of inquiry appointed by parliament went to work in the 1820s, the relevant statistics are available

---

[4] They are classified in the PRO, IND series.

[5] For a description of the docket rolls for the period up to 1640, see C. W. Brooks, *Pettyfoggers and Vipers of the Commonwealth: The 'Lower Branch' of the Legal Profession in Early Modern England* (Cambridge, 1986), pp. 48–51. The docket rolls (PRO, IND) of the King's Bench survive in a continuous series up to 1702, when they were converted to docket books (PRO, IND). This coincided with the creation of the judgment rolls (PRO, KB 122) as the formal record of civil pleas. Before 1702 both criminal and civil pleas had been enrolled on the *coram rege* rolls (PRO, KB 27), but even before 1702 the docket rolls referred to civil cases only.

[6] PRO, CP 36.

[7] See Brooks, *Pettyfoggers and Vipers of the Commonwealth*, pp. 57–71. After the creation of the King's Bench judgment rolls in 1702, the warrants of attorney for cases in that court were recorded in the plea rolls on the same piece of parchment as the full record of the case and no longer compiled into a roll of their own.

only for Chancery.[8] This is a difficulty because, as we shall see, the use of arrest as the leading process in cases of debt in the common law courts may have significantly reduced the ratio of cases which reached advanced stages as the period progressed. At the same time, none of the figures permit a proper appreciation of the differences between cases which were of general significance, or involved large outlays of financial and emotional capital, and those which were of much less consequence. For instance, a cause in Chancery might arise from a dispute over manorial customs between tenants and their landlord. On the other hand, many 'cases' in the King's Bench involved little more than the enrolment of a record on the plea rolls in order to back up a business transaction.[9] Court business did not invariably involve contention.

The statistics are interesting because, as the first part of this chapter shows, they point, first, to a massive decline; and, secondly, to unusually low levels of litigation in the central courts during the course of the eighteenth century. The remainder of the chapter goes on to explain the causes of these phenomena and to investigate their implications. Since it involves an interpretation of alterations in mass behaviour over nearly two centuries, the resulting picture is inevitably complex. Broad social and economic changes are discussed in conjunction with legal developments, such as the establishment of urban small-debt jurisdictions known as courts of requests, and within a context of public dissatisfaction with the common law system. Next, an analysis of social composition of litigants and the nature of their lawsuits considers the significance of changes in levels of contentiousness and in the behaviour of different social groups with regard to the keeping of promises. The conclusion briefly compares the history of the civil law with that of the criminal law during the period.

The late sixteenth and, to a lesser extent, the early seventeenth centuries witnessed an expansion in central court litigation unprecedented in English history. In 1640 there was probably more litigation per head of population going through the central courts at Westminster than at any time before or since.[10] But one hundred years later, in 1750, the common law hit what appears to have been a spectacular all time low. There was subsequently a modest recovery of business between 1750 and 1830: but at the latter date, after the population of England had more than quadrupled, the number of cases entertained by the major central courts of the realm was no more than half as great as it had been in 1640.

[8] On the differences between causes commenced and causes in advanced stages, see ibid., pp. 49, 75–77.

[9] For example, in 1750 a significant number of King's Bench defendants confessed judgements against themselves on a date prior to that on which they were due to repay sums of money. This practice enabled the lender to take uncontested legal action in case of default, PRO, KB 122/242 and 243, rolls 108, 403, 640.

[10] Brooks, *Pettyfoggers and Vipers of the Commonwealth*, pp. 77–78.

The general trends over the 190 years break down into five distinct phases:
1. Although the courts were inevitably disrupted during the 1640s by the Civil War (see Figure 3.1), the 1650s, 1660s and 1670s were decades in which the increase in litigation characteristic of the post-Reformation period continued, although at a very modest pace. The total number of cases in advanced stages in King's Bench and Common Pleas (Figure 3.3) rose slightly, from 28,734 in 1640 to 29,371 in 1669–70. Equally, the first reliable figures for litigation in Chancery (Figure 3.2), those for 1673/4, show 4717 causes commenced, a level which is almost certainly higher than that reached at any stage before the Civil War. However, against these moderate increases in the work of the three most important central courts of the realm, we must set the fact that two very active pre-Civil War jurisdictions, the court of Star Chamber and the Council of the North, had been abolished during the Civil War era, and were not replaced after the Restoration.[11]

Figure 3.1

Common Pleas: Number of Cases Sent for Trial at Assizes
in the Office of a Single Prothonotary, 1645–62

1645–46	17
1646–47	218
1647–48	409
1650–51	698
1655–56	1115
1661–62	1348

Source: PRO, CP 36/1.

Figure 3.2

Number of Bills Entered in the Court of Chancery, 1673–1809

1673–74	4717
1700–1	5707
1720–21	3453
1745[a]	1836
1746[a]	2032
1750	1827
1752[a]	1023
1800–9[a]	1500 (average)

Sources: PRO, IND 1/21/36; 14,421; 14,451.

[a] *Parliamentary Papers: The Report of the Committee Appointed to Enquire into the Causes that Retard Decisions in the High Court of Chancery* (London, 1811), ii, p. 507.

---

[11] Ibid., pp. 55–56; J. H. Baker, *An Introduction to English Legal History* (2nd edn, London, 1979), pp. 106, 184.

2. By contrast, between 1680 and 1700 King's Bench and Common Pleas entered their first period of decline. The counts of records sent for trial at assizes by Common Pleas (Figure 3.4) fell by 19 per cent between 1680 and 1690, and then by another 18 per cent between 1692 and 1703. Similarly, the number of cases in advanced stages in the Common Pleas dropped by 40 per cent between 1670 and 1700. In King's Bench, the flight of litigants was even more dramatic. There were 40 per cent fewer cases in advanced stages in 1690 than there had been in 1670, and there was a further drop of 30 per cent in the 1690s. Overall by 1700, the number of causes in advanced stages in the two courts was 15,306, barely half of the level of 1670.

Figure 3.3

Cases in Advanced Stages in King's Bench and Common Pleas, 1640–1830

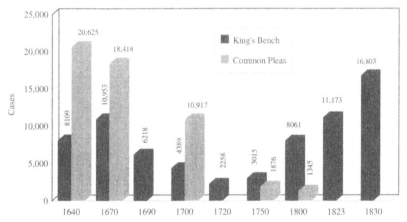

Sources: King's Bench: PRO, IND 1/1369–70, 6054–55, 6076, 6092–93, 6132, 6194–95, 6293–94, 6339–40, 6353–55. Common Pleas: PRO, IND 1/353–58, 572–80, 779–86, 997, 999, 1002–7, 1133.

3. Between 1700 and 1720 litigation in King's Bench continued to decline quite sharply,[12] but in Common Pleas the change appears to have been less dramatic (see Figures 3.3 and 3.4). The number of Common Pleas trials dropped off almost imperceptibly between 1702 and 1720. Thus it is hardly surprising that in response to a question put to him in parliament, Sir George Cooke, chief prothonotary of the Common Pleas and an official of twenty years' standing, said that he believed there was more business in the

[12] In the year 1719–20 the docket books of the King's Bench record 2258 cases in advanced stages (PRO, IND 6132–33). In 1728 John Croft, deputy to the master of the bill of Middlesex office, told the House of Commons that his records showed that the King's Bench issued about 3000 writs a year to commence actions. This may have been an underestimate, but it confirms the general trend outlined in Figure 3.3, *Journals of the House of Commons* (London, 1803ff), xxi, p. 267.

court in 1728 than there had been 'formerly'. This statement has always been taken at face value by historians,[13] and from the point of view of Cooke it may well have been true. Common Pleas business which reached advanced stages was divided between the offices of the three prothonotaries of the court, and the number of *nisi prius* records enrolled in Cooke's own office had risen slightly since the early years of the eighteenth century while that of the court as a whole more or less held steady.[14] The real significance of this episode lies not in Cooke's claim, but in the fact that he was forced to answer a question about the amount of business in his court in the first place.

Figure 3.4
*Number of Cases Sent for Trial at Assizes,
Common Pleas, 1672–1830*

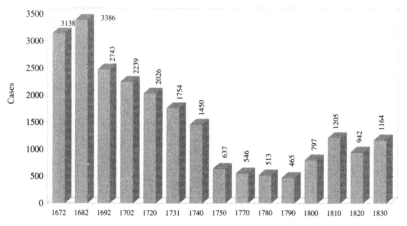

Sources: PRO, CP 36/2–4, 6–9, 11–12, 14.15–18, 21.

4. In any case, what Cooke was unable to foresee in 1728 was that during the 1730s, and especially the 1740s, both Chancery and Common Pleas would lose business at a truly spectacular rate. In 1750, only 1827 bills were filed in Chancery, just over half the number in 1720. The number of cases sent for trial by the Common Pleas fell only slightly in 1730s, but was halved in the 1740s. Although its business contracted by more than 25 per cent between 1700 and 1750, the King's Bench made something of a recovery after 1720 and sustained its position in the mid eighteenth century much better than the other two courts. It is from this period that it finally achieved

[13] Ibid. See, for example, Brooks, *Pettyfoggers and Vipers of the Commonwealth*, p. 75, and G. Holmes, *Augustan England: Professions, State and Society, 1680–1730* (London, 1982), p. 130.
[14] PRO, CP 36/3.

domination over the Common Pleas.[15] Nevertheless, the law as administered at Westminster was clearly at a nadir in 1750. Together King's Bench and Common Pleas heard only 4891 cases in advanced stages in that year, only one-third as many as in 1700, a little over a sixth of the number in 1670.

5. Nor did the position improve significantly until the end of the eighteenth century. Cases in advanced stages in King's Bench grew by more than five times between 1750 and 1830, but most of this increase came after 1790 and especially in the 1810s and 1820s. The statistics compiled by the parliamentary inquiries make the latter decade the first for which absolutely sound evidence is available on the number of actions commenced. These show an increase by one-third in the space of the four years 1823–27. Equally, in Common Pleas the number of cases sent for trial remained fairly constant between 1750 and 1800, but then rose sharply between 1800 and 1830, a trend which is also reflected in the figures for suits commenced which were collected by the House of Commons. Much the same was true of Chancery and the Exchequer of Pleas.[16]

The fluctuations in the volume of litigation across the period are surprisingly large, but most of the available evidence refers to causes in advanced stages rather than causes commenced. Hence there is an immediate question as to whether the decline observed may not be in part an optical illusion created by changes in court procedure which altered the proportion of the cases started which eventually reached advanced stages. To a limited extent this does appear to have been true.

The most important development in this respect was the increased use of the practice of arresting and holding to bail defendants in actions of debt before any pleadings had been entered in court (arrest on *mesne* process). This mode of procedure had been available from the King's Bench since the early sixteenth century, but it only became a regular feature of Common Pleas practice after the introduction of new writs by Chief Justice Francis North in the 1670s.[17] The effect on the number of cases which reached

[15] The decline of the Common Pleas seems likely to have been caused in part by a decline in the professional reputation of the serjeants at law, the lawyers who had a monopoly right of audience there. J. H. Baker, *The Order of Serjeants at Law: A Chronicle of Creations with Related Texts and a Historical Introduction*, Selden Society supplementary series, 5 (London, 1985), pp. 111–15. [Edward Wynne], *A Miscellany Containing Several Law Tracts* (n. p., 1765), p. 382–84, noted that that 'at present, the number [nine] of Serjeants is more than the business of the court'.

[16] *Parliamentary Papers 1829*, v, *First Report Made to His Majesty by the Commissioners Appointed to Inquire into the Practice and Proceedings of the Superior Courts of Common Law* (London, 1829), pp. 146–202. For the equity side of the Exchequer, a jurisdiction which has not been considered at length here, but in which litigation fluctuated in much the same pattern between 1640 and 1830, as has been outlined above, see W. H. Bryson, *The Equity Side of the Exchequer* (Cambridge, 1975), p. 168.

[17] Roger North, *The Lives of the Right Hon. Francis North, Baron Guilford; The Hon. Sir Dudley North; and the Hon. and Rev. Dr John North ... together with the Autobiography of the Author*, ed. Augustus Jessopp (3 vols, London, 1890), i, pp. 128–29. Another development which might have

advanced stages was twofold. First, arrest on *mesne* process replaced traditional methods which were more expensive and which allowed the plaintiff
to arrest defendants only after the time-consuming and expensive business
of issuing them with several summonses. The new procedures may, therefore,
have made it easier for plaintiffs to force out of court settlements on their
opponents before a case ever reached an advanced stage.[18] Equally important, impecunious debtors who were unable to raise bail could be left to
languish in prison for a considerable period of time without further action
being taken against them. For example, very few of the debtors in the
Wiltshire gaol at Fisherton Anger in the late 1760s, many of whom had
been imprisoned for well over a year, appear in the records of cases in
advanced stages in King's Bench and Common Pleas.[19]

An eighteenth-century legislative attempt to modify the impact of arrest
on *mesne* process introduced complications which also need to be taken into
consideration. A statute passed by parliament in 1725 restricted such arrests
to cases where the amount in dispute was more than £10, thereby depriving
creditors of the cheapest means of coercing the payment of small sums of
money. In these circumstances, the creditor could not have his defendant
arrested until he had pursued his case through to a verdict. This required
the outlay of additional sums of money, although these could in theory be
recovered as costs from the defendant once the court's decision had been
reached.[20]

According to the legal writer Richard Boote, the impact of this statute on
litigation was rather paradoxical. On the one hand, he claimed that creditors
attempting to recover less than £10 were reluctant to go to law at all because
they rightly feared the additional costs. Although the 1725 act is hardly ever
mentioned specifically, it no doubt contributed to the persistent claims,
which will be examined below, that the common law courts were ineffectual
for the purposes of collecting small debts. On the other hand, in Boote's
opinion the act actually added to the difficulty of debtors as well as creditors.
If the plaintiff did proceed with legal action in such circumstances, his
'Revenge is sharpened by reason of his Costs, and the same Costs in an

---

reduced litigation, the use of commissions of bankruptcy to settle the affairs of insolvent debtors,
seems unlikely to have had a significant effect. BL, MS Add. 36118 (Lord Hardwicke's legal
papers), fol. 151, an account of the number of commissions of bankruptcy issued between 1714
and 1748, shows that the rate remained constant at between 200 and 300 each year, except for
the years 1725–28, when there were between 400 and 500.

[18] Attorneys claimed that this was the effect of an earlier attempt to use similar procedures
in the Common Pleas in the 1620s, Brooks, *Pettyfoggers and Vipers of the Commonwealth*,
pp. 127–29.

[19] Wiltshire County Record Office, Trowbridge, A2/3/4, petitions of insolvent debtors.

[20] 12 George I, c. 29, 'An Act to Prevent Frivolous and Vexatious Arrests'; [Robert
Richardson], *The Attorney's Practice in the Court of Common Pleas: or An Introduction to the Knowledge
and Practice of that Court* (3rd edn, 2 vols, London, 1758), i, pp. 83–89.

Addition to the Defendant's Debt' made it all the more unlikely that the defendant would be released from prison or his creditor satisfied.[21]

The 1725 act obviously did little to diminish the hostility associated with arrest on *mesne* process, and it is also unclear how far it had an impact on the number of lawsuits in either initial or advanced stages. Imperfect evidence from the early eighteenth century suggests that most common law business at that date involved considerably more than £10, but by the 1790s a great deal of business from the London area concerned sums less than £20.[22] It is impossible to say exactly how many creditors simply did not bother to sue if the sum sank below £10. More significantly, and for the present purposes more to the point, there is little reason to doubt that there was an overall increase in the use of arrest on *mesne* process during the period from 1670 to the end of the eighteenth century. It was probably responsible for changes in the ratio of causes commenced to causes in advanced stages. In the period up to 1640, it is likely that twice as many suits were commenced as ever reached advanced stages, but the much more accurate figures available for the 1820s indicate that by then the ratio had risen to four to one.[23] The degree of distortion which this factor creates in the picture of rates of litigation at any one point before the 1820s can only be estimated. It cannot have been the primary cause of the measured decline in the volume of court business in any of the five phases, because King's Bench business declined even though the court used the procedure over the entire period. Moreover, litigation in all of the jurisdictions fell after 1700, long after the new technique had been introduced in the Common Pleas. Most importantly, we can still say with confidence that, whereas in 1640 some 1149 causes were started in the central courts per 100,000 of total population, in 1830 there were only 653.[24] If the ratio of causes commenced to cases in advanced stages in 1750 is taken to be two to one, then the number per 100,000 could at that date have been as low as 175. Even if we use the factor of four to one, the total of causes commenced per 100,000 still comes to only 350.

[21] R. Boote, *An Historical Treatise of an Action or Suit at Law: And of the Proceedings Used in the King's Bench and Common Pleas* (London, 1766), pp. 36, 59–63.

[22] A sample from the 'D' section of the King's Bench docket roll for 1700 (PRO, IND 6093), which includes only cases in advanced stages, gives the following values for debts: £600, £280, £60, £120, £1000, £5, £5 5s. 0d., £68, £60, £500, £480, £150, £170, £100, £30, £100, £27, £60, £60, £90, £3000, £74, £450, £10, £30, £40, £500, £32. In 1792 a parliamentary committee found that of 9500 bailable writs issued by the King's Bench in Middlesex (exclusive of London), 7000 were for sums under £50 and half were for less than £20. *Commons Journals*, xlvii, p. 645.

[23] Brooks, *Pettyfoggers and Vipers of the Commonwealth*, pp. 75–76; *First Report of His Majesty's Commissioners (on the) Common Law*, p. 11.

[24] Brooks, *Pettyfoggers and Vipers of the Commonwealth*, p. 77–78, for the figures and the methods of calculation.

What happened to the common law in the age of reason? The answer lies in a complex combination of demographic, economic, social, legal and behavioural characteristics of English society. Population stagnated at just below or above five million throughout the second half of the seventeenth century, only gradually reaching 5.7 million in 1750, and then doubling between 1760 and 1830. Late eighteenth- and early nineteenth-century population growth may therefore account partly for the renewed vitality of the common law in the 1790s and early 1800s. On the other hand, since population increased only marginally between 1640 and 1750, it is not surprising that central court litigation did not expand over those years, but there was nothing in this demographic regime which accounts for the massive decline in business up to 1750.[25]

The significance for court usage of long-term trends in the economy is more problematic. It is easy to see a connection between the increase in litigation after 1790 and the late eighteenth-century take-off in agricultural and manufacturing productivity later known as the 'Industrial Revolution', although both the scale of the increase and the total volume of litigation in 1830 are a surprisingly pale reflection of a conjunction of demographic and economic conditions which should have led to a massive increase in the number of economic transactions and consequently to more disputes at law. The economic state of the realm between 1660 and the mid eighteenth century is still shrouded in obscurity, but there were several economic and social changes during these years which may explain, at least in part, the fall in the amount of court business.[26]

The 1690s, the years in which the decline in litigation first became evident, were characterised by economic dislocation caused first by a shortage of specie and then by the recoinage of money in 1695–96 in an attempt to repair the problem.[27] Furthermore, quite apart from unprecedentedly high levels of taxation, the War of the Grand Alliance (1689–97) led to a revolution in finance, including the establishment of the Bank of England, which enabled the English state to borrow money at interest from the population at large in order to pay for government expenditure generally, but especially for the large outlays connected with war. Subsequently, during the first half of the eighteenth century, England was involved in three lengthy periods of war (1702–13, 1739–48, 1756–63), and there is evidence that, during each of them, people in south-eastern England with cash to invest transferred their money from the private market in loans to government stocks.[28] Since

[25] E. A. Wrigley and R. S. Schofield, *The Population History of England, 1541–1871* (London, 1981), table 7.8.

[26] D. C. Coleman, *The Economy of England, 1450–1750* (Oxford, 1977), ch. 9. See also, D. Little, *Deceleration in the Eighteenth-Century British Economy* (London, 1976).

[27] J. R. Jones, *Country and Court: England, 1658–1714* (London, 1978), p. 271.

[28] D. M. Joslin, 'London Bankers in Wartime, 1739–84', in *Studies in the Industrial Revolution Presented to T. S. Ashton*, ed. L. S. Pressnell (London, 1960), pp. 156–76.

much of the business of the central courts involved credit transactions between individuals (see Figure 3.8, p. 52), the creation of a major alternative to private lending may well have contributed to some contraction in the legal business which arose from it.

No less importantly, as studies of crime suggest, war may have helped to alleviate underemployment and low incomes amongst smaller artisans and wage-labourers, particularly in the first half of the eighteenth century when stagnant population and increased agricultural output resulted in generally high real wages.[29] Even in major royal courts, such as King's Bench and Common Pleas, a large percentage of lawsuits involved relatively small sums of money amounting to less than £20. The number of cases heard by the courts must have depended significantly on the availability of credit and the ability of shopkeepers, tradesmen, and wage-labourers to pay on time.[30]

The same conjunction of limited population growth and generally high productivity of foodstuffs which made conditions more comfortable for those involved in non-agricultural occupations had a much less beneficial effect on farmers and brought a significant decline in the number of small-holders.[31] Since nearly 30 per cent of all defendants in the Common Pleas in both 1640 and 1750 were described as yeomen or husbandman farmers (see Figure 3.7, p. 50), this change in their position had a direct impact on the overall volume of litigation. Both of the periods in which litigation dropped most dramatically, the 1690s and the 1730s and 1740s, were associated with severe bouts of agricultural depression in which many farmers were forced to sell out.[32] An important sector of the traditional market for legal services was withering away.

Changes in agricultural society are also the best explanation for the changes in the regional distribution of litigation which are displayed in Figure 3.5. For example, in the late sixteenth and early seventeenth centuries much of the prodigious boom in litigation, particularly in Common Pleas, came from East Anglia, a region noted for its large numbers of contentious freehold farmers and for its famous lawyers, including Spelman and Coke.[33] But by 1750 the cloth industry in Norwich was sagging in the face of competition from other areas, and the region as a whole was becoming a backwater.[34]

---

[29] Beattie, *Crime and the Courts*, pp. 220ff.

[30] See above, note 22.

[31] K. Wrightson, *English Society, 1580–1680* (London, 1982), pp. 132, 142–45; J. Thirsk, ed., *The Agrarian History of England and Wales*, v, *1640–1750*, part 2, *Agrarian Change* (Cambridge, 1985), pp. 64, 75, 172, 241.

[32] Ibid., p. 81; G. E. Mingay, 'The Agricultural Depression, 1730–1750', *Economic History Review*, 2nd series, 3 (1956), pp. 323–38; A. H. John, 'The Course of Agricultural Change, 1660–1760', in Pressnell, ed., *Studies in the Industrial Revolution*, pp. 134, 150.

[33] Brooks, *Pettyfoggers and Vipers of the Commonwealth*, pp. 63–65.

[34] P. J. Corfield, 'The Social and Economic History of Norwich, 1650–1850: A Study in Urban Growth' (unpublished Ph.D. thesis, University of London, 1976), pp. 115, 207, 671; A. Young, *A Farmer's Tour Through the East of England* (London, 1771).

Figure 3.5

Geographical Distribution of Litigation in King's Bench and Common
Pleas, 1606–1750 (Percentages by Assize Circuit)

	Common Pleas			King's Bench	
	1606[a]	*1640[a]*	*1750[b]*	*1606[a]*	*1750[c]*
HOME (Kent, Essex, Sussex, Hertfordshire, Surrey)	16	15	8	12	11
MIDLAND (Derbyshire, Lincolnshire, Nottinghamshire, Rutland, Northamptonshire, Warwickshire, Leicestershire)	13	13	12	11	3
NORFOLK (Norfolk, Suffolk, Cambridgeshire, Huntingdonshire, Bedfordshire, Buckinghamshire)	19	18	11	13	3
NORTHERN (Yorkshire, Northumberland, Westmorland, Cumberland)	5	4	23	2	10
OXFORD (Oxfordshire, Berkshire, Gloucestershire, Worcestershire, Shropshire, Staffordshire, Herefordshire, Monmouthshire)	13	12	12	14	12
WESTERN (Hampshire, Wiltshire, Somersetshire, Devonshire, Dorset, Cornwall)	12	15	14	25	26
LONDON and MIDDLESEX	16	22	19	21	32
LANCASHIRE, CHESHIRE, DURHAM	4	1	3		3
ILLEGIBLE	2			2	
TOTAL	100	100	100	100	100

[a] Brooks, *Pettyfoggers and Vipers of the Commonwealth*, p. 64.
[b] PRO, CP 40/3576.
[c] PRO, IND 1/6194.

Common Pleas work from the Norfolk assize circuit shrank to less than the average for the nation as a whole, and in King's Bench the decline was even steeper. On the other hand, the relative success of King's Bench in the mid eighteenth century may owe something to the fact that it was evidently more successful in attracting business from the economic centre of gravity, London. Furthermore, both courts, but especially Common Pleas, saw a significant increase in the percentage of cases from northern England. In part this was a result of the abolition of the Council of the North in 1660 as a major tribunal for hearing causes which arose north of the Trent, but it is also an indication of the extent to which some parts of Yorkshire, Northumberland, Cumberland and Westmorland had finally been integrated into the national economy.[35]

[35] Thirsk, ed., *Agrarian History of England and Wales*, p. 82; J. V. Beckett, 'The Decline of the Small Landowner in Eighteenth- and Nineteenth-Century England: Some Regional

Another major social change which contributed to the decline in litigation was a steady growth in the proportion of the English population which lived in towns. Between 1670 and 1700 urban population as a percentage of total population increased from 13.5 per cent to 17 per cent. By 1750 the figure had risen to 21 per cent, and by 1800 to 27.5 per cent.[36] Many of the new town dwellers were prosperous, self-employed merchants and tradesmen. As urbanisation progressed, however, a larger proportion of them consisted of men and women who came to towns in order to work for others and who were therefore dependent on wages.[37] The rise of this urban proletariat is directly connected with trends in litigation. They were too poor, and their economic interests too trivial, to bring them very often before the central courts at Westminster, but at the same time it is clear that they constituted the majority of defendants in new types of legal institutions which were peculiarly characteristic of the eighteenth century: the provincial courts of requests (also known in some places as courts of conscience). These were small debt jurisdictions established by statute at the petition of local communities, usually towns. The powers and administrative details of the courts varied significantly from place to place, but the petitions and statutes calling for their foundation invariably stressed the existence of a large labouring population which was frequently in need of credit, and therefore ran up debts, especially in times of sickness or unemployment.[38]

The chronology of the foundation of courts of requests reflects the course of urbanisation in England during the late seventeenth and eighteenth

Considerations', *Agricultural History Review*, 30 (1982), pp. 97–111. Similarly, the increase in central court litigation from north-eastern England which was noticed by E. Hughes, *North Country Life in the Eighteenth Century: The North East, 1700–1750* (Oxford, 1952), pp. 77ff, is attributable both to the increased affluence brought to the area by the development of the coal industry and to the concurrent decline of the palatinate courts at Durham as inhabitants of the area increasingly sought legal redress from the royal courts in London. K. Emsley and C. M. Fraser, *The Courts of the County Palatine of Durham* (Durham, 1984), pp. 38–39, 45, 76, 82–84. See also, G. Spearman, *An Enquiry into the Ancient and Present State of the County Palatine of Durham* (Edinburgh, 1729).

[36] E. A. Wrigley, 'Urban Growth and Agricultural Change: England and the Continent in the Early Modern Period', *Journal of Interdisciplinary History*, 15 (1985), p. 688.

[37] P. J. Corfield, *The Impact of English Towns, 1700–1800* (Oxford, 1982), chs 8 and 9. No less important, the eighteenth century also saw a great deal of 'industrial' expansion in the countryside, J. Rule, *The Experience of Labour in Eighteenth Century Industry* (London, 1981), pp. 18, 30.

[38] W. H. D. Winder, 'The Courts of Requests', *Law Quarterly Review*, 52 (1936), pp. 369–94. See for example, J. Brand, *The History and Antiquities of the Town and County of the Town of Newcastle upon Tyne* (2 vols, London, 1789), ii, pp. 644–47. *Commons Journals*, xxvi, pp. 368–69. H. W. Arthurs, '"Without the Law": Courts of Local and Special Jurisdiction in Nineteenth Century England', in *Custom, Courts and Counsel: Selected Papers of the Sixth British Legal History Conference Norwich 1983*, eds A. Kiralfy, Michele Slatter and Roger Virgoe (London, 1985), pp. 130–33, shows that most of the business of the courts in Bristol and Sheffield in the early nineteenth century involved shopkeepers who were suing their less well-off customers for goods sold and delivered.

centuries. The first was set up in London during the reign of Henry VIII, but pressure for the foundation of new ones did not arise again until the end of the seventeenth century. In 1673 parliament received unsuccessful petitions from Southwark and Tower Hamlets, two suburbs of London, the fastest growing metropolitan area in Europe. In the early 1690s, when several major urban centres petitioned for courts, grants were made to Gloucester, Norwich, Bristol and Newcastle, the last three being the largest towns in the realm apart from London.[39]

In contrast, no new courts were established during the first fifty years of the eighteenth century.[40] Indeed, a good series of court records from Newcastle indicates that the course of litigation in local jurisdictions during this half century generally mirrored that at Westminster, a fact which must be taken as a strong indication that the relatively high real wages of this period kept the level of indebtedness low. As Figure 3.6 shows, legal business in the town probably reached a peak a decade or so after the introduction in 1690 of a court of requests to supplement two older jurisdictions, the Sheriff's Court and Mayor's Court. Subsequently, litigation in all the courts, but especially in the Mayor's and Sheriff's Courts, dropped off to reach low levels throughout the remainder of the eighteenth century. Significant increases came only in the 1800s.

Figure 3.6

Actions in the Newcastle Town Courts, 1665–1830

	Court of Conscience [a]	Sheriff's Court [b]	Mayor's Court [c]	Sheriff's and Mayor's Court [d]
1665–66		1471		
1679–80			836	
1689–90			616	
1691–92		1578		
1696–97		1175		
1697–98	1826			
1703–04			241	
1706–07		1016		
1711–12	1789			
1729–30		418		170
1743–44	923			
1744–45		313		

[39] *Commons Journals*, ix, pp. 312, 371; x, pp. 77, 85, 277, 545.

[40] *Parliamentary Papers, 1831–32*, xxv, *Second Part of the Appendix to the Fourth Report of the Common Law Commission* (London, 1832), appendix (i) v, 'Returns of All Process Issued from Borough Courts, County Courts, Liberty Courts, Hundred Courts, Manor Courts and Courts of Requests, between the 12 February 1830 and 12 February 1831'.

	Court of Conscience [a]	Sheriff's Court [b]	Mayor's Court [c]	Sheriff's and Mayor's Court [d]
1745–46			111	
1752–53		398		
1772–73	544			
1804–05	378			
1808–09				255
1808–10	1044			
1829–30	3921			576

The spread of dates has been determined by the availability of evidence.

[a] Tyne and Wear Archives Department, Newcastle upon Tyne, NCX/CT 5/1, 3–6; *Parliamentary Papers*, 'Returns of All Process Issued From Borough Courts, County Courts [etc.]'.

[b] Tyne and Wear Archive Department, NCX/CT 2/2/2–4, 7, 15, 20–21.

[c] Tyne and Wear Archive Department, NCX/CT 1/2/1, 3–4, 6, 10.

[d] This jurisdiction was in effect created in the second half of the eighteenth century, when the records of the Sheriff's Court and the Mayor's Court were joined together, Tyne and Wear Archive Department, NCX/CT 3/3/2, 13.

Newcastle was a traditional provincial capital which shared in the urban growth of the years 1650–1750. After 1750, however, its population rose only slightly.[41] From this date newer urban centres, such as Birmingham, Liverpool and Manchester, rapidly took over the leading places in the urban league table after London. As they did so, new courts of requests quickly followed. Petitions from Birmingham and Liverpool, which stressed their recent growth and commercial success, were received by the House of Commons in 1750. There were bursts of acts enabling a variety of towns to create the new jurisdictions between 1760–65, 1775–85 and, especially, 1805–10.[42]

All told, between 1690 and 1830, there were well over one hundred acts of parliament establishing courts of requests. Although the total volume of litigation in all jurisdictions in 1830, at 2767 suits per 100,000 of the population, was significantly lower than in the early seventeenth century (4638 cases per 100,000 in 1606), the courts of requests clearly absorbed some of the legal business which departed from the central courts in the eighteenth century. In the 1820s parliamentary inquiries found that older communal jurisdictions, such as those of the manor or the borough, had long been moribund, but that the courts of requests were hearing some

[41] From 29,000 in 1750 to 33,000 in 1801. Wrigley, 'Urban Growth and Agricultural Change', p. 686. B. R. Mitchell and P. Deane, *Abstract of British Historical Statistics* (Cambridge, 1962), pp. 24–27.

[42] *Commons Journals*, xxvi, pp. 368–69, 415, 421, 426, 555, 584; xxix, pp. 433–34, 707; xxxiv, p. 72; xxxvi, pp. 671; xli, pp. 623, 855.

200,000 cases each year, or about 2.5 times the number entertained by the central courts in London.[43]

Furthermore, while social change (a contraction in the population of smaller land-owners and an expansion in urban wage labour) was a fundamental cause of this development, the rise of the courts of requests was also accompanied by a notable degree of mutual recrimination between those who advocated them and those who supported the common law establishment on both the national and local levels. The preamble to the Newcastle act of 1690 stressed that the costs of prosecuting small debts in the courts at Westminster frequently amounted to more than the cause of action itself, thereby leading to the ruin of the debtors, their wives and children, and to 'great charges to the corporation for their support and maintenance'.[44] Most petitions of the eighteenth century pointed out that costs and delays in both the royal courts and borough courts meant that creditors were unwilling to risk bringing actions for small debts, a circumstance which, it was feared, led many debtors to think that they could get away without paying.[45]

On the other hand, many lawyers were equally hostile towards the courts of requests. A number of attempts to set up the new jurisdictions were opposed, or completely frustrated, by officials in established urban small debts courts.[46] Theirs were the voices of narrow self-interest, but the courts of requests also offended legal sensibilities more generally because they bypassed formalities and limited the role of professionals. The costs of writs, documents and other procedural steps were kept to a minimum, and the use of lawyers other than local attorneys was discouraged.[47] Most importantly, the courts of requests dispensed with that 'ancient and valuable barrier of British liberty, the *trial by jury*'. The decision-making members of the tribunals were commissioners selected by town authorities, or parish vestries, from amongst local merchants and tradesmen, usually on the basis of a property qualification. Since there were no juries and no requirement that strict legal rules be followed, the commissioners had a very large degree of latitude in arriving at their judgments, a point which was latched onto by lawyers such as William Blackstone, whose *Commentaries on the Laws of England*

---

[43] *Parliamentary Papers*, 'Returns of All Process Issued from Borough Courts, County Courts'. Although it is a subject which warrants further study, and although there were particular exceptions, it is extremely unlikely that manorial courts or borough courts ever recovered much of the litigious business they lost during the course of the late sixteenth and seventeenth centuries. Brooks, *Pettyfoggers and Vipers of the Commonwealth*, pp. 96–101; S. Webb and B. Webb, *English Local Government from the Revolution to the Municipal Corporations Act: The Manor and the Borough* (London, 1924).

[44] Brand, *History and Antiquities of the Town and County of the Town of Newcastle upon Tyne*, ii, pp. 644–47.

[45] See for example the petition of Liverpool, *Commons Journals*, xxvi, pp. 368–69.

[46] Ibid., xxv, p. 984; xxxvi, p. 738; xl, p. 435.

[47] Winder, 'The Courts of Requests'.

(1765–69) attacked the 'petty tyrannies' exercised by jurisdictions where amateur judges exercised unlimited autonomy of action.[48]

Although based on the lawyers' perennial suspicion of informal means of resolving disputes,[49] such doubts about the courts of requests were not entirely without foundation. Nor did they come exclusively from the legal profession.[50] Some of the courts may have been based on earlier urban jurisdictions,[51] but the fact that commissioners were drawn from local elites, and uncontrolled by juries, meant that the customary law they administered was largely that of the better-off inhabitants of towns and that their powers were subject to abuse. The possibility of oppression of the poor was frequently referred to in petitions against new statutes. Although many courts of requests developed a tradition of encouraging debtors to make repayments of a few pence a week, their procedures for summonsing defendants, and those for executing judgments, were enforced by the sanction of imprisonment.[52] In 1780, a parliamentary bill designed to restrict this power was inspired by fears that there were too few limits on its abuse.[53] In 1792 the sheriff of the county of Lancaster petitioned the House of Commons with allegations of misconduct against the commissioners in the local court of requests, 'whereby the lower Class of People and the labouring Poor within the said County are grievously harassed and oppressed'.[54]

Even the most articulate advocate of courts of requests, the self-made Birmingham bookseller William Hutton, admitted that before his own appointment as a commissioner, in 1762, the Birmingham court had been dominated by a dipsomaniac local attorney who acted as the court clerk. Moreover, 'The Commissioners, who attended business without studying it,

---

[48] W. Hutton, *A Dissertation on Juries: With a Description of the Hundred Court as an Appendix to the Court of Requests* (Birmingham, 1789), p. 2; William Blackstone, *Commentaries on the Laws of England* (4 vols, Oxford, 1765–69), iii, p. 82. See also, Winder, 'Courts of Requests', pp. 370, 376–78.

[49] A point developed, but seriously overstressed, in H. W. Arthurs, *'Without the Law': Administrative Justice and Legal Pluralism in Nineteenth-Century England* (Toronto, 1985).

[50] See, for example, *A Letter to the Manufacturers and Inhabitants of the Parishes of Stoke, Burslem and Wolstanton, in the County of Stafford, on Courts of Request, Occasioned by the Bill Intended to be Brought into Parliament this Sessions, for the Establishment of that Jurisdiction in the Potteries*, by a Manufacturer [? James Caldwell] (n. p., 1794).

[51] M. Slatter, 'The Norwich Court of Requests: A Tradition Continued', in *Custom, Courts and Counsel*, eds Kiralfy, Slatter, and Virgoe, pp. 97–107.

[52] The extent of the use of imprisonment probably varied from place to place and over time. *Parliamentary Papers*, 'Returns of All Process Issued from Borough Courts, County Courts'. The instalment system was certainly in use in Newcastle and Lincoln: Tyne and Wear Archive Department, Newcastle, NCX/CT5/1, Court of Conscience Records, 1697–1700; Lincolnshire Archives Office, Lincoln, Lincoln City Archives, L1/2/2–3, Court of Request Minute Books, 1797–1806. See also *Commons Journals*, xxxvii, pp. 692–93, 766.

[53] *Commons Journals*, xxxvii, pp. 692, 759, 762–63, 766, 774, 783, 786–87, 792. A large number of urban communities sent in petitions opposing the measure. It was never reported to the House.

[54] Ibid., xlvii, p. 383.

sometimes forgot to treat the suitors as brethren whom they were bound to assist, but brow-beat them as little men, in little office, are apt ...'[55]

Hutton was, nevertheless, convinced that the courts of requests were necessary largely because of the even greater failings of the common law. A vituperative hatred of lawyers was a constant theme of his writings. He suggested that Blackstone's praise of the common law was nothing more than the praise of a certain kind of business activity by a man who had made a lot of money out of it. He thought that local attorneys were broken-down drunkards who stirred up unnecessary suits in order to fleece their clients with exorbitant fees. Legal process itself was long, unintelligible and costly. In sum he thought that:

> There is a striking resemblance between the law and the school-master; in *both* schools we expect to find instruction and protection, but instead of these, we find the rod. *Both* were designed for common benefit; they begin with mildness, they become burdensome, and at last, end in tyranny. Their institution was excellent, their reform is necessary.[56]

William Hutton's doubts about the quality of the legal services offered by the Westminster courts were widely shared. Fears about the high cost and increasing complexity of litigation go some way towards explaining the low levels of central court business during the eighteenth century.

Public concern about abuses in the law courts was expressed both inside and outside parliament at regular intervals throughout the late seventeenth, eighteenth, and early nineteenth centuries,[57] but the parliamentary agitation for law reform in the 1720s, just before the most catastrophic drops in central court litigation, is particularly instructive. At that time, MPs focused on a range of issues from the regulation of attorneys, solicitors and court officials to the illogicality of the fact that court proceedings were written in Latin.[58] However, the single general theme which lay behind most of the

---

[55] W. Hutton, *Courts of Requests: Their Nature, Utility and Power Described, with A Variety of Cases Determined in that of Birmingham* (Birmingham, 1787), p. 374.

[56] Ibid., pp. 7, 10, 36; idem, *A Dissertation on Juries*, pp. 9–11, 31.

[57] For investigations of the legal system by the House of Commons in the later seventeenth century, especially the 1690s, see Historical Manuscripts Commission, *The Manuscripts of the House of Lords, 1689–90*, 12th report, appendix, part 6 (London, 1889), p. 313; ibid., 13th Report, appendix, part 5 (London, 1892), pp. 17, 19, 23, 128–29; ibid., vol. 2, new series (London, 1905), pp. 69–70, 71–72, 81–82; ibid., vol. 4, new series (London, 1908), pp. 62–63, 279. *Commons Journals*, xiv, p. 12.

[58] *Commons Journals*, xxi, pp. 267, 274–77, 297, 313, 622–23, 640, 676, 741, 892–93; xxii, pp. 23, 243.258. For extra-parliamentary views see, for example, Anon., *A Bill for the More Easy and Speedy Recovery of Small Debts* (London, 1730); *A Letter to a Member of Parliament with Some Few Remarks on the Act Made for the Better Regulation of Attornies and Solicitors ... Together with Animadversions on the Grievances the Subjects of England, Especially the Poor, Labor Under, with Regard to the Great Fees Paid by Them when Prosecuting for Their Debts and Dues ... By a Gentleman of Wiltshire* (London, 1730); *Gentleman's Magazine*, 1 (1731), pp. 19, 100, 106, 213; 2 (1732), pp. 899–900, 1015, 1045; Anon., *A Discourse on Fees of Office in Courts of Justice* (London, 1736).

particular calls for reform was the claim that going to law had become excessively difficult and expensive. For example, in 1728 the House of Commons received a number of petitions from justices of the peace and other gentlemen assembled at various meetings of quarter sessions in Yorkshire and the west country which complained about the impossibility of using the royal courts to recover small debts. Like others, that from the West Riding of Yorkshire, a cloth manufacturing region, explained that 'there is in [this] Part of the Kingdom a great Number of Manufacturers, and other labourious People, who are often entitled to receive Small sums from Persons they deal with, which sometimes they cannot procure without considerable Expenses of Suit, whereby they are rendered less able to support their Families'. It then went on to suggest as a remedy that justices of the peace be granted summary jurisdiction to hear and determine small debts.[59] These petitions were almost certainly associated with disputes in the clothing districts over the payment of weavers' wages,[60] but subsequent parliamentary activity went well beyond this particular issue. The House of Commons investigated court officials, obtained the appointment of a royal commission on fees from the king, and considered several bills for the establishment of small debt courts based on the commissions of the peace.

As far as the crucial question of legal costs is concerned, there is every reason to believe that contemporary suspicions were justified. A proliferation in the number of court officials, increases in the amounts they charged for their services, the practice of making litigants pay for numerous copies of case paperwork and, from 1695, the application of government stamp duties to legal documents all contributed to the rising costs of lawsuits. Parliamentary investigations of fees in the 1690s suggest that there had by then already been significant increases. A comparison of published lists of court fees in 1654 and 1695 with those produced in response to parliamentary investigations in 1730 show both a multiplication in the numbers of officials and an uneven, but clearly detectable, increase in some court fees.[61] In addition, the fees of barristers, which accounted for a significant proportion of the costs of any suit which went to trial, and especially those in the court of Chancery, had been increasing steadily throughout the course of the seventeenth century. During the reign of James I, the accepted normal fee was 10s. for appearances or the signing of bills and pleadings. By 1700, however, young

---

59 *Commons Journals*, xxi, pp. 274, 236–37, 313, 622–23. Petitions were also received from the other Yorkshire Ridings and from Wiltshire and Devon.

60 J. De L. Mann, 'Clothiers and Weavers in Wiltshire during the Eighteenth Century', in Pressnell, ed., *Studies in the Industrial Revolution*, pp. 69–71. Political conflicts between Whigs and Tories, which have not been investigated here, may also have been significant.

61 E. Hughes, 'The English Stamp Duties, 1664–1764', *English Historical Review*, 56 (1941), pp. 234–44; *The Practick Part of the Law: Shewing the Office of a Complete Attorney* (London, 1654 and 1696); *Lists, Accounts and Tables of Fees of the Officers and Servants Belonging to the Judges of the Several Courts in Westminster Hall, and the Circuits, the Associates and Clerks of Assize Presented to the House of Commons Pursuant to their Order of the 23rd Day of March 1729* (London, 1730).

counsel could expect a guinea (21s.) for the same services, while important lawyers involved in major causes took up to four or five times that amount.[62]

No less importantly, the decline in litigation itself appears to have had a profound impact on the structure and fee-taking conventions of the lower branch of the legal profession, the attorneys and solicitors who were usually the practitioners most often in contact with potential litigants. The account books of the King's Bench attorney Henry Travers and of the Cambridgeshire practitioner Ambrose Benning show that the decline in the general levels of litigation from the 1690s onwards was reflected in the private practices of individuals.[63] Furthermore, as the amount of business they handled in London melted away, so the typical seventeenth-century pattern of practice which saw attorneys making regular termly trips to the capital began to be abandoned.[64] Admissions to the inns of chancery in London, the term-time residences of such practitioners, fell significantly in the first half of the eighteenth century, and the lower branch as a whole gradually became much more oriented towards purely provincial work, most of which was not litigious, than it had been before 1690.[65] In 1730 William Heron of Harbury in Yorkshire found it extremely irksome to have to go to London at all; by that date most country attorneys were regularly conducting their business in the Westminster courts through London agents.[66]

This development compounded the decline in litigation in two ways. Rather than charging clients a flat rate of 3s. 4d. per term for litigious work, as had previously been the practice, attorneys in the eighteenth century began to add on fees for the time they spent consulting with clients, writing letters for them and travelling to London or assizes. For instance, in the fee book which he began in 1681, Ambrose Benning made his first charges for travelling to London in 1701.[67] Over the course of the century, these additional fees became commonplace and thereby contributed significantly to the cost of litigation.[68]

[62] W. R. Prest, 'Counsellors Fees in the Age of Coke', in *Legal Records and the Historian*, ed. J. H. Baker (London, 1978), pp. 168, 182; D. F. Lemmings, 'The Inns of Court and the English Bar, 1680–1730' (unpublished D. Phil. thesis, University of Oxford, 1985), pp. 232–38.

[63] BL, MS Harleian 569. Travers recorded cases he entered on the plea rolls between 1653 and 1699. Cambridge County Record Office, 423/B1 (a), 'This book belongs to Ambrose Beninge Liber C of Triplow in Cambridgsheire or of Bernards Inn in Holborne London, gent'.

[64] Brooks, *Pettyfoggers and Vipers of the Commonwealth*, p. 31–34, 146–49.

[65] Gray's Inn Library, London, 'The Admissions Registers of Barnard's Inn, 1622–1753', fos 30–53; M. Miles, 'Eminent Practitioners: The New Visage of Country Attorneys, c. 1750–1800', in *Law, Economy and Society, 1750–1914: Essays in the History of English Law*, eds G. R. Rubin and D. Sugarman (Abingdon, 1984), p. 491.

[66] Leeds City Archive Department, Acc. 1361, letter book of William Heron, 1728–33, letters of 20 April, 17 and 31 October 1730.

[67] Account book of Ambrose Benning, fol. 69. He charged £2 for travel to London and four days' work there.

[68] Calderdale District Archives, Halifax, HAS 759, bill book of John Howarth of Ripponden, 1748–53.

The new provincial orientation of the profession was also damaging to the central courts, because it discouraged some practitioners from advising people to go to law at all. As the perceptive legal writer Richard Boote pointed out in 1766, attorneys received only a modest proportion of the money clients laid out for the procedural steps which accompanied any lawsuit.[69] In fact, the fee structure by then worked in such a way that they could make just as much money out of a dispute by encouraging a settlement through arbitration which might, or might not, be undertaken in connection with the purchase of London writs. Late eighteenth-century critics of the profession, who wrote mainly from London, continued to attack pettyfogging practitioners who stirred up lawsuits, but the letters of the Bath solicitor John Jeffreys suggest that by the 1780s he frequently found his income from litigious work scarcely worth the trouble it caused him.[70] A recent study of the Bradford attorney John Eagle shows that he in fact handled more arbitrations than cases which went the course through the courts.[71] The full extent of this practice is virtually impossible to measure but it may have had a powerful influence on the volume of central court litigation.

These changes in the structure of the legal profession attracted little attention from the law reformers. Nor was very much achieved in correcting those abuses which they did notice. Despite the complaints and parliamentary agitation of the years around 1730, virtually nothing was done to tackle the problem of high legal costs in general or about the particular issue of the excessive expense involved in bringing actions to recover small debts. Statutes were passed to regulate the training of attorneys and solicitors, and to translate legal proceedings into English, but bills for the establishment of small debt courts floundered on the vested interests of office-holders.[72] The royal commission appointed in 1732 to investigate fees was wound up in 1746 with little to show for its efforts apart from a bill for the clerk's salary.[73]

As a result of the unchecked increases in fees, the overall cost of litigation in the central courts doubled between 1680 and 1750. In the 1660s and 1670s, the overwhelming majority of the clients of the Hertfordshire attorney George Draper paid less than £10 for their suits at common law.[74] Between

---

69 Boote, *An Historical Treatise*, pp. xi, xiv.

70 A. Grant, *The Progress and Practice of a Modern Attorney: Exhibiting the Conduct of Thousands Towards Millions* (London, n. d., *c.* 1790s). Somerset Record Office, Taunton, DD/WLM, box 1, letter books of John Jeffreys, solicitor of Bath, 1773 to *c.* 1800: vol. i, 11 October 1774, 13 February 1775, 13 October 1777; vol. ii, 11 January 1784.

71 Miles, 'Eminent Practitioners', pp. 495–96.

72 2 George II, c. 23, and 4 George II, c. 26. *Commons Journals*, xxiii, pp. 234, 287, 298, 699, 636, 653.

73 BL, MS Add. 36118, fol. 575. The commission completed its investigation of the court of Chancery in 1740, but had not sat since then. Lord Chancellor Hardwicke, who was responsible for the activities of the commission, evidently did little to encourage it. But also, see below, Chapter 4, p. 95.

74 Brooks, *Pettyfoggers and Vipers of the Commonwealth*, p. 105.

1750 and 1830, figures of between £20 and £30 for the same kind of work appear constantly in the fee books of attorneys, in literature calling for reform and in the reports of parliamentary inquiries.[75] It became an eighteenth-century commonplace that most people would rather loose their rights than risk their money in going to law. Richard Boote linked the decline in litigation at Westminster with the effects of high clerical fees and stamp duties.[76] Another legal observer pointed out that high office fees also accounted for the fact that by 1730 attorneys were no longer extending credit to less well-off litigants, thereby identifying the decline of a practice which had been important in fuelling the late Elizabethan and early Stuart boom in litigation.[77] As we have seen, eighteenth-century petitions for the establishment of courts of requests constantly complained about the difficulties of suing for small debts. In 1823 a parliamentary committee collected evidence from tradesmen who unanimously agreed that no prudent businessman would risk going to law for a debt of less than £15. In their view, the difficulty this imposed on collecting for goods sold on credit meant that they had to charge all customers more than would have been the case if there had been a reliable means for forcing payment.[78]

Some people, most notably Sir William Blackstone, continued to defend the common law system. Many others paid lip-service to the notion that in substance the English enjoyed the best of all possible laws.[79] But the periodical literature of the eighteenth century reveals a very articulate body of public opinion which saw excessive fees as only one aspect of an 'oppressive' system of justice which was also subject to delay and unreasonable complexity. A writer in the *Universal Spectator* (1731) explained that while the law began as customs which were well suited to the needs of the people, as circumstances changed, new forms of practice were introduced – until the legal system was precipitated into a miserable state of intricacy, expense

[75] Calderdale District Archives, bill book of John Howarth; [A. Grant], *The Public Monitor; or A Plan for the More Speedy Recovery of Small Debts; Wherein the Expediencey of Erecting County Courts and of Enlarging the Powers of the Courts of Request is Pointed Out* (London, 1789), pp. vi–viii; Hutton, *Courts of Request*, p. 81; *Parliamentary Papers 1829*, ix, *First Report of the Commissioners on the Practice and Proceedings of the Superior Courts of Common Law with a Supplement and Appendix* (London, 1829), appendix (M), no. 1. 'Bills of Costs, pp. 687–716; C. W. Francis, 'Practice, Strategy, and Institution: Debt Collection in the English Common-Law Courts, 1740–1840', *Northwestern University Law Review*, 80 (1986), p. 858.

[76] *A Letter to A Member of Parliament with Some Few Remarks on the Act Made for the Better Regulation of Attornies and Sollicitors*, pp. 2–3; *Commons Journals*, xxi, p. 640; Boote, *An Historical Treatise*, p. x.

[77] *A Letter to A Member of Parliament with Some Few Remarks on the Act Made for the Better Regulation of Attorneys and Sollicitors*, p. 9; Brooks, *Pettyfoggers and Vipers of the Commonwealth*, pp. 105–6.

[78] *Parliamentary Papers 1823*, iv, *Report from the Select Committee on the Recovery of Small Debts in England and Wales* (London, 1823), pp. 3, 13–15.

[79] See also, Daines Barrington, *Observations on the Statutes, Chiefly the More Ancient, from Magna Charta to the Twenty-First of James the First* (London, 1766), pp. iv, 337–38.

and confusion.[80] In 1749, the *Gentleman's Magazine* approvingly outlined law reforms recently undertaken by the king of Prussia and compared them favourably with the 'engine of oppression' which English law had become.[81] Writing in 1792, Jeremy Bentham mockingly sparred with a speech in praise of the law which had been delivered by Sir William Ashurst to the Middlesex grand jury. In response to Ashurst's claim that 'No man is so low as not to be within the law's protection', Bentham wrote:

> Ninety-nine men out of a hundred are thus low. Everyman is, who has not from five-and-twenty pounds, to five-and-twenty times five-and-twenty pounds, to sport with, in order to take his chance for justice.[82]

At about the same time, another critic complained about the difficulty of using the law to recover property; as well as about the injustices, particularly the practice of arrest on *mesne* process, which had grown up on the fringes of the legal system so that an essentially litigious society could carry on its business. 'Either John Bull must be a contentious wicked fellow, or else there must be some strange and unaccountable defect in the Laws by which he is governed.' There was little that was new in the conclusion of the parliamentary investigators in 1830 that excessive costs and defects in legal administration amounted to a 'denial of justice' in the face of greater demands for justice which had by then been created by the increased population, wealth and commerce of the nation.[83]

By the 1730s social change, alterations in the legal profession and increased fees were putting the great 'Law Shops' at Westminster Hall beyond the reach of many potential litigants. Nevertheless, these factors do not necessarily rule out the possibility that the decline in litigation was also a consequence of a general change in attitudes and behaviour which led to a decline in contentiousness between 1640 and 1750. This is an hypothesis which has been stressed by Lawrence Stone. Along with an apparent fall in the rate of homicide, it is in his view further support for the broader claim that the social tension which characterised English society before 1650 gradually gave way to an eighteenth-century world of less violence and less contention.[84] The issue raises questions of almost unlimited scope, but an analysis of those litigants and disputes which did come before the central courts is a logical first step in dissecting them.

---

80 Reprinted in the *Gentleman's Magazine*, 1 (1731), p. 100.

81 Ibid., 20 (1750), pp. 215–17.

82 'Truth versus Ashurst; or Law as It Is, Contrasted with What It Is Said to Be', in *The Works of Jeremy Bentham, Published under the Superintendence of His Executor, John Bowring* (11 vols, Edinburgh, 1843), iv, p. 233.

83 Grant, *The Progress and Practice of a Modern Attorney; Fourth Report of the Commissioners on the Practice and Proceedings of the Superior Courts of Common Law: With a Supplement and Appendix*, part 1 (London, 1831–32) pp. 5–45.

84 Stone, 'A Rejoinder', pp. 216–24.

Figure 3.7

Social Status of Litigants in Common Pleas, 1640 and 1750
(percentages, numbers in round brackets)

	1640 [a]			1750 [b]		
	Plaintiffs	*Defendants*	*Total*	*Plaintiffs*	*Defendants*	*Total*
Gentleman and above	25 (271)	39 (561)	33 (832)	11 (114)	16 (171)	12 (285)
Yeoman	—	22 (314)	13 (314)	—	25 (265)	13 (265)
Husbandman ('Farmer')	—	6 (88)	4 (88)	—	4 (38)	2 (38)
Total landed	25 (271)	67 (963)	50 (1234)	11 (114)	45 (474)	29 (588)
Commercial/ artisan	0.5 (5)	18 (255)	10 (260)	1 (13)	25 (269)	13 (282)
Clergy	1 (15)	3 (43)	2 (58)	2 (16)	0.5 (8)	1 (24)
Attorneys	0.7 (7)	3 (37)	2 (44)	4 (41)	2 (26)	3 (67)
Widows	6 (60)	2 (23)	3 (83)	3 (29)	3 (35)	3 (64)
Miscellaneous	0.2 (2)	6 (92)	4 (94)	0.7 (8)	6 (65)	3 (73)
Not given	66 (706)	1 (13)	29 (719)	79 (815)	19 (203)	48 (1018)
Grand Total	100 (1066)	100 (1426)	100 (2492)	100 (1036)	100 (1080)	100 (2116)

[a] Brooks, *Pettyfoggers and Vipers of the Commonwealth*, p. 283.
[b] PRO, CP 40/3575. In connection with this table, and Figure 3.8, there is no reason to think that the dates 1640 and 1750 were atypical from the point of view of litigation. Since inaccuracies in the styles given to defendants were a ground for non-suiting plaintiffs, it is likely that most of the defendants for whom no style is given were of non-armigerous status.

Changes in court record-keeping, a decline in the accuracy and regularity with which men attached styles to their surnames and the need for further study all dictate caution in jumping to conclusions about the nature of litigants in the main Westminster courts in the mid eighteenth century. Even so, a glance at Figure 3.7, which compares the social status of Common Pleas litigants in 1640 and 1750, reveals a very significant decline in the percentage of both plaintiffs and defendants styled as gentlemen, esquires, knights or one of the ranks of the peerage. The trend is further corroborated by the dramatic drop in the levels of business in Chancery, a court which was particularly concerned with the affairs of the gentry. In addition, it can be illustrated more concretely through the accounts of the legal work handled by the attorney John Donne for a wealthy Somerset family, the Pauletts. Between 1729 and 1773, the Pauletts ran up legal costs totalling some £953 (an average of about £22 per annum). However, apart from the relentless prosecution of a man who had aided a gaol break and invaded the family's garden at Hinton St George, two Chancery suits and a couple of ejectments against tenants, most of Donne's work over the course of forty-four years involved miscellaneous errands and the drawing of instruments such as deeds, wills and warrants for gamekeepers.[85]

A more stable land market and the development of mortgages as a way of raising capital, as well the effectiveness of the strict settlement as a means of reducing inter-familial conflict over property, may well account for a large part of this decline in gentry litigation.[86] So, too, may the reputation of the law. Some parts of the gentry community must have been aware of the criticisms of the law which were circulated in the press and sometimes debated in parliament. All squires would have recoiled in anger from an account published in the 1730s which described how the masters in Chancery exploited estates which had been put into their hands in connection with litigation over mortgages.[87] At the same time, some gentlemen may have thought that it besmirched their honour to have their affairs discussed publicly in court or press reports.[88]

On the other hand, the decline in gentry litigants may reflect little more than the fact that it was hard to get the elite to pay their debts. For instance, at the time of his death the attorney John Donne had received only £41 18s. 0d. of the £953 due to him from Lord Paulett for legal services; if his case is typical then the legal profession obviously had a vested interest in keeping the aristocracy out of court.[89] More generally, tradesmen frequently complained that it was difficult to get gentlemen to settle their accounts. Peers of the realm could not be arrested for debt. Given the high cost of litigation, richer gentlemen may have been protected from the law by their potential ability to outpurse creditors who were thinking of taking legal action against them.[90] Although army and navy officers, most of whom were the offspring of the lesser gentry, appear sometimes to have ended up in debtors' prison, Alexander Grant must have been largely correct in claiming that the richer part of the nation had little experience which would enable them to imagine the horrors of the Fleet or the King's Bench prisons.[91]

---

85 Somerset Record Office, Taunton, DD/MR 101, fee book of John Donne, fos 52–73v. It took over two years and the staggering sum of £321 14s. 6d. to get Thomas Burridge transported for seven years in 1735. Two other prosecutions for theft, one involving a silver spoon, were brought for less than £10. By comparison, one Chancery case which ran for four years cost £107 18s. 5d.; the other, which lasted three years, came to a minimum of £62 11s. 2d.

86 For the strict settlement, see L. Stone and J. F. C. Stone, *An Open Elite? England, 1540–1880* (Oxford, 1984), p. 74.

87 *Gentleman's Magazine*, 3 (1733), p. 467.

88 Anon., *The Locusts: or Chancery Painted to the Life and the Laws of England Tryed in Forma Pauperis. A Poem* (London, 1704), preface.

89 Somerset Record Office, fee book of John Donne, fol. 73v.

90 Grant, *The Progress and Practice of a Modern Attorney*, pp. 73–75; J. Brewer, 'Commercialization and Politics', in *The Birth of a Consumer Society: The Commercialization of Eighteenth Century England*, eds N. McKendrick, J. Brewer, and J. H. Plumb (London, 1982), pp. 198–99.

91 *The Most Humble Petition of the Several Persons in the Fleet-Prison in Behalf of Themselves and Several Thousand Imprison'd Debtors in the King's-Bench and the Several Goals of this Kingdom* (London, n.d., but *c*. 1727); [Grant], *The Public Monitor*, p. 28.

The decline in the percentage of Common Pleas business which involved landed society suggests that the work of the courts was being concentrated increasingly on the affairs of merchants, tradesmen and artisans, and this is in fact quite consistent with an overall drop in litigation. We have seen already how these groups benefited from early eighteenth-century economic trends. In addition, from the later middle ages, if not long before, the culture of urban communities stressed fair dealing and probity in business transactions. Towns maintained their own institutions, such as guilds, which were essentially hostile to the adversarial nature of deciding disputes at common law.[92] Commercial opinion is well reflected in John Marius's famous remark that 'The right dealing merchant doth not care how little he hath to do in the Common Law'.[93] Tradesmen like William Stout and Thomas Turner were probably not atypical in their extreme reluctance to use the law against those who owed them money.[94] By 1750 the older institutional fabric in which these values had grown was in decline, but the customs of merchants continued to colour transactions, and newer social organisations, such as the ubiquitous tradesmen's clubs of the eighteenth century, promoted the virtues of honesty and fair dealing, including the payment of debts on time.[95] Furthermore, between 1650 and 1750, a number of changes were introduced into the common law which helped to accommodate it better to commercial needs; these may also have contributed to the reduction in the number of lawsuits.

Table 3.8

Forms of Action at Common Law, 1640–1750 (percentages)

	Common Pleas		King's Bench	
	1640[a]	*1750*[b]	*1640*[a]	*1750*[c]
Debt	88	32	80	32
Actions on the case	5	37	13	42
Ejectment	1	16	2	13
Trespass	3	13	5	10
Miscellaneous	3	2	—	3
Total	100	100	100	100

[a] Brooks, *Pettyfoggers and Vipers of the Commonwealth*, p. 69.

[b] PRO, CP 40/3575.

[c] PRO, IND 1/6194.

[92] S. Thrupp, *The Merchant Class of Medieval London* (Chicago, 1948), p. 21; Brooks, *Pettyfoggers and Vipers of the Common Wealth*, p. 35.

[93] Quoted in J. Milnes Holden, *The History of Negotiable Instruments in English Law* (London, 1955), p. 42.

[94] *The Autobiography of William Stout of Lancaster, 1665–1752*, ed. J. D. Marshall, Chetham Society, 3rd series, 14 (1967), pp. 119–20; Thomas Turner, *The Diary of a Georgian Shopkeeper*, ed. R. W. Blencowe and M. A. Lower (2nd edn, Oxford, 1979), p. 26.

[95] Brewer, 'Commercialization and Politics', pp. 200, 214, 217, 229.

As Figure 3.8 shows, in 1640 actions of debt made up the vast majority of cases in King's Bench and Common Pleas. In turn most of these lawsuits involved written obligations under seal which were associated with loans or other financial arrangements. In the sixteenth and seventeenth centuries the action was frequently called upon in connection with a legal instrument known as the conditional bond, which was widely used to enforce agreements to perform certain actions or pay off debts. The form of the bond was usually that a debt should be paid or an action undertaken by a specified date. If there was a default, the defaulter was obliged to pay a penal sum of money which had been agreed beforehand by both parties. Bonds were a relatively secure way of carrying out business which left both the details of the agreement and the degree of the penalty to be exacted for non-compliance largely up to the parties themselves.[96] Moreover, bonds and other written obligations were enforced rigorously by the courts: if the writing could be produced in court, there was little the defendant could do to prevent a judgment being given against him. On the other hand, one disadvantage of such instruments was that they had to be written out and sealed. Another was that debts created in this way were not assignable: a debt owed to a designated creditor could not be used by the creditor to pay his own debts. By the early seventeenth century, this was a source of constant complaint from the merchant community: it limited the fluidity of credit and was contrary to business practices which English merchants found common elsewhere in Europe.[97]

By the later seventeenth century, the rigours of the common law of contract were being relaxed in favour of the generally more forgiving customs of merchants. The court of Chancery led the way by providing debtors with relief from the stringent penalties of the conditional bond if it appeared that they had been defrauded or had some genuine reason for failing to carry out the conditions.[98] The common law courts followed suit. By 1750 they were regularly using mechanisms which eased the rules that obligations had to be performed on a certain day and which forced creditors to accept partial payments of debts. Although the exact chronology is somewhat obscure, during the course of the eighteenth century the superior courts, like the courts of requests, were facilitating the repayment of debts by weekly or monthly instalments.[99] In addition, after 1640, there were two important changes associated with litigation which came into the common law courts under a broad category of legal remedies known as actions on the case.

[96] Brooks, *Pettyfoggers and Vipers of the Commonwealth*, pp. 67–68.

[97] Holden, *The History of Negotiable Instruments in English Law*, pp. 66–68.

[98] A. W. B. Simpson, *The History of the Common Law of Contract: The Rise of the Action of Assumpsit* (Oxford, 1975), pp. 118–24.

[99] PRO, KB 125/151, King's Bench Rule Book, 1750; William Bohun, *Institutio Legalis: or An Introduction to the Study and Practice of the Laws of England as Now Regulated and Amended by Several Late Statutes* (3rd edn, London, 1724), p. 4; Francis, 'Practice, Strategy, and Institution', p. 827.

Actions on the case for assumpsit were used more and more widely to enforce informal written or verbal contracts of all kinds. What is no less important, by 1704 the courts were allowing actions on the case to be used to enforce the honouring of bills of exchange and promissory notes, both of which were negotiable instruments of credit.[100]

The rise between 1640 and 1750 in the percentage of actions on the case sued in both King's Bench and Common Pleas was largely the result of these changes in the way men did business. Moreover, it is possible that the development of negotiable promissory notes helped to cut down the number of lawsuits. Because of the ubiquity of small-scale borrowing and lending, most landowners and businessmen were simultaneously creditors and debtors. When the conditional bond was the primary means of arranging loans, creditors could not be lenient with their debtors because they themselves might need cash in order to pay debts of their own which were due under the strict terms of the bond. Hence one reason for the large number of lawsuits in the period from 1560 to 1640.[101] By contrast, since they enabled debts to be transferred, promissory notes helped to take some of the urgency, and hence some of the hostility, out of the debtor-creditor relationship. So, too, did the practice of encouraging partial payment or payment by instalment.

Although it may have contributed to a general drop in the amount of litigation, the growth in the number of actions on the case for debt also meant an increase in the percentage of all suits at Westminster which eventually ended up going for trial before a jury. Since a defendant who had signed his name to a written agreement usually had little to gain by putting his case to a jury, relatively few cases of 'debt on specialty', as they were known, entered the records of suits sent for trial at assize. But actions on the case, where the promises to be kept were sometimes complicated or ill-defined, and the penalties had not been prescribed by the litigants, were potentially much more likely to involve both fraud and contention. Over 50 per cent of all actions on the case which reached advanced stages in the King's Bench in 1750 went for trial at *nisi prius*.[102] Therefore, as the total number of actions on the case increased, so too did the percentage of all cases which were heard by a jury. In the Common Pleas between 20–25 per cent of all cases in advanced stages went to trial in the 1680s and 1690s. In the King's Bench 40 per cent did so by 1750.[103]

Litigation about debts and contracts was important because it was so frequent; the history of civil litigation between 1640 and 1750 is primarily the history of how English society made and enforced promises. Nevertheless,

---

[100] Holden, *The History of Negotiable Instruments*, pp. 30, 32, 36, 52, 66, 79, 99–100.

[101] Thomas Wilson, *A Discourse upon Usury*, ed. R. H. Tawney (London, 1925), p. 235.

[102] PRO, IND 1/6194.

[103] PRO, CP 36/11, which contains a contemporary analysis of the number of cases sent for trial versus those ('common judgments') which were not; PRO, IND 1/6194.

other types of legal business entered the court records. Figure 3.8 (p. 50), which displays the relative frequency of each of the forms of action at common law, provides a means of tracing its profile.[104]

We have seen already that many actions on the case involved debts or contracts but, although it is impossible to break it down statistically, this category also includes other important types of case including slander (malicious words), malfeasance (the inadequate performance of a task or obligation) and negligence. On the other hand, actions of ejectment were made up of a large number of collusive actions to establish titles to land – as well as cases in which landlords were suing for rent or evicting tenants. Finally, trespass was another broad category which housed a wide range of disputes. It included allegations of assault resulting in personal injury, as well as actions of false imprisonment. At the same time, trespass frequently involved mishaps or disagreements associated with agricultural life, such as the destruction of crops or the damaging of sheep by dogs. The action was sometimes associated with cases which hinged on the disputed title to land. It was also used by husbands to sue men who had committed adultery with their wives. For example, in 1750, an Oxfordshire man asked for £1000 damages against a victualler of Wallington, accusing him of adultery with his wife.[105]

Thanks to the notes which the judge Sir Dudley Rider made of civil cases tried before him at the Middlesex assizes between 1754 and 1756, it is possible to penetrate more deeply into the complex issues which some of these civil actions actually involved. Predictably, actions on conditional bonds were settled with relatively little controversy once the existence of the bond had been proven. But a suit over a promissory note which was given in connection with the sale of 'slops', or civilian clothing, to a regiment of marines had to be put out to arbitration by three people who were familiar with the exact functions of military quartermasters.[106] In general, the striking feature of what can be described as the commercial cases is both the extent to which legal process was allowed to intervene in business affairs and the wide discretion left to juries. For example, a case in which the plaintiff accused an organ-maker of overcharging for an incompetent repair job raised questions about whether the work was done properly; whether the price was fair; and whether the organ-maker had taken too much profit from the work of his employees. Similarly, a suit for wages which Ann Byers brought against her employer, Sarah Mackay, led to a series of witnesses

---

[104] For more detail on the forms of action see Brooks, *Pettyfoggers and Vipers of the Commonwealth*, pp. 66–71.

[105] PRO, CP 40/3574, rolls 567, 594. In 1750 6 per cent of all Common Pleas, and 3 per cent of King's Bench cases, involved the action of trespass and assault.

[106] Lincoln's Inn Library, London, transcript of Dudley Ryder's law notes by K. L. Perrin, document 12, p. 12; document 16, p. 16.

discussing the levels of pay due for various kinds of work in the mantua-maker's trade.[107]

Actions of assault, slander and unlawful imprisonment were also common. As in the seventeenth century, these appear frequently to have arisen out of the processes by which criminal accusations were brought during the early modern period. Since there was no professional police force, people who thought that crimes had been committed against them had to be active personally in getting constables to make arrests and in presenting accusations to justices of the peace or judges. Hence actions for damages as a result of unlawful imprisonment, or for slander for words which implied that the plaintiff had committed a crime, constituted a method of countering unjust prosecutions or malicious rumours.[108] Equally, some people sought compensation for assaults through the civil rather than the criminal court system. A Dutchman who had been impressed on an English East Indiaman won both a moral case and £10 damages from the Middlesex jurors by bringing an action of assault against the ship's mate for immoderately punishing him. More surprisingly, a young distillery worker successfully sued a squire for threatening him with a gun, tearing his clothing and keeping him prisoner for several hours.[109]

Other actions of assault or slander seem to have originated from relatively more trivial petty quarrels. In many suits for assault tempers had flared suddenly, sometimes in conjunction with provocative words. In one such, a defence lawyer commented that 'this sort of action ought to be discouraged'. In several of the others, Ryder was understandably uncertain as to how to direct the jury. The derisory damages of a shilling or so awarded by the jurors suggest that they found the task of assessing blame virtually impossible or hardly worth the effort.[110] It was much the same with many cases of slander, some of which involved business rivals making unkind remarks about each other, while many others seem the product of little more than personal hostility.[111] Nor was mid eighteenth-century London short of litigious souls. A glazier who had slandered his local churchwarden

---

[107] Ryder's law notes, document 12, p. 12; document 13, p. 17.

[108] Brooks, *Pettyfoggers and Vipers of the Commonwealth*, pp. 107–111, 279; J. Kent, *The English Village Constable, 1580–1642: A Social and Administrative Study* (Oxford, 1986), pp. 246, 261; R. H. Helmholz, 'Civil Trials and the Limits of Responsible Speech', in R. H. Helmholz and T. A. Green, *Juries, Libel, and Justice: The Role of English Juries in Seventeenth- and Eighteenth-Century Trials for Libel and Slander* (Los Angeles, CA, 1984), pp. 3–36. Interestingly, John Jeffreys of Bath told Lord Camden that many men refused to become justices of the peace because of the 'great application necessary to avoid being entangled in Vexatious, harassing Law Suits, even for a slip, an Error, not a premeditated wrong'. Somerset Record Office, letter books of John Jeffreys, vol. ii, 10 August 1783.

[109] Ryder's Law Notes, document 12, pp. 1, 8, 30; document 13, pp. 26; document 16, p. 34, 54.

[110] Ibid., document 12, pp. 1, 11, 24, 59.

[111] Ibid., document 12, pp. 15, 37, 50, 59; document 16, p. 19, 50.

at one point in their quarrel boasted that he 'liked a little law now and then'.[112]

Although they refer only to cases from metropolitan London, Ryder's notes suggest that much petty contention existed alongside more serious disputes, a conclusion which also emerges from the more general picture found in Figure 3.8. The significant increase between 1640 and 1750 in the percentages of trespass, ejectment and actions on the case is a warning against assuming that the mid eighteenth century was much more tranquil than the mid seventeenth. If we make the admittedly risky calculation of the actual number of cases involving actions of trespass or ejectment in 1640 as opposed to 1750, there appears to have been a decline of only 20 per cent compared with a much greater decrease in the overall volume of litigation. Unfortunately, it is impossible to discover how many actions on the case involved slander as opposed to debt or other kinds of commercial case, but the great increase in the percentage of such suits raises doubts about whether there was in fact any significant drop in disputes over contentious words.

The most clear-cut changes in the nature of litigation between 1640 and 1750 appear, therefore, to have occurred in the field of interpersonal promises. Although bound up inextricably with technical legal developments, these changes reflect alterations in behaviour and attitude amongst the urban middling sort and gentry which may have contributed to the decline in litigation. Much depends on the significance attached to the fact that the widespread use of sealed written agreements before 1640 gave way by 1750 to the informal written agreement or verbal promise as the primary means through which business transactions were conducted.

The conditional bond, the most common legal device of the period before 1640, presupposed the importance of having an agreement written down on parchment or paper and sealed with wax, presumably because one's neighbours, or potential jurors, could not otherwise be trusted. It was associated with a social world of contentious gentry and small-holders, and the psychological context in which it flourished is reflected in the writings of political and social observers. Thomas Hobbes's obsession with the problem of how people could be made to keep their promises was typical of English legal thinking from the 1520s until the time he himself wrote in the middle of the seventeenth century.[113] The quip of the Chancery official

---

[112] Ibid., document 12, pp. 22–23.

[113] 'A Replication of a Serjeant at the Laws of England', in *Christopher St German on Chancery and Statute*, ed. J. A. Guy, Selden Society supplementary series, 6 (London, 1985), pp. 99–105; Anon., *A Petition to the Kings Most Excellent Maiestie, the Lords Spirituall and Temporall and Commons of the Parliament Now Assembled, Wherein is Declared the Mischiefes and Inconueniences, Arising to the King and Commonwealth, by the Imprisoning of Mens Bodies for Debt* (London, 1622), p. 16; Thomas Hobbes, *Leviathan* (London, 1914), pp. 66, 68, 70–71, 75–76.

George Norburie in the 1620s – that a man's word without his signature on a bond was worthless – is characteristic of his age.[114]

By contrast, the radically divergent viewpoint suggested by the phrase 'a man's word is his bond' seems to have arisen in the eighteenth century, and is consistent with the ways in which contracts were made at that date, at least amongst the urban middle classes.[115] It also corresponds with the observations of the eighteenth-century economist Adam Smith. In his lectures on jurisprudence, Smith postulated that peoples with highly developed commercial habits were more likely to keep their promises than those living in less civilised times and places. In this respect he thought the Dutch were ideal, but he also believed that, by the second half of the eighteenth century, the British were catching up.[116] There is evidence that such values were shared even in professional legal circles. The papers of the attorney and town clerk of Bath, John Jeffreys, which include letters to the sometime Whig chancellor, Lord Camden, reveal a man who was tediously proud of his elevated sensibilities, who believed that 'Natural Justice ... obliges every man ... to render unto every Man what is substantially just and right', and who expressed revulsion at the contentiousness he found in some of the people with whom he had to deal.

It is nevertheless noteworthy that Jeffreys' patience could only be stretched so far. In 1778 he warned a man who owed him money that he was 'resolved ... to be trifled with no longer, for I will use the means that the Law has given me for recovering money, let the consequences be what it will'.[117] More generally, there are three serious flaws in any explanation of the decline in litigation which concentrates exclusively on the emergence during the eighteenth century of more urbane views such as his.

First, many legal authorities were convinced that the replacement of the bond by verbal promises made fraud endemic.[118] Secondly, the great trough in litigation was relatively short-lived. Central court business increased from the 1790s onwards. From 1700, and particularly after 1750, the erection of more and more courts of requests was accompanied by an overall increase in the number of lawsuits,[119] bringing growing numbers of the urban poor within the ambit of a very strict discipline which taught the necessity of honouring obligations. For instance, William Hutton claimed that he was deeply moved by the predicament of the great number of indebted families where the husband was both an apprentice and under age, but he was clear

---

[114] G. Norburie, 'The Abuses and Remedies of Chancery', in *A Collection of Tracts Relative to the Laws of England*, ed. F. Hargrave (London, 1787), p. 433.

[115] Brewer, 'Commercialization and Politics', p. 214.

[116] Adam Smith, *Lectures on Justice, Police, Revenue and Arms Delivered in the University of Glasgow ... Reported by a Student in 1763*, ed. E. Cannan [1896] (New York, 1964), pp. 253–59.

[117] Somerset Record Office, letter books of John Jeffreys, vol. i, 12 October 1775; 21 December 1776; 24 September 1779; vol. ii, 1 April 1783.

[118] Simpson, *Common Law of Contract*, pp. 592, 603.

[119] Brooks, *Pettyfoggers and Vipers of the Commonwealth*, pp. 77–78.

that the Birmingham court of requests seldom accepted a plea of minority in favour of a defendant, because that would teach him a 'wicked argument' against paying his just debts.[120] Thirdly, in the eighteenth century, as in the seventeenth, the sanction of imprisonment stood behind every business deal, behind the implicit bargain which took place every time a shopkeeper extended credit to an urban wage-labourer. In the common law courts, and in the courts of requests, every stage in a lawsuit, from the first writ of summons to that which called for a settlement at the conclusion, was backed up by the threat of imprisonment.[121] In fact, many courts of requests laid down schedules which specified the number of days in gaol which were necessary in order to purge a debt of so many tens of shillings.[122]

Despite the decline in litigation, it is unlikely that there was a proportionate decline in the number of prisoners, and in particular of the numbers imprisoned for relatively small debts. A list of 359 debtors in the King's Bench prison in 1654 shows that most of them were there because they owed considerable sums of money (an average of £2439 each).[123] In the early eighteenth century statutes for the relief of insolvent debtors frequently set the upper limit on the amount to be relieved at £100, which suggests that large numbers of people were imprisoned for less than that relatively small sum. In the 1720s petitions for the relief of imprisoned debtors came not just from London, but from the provinces as well.[124] Samuel Johnson was only one of many in the mid eighteenth century who thought that more men died as a result of imprisonment for debt than in war.[125] In the 1780s the population of the King's Bench Prison fluctuated at between 400 and 500 debtors each year, and a survey of 1789 suggested that no less than 165 of them owed less than £20. Arrest on *mesne* process out of the Westminster courts had become a fearful scourge which, it was claimed, ruined thousands. With the introduction of additional courts of requests, many more

---

120 Hutton, *Courts of Requests*, pp. 25, 53.

121 For a good outline of the procedure in the central courts, see J. Innes, 'The King's Bench Prison in the Later Eighteenth Century: Law, Authority and Order in a London Debtor's Prison', in *An Ungovernable People*, ed. Brewer and Styles, p. 252.

122 *Parliamentary Papers: Appendix [Part II] to the Fourth Report, 1831–32*, appendix (i), v, 'Returns of All Process Issued from Borough Courts, County Courts, Liberty Courts, Hundred Courts, and Courts of Requests'.

123 *A List of All The Prisoners in the Upper Bench Prison, Remaining in Custody the Third of May 1653: Delivered in by Sir John Lenthall to the Committee Appointed by the Councell of State, for Examining of the State of the Said Prison. With the Times of Their First Commitment* (London, 1654). While the average is inflated by some extremely large sums (including one of £98,000) which must be associated with the recent wars, the majority of the debts listed run to hundreds or thousands rather than tens of pounds. The smallest debt mentioned was for £20.

124 2 George II, c. 22. Petitions in 1728 were received from Bristol, Lincoln and Coventry. *Commons Journals*, xxi, pp. 228, 236. A report on the Fleet prison in London suggests that as many as 520 were incarcerated there, ibid., pp. 275–76.

125 P. Haagen, 'Eighteenth-Century English Society and the Debt Law', in *Social Control and the State*, ed. S. Cohen and A. Scull (Oxford, 1983), p. 224.

poorer people than ever before were involved.[126] Alexander Grant calculated the total number of prisoners for debt in 1789 at 16,409. Not surprisingly, this period also saw the establishment of charitable foundations to relieve their plight.[127]

In conclusion, since it was a period of very low overall levels of litigation, there was in one sense certainly less contention in the eighteenth century than there had been before or there was to be afterwards. What we do not know is how many people were prevented from using the law because of its inaccessibility; who therefore turned to arbitration to settle their disputes, or who suffered the frustration of having to lose what they considered their just causes. The numbers are impossible to measure, but the volume of complaint was loud. Whereas much pre-1640 criticism of the legal system stressed the disruptive social consequences of ready access to the law amongst the lower orders,[128] after 1700 the reiteration of the difficulty of finding justice in the English legal system is too persistent to be ignored. Moreover, while it is certainly true that recourse to law became less frequent during the eighteenth century in rural areas, imprisonment for debt and payment through the instalment plan, as promoted by the courts of requests, emerged as major features of urban life.

While there is some evidence from the gentry and middle ranks of society to support Lawrence Stone's view that the drop in litigation was associated with a spread of urban values which led to a decline in contentiousness and, perhaps, a growing willingness to honour obligations, it is hard to disentangle this conclusively from the consequences of social and legal change, or the unsavoury reputation of the law. The middling orders in particular found the common law itself a constant source of irritation and injustice. Meanwhile, the courts of requests and imprisonment for debt subjected the urban poor to arbitrary control over their personal liberty by their creditors and local worthies which hardly contributed to a relaxation of social tension. William Hutton of Birmingham never forgot the night in 1791 when a group of rioters manhandled him and set fire to his house. The mob shouted 'Down with the Court of Conscience'; significantly, their rage appears to have been associated with the way in which the court dealt with tallies run up in alehouses.[129]

---

[126] Innes, 'The King's Bench Prison', p. 263; [Grant], *The Public Monitor*, p. vii. Grant underestimated the total population of the King's Bench Prison at about 300 persons. Grant, *The Progress and Practice of a Modern Attorney*, pp. 62–73.

[127] Ibid., p. 19. J. Neild, *An Account of the Rise, Progress and Present State of the Society for the Discharge and Relief of Persons Imprisoned for Small Debts Throughout England and Wales* (London, 1802).

[128] Brooks, *Pettyfoggers and Vipers of the Commonwealth*, pp. 133–36.

[129] William Hutton, *The Life of William Hutton, FASS, including a Particular Account of the Riots at Birmingham in 1791: Written by Himself* (London, 1816), pp. 180–85.

Changes in the patterns of litigation in eighteenth-century England are best explained by social and economic change in both urban and rural society, and by the further ossification of the 'ancien régime' bureaucratic practices of the common law courts. Furthermore, there are a number of striking similarities and interconnections between the administration of the criminal and the civil law during the period.[130] In both fields, urban growth and the process of proletarianisation were the most important stimulants to change. If by 1750 concern about rising levels of crime and the emergence of alternatives to the death sentence was associated largely with questions about how to deal with the crimes of the urban poor and the reform of their behaviour, the debates over the establishment of the courts of requests hinged on the necessity of exercising financial discipline and moral regulation over the same groups of people. Just as transportation to the colonies and terms of imprisonment were developed as alternative punishments to the death sentence, so too the growing use of repayment of debts by weekly instalments was an alternative to the hopelessness of imprisoning poor people for debt. The plight of imprisoned debtors had been, since the later sixteenth century, the subject of an endless debate in which humanitarian concern, and despair about the illogical economic consequences of the practice, contested with a fear of deceit and the dangers of allowing people to get away without honouring their obligations. The injustice of a system, which was frequently perceived as one in which unfortunate people were punished as if they were criminals, became even more obvious in the later eighteenth century when men were thinking increasingly that punishments ought to be proportionate to crimes, and when imprisonment was being adopted as an alternative to hanging for the punishment of more serious offences.[131] At the same time, the growing involvement of the legal profession in criminal trials for felonies fits well into the chronology of the early eighteenth-century decline in litigation; it is impossible not to suspect that lawyers sought a share in criminal business at least in part to make up for the difficulty of earning a living in the civil courts.

The greatest differences between the administration of the civil and the criminal law appears to lie in the attitudes of members of the public towards each. After 1750, there is evidence that people who felt themselves to be victims of crime, like those who were owed bad debts, were put off from using the law because of high costs. Yet, according to Professor Beattie, before the mid century, and outside London afterwards, there was very little hostility to the existing system of criminal law. By comparison, the civil law was subject to a constant stream of criticism which reached particularly acute

---

130 The view of the criminal law discussed here is taken largely from Beattie, *Crime and the Courts in England*, especially ch. 11.

131 Arrest on *mesne* process was abolished in 1838, but aspects of the system continued into the twentieth century. G. R. Rubin, 'Law, Poverty and Imprisonment for Debt, 1869–1914', in *Law, Economy, and Society*, ed. Rubin and Sugarman, p. 241.

levels in the 1690s, the later 1720s, the 1790s, and the 1820s and 1830s. In this respect, the crucial differences between the two systems lay in the role played by bureaucracy and the legal profession. Eighteenth-century criminal law was still largely a local and non-professional process. Judges from Westminster delivered the gaols all over the country, but in rural areas all of the steps leading to a trial took place in the neighbourhood where the alleged offence had occurred, and the most important officials involved, the constables and justices of the peace, were largely unpaid members of the local elite. On the other hand, a civil lawsuit which went to Westminster could not proceed without paying off sinecurists in London for largely incomprehensible steps which were necessary if the case was to progress. Lawyers, never the most popular of social groups in England, were usually seen as being busy manipulating the system for largely unscrupulous ends.

Thanks to the high profile of the court officials in London, and to the fact that in matters of civil law a squire paid as much as a cottager, some gentry MPs in the years around 1730 actively led demands for law reform. However, the middling sort, particularly the urban middling classes, were the main forces calling for substantial change in the civil side of the common law in the eighteenth century. Always an important source of litigants, they became increasingly the primary customers of the courts as the eighteenth century progressed. This is not to say that the landed gentry had no interest in the law and the legal system, but by 1750 their economic and social preeminence was evidently sufficiently secure to render recourse to law less frequent than it had been before, a point which is particularly noticeable in the decline of Chancery litigation. By contrast, it was the urban middling orders who were responsible for parliamentary legislation which enlarged the use of promissory notes, petitioned for the establishment of courts of requests, and gave hostile evidence to parliamentary inquiries into the common law in the 1820s. Much of eighteenth-century substantive law must have been shaped to a very significant extent by these same social groups, albeit with the intervention of lawyers. It is clearly no longer tenable to think of English law in the eighteenth century as simply a matter of gentry hegemony over the rest of the population.

4

Litigation and Society in England, 1200–1996

The purpose of this chapter is simple. It puts forward and discusses a series of statistics on civil litigation and court usage in England during the past eight hundred years.[1] Some of the statistical data has been extracted from court records in the Public Record Office and other archives, but a great deal of it has also been found readily available in *Parliamentary Papers* and officially published statistics.[2] In addition, the past twenty years have seen a steady stream of new work on courts, court usage and the settlement of disputes. Studies covering a wide chronology from the middle ages to the present, and looking at courts in the localities as well as the central courts in London, have added significantly to what we know about how the institutions worked and how they interacted with the communities in which they operated.[3]

Many of the interpretative problems concerning causality and the ways in which we can explain alterations in the landscape of court usage have been ably discussed in some of the work on litigation that has been generated by contemporary concern about 'hyperlexis', especially, but not exclusively, in the USA, and about 'access to justice' in England and other European countries.[4] It is, for example, important to consider whether the role of courts in the past was the same they play today. Equally, it is evident that a statistical study covering such a long chronology constantly runs the risk of failing to give adequate attention to the changing social, economic, legal

---

[1] England is the primary focus, although some of the nineteenth- and twentieth-century statistical material applies to England and Wales. Very tentative discussions of the evidence were presented at LaTrobe University in Melbourne, Australia in 1983 and at a seminar of the Centre for Seventeenth-Century Studies in Durham in 1986. A fuller account was delivered at the Tenth British Legal History Conference in Oxford in 1991. This chapter is a much expanded and rewritten version of the the latter.

[2] See below, p. 108.

[3] In addition to the numerous works referred to below, see, for example, John Bossy, ed., *Disputes and Settlements* (Cambridge, 1983); and W. Davies and P. Fouracre, eds, *The Settlement of Disputes in Early Medieval Europe* (Cambridge, 1987).

[4] Mauro Cappelletti, James Gordley and Earl Johnson, Jr, eds, *Toward Equal Justice: A Comparative Study of Legal Aid in Modern Societies* (Milan and New York, 1975); Marc Galanter, 'Reading the Landscape of Disputes: What We Know and Don't Know (and Think We Know) about Our Allegedly Contentious and Litigious Society', *UCLA Law Review*, 31 (1983), pp. 4–71; and the series of articles in a special issue on 'Longitudinal Studies of Trial Courts', *Law and Society Review*, 24 (1990). See also J. Starr and J. F. Collier, eds, *History and Power in the Study of Law: New Directions in Legal Anthropology* (Ithaca, NY, 1989).

and political contexts in which disputes took place.[5] Perhaps surprisingly, the historical material available for making what is known as a 'longitudinal' study in England is in many respects quite good. The records of central common law courts stretch back to last decade of twelfth century and survive in unbroken runs from third quarter of the thirteenth century.[6] Court officials in a number of different periods have been interested from time to time in trying to measure court usage in order to calculate their income from it. Since the third decade of the nineteenth century, governments have collected statistics as a means of measuring the performance of courts on the local as well as the national level.[7]

Even so, any attempt to turn such a disparate body of source material into quantitative measurements inevitably confronts many technical and conceptual hazards. Some of the former are discussed in Chapters 2 and 3, and are, quite consciously, not dealt with in any detail here.[8] Of the latter, the most important for present purposes is simply the question of what constitutes a lawsuit. In the medieval and early modern periods, for instance, the fact that the victims of crime were expected to play a large part in bringing charges against those whom they suspected of committing the offence means that criminal cases, whether brought before justices of the peace or the courts of assize, can be said to have had much in common with the more familiar categories of 'civil litigation' between private parties.[9]

While such cases have been excluded from detailed consideration here by focusing primarily on the civil versus the criminal courts, there is even good reason for questioning how a civil lawsuit should be defined. One of the constant features of court usage in England has always been that only a very small proportion (less than 10 per cent) of the cases started are ever heard in court before a judge, let alone a judge and jury.[10] Most disputes never appear in court records as anything more than a summons, while many others reappear more than once because they advanced in procedural terms even though they never reached trial or formal disposition. These characteristics of lawsuits mean that the traces they have left on the records of different courts at different points in time are not always directly comparable; in some instances we can measure actions commenced, in others only those

---

[5] L. M. Friedman, 'Opening the Time Capsule: A Progress Report on Studies of Courts over Time', *Law and Society Review*, 24 (1990), pp. 237–28; Richard Lempert, 'Docket Data and "Local Knowledge": Studying the Court and Society Link over Time', ibid., pp. 321–33.

[6] Paul Brand, *The Making of the Common Law* (London, 1992), pp. 94–96.

[7] The history of nineteenth-century quantification is well told in O. R. McGregor, *Social History and Law Reform* (London, 1981), chs 3–4.

[8] See above, pp. 9ff, 28–29.

[9] See for example, J. A. Sharpe, *Crime in Early Modern England, 1550–1750* (London, 1984), and Cynthia B. Herrup, *The Common Peace: Participation and the Criminal Law in Seventeenth-Century England* (Cambridge, 1987).

[10] See below, p. 80.

cases 'in advanced stages', and in still others little more than the number of rolls of parchment the clerks filled up with proceedings.

At the same time, it is arguable that the role of a court, and what constitutes litigation, differs as a case moves from commencement to the joining of issue between the parties, and eventually to a trial. Initial summonses, for example, have been described as little more than a version of the final notice in red which arrives from the gas or electricity utility demanding immediate payment. While there is some truth in this view, the initial writ does after all carry the threat of sanctions or further proceedings, and it is evident that the threat of proceedings is as important a feature of the role of law in society as are trials or judicial decisions. More mundanely, the surviving records of many courts, especially local jurisdictions, often consist of little more than notes of initial summonses. Statistics about the number of cases commenced have also been the measures most commonly assembled in compilations of official statistics undertaken since the early nineteenth century. For all of these reasons, in what follows the aim has been to provide a profile of court usage which is based as far as possible on the initiation of actions.

Of all the difficulties which remain, there are two which are particularly troubling. First, it is very difficult to make comparisons between legal and non-legal modes of conflict resolution, not least because so much of our evidence about social relations in the past comes from court records. Secondly, there is no way to know for certain what proportion of the population at any given time may have been deterred by the cost of litigation, procedural complexity or corruption from going to law; and so either found other ways to settle their grievances or suffered the discomfort of having them remain unresolved. As we shall see, this is a particular concern in connection with the fifteenth and eighteenth centuries, but it is also significant today.[11]

More generally, the discussion attempts to maintain a consumer-oriented approach, although it is also evident that changes in the volume of litigation have also had a very significant impact on the size and nature of the legal profession, as well as on the courts in which the lawyers worked and therefore, on the legal culture of the country as a whole.[12] The patterns of change and continuity in the rates of litigation are complex and no doubt subject to alternative interpretations. My expectation is that the data and the discussion of it will raise as many questions as they answer.

The pattern of court usage over the past 800 years is most easily described in terms of five secular waves of increases in litigation, four of which have been followed by substantial troughs or drops in court business (Figure 4.1).

11 Gallenter, 'Reading the Landscape of Disputes', pp. 26–32, 34ff.
12 For further discussion of this, see Chapter 7, p. 182–86.

Figure 4.1
*Impressionistic Sketch of the Volume of Central Court Litigation,
c. 1200–1750*

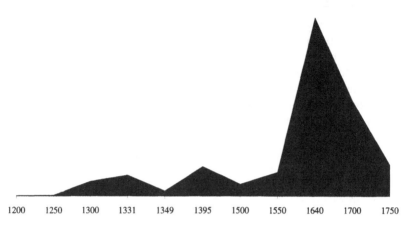

| 1200 | 1250 | 1300 | 1331 | 1349 | 1395 | 1500 | 1550 | 1640 | 1700 | 1750 |

If we take as our starting point the reign of Henry II and the later years of the twelfth century, it would appear that what has been described as the professionalisation of justice during this period was accompanied by a steady rise in the recourse litigants had to the royal courts in London. Judging from the amount of parchment clerks used in order to record it, business in the court of Common Pleas may have grown by a factor of as much as thirty between 1200 and 1306, with the most striking increases taking place from the 1260s onwards, and especially after 1300.[13] Furthermore, although the statistical evidence continues to be fairly rough and ready, it is likely that this first wave continued on a rising curve into the fourteenth century. Robert Palmer estimates that some 8500 actions were commenced in the court of Common Pleas in 1331. Levels remained quite high until the catastrophic impact of the Black Death resulted in a trough which lasted from 1348 to the late 1360s.[14] But this drop was in fact relatively brief in historical terms. Statistical evidence, assembled by Marjorie Blatcher about the fees which the two principal common law courts, King's Bench and Common Pleas, collected for the writs they issued between 1358 and 1558, indicates that there was a very significant increase in court business during the later fourteenth century; an increase which was largely maintained until the later 1440s, when a second long, but not very deep, trough opened up (Figure 4.2).[15]

---

[13] P. Brand, *The Origins of the English Legal Profession* (Oxford, 1992), pp. 16, 23–24.

[14] Robert C. Palmer, *The Whilton Dispute, 1264–1380: A Socio-Legal Study of Dispute Settlement in Medieval England* (Princeton, 1984), p. 5; idem, *English Law in the Age of the Black Death, 1348–1381* (Chapel Hill, NC, 1993), p. 3.

[15] M. Blatcher, *The Court of King's Bench, 1450–1550: A Study in Self-Help* (London, 1978).

Figure 4.2

Income (in Pounds) from the Seals of King's Bench and Common Pleas, 1358–1558

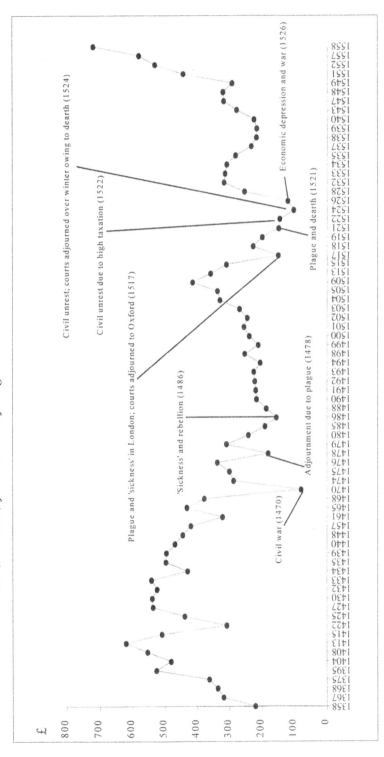

Sources: Blatcher, *The Court of King's Bench*, Appendix; Brooks, *Pettyfoggers and Vipers of the Commonwealth*, pp. 79–81.

There were slight increases in business around 1500, but the volume of work reached an historic low point in the 1520s. After faltering fortunes in the 1530s and 1540s, there was a massive increase in central court litigation which dated from just before the accession of Elizabeth in 1588, reaching a peak in the years around 1600. Thereafter this third wave rolled on (despite a brief drop during the Civil War of the 1640s) for another seventy or eighty years, before contracting in the early 1700s.[16] This comparatively bleak period for lawyers continued until the latter part of the eighteenth century, when a fourth wave of increases in litigation began again which became particularly sharp in the 1820s, and which was particularly notable in local jurisdictions known as courts of requests.[17]

Figure 4.3

Cases in Advanced Stages in Common Pleas and King's Bench, 1490–1830

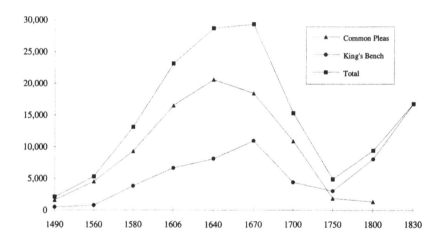

The rate of litigation (per 100,000 of total population) in central courts (653) in 1847 was much lower than it was in 1600 (1351),[18] but between 1847 and the end of the 1880s a further overall growth in the number of plaints coincided with the expansion of a new county court system.[19] Finally,

---

[16] C. W. Brooks, *Pettyfoggers and Vipers of the Commonwealth: The 'Lower Branch' of the Legal Profession in Early Modern England* (Cambridge, 1986), chs 4–5.

[17] Above, Chapter 3, p. 39–42. See also the detailed discussion of Chancery's business and litigants in Henry Horwitz, *Chancery Equity Records and Proceedings, 1600–1800: A Guide to Documents in the Public Record Office* (London, 1995), ch. 2; also Henry Horwitz and Patrick Polden, 'Continuity or Change in the Court of Chancery in the Seventeenth and Eighteenth Centuries?', *Journal of British Studies*, 35 (1996), pp. 24–57. These works both confirm and refine some of the conclusions in Chapter 3.

[18] Brooks, *Pettyfoggers and Vipers*, pp. 78–79. The figure for 1975 was 560.

[19] See below, p. 105–8.

in what is perhaps best described as a muted echo of previous cycles, a gradual but significant drop in rate of litigation per head of population, which reached a low point in the 1950s, has been followed by an epoch which has seen a more comprehensive system of legal aid in place than has ever existed before, with an increase in the amount of litigation which seems to have reached a brief, but historic, peak in 1992.[20]

Given the variety of methods which have been used by different scholars to measure court business in periods before the nineteenth century, it is obviously necessary to take great care in interpreting the results. Most importantly, in nearly every epoch before that of the Victorians, extrapolating from measures of central court activity to global statistics for court usage, which take account of local jurisdictions such as those of the manor or the borough, poses nearly insurmountable difficulties. Nevertheless, although legal historians have traditionally hypothesised that an unrelenting decline in local courts throughout the later middle ages and early modern period was a precondition for a the rise of the central jurisdictions which sat in Westminster Hall,[21] a number of recent studies have suggested instead that, before the nineteenth century, fluctuations in local court business have in fact frequently followed similar patterns to those in the central courts. They confirm and sharpen the contours of the five waves.

Although it does not lend itself to resolution through quantitative measurements, the problem of the relationship between central and local justice is encountered at the very beginning of our period in connection with the 'birth' of the common law in the twelfth and thirteenth centuries. Administrative reforms in the central royal courts were accompanied by the gradual development of remedies, such as the action of replevin, which enabled litigants to challenge decisions in local jurisdictions, including the county courts and those of seigniorial lords.[22] Yet whether or not these changes should be seen as indicative of a massive jurisdictional shift of business away from local and towards the central courts is much less clear.[23] Thirteenth-century local courts appear to have had plenty of business, and it has been argued recently that the emergence of manorial court rolls as written records at this time reflects an effort by landlords to bring their jurisdictions into line with the royal courts and to improve the services they offered in an attempt to attract litigants.[24] Furthermore, quantitative measures of local

---

[20] See below, p. 113–14.

[21] The present author must also admit guilt; see *Pettyfoggers and Vipers*, pp. 98–100.

[22] Brand, *Origins of the English Legal Profession*, pp. 31–32. There is of course a huge literature on this issue.

[23] P. Brand, 'The Formation of the English Legal System, 1150–1400', in Antonio Padoa-Schippa, ed., *Legislation and Justice* (Oxford, 1997), pp. 104–111, provides a balanced picture of the strengths and weaknesses of the local versus royal jurisdictions.

[24] R. C. Palmer, *The County Courts of Medieval England, 1150–1350* (Princeton, 1982); Zvi Razi and Richard Smith, 'The Origins of the English Manorial Court Rolls as a Written Record: A Puzzle', in Razi and Smith, eds, *Medieval Society and the Manor Court* (Oxford, 1996), p. 36.

court business, especially that of towns, from quite early periods reveal
fluctuations in line with those of the central courts. Two studies from Essex,
one of the town of Colchester and the other of the manor of Writtle, have
found generally rising levels of business before and after the Black Death in
the fourteenth and into the first half of the fifteenth century.[25] Similarly,
although the evidence is of necessity somewhat speculative, it appears that
the amount of business which was handled in the 1470s by one of the principal
local municipal courts of London, the Sheriff's Court, was roughly half that
which existed in the early to mid fourteenth century, a finding which is
consistent with an overall pattern similar to that of central common law
courts.[26] It is also notable that the number of plaints brought in Colchester
and at Writtle was markedly lower in the later fifteenth century than they
had been before. At Colchester, for example, there was during the fourteenth
century a five- to tenfold increase which reached a high point of 878 plaints
in 1387/88. By contrast the numbers probably dropped off slightly during
the early fifteenth century but were notably lower in the 1490s and 1510/1,
when the highest recorded number of plaints came to only 322.[27]

These indications that rates of litigation in the central common law courts
were tracked by other jurisdictions is confirmed by work on local courts in
the sixteenth, seventeenth and eighteenth centuries. Meticulous studies of
the Battle Abbey manorial court, the Shrewsbury *curia parva* and the court
of pleas at King's Lynn have found that the sixteenth and seventeenth
centuries saw increases in litigation which match those in the central courts,
but which may place the peak in the amount of litigation in the second half
of the reign of Elizabeth rather than the early years of the seventeenth
century.[28] Indeed, the most recent findings of Craig Muldrew, about the
vitality of local jurisdictions associated with market towns and boroughs,

---

[25] R. H. Britnell, 'Colchester Courts and Court Records, 1310–1525', *Essex Archaeology and History*, 17 (1984), pp. 133–40; Elaine Clark, 'Debt Litigation in a Late Medieval English Vill', in *Pathways to Medieval Peasants*, ed. J. A. Raftis (Toronto, 1981), pp. 247–79. See also T. Foulds, J. Hughes and M. Jones, 'The Nottingham Borough Court Rolls: The Reign of Henry VI (1422–57)', *Transactions of the Thoroton Society*, 97 (1993), pp. 74–85.

[26] P. Tucker, 'Relationships between London's Courts and the Westminster Courts in the Reign of Edward IV', in *Courts, Counties and the Capital in the Later Middle Ages*, ed. Diana E. S. Dunn (Gloucester, 1996), p. 121; idem, 'London's Courts of Law in the Fifteenth Century: The Litigants' Perspective', in C. Brooks and M. Lobban, eds, *Communities and Courts in Britain, 1150–1900* (London, 1997), pp. 26–27. Although some of the shortfall in the Sheriff's Court may have been made up for by increases in the Mayor's Court.

[27] Clark, 'Debt Litigation', p. 251; Britnell, 'Colchester Courts', pp. 133–40.

[28] J. H. Baker, 'Personal Actions in the High Court of Battle Abbey, 1450–1602', *Cambridge Law Journal*, 51 (1992), p. 528; Craig Muldrew, 'Credit and the Courts; Debt Litigation in a Seventeenth-Century Urban Community', *Economic History Review*, 46 (1993), pp. 23–38; W. A. Champion, 'Litigation in the Boroughs: The Shrewsbury *Curia Parva*, 1480–1730', *Journal of Legal History*, 15 (1994), pp. 201–22. At Shrewsbury the annual average number of actions increased from 448 in the decade 1490–1500 to a high of 1516 actions between 1580 and 1590, a level which was not quite exceeded in the 1620s (1440 actions).

have led him to calculate that they were entertaining as many 1,036,842 actions a year at the end of the reign of Elizabeth. If these figures are combined with those for the central courts, the palatinate courts, the councils in the North and in Wales, plus the ecclesiastical courts, then the overall rate of litigation would then have been about twice as great per 100,000 of population as it was in 1992.[29]

The great boom in legal business which made the late sixteenth and early seventeenth centuries the most litigious age in English history was, moreover, a phenomenon of the ecclesiastical as well as the civil courts. Although it was partly associated with successful attempts by the common lawyers to limit the church courts' jurisdiction over matters such as debt and some types of defamation, there were significant declines in the amount of business entertained by the ecclesiastical courts between the accession of Henry VII and the early 1530s, a decline which matches that of business in the common law courts and with similar causes.[30] For example, while the consistory court at Canterbury handled 636 cases in 1482, the number had shrunk to 223 by 1522.[31] Yet while business in the church courts remained static throughout the years up until the accession of Elizabeth, the English Reformation did not by any means extinguish the jurisdiction. Although the amounts of business may not have risen in absolute terms above those of the mid fifteenth century, the records in a number of dioceses show that litigation probably doubled over the course of the reigns of Elizabeth and James I.[32] By the early seventeenth century the work of the church courts included matters concerned with the maintenance of ecclesiastical discipline within the English church; sexual continence; and matrimonial causes which arose primarily from the making, as opposed to the breaking, of unions.[33] Some of this activity, most notably that having to do with sexual and ecclesiastical offences, must be classified as criminal or disciplinary. But by the early seventeenth century an increasingly significant proportion of the total number of church court cases, between 25 and 50 per cent, were actions concerned with accusations of slander brought primarily by women evidently defending either their own reputations or those of their husbands.[34]

[29] C. Muldrew, 'Rural Credit, Market Areas and Legal Institutions in the Countryside in England, 1550–1700', in Brooks and Lobban, eds, *Communities and Courts*, pp. 155–78; idem, *The Economy of Obligation: The Culture of Credit and Social Relations in Early Modern England* (forthcoming), ch. 8.

[30] See, for example, R. M. Wunderli, *London Church Courts and Society on the Eve of the Reformation* (Cambridge, MA, 1981), pp. 18–23.

[31] R. H. Helmholz, *Roman Canon Law in Reformation England* (Cambridge, 1990), ch. 2.

[32] Ibid.; M. Ingram, *Church Courts, Sex and Marriage in England, 1570–1640* (Cambridge, 1987), p. 69; R. Houlbrooke, *Church Courts and People during the English Reformation, 1520–1570* (Oxford, 1979), pp. 273–74.

[33] Ingram, *Church Courts*.

[34] Ibid., p. 69; Helmholz, *Roman Canon Law*, p. 58, for a consideration of the relevant legal issues. Laura Gowing, *Domestic Dangers: Women, Words and Sex in Early Modern England* (Oxford, 1996); and eadem, 'Language, Power, and the Law: Women's Slander Litigation in Early Modern

Unlike the civil courts, the ecclesiastical courts suffered a complete collapse during the 1640s and Interregnum, a crisis from which they never fully recovered. Though restored in 1660, a declining volume of litigation, which seems to have reached its nadir in the third and fourth decades of the eighteenth century, was dominated statistically by actions of defamation, primarily involving female litigants.[35] While nature of the ecclesiastical jurisdiction may mean that it should be treated as a special case, it is notable that this decline in fact mirrored that which was taking place in the central common law courts and which has also been observed in the local courts. There were by the mid eighteenth century falls in the amount of business as precipitate as those in the central courts or the ecclesiastical courts in Newcastle, Shrewsbury, King's Lynn, Bristol and other places, as well as in the Lord Mayor's Court of London.[36] It is true, of course, that the eighteenth century also saw the proliferation of a newer type of jurisdiction, the courts of requests (also known as courts of conscience), which were established by statute, and which dealt with small debts speedily, dispensing with legal formalities and trial by jury. But a closer look at the history of the courts of requests indicates that they can have done little to offset the overall decline of litigation in the first half of the century. There were in fact no new courts of requests established between 1700 and 1750, and it would appear that litigation either declined or remained stagnant in those which already existed during these years.[37] Although over one hundred new courts of requests came into existence between 1690 and 1830, the vast majority of these were created in the later eighteenth century and most notably in the period 1805–10.[38] The courts of requests, like the comprehensive system of county courts which superseded them in 1846, were the venue for most of the increases in litigation which have taken place in the nineteenth and twentieth centuries; but they were hardly the causes of it.

London', in J. Kermode and G. Walker, eds, *Women, Crime and the Courts in Early Modern England* (London 1994), pp. 26–47. But compare Gowing's conclusions with Elizabeth A. Foyster, 'The Concept of Male Honour in Seventeenth-Century England' (unpublished Ph.D. thesis, University of Durham, 1996).

[35] J. A. Sharpe, *Defamation and Sexual Slander in Early Modern England: The Church Courts at York*, Borthwick Papers, 58 (York, 1981); L. Stone, *The Road to Divorce: England, 1530–1987* (Oxford, 1990), pp. 41–42; Tim Meldrum, 'A Women's Court in London: Defamation at the Bishop of London's Consistory Court, 1700–1745', *London Journal*, 19 (1994), pp. 1–20.

[36] Chapter 3, p. 40; W. A. Champion, 'Recourse to Law and the Meaning of the Great Litigation Decline, 1650–1750: Some Clues from the Shrewsbury Local Courts', in Brooks and Lobban, eds, *Communities and Courts*, p. 179; Corporation of London Record Office, Guildhall, London, typescript schedule of Mayor's Court records, p. iv; *Parliamentary Papers, 1831–32*, xxv, *Second Part of the Appendix to the Fourth Report of the Common Law Commissioners* (London, 1832), appendix (i), v, 'Return of All Process Issued from Borough Courts, County Courts, Liberty Courts, Hundred Courts, Manor Courts and Courts of Requests between 12 February 1830 and 12 February 1831'.

[37] Chapter 3, p. 40.

[38] Chapter 3, pp. 41–42.

If nothing else, the general shape of the pattern of court usage over eight centuries suggests that there is no simple connection between 'modernisation' and levels of litigation.[39] The total rate of litigation per head of population in 1400 was probably higher than that in either 1530 or 1750. The later fifteenth century in some respects looks like the early eighteenth century; the seventeenth century arguably allowed less scope for informal conflict resolution than the twentieth. At the same time, while there have been important changes in the constitution of courts, especially at the local level (and despite the fluctuations in the volume of litigation which have taken place),[40] there are two persistent features which demand attention. First, if we consider that litigation is a phenomenon which went on at a number of different jurisdictional levels, the percentage of the population which resorted to courts has always been much greater than has normally been assumed. Secondly, the vast majority of the work of civil courts has always involved a wide range of economic transactions which are reflected in the perennial importance of actions for debt. As the barrister, and recently appointed Lord Chancellor, Henry Brougham pointed out in the momentous speech on law reform which he delivered in parliament in 1830 the 'great bulk of the suits which came for decision before the ordinary tribunals [originate] with the middling and poorer classes of society, to whom ... the interest involved, be they great or be they small [are] as real and as important as matters of great moment to persons in higher and wealthier stations in society'.[41]

A glimpse at the kind of concerns at stake is provided by an account of the business in the London Court of Requests, which a clerk, John Holmes, drew up in 1799. He began with cases brought by persons who purchased goods that turned out to be damaged or not what they were warranted to be by the seller. Then there was the loss of, or damage to, parcels and money sent from the country by carriers to persons in London. Next, we have losses on the sale of goods delivered and returned, or on goods ordered and not taken, or bought at sales and not taken away. There were actions against drovers who lost, lamed or damaged sheep and cattle entrusted to their care. There were suits for the money which parties had agreed before magistrates to pay as satisfaction for assaults and damages; others involved the recovery of damages by persons who had their windows and window frames broken or otherwise damaged by carts, carriages, horses and foot-passengers. Carmen, ticket and tackle porters, hackney coachmen and

[39] See below, Chapter 7, pp. 180–82.

[40] See below, pp. 104–5.

[41] *The Speech, Delivered in the House of Peers, on Thursday 2nd December 1830 by Henry Baron Brougham and Vaux, Lord High Chancellor of Great Britain Introducing his Bill to Reform the Existing Legal Abuses of the Country* (London, 1830), p. 25. The first speech on law reform was delivered in 1828. *The Speech of Henry Brougham, Esq. as Delivered in the House of Commons, on Thursday, February 7, 1828, on his Motion Touching the State of the Law in this Country and its Administration in the Courts of Justice* (London, 1828)

watermen sued for payment of their fares. Still other litigants went to law as a result of breakdowns in a myriad of economic transactions: money lent and advanced; money due on account; work done and materials provided; meat, drink, washing and lodging; travel, horse hire and expenses; money due on hand notes and bills of exchange; rent where the contract was not under seal and where the tenant had before paid rent to the landlord in possession; the bills of attorneys, apothecaries or surgeons; alehouse scores; bills for the carriage of freight or goods. Servants sued for wages or for being turned out of doors by their masters or mistresses, while journeymen and labourers sued masters for unlawfully detaining their tools.[42]

Holmes's list does not of course mention the work of the central courts operative in his own day, and in its detail his account obviously reflects no more than the particular social world of late eighteenth-century London. A more comprehensive picture of the concerns of courts over the ages would have to include, amongst others, debts on conditional bonds, defamation, negligence in the performance of a trade or profession, and accidental injury; not to mention disputes over the titles to land which were heard before central courts such as King's Bench, Common Pleas and Chancery.[43] At the same time, it is also clear that the social range of litigants has often reached well beyond the poor and middling classes identified by Brougham. Given the vast scope of their landed interests, it is not surprising that in earlier centuries the gentry and aristocracy were always important employers of lawyers. In 1606, for instance, people who styled themselves gentleman, esquire or a member of peerage accounted for 31 per cent of all litigants in the court of Common Pleas;[44] in the thirteenth and early fourteenth centuries the majority of cases brought before the central courts concerned land.[45] On the other hand, from at least the early fifteenth century, actions of debt and trespass, actions which were directly associated with money transactions and other kinds of interpersonal relationships, have made up the vast bulk of the business, including that of the central courts. In 1441, for example, 82 per cent of the actions in Common Pleas involved either debt (65 per cent) or trespass (17 per cent), while in borough and manorial jurisdictions the proportion of cases for debt usually approached 90 per cent.[46] Equally, if 31 per cent of the litigants in Common Pleas in 1606 claimed gentry status, this none the less means that the remaining 69 per cent were from social groups outside the gentry, most notably the yeomanry and those in the commercial and artisan classes.[47] In a seventeenth-century borough such as

[42] Corporation of London Record Office, MS Court of Requests Precedent Book 1799, including the 'Memorial' of John Holmes, clerk of the court.

[43] Brooks, *Pettyfoggers and Vipers*, chs 4–5.

[44] See above, Chapter 2, pp. 14–16.

[45] Palmer, *The Whilton Dispute*, p. 22–24; compare the account in idem, *English Law in the Age of the Black Death*, chs 6–10.

[46] See below Figure 4.5, p. 78.

[47] Chapter 2, pp. 14–16; see also Brooks, *Pettyfoggers and Vipers*, pp. 58–63.

King's Lynn, or a market town such as Hexham in Northumberland, every adult male no matter what his station was likely to find himself a suitor in the local court of pleas at one point or another in his life.[48] Indeed, judging by the figures available for the central and ecclesiastical courts, women were much more likely to be named as litigants before 1800 than they were afterwards.[49]

Given the social composition of litigants and the nature of their business throughout the centuries, it is not surprising to find that there is a strong, if not absolute, correlation between overall changes in the levels of litigation and demographic, social and economic conditions. While the creation of the royal court system in the later twelfth century must be credited to some degree to the political initiatives of King Henry II,[50] and while the jurisdiction was enhanced both by a broadening in the scope of remedies available through royal writs, and by the restrictions, most notably the forty shilling jurisdictional ceiling, placed on the competence of seigniorial courts,[51] the growth in central court litigation through the later thirteenth and early fourteenth centuries should also be considered in the light of the prevailing economic and demographic conditions. The three centuries between 1000 and 1300 may have seen population increases from perhaps two million to as many as six million just before the outbreak of plague in 1348, a figure which was not exceeded again until after 1750. Pre-plague England has, furthermore, been cautiously described as a 'commercialising society' with a growing urban population. The use of coinage increased to the extent that by the end of the thirteenth century manorial rents were being paid in money rather than kind.[52]

Equally, although the Black Death was devastating insofar as it cut population by as much as two-thirds, the depressing effect on court business was short-lived. An increase in litigation at all levels coincided with a new burst of economic activity which accompanied the social transformations that followed in the wake of the demographic disaster. Associated with the greater freedom of smallholders from the restrictions of unfree tenure and the advantage of low rents, the late fourteenth and early fifteenth centuries constituted an epoch of relative economic vitality, although one susceptible

[48] Muldrew, 'Rural Credit, Market Areas and Legal Institutions in the Countryside in England, 1550–1700', p. 160; Anna Rossiter, 'Economy, Society and Government in Seventeenth Century Hexham' (unpublished M. Litt. thesis, University of Newcastle, 1997), pp. 268–76.

[49] See below, p. 111.

[50] It is worth noting that John Hudson, *Land, Law and Lordship in Anglo-Norman England* (Oxford, 1994), argues for the importance of the rule of law before the Angevin administrative changes.

[51] Brand, *Origins of English Legal Profession*, pp. 23–32. Brand does not, however, claim that developments in the central courts necessarily led to a decline in local court business.

[52] R. H. Britnell, 'Commercialisation and Economic Development in England, 1000–1300', in R. H. Britnell and Bruce M. S. Campbell, eds, *A Commercialising Economy: England, 1086 to 1300* (Manchester, 1995). pp. 7–26.

to the adverse impact of war and high taxes.[53] Exactly how far the recovery in central court business after the Black Death was a product a government initiative to enforce interpersonal obligations in a new and uncertain environment, as against a greater propensity for litigants and their lawyers to exploit possibilities which were already available, is a matter currently under debate.[54] No matter what the conclusion, this was an important period for the common law which has hitherto been overlooked by general historians.

There is no better way to illustrate this point than by considering the changing fortunes of the lawyers. As Paul Brand has shown, the rise in the business of the royal courts in the thirteenth century was accompanied by an increase in the number of professional lawyers who worked in them. By 1300 there were as many as thirty serjeants, plus 250 attorneys, active in King's Bench and Common Pleas in London; and there may also have been a fairly large cohort of professionals who worked in local jurisdictions such as county courts.[55] There is evidence from the late thirteenth century that the common law was being formally taught in London, while the judiciary from time to time took steps to exercise some control over the number and standards of practitioners. For example, in the first known instance of what became a well-known formula, an ordinance of 1292 concerning the regulation of attorneys evidently arose out of suspicions of malpractice and the view that inordinate numbers caused excessive litigation.[56]

By comparison, relatively little is known about the size of the profession during the fourteenth century, and especially between the Black Death and 1450. But the increase in the volume of business in the courts must have made this a reasonably prosperous time for lawyers. There is circumstantial evidence that their numbers were high. J. R. Maddicott has noted the importance of attorneys in 'county communities' of the fourteenth century.[57] A statute of 1402/3 for the better regulation of the lower branch of the profession evidently arose out of complaints about the mischiefs caused by the excessive numbers of practitioners. Another measure, which was put forward in 1455, but which did not become law, proposed to limit the numbers of practitioners in two of the counties, Norfolk and Suffolk, which were the amongst the most litigious in the country.[58]

Of no less importance, the late fourteenth and early fifteenth centuries

---

[53] J. Hatcher, 'England in the Aftermath of the Black Death,' *Past and Present*, 144 (1994), pp. 3–35.

[54] Palmer, *English Law and the Black Death*, as against earlier writers, stresses a government initiative but, as he himself acknowledges, he is unable to produce a decisive piece of evidence to prove the case.

[55] Brand, *Origins*, ch. 5.

[56] Ibid., ch. 7, p. 115.

[57] J. R. Maddicott, 'The County Community and the Making of Public Opinion in Fourteenth-Century England', *Transactions Royal Historical Society*, 5th series, 28 (1978), pp. 27, 37–38

[58] Brooks, *Pettyfoggers and Vipers*, p. 20.

were a particularly notable period in the history of legal education. Evidence from the 1340s provides the earliest proof of the existence of three of the four inns of court, the Inner Temple, Gray's Inn and the Middle Temple. More abundant evidence about the vitality of the fourth 'greater' house, Lincoln's Inn, as well as the 'lesser' inns of chancery comes from the early fifteenth century, by which time it is clear that a thriving culture of legal education, including lectures and moots, had been established.[59]

Whether or not legal education as it appears in the early fifteenth century was newly founded in the wake of the Black Death or, as seems equally likely, merely built upon earlier foundations, the institutions and practices which were then established continued in place until the second half of the seventeenth century. So, too, it would appear that the general patterns of litigation which were typical of the common law courts for the remainder of the early modern period had already become established by the middle of the fifteenth century.

Figure 4.4
Social Status of Litigants in the Court of Common Pleas, 1441

	First Party		Second Party		Total	
	Number	Percentage	Number	Percentage	Number	Percentage
Gentleman and above	20	1	100	5	120	6
Yeomen	14	1	160	8	174	8
Husbandmen	39	2	319	15	358	17
Ecclesiastics	108	5	51	2	159	8
Commercial and artisan	120	6	382	18	502	24
Widows	29	1	19	1	48	2
Other women	34	2	31	1	65	3
Unknown	494	24	168	8	662	32
Grand total	858	41	1230	59	2088	100

Source: PRO, CP 40/723 (Michaelmas 20 Henry VI), 'Roll of Warrants of Attorney'.

Thanks to the passage of the Statute of Additions, which required litigants in the king's courts accurately to 'style' their opponents or else be non-suited, it is possible after 1413 to begin to put together a social profile of the litigants who used the courts.[60] As Figure 4.4 indicates, although the proportion of

---

[59] *Readings and Moots at the Inns of Court in the Fifteenth Century*, ed. S. E. Thorne and J. H. Baker, Selden Society, 105 (London, 1990), introduction; J. H. Baker, *The Third University of England: The Inns of Court and the Common-Law Tradition*, Selden Society Lecture (London, 1990). For the inns of chancery, see also, C. W. Brooks, *The Admissions Registers of Barnard's Inn, 1620–1869*, Selden Society supplementary series, 12 (London, 1995), pp. 15–20.

[60] 1 Henry V, c. 5. The best account of the statute of additions is Sir George Sitwell, 'The English Gentleman', *The Ancestor*, 1 (1902), pp. 73–75, who also notes that the use of the status term 'gentleman' was not widespread in the first half of the fifteeenth century.

litigants styled as members of the landed gentry or peerage was low in comparison with later periods, there was a roughly similar distribution of rural litigants (perhaps as many as 39 per cent) versus those who came from other walks of life.[61]

Figure 4.5
Forms of Action, Common Pleas, 1441

Action	Number	Percentage
Debt	511	65
Detinue	18	2
Trespass	132	17
'Land'	63	8
Waste	4	0
Account	11	1
Miscellaneous	13	2
Illegible/Unknown	37	5
Total	789	100

Source: PRO, CP 40/723, 'Roll of Warrants of Attorney'.

At the same time, the bulk of the work of the court was concerned with debts or various 'wrongs' which came under the category of trespass (Figure 4.5), and

Figure 4.6
Geographical Distribution of Litigation in Common Pleas, 1441
(by Assize Circuit)

	Number	Percentage
HOME (Kent, Essex, Sussex, Hertfordshire, Surrey)	101	13
MIDLAND (Derbyshire, Lincolnshire, Nottinghamshire, Rutland, Northamptonshhire, Warwickshire, Leicestershire)	83	11
NORFOLK (Norfolk, Suffolk, Cambridgeshire, Huntingdonshire, Bedfordshire, Buckinghamshire)	184	24
NORTHERN (Yorkshire, Northumberland, Westmorland, Cumberland)	54	7

---

[61] See also Philippa C. Maddern, *Violence and Social Order; East Anglia, 1422–1442* (Oxford, 1992), p. 39, who finds that nearly 24 per cent of plaintiffs in the King's Bench were gentry. Timothy S. Haskett, 'The Medieval English Court of Chancery', *Law and History Review*, 14 (1996), p. 290, details the status of Chancery litigants. Esquires were the most common of those given styles (34 per cent), followed by knights (23 per cent), gentleman (18 per cent) and yeoman (7 per cent).

	Number	*Percentage*
OXFORD (Oxfordshire, Berkshire, Glouces-tershire, Herefordshire, Worcestershire, Shropshire, Staffordshire, Monmouth-shire)	65	8
WESTERN (Hampshire, Wiltshire, Somerset-shire, Dorset, Devonshire, Cornwall)	103	13
MIDDLESEX	20	3
LONDON	122	16
UNKNOWN or ILLEGIBLE	46	6
TOTAL	778	100

Source: PRO, CP 40/723, 'Roll of Warrants of Attorney'.

the most notable geographical sources of litigants were London and Middle-sex along with East Anglia, a part of the country which was evidently already earning its reputation for being notoriously litigious (Figure 4.6).[62]

If this generally optimistic picture of the fortunes of the common law and the common lawyers between the Black Death and the mid fifteenth century is sustained by the further research, it offers a potentially important revision of the general historical view of the period as one in which weak kingship, a factious nobility and procedural sclerosis struck serious blows against the rule of law.[63] It is furthermore a thesis which has in the past enjoyed support from the legal fraternity. Writing in 1787, the barrister John Reeves con-cluded his multi–volume history of the common law with the observation that in the reign of Henry VI, while the nation was in arms and the throne overturned, the courts of law enjoyed an entire peace and justice was admin-istered with a precision, learning and effect not surpassed at any time before or since.[64] Even more convincingly, at the end of the 1460s or early in the 1470s, a former lord chief justice of the King's Bench, Sir John Fortescue wrote *De laudibus legum Angliae*, a famous assertion of the importance of the rule of law in the English polity, which compared the English common law favourably with the legal institutions of France, and described the legal inns in London as thriving educational societies which numbered perhaps as many as 2000 members. Often criticised for being over-optimistic about the state

---

[62] For comparisons see, Brooks, *Pettyfoggers and Vipers*, pp. 63–66, and Chapter 3, p. 38.

[63] The extensive literature is discussed ibid., pp. 84–93. See also M. Hicks, *Bastard Feudalism* (London, 1995).

[64] John Reeves, [Barrister at Law], *History of the English Law: From the Time of the Saxons to the End of the Reign of Philip and Mary* (2nd edn, 4 vols, Dublin, 1787), iv, pp. 108–20. Reeves admired the developments in legal education which he observed, and, although he acknowledged that there were some occasional irregularities in the application of the criminal law, he concluded the reigns of Henry VI and Edward IV 'abounded with eminent lawyers'. One of the very few modern historians to agree generally with this optimistic conclusion is Maddern, *Violence and Social Order*.

of the common law in the fifteenth century,[65] Fortescue's perspective may be easier to understand when it is recalled that he was a student and then a member of the governing body of Lincoln's Inn at the dawn of its recorded history in the 1420s; for most of his professional life, both as a student and as a judge, levels of litigation in the central courts had been generally high.[66] It was only from around the time of Fortescue's death, in the later 1470s, that court business, both in London and in the localities, dropped down for fifty years onto a lower plateau before suffering the drastic contractions of the late 1510s and early 1520s.[67]

Since the time of F. W. Maitland, this has been identified as a period of crisis for the common law.[68] Furthermore, two pioneering twentieth-century works on the history of King's Bench and Common Pleas in the late fifteenth century singled out high costs, dilatory procedures and the unreliability of the gentry who acted as sheriffs as prime causes for the generally ineffective state of the courts. This line of interpretation correlated well with the predominant late twentieth-century view of the reign of Henry VIII, which depicted it as a time of reform and the reassertion of the authority of the state after a period of decline and uncertainty.[69] It is worth noting, however, that while one of the strongest pieces of evidence against the common law courts of the later fifteenth century is the statistical finding that very few of the suits which were commenced in them ever reached a conclusion, the comparative study of litigation enables us to see that there was very likely nothing in the least unusual about this.[70] It has always been a characteristic of English forums that the vast majority of civil suits are settled out of court before they ever come to trial. In 1975, for instance, only 4.5 per cent of some 1,815,461 actions commenced in the English county courts had judgments entered after trials before judges, registrars or arbitrators.[71]

Similarly, although a number of recent researchers have discovered that

---

[65] Sir John Fortescue, *De laudibus legum angliae*, ed. S. B. Chrimes (Cambridge, 1942). Fortescue also praised the wide distribution of landed wealth in the country which made it possible to find honest jurors. On the other hand, he also said that learning the law was so expensive that only those sprung of noble blood could afford to do it.

[66] *Dictionary of National Biography*. Fortescue is thought to have died in 1476. W. P. Baildon, ed., *The Records of the Honourable Society of Lincoln's Inn: The Black Books* (4 vols, London, 1897–1902), i, p. 2, 3, 4, 6, 8, 15.

[67] See Figure 4.2, p. 67.

[68] F. W. Maitland, 'English Law and the Renaissance', in *Select Essays in Anglo-American Legal History by Various Authors* (3 vols, Boston, 1907), i, pp. 185–95. See Brooks, *Pettyfoggers and Vipers*, p. 307 n. 39, for a fuller account of the historiography.

[69] M. Hastings, *The Court of Common Pleas in Fifteenth-Century England* (Ithaca, NY, 1947); Blatcher, *The Court of King's Bench, 1450–1550*.

[70] Ibid., pp. 64–77.

[71] *Judicial Statistics Relating to the Judicial Committee of the Privy Council, the House of Lords, the Supreme Court of Judicature, the Crown Court, County Courts and Other Civil Courts: For the Year 1975. Compiled by the Lord Chancellor's Department* (London, 1976), pp. 31–32, 34. Most cases were resolved by consent or in default of appearance or defence.

arbitration was an important feature of dispute resolution in the fifteenth century, the consequences of this for our picture of the overall number of disputes and the ways in which they were settled must be weighed carefully.[72] Arbitration, sometimes in connection with actions in court and sometimes without it, appears as a significant factor in all studies of dispute processing, including those for the twentieth century.[73] One important feature of the practice in the fifteenth century was that it sometimes took place within baronial councils, but it was also frequently associated with legal action either within the central courts, or indeed lesser jurisdictions such as those of the principalities.[74]

On the basis of the studies completed so far, it is difficult to say whether there was any change in the use of arbitration which seriously affected trends in central court litigation. Equally, it is unclear whether arbitration in the fifteenth century should be seen as evidence of the sinister power of the great to corrupt the course of justice, or as a sign that one advantage of good lordship was that it could provide relatively painless, and perhaps less expensive, ways of settling local disputes. It is plain that some of the overmighty, or would-be overmighty, indulged in violence, attempted to influence juries and brought the power of the purse to their disputes,[75] but a catalogue of instances from the fifteenth century could certainly be matched with a similar one for the later sixteenth and seventeenth centuries when the rate of litigation was high. For instance, J. G. Bellamy has recently drawn attention to way in which the disputes of the gentry over land in the fifteenth century were frequently accompanied by the violence of forcible entry.[76] But his evidence is drawn from Star Chamber cases, a court whose records reveal much the same levels of alleged violence in Elizabethan and early Stuart times.[77] A general feature of all litigation about land in the early modern

[72] For example, I. Rowney, 'Arbitration in Gentry Disputes of the Later Middle Ages', *History*, 67 (1982), pp. 367–76. E. Powell, 'Settlement of Disputes by Arbitration in Fifteenth-Century England', *Law and History Review*, 2 (1984), pp. 21–43.

[73] J. H. Baker, *Reports from the Lost Notebooks of Sir James Dyer*, Selden Society, 109–10 (2 vols, London, 1994), p. lxxxv, notes that Dyer, a chief justice of Common Pleas, was frequently in demand as an arbitrator. H. Horwitz and J. Oldham, 'John Locke, Lord Mansfield and Arbitration during the Eighteenth Century', *Historical Journal*, 36 (1993), pp. 137–59.

[74] C. Rawcliffe, 'The Great Lord as Peacekeeper: Arbitration by English Noblemen and their Councils in the Later Middle Ages', in *Law and Change in English History*, ed. J. A. Guy and H. G. Beale (London, 1984). Tim Thornton, 'Local Equity Jurisdiction in the Territories of the English Crown: The Palatinate of Chester, 1450–1540', in Dunn, ed., *Courts, Counties and the Capital*, pp. 39–41.

[75] See for example, N. Saul, *Knights and Esquires: The Gloucestershire Gentry in the Fourteenth Century* (Oxford, 1981), pp. 90–91, who argues that magnate interference in the working of the courts in the form of maintenance incurred the wrath of the commons on many occasions. Support in litigation was probably the quality of good lordship that the retainer valued most.

[76] J. G. Bellamy, *Bastard Feudalism and the Law* (London, 1989), esp. pp. 1–8.

[77] Roger B. Manning, *Village Revolts: Social Protest and Popular Disturbances in England, 1509–1640* (Oxford, 1988), pp. 27, 39, 65, 317.

period was that the procedure for someone who wanted to make a claim was to make an entry, which would then have to be prosecuted in court by the claimant who was being challenged. The importance of the public claim to seisin, like the importance of public livery of seisin, appears to have made a certain level of force endemic to disputes over real property. Yet, as Professors Sutherland and Palmer have pointed out, the greater availability of the action of trespass as a means to try titles probably led to an overall drop in the level of violence which was connected with such disputes well before the fifteenth century.[78] It is notable that a statute passed in the reign of Henry VI, which gave justices of the peace powers to make restitution after forcible entries, still formed one of the most important measures against the practice in the seventeenth century.[79]

It is most likely that the low level of court usage in the later fifteenth century was the consequence primarily of population stagnation and what has recently been described as a 'great slump' affecting all sectors of the economy. While at its most severe in the years between the later 1440s and the 1470s, it also cast its shadow well into the first three decades of the sixteenth century, with towns in particular claiming economic desolation as late as the 1520s.[80] R. H. Britnell observes, on the basis of his extremely detailed study of Colchester's economy, that the period of most notable contraction in the number of debt cases there coincided with economic decline.[81] Towards the end of this period, in the 1510s and 1520s and thanks largely to the observations of the London lawyer Edward Hall, there are good illustrations of how a combination of poor harvests, unrest over taxation and severe outbreaks of plague in the capital led to catastrophic falls in the business of King's Bench and Common Pleas which evidently had nothing to do with the failings of the common law.[82]

Although the biographies of successful lawyers of this period hardly smack of either a loss of professional self-confidence or a failure to make substantial profits out of a legal career, it may be that the years between 1480 and 1530 were significantly more difficult for the legal profession as a whole.[83] From the late 1480s into the early sixteenth century, the principal of Barnard's Inn, one of the inns of chancery, had trouble collecting dues from his

---

[78] Palmer, *Whilton Dispute*, pp. 11–13, 17–18; D. Sutherland, *The Assize of Novel Disseisin* (Oxford, 1973).

[79] 4 Henry VI, c. 9.

[80] John Hatcher, 'The Great Slump of the Mid Fifteenth Century', in *Progress and Problems in Medieval England: Essays in Honour of Edward Miller*, eds, Richard Britnell and John Hatcher (Cambridge, 1996), pp. 237–272. The evidence is rehearsed extensively in Brooks, *Pettyfoggers and Vipers*, pp. 79–84.

[81] Britnell, 'Colchester Courts', pp. 133–40.

[82] See Figure 4.2, p. 67, and Brooks, *Pettyfoggers and Vipers*, pp. 80–84 for the details.

[83] See, for example, E. W. Ives, *The Common Lawyers of Pre-Reformation England. Thomas Kebell: A Case Study* (Cambridge, 1983); C. E. Morton, *The Townshends and Their World: Gentry, Law, and Land in Norfolk, c. 1450–1551* (Oxford, 1992).

membership and in paying the rent for the premises occupied by the inn.[84] Admissions to the four inns of court were so low in the early sixteenth century that Wilfrid Prest has expressed doubt about whether they could have sustained a membership as large as that described by Sir John Fortescue.[85] If we define it as being solely comprised of lawyers who were qualified to practise either as attorneys or pleaders in the central courts, it is likely that the London legal profession, numbering perhaps 200 men in 1480, was a good deal smaller than that described by Paul Brand for the late thirteenth century, and it may well have been smaller than that of the early fifteenth century.[86] Studies of local jurisdictions have found that 'professionals' were making some, albeit limited, impact on the localities during the mid fifteenth century, largely through their presence in borough courts and as agents for litigants, but this trend may not have been sustained.[87] By the middle of the sixteenth century purely local practitioners and amateurs are encountered much more frequently than 'professionals' in borough and manorial court records.[88]

The relatively small number of 'professional' lawyers associated with central courts is a reminder that much legal activity in this period went on outside of London, in the boroughs on the one hand and within manorial jurisdictions on the other. Although they are still insufficiently studied, especially by those interested in the sixteenth and seventeenth centuries, it is likely that the volume of litigation in courts leet and courts baron (whose jurisdictional competence was determined largely by tenurial obligations) fluctuated in much the same way as that of the central courts during the later fifteenth and early sixteenth centuries.[89] But the simpler and no less significant point is that, well into the sixteenth century, they were the institutions most ordinary people in England would have come into contact with both in connection with the transmission of their land-holdings and in order to settle their disputes and regulate behaviour within the community.

[84] Brooks, *Admissions Registers of Barnard's Inn*, pp. 15–16; idem, *Pettyfoggers and Vipers*.

[85] W. R. Prest, *The Inns of Court under Elizabeth and the Early Stuarts, 1590–1640* (London, 1972), pp. 5–7.

[86] J. H. Baker, 'The Attorneys and Officers of the Common Law in 1480', *Journal of Legal History*, 1 (1980), p. 185; Brand, *Origins of the English Legal Profession*, ch. 5.

[87] Britnell, 'Colchester Courts', pp. 138–40; Christine Carpenter, *Locality and Polity: A Study of Warwickshire Landed Society, 1401–1499* (Cambridge, 1992), p. 146; T. S. Haskett, 'Country Lawyers? The Composers of English Chancery Bills', in P. Birks, ed., *The Life of the Law* (London, 1993), pp. 9–23; R. Griffiths, 'Public and Private Bureaucracies in England and Wales in the Fifteenth Century', *Transactions of the Royal Historical Society*, fifth series, 30 (1980), p. 119, suggests that vocational training in 'business studies' offered at Oxford by private teachers may have declined in the fifteenth century as the 'emergent' inns of court and inns of chancery attracted more students.

[88] Brooks, *Pettyfoggers and Vipers*, pp. 112–18; Baker, 'Battle Abbey', pp. 511–14; Champion, 'Recourse to Law and the Great Litigation Decline', pp. 184–90.

[89] Baker, 'Battle Abbey', p. 528; C. Harrison, 'Manor Courts and the Governance of Tudor England', in Brooks and Lobban, eds, *Communities and Courts*, pp. 43–60. See also the pioneering J. P. Dawson, *A History of Lay Judges* (Cambridge, MA, 1960).

In addition to hearing cases between party and party over trespasses and debts, the courts frequently dealt with minor fights, thefts and affrays.[90] Although it is a mistake to assume that the world of the manor was completely isolated from that of Westminster Hall or the legal inns in London, much of the business in such courts during the later middle ages was handled largely within the communities which constituted the manors and (more often than not) without the presence of professional lawyers.[91]

It is appropriate to end the discussion of the first two cycles of fluctuations in litigation with communal justice because the third wave of increases in the amount of court business, which lasted from late in the reign of Henry VIII to well after the Restoration of Charles II in 1660, was by contrast one in which the royal courts at Westminster, and the lawyers who worked in them, made an unambiguous impact. Once again, long-term demographic and social trends, particularly the enrichment of the yeomanry and gentry, plus the opportunities and uncertainties associated with the dissolution of the monasteries and reforms over technical matters such as uses, provide the background against which the rate of litigation began to grow. Once again, temporary reversals of the trend, like that which occurred in the 1620s, can be associated with short-term crises such as the interruption of the cloth trade or outbreaks of epidemic disease in London.[92] In fact, there is enough evidence from the sixteenth century to test the age-old conundrum about whether lawsuits create lawyers or vice-versa. Although the size of the legal profession increased prodigiously under the Tudors and Stuarts, a comparison of the chronology of the increase in the number of suits with the multiplication in the numbers of lawyers indicates that the surge in litigation came first. By the early seventeenth century there are even indications that the average size of caseloads was declining, a finding which suggests that by then too many practitioners were chasing too few potential clients.[93]

Apart from its role in creating uncertainty by undertaking religious change, suddenly threatening inheritances by attacking the validity of the use, and transferring landed wealth from the church to the laity, it is far from clear that the Tudor increase in litigation was a deliberate consequence of any government policy or of any single technical legal innovation.[94] Declarations, such as those made by Cardinal Wolsey in the 1510s and 1520s, about the

---

[90] For an account of fifteenth-century manorial business, see M. K. McIntosh, *Autonomy and Community: The Royal Manor of Havering, 1200–1500* (Cambridge, 1986), pp. 183–209. Interestingly this study identifies a decline in the business of the court at Havering during the early fifteenth century.

[91] This subject is pursued in more detail in Chapter 7 and at p. 191 below.

[92] Some of the detailed statistics are given in Chapter 2, p. 11. For the general interpretation, see also, Brooks, *Pettyfoggers and Vipers*, chs 4–6.

[93] For the numbers of lawyers, see Chapter 2, pp. 20–22, and Chapter 7, p. 184.

[94] The late fifteenth- and early sixteenth-century legal history is treated masterfully in J. H. Baker, *The Reports of Sir John Spelman*, Selden Society, 94 (London, 1978).

importance of the due administration of justice, were conventional common-places of the later middle ages, while from the Elizabethan period onwards contemporary comment and official pronouncements tended to condemn excessive litigiousness.[95] On the other hand, J. H. Baker has convincingly demonstrated the importance of an intellectual transformation of the early sixteenth century, which saw an older view of law as 'common erudition' replaced by a newer one which put more emphasis on the decisions of judges, and which subsequently made law reports (such as those printed under the names of luminaries such as Plowden, Dyer, and Coke) authoritative sources on legal doctrine in a way that the Year Books of the later middle ages had not been.[96] Although the exact relationship between cause and effect is still unclear, it is unlikely to have been coincidental that this occurred when central court business was increasing, and when there was evidently a more contentious spirit abroad which meant that 'litigants, as advised by their lawyers, did not merely want their disputes settled: they wanted them settled with reasons, and they wanted the judges to elaborate the law'.[97] Part of a more general European development, these changes were also associated with Renaissance humanism as well as an intellectual and political climate in which ideas about the rule of law became even more important constituents in social and political discourse than they had been before – not least because there were so many more practitioners who proclaimed that this was the case. In an age when questions of conscience regularly raised the problem of political allegiance, lawyers, with the support of royal ministers like Nicholas Bacon, Elizabeth's first lord keeper, and William Cecil, the principal secretary of state, promoted a vision of civil society in which the provision of the rule of law, and the protection of the person and property of the individual which it offered, were in themselves good reasons for supporting authority as it existed, regardless of its religious complexion.[98] While seventeenth-century lawyers espoused a variety of theories about the nature of political obligation, for all of them the maintenance of justice was one of the qualities which distinguished legitimate government from tyranny.[99]

Thanks to the survival of account books and bills of costs, this is also the first age for which it is possible to make a detailed study of costs. On the whole these were surprisingly low in historic terms. Even in the central courts, common law actions could be launched for a matter of a few shillings and prosecuted through to a trial at assizes for less than £10; in the localities

---

[95] Brooks, *Pettyfoggers and Vipers*, pp. 84–93. The early Elizabethan judiciary appears to have been generally conservative about innovation; Baker, *The Lost Notebooks of Sir James Dyer*, i, pp. xxvi–xxvii.

[96] Idem, *The Legal Profession and the Common Law* (London, 1986), ch. 23.

[97] Ibid., p. 476.

[98] See Chapter 8, pp. 205ff.

[99] See Chapter 9, pp. 245, 249, 257.

court fees were considerably lower than this.[100] Attorneys, who generally
handled the procedural aspects of getting a case through the court
machinery, usually adhered to a fixed tariff of fees. By the early seventeenth
century, although there were certainly pressures for increases, most notably
in the fees paid to counsel, many of the most basic charges, including the
termly attorney's fee of 3s. 4d., had remained largely unchanged for as
much as a century.[101] Since the intervening period had been one of something like fourfold inflation, it must have been the case that going to law
was cheaper in real terms under the Tudors and Stuarts than it had ever
been before.[102]

Some contemporaries, like some modern historians, were nevertheless
convinced that high levels of litigation were less an illustration of the effective
rule of law than a symptom of social stress, conflict and disharmony.[103] Here
we come up against the question, so often asked today, of how much litigation
is too much litigation. Then, as now, it was not an easy question to answer.
In the early modern period, although many people saw lawsuits as a worrying
example of the decline of the Christian values of charity and love, it is
arguable that the most persistent critics of hyperlexis reflected the views of
the social elite.[104] When we hear character writers lamenting the fact that
lowly attorneys were helping tenants to vex their landlords, or the duke of
Newcastle telling Charles II that the lawyers had taught subjects to wrangle
about everything, including the king's prerogative, we are hearing the voices
of the social and political elite lamenting potential challenges to their
hegemony. In contrast there is no doubt that many quite ordinary people
were empowered by their ability to take out actions at law.[105] Some traditionalists, such as the Jacobean recorder of London, Sir Anthony Benn, even
complained that women liked to go to law because speaking in court gave
them the capacity to make themselves heard in a public forum.[106] While the
voices of ordinary people are, of course, harder to detect, attitudes towards
the law no doubt had much to do with an individual's position in any given
case. For example, the early seventeenth-century memorial brass of John
Gladwin, a ninety-five-year-old Essex farmer, records how he undertook
'long and tedious suits at law' in order to prove the custom of the manor

[100] Brooks, *Pettyfoggers and Vipers*, pp. 101–7; Champion, 'Recourse to Law and the Great
Litigation Decline', pp. 185–86.

[101] For the fees and incomes of counsel see W. R. Prest, *The Rise of the Barristers* (Oxford, 1986),
ch. 2

[102] Although this is not to say that there were not many quarrels within the legal system during
this period over fees and the profits of office. See Brooks, *Pettyfoggers and Vipers*, ch. 7.

[103] L. Stone, 'Interpersonal Violence in English Society, 1300–1980', *Past and Present*, 101
(1983), pp. 22–23.

[104] See, for examples, Chapter 2, pp. 24–25.

[105] For some illustrations of this see below, Chapters 7 and 9.

[106] As quoted in W. R. Prest, 'Law and Women's Rights in Early Modern England', *The
Seventeenth Century*, 6 (1991), pp. 182–83.

of Harlow to the 'great benefit of posteritie for ever'. On the other hand, in 1632 the London craftsman Nehemiah Wallington and his wife were devastated when the bailiffs came to distrain some of their household goods because of the default of a friend for whom he had stood bail.[107]

The reality was that the vast majority of actions concerned some form of the debtor-creditor relationship. Craig Muldrew has argued that the court of pleas at King's Lynn, for example, successfully handled its work with a high degree of involvement from groups throughout the community, principally in the form of jury service.[108] Furthermore, Christian charity, and its pagan analogues, the concepts of natural law and equity, were as much a part of the legal as any other early modern world view. Attorneys, like many ordinary lay testators, often gave significant bequests to the inhabitants of London's debtors' prisons, and practitioners themselves were generous with credit.[109] According to William West, the most authoritative writer on contracts, the law of nature was the first cause of promises between people. Human agency was only secondary, and it is of course true that the theoretical basis of equitable relief in Chancery was the idea that the rigour of the law should be malleable in order to ensure that natural justice was done.[110] Yet the sheer weight of numbers of cases which found their way into courts is at the same time a reminder of a harder, more cynical, side to human relations in the early modern period. The most important legal instrument of the period, the penal bond, which was backed up by the sanction of

[107] Mill Stephenson, *A List of Monumental Brasses in the British Isles* (London, 1926), p. 121, John Gladwin, of Harlow, dated 1615; Nehemiah Wallington, *Historical Notices of Events Occurring Chiefly in the Reign of Charles I* (2 vols, London, 1869), i, pp. xxix–xxx. Wallington noted that this cost him two weeks of 'vexation and sorrow' during which time he neglected his shop. Later in the 1630s, he also had to face an intimidating appearance in Star Chamber because of his association with the religious dissidents Bastwick, Prynne and Burton. See P. S. Seaver, *Wallington's World: A Puritan Artisan in Seventeenth-Century London* (Stanford, CA, 1985), pp. 159–60.

[108] Muldrew, 'Credit and the Courts; Debt Litigation in a Seventeenth-Century Urban Community', pp. 23–38; idem, 'Credit, Market Relations and Debt Litigation in Late Seventeenth-Century England, with Special Reference to King's Lynn' (unpublished Ph.D. thesis, University of Cambridge, 1990), pp. 348–64.

[109] For example, in his will which was dated 1577, Thomas Went gave bequests to the poor of six debtors' prisons in London, (PRO, PROB 11/59, 18 Daughtry). In 1624 William Payne of Podington, Bedfordshire, wrote that he willed 'that my late Clientes be well dealt withall both in theire writinges and otherwise and like wise that my tenantes be well dealt withall' (PROB 11/143, 41 Byrde). Thomas Green of Knapton, Norfolk willed that 'if any person or persons whatsoever they be that can of right complain of any injury or wrong that I did to them in my life', then his executors should make restitution (Norfolk Record Office, Consistory Court Wills, 380 Clearke. Dated 1586). Like many others Francis Bennett of Warminster, Wiltshire, left benefactions to the poor, but also provided £5 to be used as a 'stock' for local tradesmen in need (Wiltshire Record Office, Awdry Collection, 212 B/6852, copy of will dated 1665).

[110] *Symbolaeographia: Which May be Termed the Art, Description, or Image of Instruments, Covenants, Contracts, etc. or The Notarie or Scrivener, Collected and Disposed by William West of the Inner Temple Gentleman, Atturney of the Common Law in Fower Severall Bookes* (London, 1590); and idem, *Three Treatises of the Second Part of Symbolaeographie: First of Compromises and Arbitrements* (London, 1594).

imprisonment for debt, at one and the same time allowed the parties to an agreement a great deal of scope in arranging their own affairs, while depending on the courts for the enforcement of draconian penalties for failure to comply.[111] A rare document in the papers of Sir Robert Phelips, who was sheriff of Somerset in the 1620s, gives us a glimpse of satisfied customers of the courts of King's Bench and Common Pleas. Nearly one hundred of them consisted of small farmers who put their marks on warrants to release from gaol people who had finally satisfied the debts they owed them.[112]

In the end it is hard not to ask why so many people had to be taken to court in order to keep their obligations; or why the Elizabethan period saw the plight of prisoners for debt become a major social problem, one which was to persist well into the eighteenth century and beyond.[113] Chronic shortages of coin made the extension of credit a commercial necessity. Uncertainties in a society whose economic life involved an enormous amount of geographical mobility, and hence fluidity in relationships, provides another part of the answer. There was certainly also a strain of deep distrust in human nature and doubt that people would keep their promises if they were not subject to coercion. The London poet John Taylor described the 1620s and 1630s as a 'brasen age', in which most forms of fraternity had collapsed.[114] Even clerical lord chancellors, such as Stephen Gardiner, accepted the common law principle that too much relaxation of the strict

---

[111] Brooks, *Pettyfoggers and Vipers*, pp. 67–68; Palmer, *English Law and the Black Death, 1348–1381*, p. 60, suggests that the common law courts encouraged the development and use of the penal bond in the uncertain conditions which followed the Black Death.

[112] Somerset Record Office, Taunton, MS Phelips DD/Ph/197. Another document, MS DD/Ph 223/50, which is dated 1635, makes it clear that the town of Ilchester depended heavily on the debtors' prison there for its livelihood.

[113] Lord Treasuer Burghley and Sir Thomas Egerton, then solicitor general, corresponded in 1585 about the establishment of commissions for the relief of prisoners for debt. J. Payne Collier, ed., *The Egerton Papers*, Camden Society, old series, 12 (1840), p. 111. The correspondence and draft instruments are in Henry E. Huntington Library, San Marino, CA, MSS Ellesmere 6210–14. Interestingly, what appears to be the first draft of the commission from Burghley contains an attack on the unjust practices of attorneys, which was deleted by Egerton. Otherwise the arguments against the practice of imprisonment for debt were much the same as those rehearsed regularly over the next three centuries. For an account of the hardship of imprisonment, see Moses Pitt, *The Cry of the Oppressed: Being a True and Tragical Account of the Unparalleled Sufferings of Multitudes of Poor Imprisoned Debtors, in Most of the Gaols in England, under the Tyranny of the Gaolers, and Other Oppressors, Lately Discovered upon the Occasion of this Present Act of Grace, For the Release of Poor Prisoners for Debt, or Damages; Some of Them Being Not Only Iron'd, and Lodg'd with Hogs, Felons, and Condemn'd Persons, but Have Had Their Bones Broke; Otheres Poisoned and Starved to Death; Others Denied the Common Blessings of Nature, as Water to Drink, or Straw to Lodge on; Others Their Wives and Daughters Attempted to be Ravish'd; With Other Barbarous Cruelties, Not to be Parallel'd in Any History, or Nation; All Which is Made Out by Undeniable Evidence. Together with the Case of the Publisher ... Illustrated with Copper-Plates* (London, 1691). I am grateful to Professor John Beattie for drawing my attention to this work.

[114] *All the Workes of John Taylor the Water Poet Being Sixty-Three in Number Collected into One Volume by the Author* (London, 1630), preface.

enforcement of agreements would encourage people to break their promises. Far from being a precursor of the future, when Thomas Hobbes described the enforcement of obligations as the major benefit of political society he seems to be addressing the same problem as many of the litigants before the courts.[115]

While the social relationship most often reflected in early modern litigation was that between debtor and creditor, the full range of court usage extended to disputes over land, the arrangement of marriage agreements, the maintenance of personal and professional reputations, and, if we include the ecclesiastical court jurisdictions, matrimonial disputes and the regulation of religious observance as well as personal morality. Large numbers of people of modest wealth had much of their lives tied up in parchment and paper, and many of their lawsuits are best explained largely in functional terms. Actions of slander were brought to maintain reputations in a face to face society where the ability to raise credit depended on being known as creditworthy. Ecclesiastical court sanctions against personal immorality, and litigation over the making of marriage, supported a demographic regime in which most people married in their late twenties – ideally, only after they had established a means of supporting their household.[116] In the early seventeenth century, such matters accounted for perhaps a third of ecclesiastical court business, and maybe 1 per cent of total actions. In the modern era by contrast family matters make up about 6 per cent of all litigation. By this measure, although the seventeenth century was more censorious, the greater ease with which marriages can be dissolved today means that twentieth-century lawyers probably make more money out of sex and marriage than did their early-modern predecessors. As we shall see, this has had a profound influence on the general shape of modern civil litigation.[117]

Another consequence of greater access to the central courts in the late sixteenth and seventeenth centuries was that the intensity of social regulation was to some degree diluted. There were important exceptions, but by the early seventeenth century the manorial courts, which figured so prominently in the fifteenth century, appear to have been the one jurisdiction which had failed to flourish. Apart from those which were associated with growing market towns, in court after court civil actions of debt and trespass appear regularly, if not at all that high a rate, during the later sixteenth century. They then disappear after 1600; and at the same time the presentments of courts leet deal less and less with neighbourhood regulation.[118] By the

115 Chapter 3, pp. 57–58; C. W. Brooks, R. H. Helmholz and P. G. Stein, *Notaries Public in England Since the Reformation* (Norwich, 1991), pp. 89–91; C. Muldrew, 'The Culture of Reconciliation: Community and the Settlement of Economic Disputes in Early Modern England', *Historical Journal*, 39 (1996), pp. 915–42.

116 Ingram, *Church Courts*.

117 See below, pp. 117ff.

118 It was of course S. and B. Webb, *English Local Government from the Revolution to the Municipal Corporations Act: The Manor and the Borough* (London, 1924), p. 31, who wrote that by the

Restoration period, manorial customs were literally the subject of professional jokes.[119] Tenurial changes, inflation in the value of money and the preferences of litigants, as well as a quite distinct legal imperialism from Westminster which subjected the powers of customary courts to close scrutiny and limitation, all contributed to the decline.[120] One of the most obvious consequences of this was that local communities lost forever the power of selecting their own constables (police), and much of the responsibility for the regulatory functions of the court were shifted to the justices of the peace, who were, of course, drawn largely from the gentry. There were powerful social and religious impulses which led county benches to regulate alehouses and to attack immorality whilst having to deal with the consequences of illegitimacy, but many of the more mundane regulatory activities of the court leet, including economic and social sanctions, do not appear to have taken up much of their time. Furthermore, as social offences such as bearing illegitimate children, or loitering in the alehouse during divine service, became enshrined in statute and were adjudicated before the justices of the peace, professional lawyers became involved more frequently. A significant number of cases which were brought before the royal courts in one way or another challenged regulatory authority, very often using arguments based on due process. A number of attempts by puritan minorities to enforce a reformation of manners against individuals in the localities ended up being challenged in the courts. Star Chamber cases reveal plaintiffs who questioned the way in which justices of the peace had used their powers. In actions of slander at common law, very significant damages could be allowed to plaintiffs who claimed that false accusations, which might lead to prosecution, had been made against them.[121] Lawyers had something to offer to clients who bridled at either customary or moral prescriptions; or, indeed, as the history of the Quakers suggests, to those who found themselves the targets of religious persecution.[122]

Restoration period there was no place where the manorial court was what it used to be. However, on p. 116, they note that regulatory activity was still greater than they had expected in the period up to 1689. Muldrew, 'Rural Credit, Market Areas and Legal Institutions in the English Countryside', pp. 166–67, suggests that manorial courts associated with market towns were much more likely to have remained lively venues for civil litigation than those connected with smaller villages.

[119] T[homas] B[lount] of the Inner Temple, *Fragmenta Antiquitatis: Ancient Tenures of Land and Jocular Customs of Some Mannors* (London, 1679). However, professional amusement at local peculiarity seems not to have been all that new. In 1300 Justice Bereford facetiously reminded Serjeant Mutford of a manor where the customary service was 'a leap, a whistle and a fart', BL, MS Add. 31826, fol. 91v. I owe this reference and the translation to Paul Brand.

[120] F. J. C. Hearnshaw, *Leet Jurisdiction in England* (Southampton, 1908) contains much valuable illustrative material.

[121] See below, Chapter 7, pp. 195ff.

[122] Craig W. Horle, *The Quakers and the English Legal System, 1660–1688* (Philadelphia, PA, 1988).

Lawyers had an extremely high profile in sixteenth- and seventeenth-century society, and of course in the political debates of the period as well. Against this background, the dramatic decline in court usage in the early eighteenth century appears all the more remarkable and at first (or second sight) all the more difficult to explain.[123] There is also another intriguing factor: similar trends have been identified in France, Germany and Spain, although, interestingly, Ireland appears to be an exception that proves the rule.[124]

One or two longitudinal studies of other places and other times have suggested what is known as the 'curvilinear thesis' in order to explain similar patterns of peaks and troughs. According to this line of thinking, periods of rapid social change produce a great deal of litigation as the law is adapted to new economic and social relationships.[125] Once the adjustment is made, levels of contention drop as patterns of behaviour conform to the new conventions. Some, including the historian of Spanish lawsuits Richard Kagan, argue that the legal professions can themselves act to cool litigiousness by discouraging those with unlikely cases or by channelling disputes into arbitration rather than by offering to take out a writ.[126]

Although the fit is by no means perfect, some of the English evidence seems to conform to this hypothesis. The increased availability of the action of assumpsit for debt, and particularly its adaptation to enforce promissory notes, undoubtedly helped to institute much more flexible credit arrangements than were possible in connection with the conditional bond. Lines of credit were no longer quite so threatened by the refusal or inability of a single person to pay. This may have taken some of the urgency out of going to law. It can even be argued that the extensive use of law to enforce agreements in the seventeenth century exercised a kind of pedagogic effect on debtor-creditor relationships. At the same time, although it is certainly more of a social and economic than a legal argument, the early eighteenth century may well have been a period in which a stable demographic and social regime combined with some economic expansion to increase individual prosperity and reduce indebtedness.[127]

On the other hand, the idea that a greater sense of professionalism may

---

[123] For a detailed consideration see Chapter 3.

[124] R. L. Kagan, *Lawsuits and Litigants in Castile, 1500–1700* (Chapel Hill, NC, 1981); Colin Kaiser, 'The Deflation in the Volume of Litigation at Paris in the Eighteenth Century and the Waning of the Old Juridical Order', *European Studies Review*, 10 (1980), pp. 309–36; Christian Wollschläger, 'Civil Litigation and Modernization: The Work of the Municipal Courts of Bremen, Germany in Five Centuries, 1549–1984', *Law and Society Review*, 24 (1990), pp. 261–82; T. C. Barnard, 'Lawyers and the Law in Later Seventeenth-Century Ireland', *Irish Historical Studies*, 28 (1993), pp. 256–82, especially p. 260.

[125] F. Van Loon and E. Langerwerf, 'Socioeconomic Development and the Evolution of Litigation Rates of Civil Courts in Belgium, 1835–1980', *Law and Society Review*, 24 (1990) p. 286.

[126] Kagan, *Lawsuits and Litigants in Castile*, chs 4, 7.

[127] Chapter 3, pp. 36ff. See also, C. W. Francis, 'Practice, Strategy and Institution: Debt Collection in the English Common-Law Courts, 1740–1840', *Northwestern University Law Review*, 80 (1986), pp. 807–955.

have led lawyers to discourage litigation seems improbable. It is unlikely that men would change their outlook towards their trade in a single generation. The best evidence that this was not the case comes from the account books of attorneys who worked over the two or three crucial decades in the 1690s and early 1700s, since they reveal a drop in the amount of litigious work within the careers of individuals.[128] What is striking about the century and a half from 1690 to 1850 is that there was a constant stream of complaint about the inefficiency of the administration of justice. This lasted from the parliamentary investigations into fees in the 1690s, to the fulminations of Jeremy Bentham and other critics in the second half of the eighteenth century, to even more widespread nineteenth-century calls for reform which were eventually to some degree realised. While it is true that criticism of the legal system and lawyers was already a very familiar refrain during the seventeenth century, if not well before, there was a difference between the two periods. The eighteenth century saw significantly more discussion of the way in which the courts had priced themselves out of the market, and of how the workings of the legal system were so unpredictable that ordinary people would rather suffer injuries than risk additional losses by trying to use the law. There is, moreover, every reason to believe both that higher fees were indeed being demanded by lawyers and by the clerical officials of the courts, and that eighteenth-century practitioners were in fact concerned about the lack of business.[129]

W. A. Champion has shown that one of the causes of the decline of business in the local court at Shrewsbury was that fees there began to increase significantly as the local legal establishment came to be dominated by professional lawyers who also had ties with London. The impact was felt first in the early seventeenth century and was subsequently compounded by later developments, such as the introduction of stamp duties on legal documents in the 1690s.[130] In the case of the central courts, the relative stability of the Elizabethan and early Stuart years were followed by the beginning of the next century by a renewed wave of concern. While it is difficult to determine with precision whether the more ruthless exploitation of the potential economic rewards of office was a cause or a consequence of the decline in litigation, the two certainly remained closely intertwined until the major administrative reforms of the royal courts in the period between 1830 and 1850. It seems unlikely that the initial drop in business was caused primarily by bureaucratic and cost factors, but these very soon began to compound the process. While little is known at present about the exact

---

[128] Chapter 3, p. 46.

[129] Ibid., pp. 44–49.

[130] Champion, 'Recourse to Law and the Great Litigation Decline', pp. 184–86. Indeed, the House of Commons was worried that attorneys were evading the stamp duties by failing to take out legal process, and this should be borne in mind in evaluating the extent of the 'decline' in litigation, *Journals of the House of Commons* (London, 1803ff), xv, pp. 569, 618–19.

configuration of legal office-holding in the early eighteenth century, it is evident that many posts were held by sinecurists, who may not have been interested in anything more than the potential income which an office might generate.[131] Under such conditions, the level of fees was bound to be an important consideration.[132] As early as 1712 an anonymous reformer, himself an attorney, identified the payment of fees to office-holders as the greatest single hindrance to the effective administration of justice. During the later seventeenth and eighteenth centuries, there was certainly an upward trend in official fees compounded by quite significant rises in the charges made by counsel.[133]

Significantly, the fee which was more successfully fixed than any of the others was the termly fee of 3s. 4d. due to attorneys for each action that they handled. Predictably, some practitioners considered it an injustice that, while those of barristers had risen from 10s. to as much as £10, the fees of attorneys had been fixed at a rate whose value had been seriously eroded by inflation.[134] Also, although it is a point historians rarely acknowledge, the establishment and maintenance of a legal practice involved by this date the necessity of paying for premises, paper, ink and stamped parchment – as well as extras such as snuff and tobacco.[135] Early eighteenth-century accounts reveal the ways in which such factors led lawyers to consider carefully whether their costs were covered by their incomes. For instance, although he conducted much of his work that involved the central courts through a London agent, the Sheffield attorney Thomas Wright noted with some irritation in 1701 that the business of a single client took him to London for eight days. During the first four of these he 'did nothing but run all the Towne' trying to arrange a meeting, and during the next four, he spent much of his time waiting in coffee houses to see people.[136]

In the early seventeenth century, when the volume of business was high,

[131] Chapter 3, p. 45.

[132] Horwitz, *Chancery Equity Records*, pp. 10–11, 30–31, illustrates some of the consequences of the decline of business on the fee-taking of officials in the very early eighteenth century. The dragging out of business and not replacing office-holders who died were amongst the alternative remedies. See also, for example, *The Case of the Filacers of His Majesty's Court of Common Pleas, in Regard to the Bill Now Depending before the Honourable House of Commons, For the More Easy and Speedy Recovery of Small Debts. Read 4 March 1730* (London, 1730), which says that since the income of the filacers will suffer if the bill passes, they hope for a 'proportionable Consideration for their loss'. They give a number of examples where 'the Rights and Properties of Private Persons in publick offices, which being long enjoyed, were preserved, or an adequate Compensation given'.

[133] *Proposals Humbly Offer'd to the Parliament for Remedying the Great Charge and Delay of Suits at Law and in Equity: By an Attorney* (3rd edn, London, 1729; first published 1712), pp. v, 1–3, 10–11. See also, Chapter 3, pp. 45–46.

[134] *Proposals Humbly Ofer'd to the Parliament*, p. 26.

[135] These expenses are nicely illustrated by the office accounts of Thomas Wright of Sheffield. Sheffield City Archives, MS TC 383 (*c.* 1714).

[136] Sheffield City Archives, MS TC 379, fol. 15.

provincial attorneys were more likely to be able to cover the costs of such a journey by having enough work to make the trip worthwhile.[137] As litigation declined this was no longer the case. Costs (both in terms of a provincial attorney's time, and in terms of what he would have to lay out to agents and officials) may well have been positive incentives against encouraging people to sue.[138] What is certain is that, in the absence of any increase in the standard 3s. 4d. fee, additional income was generated by making additional charges. Thomas Wright, who calculated that his trip to London had cost him 14s. in expenses over and above 'the pains' he took over the work itself, was determined that he would leave it to his client 'to gratify' him.[139] Similarly, the fee books of the Cambridgeshire practitioner Joshua Eversden show that, in the years around 1710, he supplemented the standard attorney's fee by making a number of additional charges for each piece of work done for a client. He charged for journeys undertaken to consult with litigants, to speak to witnesses and, in what becomes a common phrase in fee books of the eighteenth century, as much as £2 for his 'troubles' in a matter.[140]

Coupled with what appears to have been a greater reluctance of lawyers to allow litigants to conduct their business on credit, these seemingly trivial changes in the way fees were taken not only help to explain the contraction of court business in the eighteenth century, they also amount to a profound watershed in the way legal services were financed in England. They mark the replacement of the principle of a fixed tariff by a system of remuneration in which attorneys and solicitors charged essentially on the basis of some kind of calculation of how much time and effort they had expended.[141] It is true, of course, that some control over the fees of both officials and attorneys (but not barristers) was exercised through the powers of the courts to assess the validity of costs which losing parties were obliged to pay; but, as one writer plausibly pointed out in 1759, at a time when its business was haemorrhaging badly, it was unlikely that prothonotaries of the Common Pleas, responsible for determining costs, would have been anxious to alienate attorneys by attacking their profits.[142] More generally, it appears that two important mechanisms, which had operated in the earlier periods to help control procedural complexity and the inexorable escalation of fees, were largely ineffective in the eighteenth century. In the early seventeenth century

---

[137] Brooks, *Pettyfoggers and Vipers*, ch. 11. Brand, *Origins of English Legal Profession*, pp. 89–94, discusses the various methods of remuneration which operated in the thirteenth century.

[138] See above, Chapter 3, p. 47.

[139] Sheffield City Archives, MS TC 379, fol. 15.

[140] PRO, C 106/6, papers of Joshua Eversden. I am grateful to Henry Horwitz for this reference.

[141] See below, p. 104 and pp. 123–24, for the later consequences of this development.

[142] Anon., *Reflections or Hints Founded upon Experience and Facts Touching the Law, Lawyers, Officers, Attorneys and Others Concerned in the Administration of Justice: Humbly Submitted to the Consideration of the Legislature* (London, 1759), p. 41.

pressure from litigants led common law attorneys to press for procedural simplification: royal commissions on fees, although frequently little more than government money-raising exercises, appear to have produced set tables of fees which were generally adhered to by officials.[143] In the eighteenth century neither of these disciplines operated effectively and court fees slipped further out of control. A select committee of the House of Commons reported in 1732 that orders which had been made in the past for officers publicly to display lists of fees had since been withdrawn or 'suffered to decay, and become so useless, that the Officers themselves seemed often doubtful what Fees to claim'.[144] The committee resolved to request a royal commission to investigate fees but, for reasons that are unclear, Lord Chancellor Hardwicke seems to have effectively smothered its activities.[145] Arising from a state of public opinion in which practitioners themselves evidently wanted limitations on numbers, whilst laymen were calling for cheaper and more effective means of recovering small debts, the most significant reforms achieved in the early eighteenth century (the 1729 act which required attorneys and solicitors to register indentures of clerkship if they wanted to be admitted into practice and the measure of 1730 abolishing the use of court hands, Latin and French) evidently had little impact on the problem of access or in halting the increasingly precipitate decline in court usage.[146] Throughout the remainder of the eighteenth century there is a strong case to be made that successive governments were more interested in taxing the legal profession, which they did successfully, than in regulating its standards of education and practice.[147] According to Sir William Blackstone, it was even arguable that the abolition of Law French and Latin as the languages of record made matters worse rather than better. In his view, since the changes had been instituted, documents, and in particular special pleadings, had become longer (and hence more costly) than ever before.[148]

Exactly how far these circumstances were associated with a withdrawal of the law from the general cultural currency of the period, and the emergence of a society which contained a large number of embittered 'lumpers' who felt they had to accept injustice because the law was beyond their means,

---

[143] Brooks, *Pettyfoggers and Vipers*, ch. 7.

[144] *Commons Journals*, xxi, p. 892.

[145] Above Chapter 3, p. 47, but compare the remarks of in *Relections or Hints Founded upon Experience*, p. 6, whose author thought the commission, which had been launched out of sheer animosity towards the profession, was suppressed because it could find no evidence of increases 'for many years past'.

[146] See Chapter 3. A more optimistic assessment of piecemeal reform in the early eighteenth century is made in Wilfrid Prest, 'Law Reform in Eighteenth-Century England', in P. Birks, ed., *The Life of the Law* (London, 1993), pp. 113–24.

[147] See also Chapter 6 and Chapter 7, pp. 140, 155–56.

[148] William Blackstone, *Commentaries on the Laws of England* (4 vols, Oxford, 1765–69), iii, pp. 322–23. The point was also made at length by the author of *Reflections or Hints Founded upon Experience*, pp. 10–17.

are subjects which still need further investigation. It is possible, of course, that the period could be put forward as a shining example of one in which the social and moral evil of litigation had been greatly contained, but the volume of contemporary criticism appears instead to focus on the failings of the law in terms of its inaccessibility. In any case the great trough in litigation meant that by 1750 many fewer people used courts to resolve their conflicts than had done so the a century earlier. This is true whether or not we are considering courts leet or borough courts, ecclesiastical courts or those which sat in Westminster Hall at London.[149]

An important consequence of this was that the middle years of the eighteenth century were difficult ones for legal practitioners.[150] For example, a meeting of London attorneys held at a Tavern in Fleet Street in 1749 is reported to have resolved that a further reduction in the number of practitioners was an essential ingredient in the regulation of the profession. The reason was that 'where there are more Professors than the honest Gains of the Profession can maintain, Necessity may excite Practices, as injurious and troublesome ... to the Property and Peace of Individuals, as the Want of Justice, in Countries not governed by Law ...'[151] A tract written at mid century in defence of the monopoly of the serjeants at law in the Common Pleas commented that 'at present the number of Serjeants is more than the business of the court'.[152] The experiences of the circle of professional friends of a future chief justice of the King's Bench, Lloyd Kenyon, who was called to the bar in 1757, indicates that the patient endurance of long years of relative penury, and an element of luck, were necessary before a life at the bar could be turned into a comfortable living.[153] As late as the 1840s these times were frequently referred to by legal biographers as exemplifying the kind of perseverance which was necessary to make a success of the law.[154]

As the numbers of lawyers dropped to a level which may not have been

---

[149] Champion, 'Recourse to Law and the Great Litigation Decline', pp. 192–96, for a pioneering discussion of the simultaneous decline of leet business and that of the civil courts at Shrewsbury during the eighteenth century.

[150] For the numbers of practitioners see Chapter 7, p. 184.

[151] *Animadversions upon the Present Laws of England; or An Essay to Render Them More Useful and Less Expensive to All His Majesty's Subjects. To Which is Added a Proposal for Regulating the Practice and Reducing the Number of Attornies and Sollicitors. With a Supplement Humbly Submitted to the Serious Consideration of Both Houses of Parliament* (London, 1750), pp. 35–37.

[152] [Edward Wynne], *A Miscellany Containing Several Law Tracts* (n. p., 1765), p. 382–84; James Oldham, *The Mansfield Manuscripts and the Growth of English Law in the Eighteenth Century* (2 vols, Chapel Hill, NC, 1992), i, pp. 124–28, fills in the detail of the problems of the Common Pleas.

[153] George T. Kenyon, *The Life of Lloyd, First Lord Kenyon* (London, 1873), pp. 16–22. Oldham, *The Mansfield Manuscripts and the Growth of English Law*, i, p. 79, concludes that twenty or thirty barristers shared the bulk of the work in King's Bench during the Mansfield era.

[154] [Archer Polson], *Law and Lawyers: or Sketches and Illustrations of Legal History and Biography* (2 vols, London, 1840), i, pp. 43–49. P. Corfield, *Professions and Power in Britain, 1700–1850* (London, 1995), pp. 70–72, puts forward a more optimistic picture, but it does not take much account of the changes described here.

any greater than that which had existed a century before, the legal inns in London fell into a torpor, which was evident from the early decades of the eighteenth century, and which meant that they thenceforth contributed little to legal education or the maintenance of standards within the profession.[155] If lawyers as an occupational group were characterised, or caricatured, as dealers in a confused and unintelligible science which they exploited for their own ends, it may well have been partly because, during most of the eighteenth century, they lacked the institutional foundations on which to build a better reputation. It also seems reasonable to suggest that lay ignorance of the law which writers, including Sir William Blackstone and Jeremy Bentham, detected was in part a reflection of the simple fact that in their day relatively few people ever had anything to do with a court. Interestingly, Bentham's belief that the society in which he lived was an anachronistic one, in which personal loyalties and shared traditions created a subservient and deferential population rather than a society of equal freeman citizens, tallies more closely with the relatively non-litigious eighteenth century than with the highly litigious sixteenth and seventeenth.[156]

It would, on the other hand, be misleading to paint an entirely bleak picture. While some critics went so far as to suggest that the only way to rejuvenate business was to undertake codification and make a drastic reduction in legal costs, most commentators of the early eighteenth century frequently went out of their way say that their complaints focused on procedures and costs rather than on the quality of the judiciary, which was often praised.[157] Although a newspaper report of 1778 expressed surprise at how few cases there were before the Court of Common Pleas, the regularity with which they were reported in the provinces as well as London indicates that lawsuits were clearly of interest to the wider populace. During the second half of the century, the King's Bench, if not the Common Pleas, made a significant recovery. This began during the tenure of the Scottish-born judge

---

[155] See Chapters 5 and 6, pp. 132, 150ff.

[156] Gerald J. Postema, *Bentham and the Common Law Tradition* (Oxford, 1986), pp. 267, 273, 294–95, 310, 396, 426.

[157] For example, *The Gentleman's Magazine*, 1 (1731), pp. 19, 100, 213; 2 (1732), pp. 899, 1045; *The Law-Suit: or The Farmer and Fisherman. A Poem in Hudibrastic Verse* (London, 1739); Joshua Fitzsimmons, *Free and Candid Disquisitions on the Nature and Execution of the Laws of England Both in Civil and Criminal Affairs* (London, 1751). A more favourable view is expressed by John Brown (of Newcastle), *Estimate of the Manner and Principles of the Times* (Dublin, 1758), p. 16. 'Another Virtue, and of the highest Consequence, as it regards the immediate and private Happiness of Individuals, yet left among us, is the pure Administration of Justice, as it regards private Property'. Brown thought that the 'spirit of commerce' produced a self-regulating selfishness which contributed to the increase in wealth. For a professional defence of the law, see Daines Barrington, *Observations on the Statutes, Chiefly the More Ancient from Magna Charta to the Twenty-First of James I* (London, 1766), p. 337, 'Those who ridicule the laws of Engalnd can never have been witnesses to that constant, deliberate, and upright administration of justice, which hath prevailed in different courts ... since the Revolution and that upon the most solid and rational principles'.

William Murray, Lord Mansfield, as chief justice between 1762 and 1778.[158] Although some of this activity may reflect the ability of the lawyers to draw out what business they had, rather than a dramatic increase in the number of new cases, by the latter date he was hearing upwards of one thousand cases each year and finding it difficult to keep pace with the volume of work.[159] From about the same time, the numbers of attorneys admitted to practice increased significantly. By the 1790s there was a very distinct interest in finding ways to breathe new life into legal education.[160]

Mansfield is frequently credited with helping to adapt the common law to the conditions of the newly emerging economic world associated with the 'Industrial Revolution', and it is evident that all of the central courts saw a rise during the eighteenth century in business generated from the non-agricultural sectors of society, with litigants coming increasingly either from the industrialising north of England or from the London metropolitan area.[161] Nevertheless, the increases in central court business during the late eighteenth and early nineteenth centuries hardly kept pace with the growth in population, which doubled from around 5,500,000 in 1750 to 11,000,000 in 1830. Consequently, it is probable that the recovery which took place owed more to historically unique demographic and economic circumstances than to administrative or judicial reform.[162]

While even less is known about the functioning of local courts in the eighteenth century than about the major common law courts and Chancery, it appears that one of the most significant consequences of the decline in business was that it eventually undermined traditional borough jurisdictions to such an extent that, when the upturn in litigation began, many of them were superseded by the courts of requests.[163] But even the latter at times had trouble adapting to changing circumstances, a point which is well documented in the case of the oldest court of requests in the country, that of the City of London.[164] In 1758 the court was issuing more than 3873 summonses each year but, over the next forty to fifty years, business

---

[158] See Figure 4.3 and Chapter 3, p. 33.

[159] See generally, Oldham, *The Mansfield Manuscripts and the Growth of English Law*.

[160] See Chapters 6 and 7, pp. 164ff, 184.

[161] See Chapter 3, pp. 37–39, and Horwitz and Polden, 'Continuity or Change in the Court of Chancery', p. 46.

[162] Ibid., p. 38.

[163] See Chapter 3, pp. 41–42, and below, pp. 104ff, for the later consequences of this development.

[164] The best brief account of the history of the court is Corporation of London Record Office, the Guildhall, London, MS Miscellaneous 135.3, 'Historical Notes on the Court of Requests' (typescript). The court was founded by act of the Common Council in 1518, which laid it down that the court of aldermen should make monthly appointments of two aldermen and four commoners who were to sit as commissioners on Wednesdays and Saturdays to hear actions of debt involving less than 40s. The jurisdiction of the court was confirmed and regulated by 3 James I, c. 15 and 14 George II, c. 10. In the nineteenth century the commissioners were two aldermen and twenty inhabitant householders, possessed of property worth not less than £1000.

increased, steadily during the 1760s and then more quickly in the 1770s and 1780s.[165] As it did so, the committees appointed by the City to oversee the affairs of the court found that past procedures occasionally cracked under the strain. In 1759 all seemed well.[166] The court's clerk, William Priest, had been in place since 1733, and the City of London's committee for letting lands and tenements could find men who were willing to pay as much as £950 for each of the two offices of beadle.[167] But during the next two decades there were difficulties. The clerk and the beadles quarrelled over fees. William Priest was suspended from office twice. In 1774 George Green, the beadle who had paid £950 for his position, was suspended on a charge of malpractice and died soon afterwards.[168] From his point of view the problem was that the profits of his office, and the amount of work it entailed, did not amount to a very satisfactory return on the capital sum which he paid in order to obtain it.[169]

On the other hand, in evidence which they gave to an investigation in the 1770s, plaintiffs complained that the laxity of the court's procedures caused them to spend a great deal of time in fruitless attendance before a tribunal which met amidst much commotion and confusion.

The Eccho in the Hall occasioned by the great resort of People thither, and also a great Number of Idle People constantly assembling during the time of the Court, render the Hearing very disagreeable to the Commissioners and subjects the Clerks to the Commission of many Errors.[170]

[165] Corporation of London Record Office, MS Miscellaneous 259.9, papers connected with an investigation into the affairs of the court in 1768. William Priest's account of 'how many Summonses are issued in a Year that do not come to a hearing for Ten years past':

1758	3872	1763	3056
1759	3536	1764	3914
1760	3108	1765	4043
1761	2732	1766	4499
1762	2987	1767	4252

He made the total 35,999; an average of 3599 summonses each year.

[166] Corporation of London Record Office, MS Miscellaneous 259.8, minutes of committee appointed to investigate the court of requests, 1759. Printed report of the Committee Appointed by the Common Council, 4 December 1759. However, there was, in 1760–61, a dispute between Priest and one of the beadles, Samuel Farley, minutes of 20 December 1760 and 14 April 1761.

[167] Corporation of London Record Office, MS Miscellaneous 259.8, minutes of committee appointed to investigate the court of requests, 1759, deposition of Priest, dated 2 October 1759; MS Miscellaneous 284.5, papers concerned with the court of requests, including a table of fees, 1755, and the printed agreement between the 'Committee of City Lands' and George Green of Great Coxwell, Berkshire.

[168] Ibid., Priest claimed that in 1761 he himself acted as beadle during a period when the office was unfilled, suggesting perhaps that he was attempting to increase his income. Corporation of London Record Office, MS Miscellaneous, minute book of committee appointed to inquire into the court of requests, 1774–1788, pp. 109ff.

[169] Ibid., p. 88. Having paid nearly £1000 for the office, Green evidently owed interest of nearly £80 p. a. on this sum, but recovered fees worth no more than £50 p. a.

[170] Ibid., p. 36. Interestingly, it appears that litigants employed agents, who were frequently

Business was also interrupted by the drawing of lotteries and the taking of polls, but even when plaintiffs managed to get a judgment, they could not be confident that the beadles would serve executions or, indeed, hand over to them money which had been collected on the payment of debts. Achieving satisfaction involved chasing around after the beadles, a task which frequently included making several visits to the public house that was run by one of them.[171] For his part, William Priest reported that the neglect of the beadles was often communicated to himself in the form of the innumerable insults and abuses he received from irritated and 'injured' plaintiffs, and even the beadles admitted that they might have had a case. It was clearly an advantage to defendants that the beadles were often too busy to deliver attachments and executions; at the same time, defendants were known to refuse to accept process on the plausible grounds that the servants delivering it were not *bona fide* officials. The beadles also alleged, however, that much of the litigation they encountered was purely vexatious, arising simply because people had a 'falling out' with each other. They pointed out that defendants who were imprisoned for defaults often found themselves in gaol for years because the fees they were obliged to pay were often double or triple the value of the original debt.[172]

The committee appointed by the City of London to investigate the affairs of the court in 1774 condemned the beadles, claiming that their negligence had been to the great detriment of suitors, 'many of whom [were] of the lower Class of People, whose Time is the sole Support of themselves and Families'.[173] A new set of rules regarding summonses, writs and the keeping of records was instituted. The committee ordered that some of the money raised in fees should be spent to purchase gowns that the clerks and beadles were henceforth obliged to wear in court. More significantly, they decided that the number of beadles should be increased from two to four, and that the office should be disposed of by annual election rather than by sale, not least because Green and the others had formerly claimed that their purchase of the position gave them a 'right' to act without control.[174] Over the next twenty-five years, although the affairs of the court still continued on occasion

women, to act for them. Corporation of London Record Office, Court of Requests Register Books, 1770–90, vol. 1, August 1770 to July 1771, records their names, including 'Sarah', 'Ann', 'Buff', 'Phebe' and 'Jane'. In the face of questions from a parliamentary committee in the 1820s, the clerk was evasive about the use of agents, but acknowledged that 'friends' might be employed when it was inconvenient for someone to attend in person. *Parliamentary Papers, 1823,* iv, *Report from the Committee on the Recovery of Small Debts* (London, 1823), pp. 205–6.

[171] Corporation of London Record Office, MS Miscellaneous, minute book of committee appointed to inquire into the court of requests, 1774–1788, pp. 52ff, 89–90.

[172] Ibid., pp. 89–90, 93–104.

[173] Corporation of London Record Office, Reports of the Committee on the Practice and Fees of the Court of Requests, 1774–1790, p. 41, printed order of the Common Council of London, 29 July 1774. It goes on to mention women, servants, journeymen, handicraftsmen and labourers.

[174] Ibid., pp. 41–46.

to give rise to mutual recriminations amongst the officials, this arrangement appears to have worked reasonably well.[175] In 1800 the City spent a considerable sum of money to extend its jurisdiction to £5 and undertook a further major change in the way in which the officials were paid.[176] Anticipating an increase in business, they considered (but rejected) the idea that suitors should be allowed to call on legal representation.[177] They did advise, however, that 'for the better service of the poorer Classes of the Community', the fee-taking system should be abolished and a schedule of salaries introduced for the officials.[178]

It is not at present possible to say whether the court of requests of the City of London was the first court in the realm to follow this course of reform, but its story is in many respects a template of a drawn out series of changes which eventually spread throughout England during the half century between 1820 and the passage of the Judicature Act of 1875.[179] Although the number of cases brought in the central courts, as well as the number sued in the courts of requests, increased during the first two decades of the nineteenth century, there was a constant stream of complaint in the 1820s and 1830s about delays and high costs which impeded those with grievances, especially concerning unpaid debts, from taking their cases to law.[180] As Henry Horwitz and Patrick Polden have recently suggested in their analysis of Chancery, the problem faced by courts in the early nineteenth century was that

---

[175] Corporation of London Record Office, MS Miscellaneous 260.1, papers and rough minutes relating to the court of requests 1790–1832: minutes of the general purposes committee. In 1790 Priest, the clerk, claimed that one of the beadles had died insolvent and had £40 of suitors' money in his hands at the time. In 1791, he complained about another beadle, Holloway Brecknock, who wrote to the committee in 1792 that he was a 'poor unfortunate Mortal', who was down on his luck and frequently called a 'blockhead' by Priest.

[176] Corporation of London Record Office, MS Minutes of the Committee to Enquire into the Court of Requests, 1774–78. The committee seems to have met infrequently in the late 1770s and 1780s.

[177] Corporation of London Record Office, P. A. R. Book 12, p. 52. 'Having taken into Consideration the Expediency of admiting Counsel to plead in the Court of Requests, we are decidedly of Opinion, that as no Points of Law can be agitated before the Commissioners, it would be extremely improper to admit either Counsel or Attorneys at Law, to plead or act for any Plaintiff or Defendant in the said Court.'

[178] Ibid., pp. 52–55. The salaries were £400 for the principal clerk and £60, exclusive of their fees due for serving attatchments, levying executions and summonsing witnesses, for the beadles. This was based on a calculation that the fee income for 1799 had been £294 13s. 6d. for the clerk and £68 2s. 3d., exclusive of fees, for the beadles.

[179] A parliamentary committee heard in 1823 how a significant increase in business had taken place in the Cambridge county court, mainly because of the arrival in town of two new and active attorneys. In the ten years since 1814, the number of actions had increased from 82 p.a. to 484 p. a., *Report from the Select Committee on the Recovery of Small Debts*, p. 243.

[180] See, for example, *Parliamentary Papers 1833*, xxii, *Fifth Report Made to His Majesty by the Commissioners Appointed to Inquire into the Practice and Proceedings of the Superior Courts of Common Law* (London, 1833).

increasing amounts of litigation, which was due primarily to population increases and economic change, put pressure on institutions and a legal profession whose characters had most recently been influenced by a relative lack of business and bureaucratic ossification.[181] Indeed, for radical critics like John Wade, it was evident that the 'old corruption' of sinecures and reversions infected the legal system in much the same way as they did most of the other branches of English government.[182]

In his 1828 speech on law reform, Henry Brougham observed that there were faults in the legal system which had been there from the beginning, as well as others which had been recently introduced. His prime example of the latter was the mid eighteenth-century collapse of the court of Common Pleas. The lack of business eventually affected the appointment of judges, so that suitors, losing confidence, became inclined to go elsewhere. Yet he also pointed out that the recent increases in business placed strains on the relatively small number of judges who were available in his own day. According to Brougham, 'It could not be argued, when there were 800 causes for trial at Guildhall, that twelve judges were sufficient. That number might have sufficed when Lord Mansfield lived, in the late reign, at which time perhaps, sixty causes might have been set down for trial; but was it sufficient now, when six or seven hundred cases were to be heard?'[183] Meanwhile parliamentary investigations into the state of the courts during the 1820s collected statistics and the depositions of litigants, who were unanimously agreed that high costs and labyrinthine procedures prevented tradesmen and commercial people from using the law if they could possibly avoid it.[184] From the 1830s onwards, business interests and concerned professionals acted through the chambers of commerce and organisations such as the Association for the Promotion of Social Science to encourage the investigation of how the courts worked and to press for improvements in the system.[185] As late as 1852, the novelist Charles Dickens metaphorically described the court of Chancery as

---

[181] Horwitz and Polden, 'Continuity or Change in the Court of Chancery in the Seventeenth and Eighteenth Centuries', p. 55. They also emphasise Lord Eldon's preoccupation with bankruptcy, and his meticulous pursuit of the 'absolutely correct decision'.

[182] [John Wade], *The Black Book; or Corruption Unmasked! Being an Account of Places, Pensions, and Sinecures; the Revenues of the Clergy and Landed Aristocracy; the Salaries and Emoluments in Courts of Justice and the Police Department; the Expenditure of the Civil List* (London, 1820), pp. 3, 186ff, 203. *Parliamentary Papers 1818*, vii, *Report of the Commissioners into the Duties, Salaries and Emoluments of Officers of Courts of Justice* (London, 1818) seems certainly to show an increase in numbers of officers. This report also appears to have had access to material collected by the commission of 1734.

[183] *The Speech of Henry Brougham, Esq., as Delivered in the House of Commons, on Thursday, February 7, 1828, On His Motion Touching the State of the Law in this Country and its Administration in the Courts of Justice* (London, 1828), pp. 8, 13.

[184] For example, *Parliamentary Papers 1829*, ix, *First Report of His Majesty's Commissioners on the Common Law* (London, 1829); *The Special and General Reports Made to His Majesty by the Commissions Appointed to Inquire into the Practice and Jurisdiction of the Ecclesiastical Courts* (London, 1832).

[185] McGregor, *Social History and Law Reform* ch. 3.

a dingy warehouse filled with heaps of paper and parchment; he implied that an illiterate rag and bones man was likely to know as much about the causes before the court as the lord chancellor himself.[186]

There is no doubt that Dickens exaggerated, but he evidently captured the public image of the legal system, and he also conveyed something of the psychology of those who worked in it. For example, Charles Pugh, a second generation official, who occupied a position as a clerk to one of the masters in the court of Chancery, and who left a ten-volume diary covering the years between 1830 and his death in 1860, clearly approached his task, which involved sorting out the estates of litigants whose causes were in the hands of the court, with a sense of responsibility and duty. Yet he was embarrassed that his position, which was not officially recognised, made him feel more like a private than a public servant; while he acknowledged that reform was necessary, he was also deeply worried about what that might mean for his own well-being.[187] In the event, of course, Charles Pugh did not have to worry. Parliament undertook to buy out the private interests which had for centuries occupied the legal system. Writing in 1849, John Wade fumed that the present Lord Ellenborough was in receipt of a pension of £77,000, which he was awarded for giving up the chief clerkship of the King's Bench, a post for which money had been changing hands from as far back as the seventeenth century, and which was given to Ellenborough by his father, who was lord chief justice between 1802 and 1818. Even the lesser men did well. Wade's indignation also fell upon one of Charles Pugh's colleagues in the Chancery, William Henry Baines, who was only thirty-four years of age, and who received £23,511 in compensation for his post as a taxing master.[188]

According to the rapidly growing professional press, which is such a notable feature of the first half of the nineteenth century, much of the public calumny which was aimed at the inaccessibility and inefficiency of the courts also fell on the legal profession. The growth in court business had from the 1790s onwards led to rapidly accelerating increases in the numbers of practitioners, most notably attorneys and solicitors.[189] But, although social critics deplored this development in general terms, it seems to have been attacks on professional competence and integrity which touched most tellingly on sensitive nerves.[190] In 1830, for instance, Benjamin Brooks, the

---

[186] Charles Dickens, *Bleak House*, ch. 5.

[187] Bodleian Library, Oxford, MSS Eng. Misc. d. 465–73. See also Brooks, *Admissions Registers of Barnard's Inn*, pp. 63–64.

[188] John Wade, *Unreformed Abuses in Church and State: With a Preliminary Tractate on the Continental Revolutions* (London, 1849), pp. 180, 183.

[189] See Figure 7.1, p. 184.

[190] Wade, *The Black Book*, p. 96, estimated that the legal and medical professions numbered some 90,000 people each. 'We have put these two professions together, because there is betwixt them several points of resemblance: first, they are the most lucrative professions in society; secondly, in both there is a great deal of ignorance, mis-called learning, and of quackery and imposition ...'

president of the Society of Gentlemen Practisers, declared that it was time to protest against the imputations which were cast on attorneys and solicitors. In his view high barristers' fees and the antiquated court bureaucracies, rather than any faults of his fellow practitioners, were responsible for the delays and costs of legal proceedings.[191]

Although Brooks cautioned against overhasty demands for change, it is well known that the early years of the reign of Victoria were notable for reforms which were introduced in legal education and in the organisation of the lower branch, most notably the foundation of the Incorporated Law Society.[192] The preface to the first volume of the *Legal Observer and Journal of Jurisprudence*, edited by Robert Maugham, the secretary of the Law Society, and which claimed to speak for the profession, declared itself in favour of all moderate and practical reform. The pages of the periodical press between 1830 and 1860 are also full of reports on the latest reforms in the law, a steady stream which often seemed to the profession an unending torrent.[193] As David Sugarman has shown, however, the Law Society was also a very effective trade union in looking after the interests of practitioners, and it does not appear that important issues such as the control of professional costs was ever canvassed as a serious possibility. It is telling that in 1840 the legal biographer Archer Polson noted that in most German states the judges prepared tables of fees which regulated the takings of advocates, but he was also quick to observe that the social position of the lawyer in such places was neither independent or profitable.[194]

At the same time, the profession was at best divided on the nineteenth-century reform which is the most significant for the student of court usage: the creation in 1846 of a more or less completely new system of county courts. In the speech of 1830 in which he first proposed the idea, Brougham pointed out the potential advantages of such courts in terms of elimination of delays and prohibitive costs.[195] In addition, he stressed that a new system was needed to replace the 280 odd courts of requests which were then in existence and which handled the greater proportion of the litigation within

---

[191] *Legal Observer and Journal of Jurisprudence*, 1 (1830–31), p. 38.

[192] See Chapters 5 and 6, pp. 141ff, 168ff.

[193] *Legal Observer and Journal of Jurisprudence*, 1 (1830–31), p. iv. Similarly, the *Law Times and Journal of Property*, 1 (1843), p. 38, reminded its readers that 'We repeat, emphatically, that the lawyers of Great Britain, and the *Law Times*, as their public organ, are not opposed to rational, practical, well-digested reforms, aye, even if those reforms should somewhat retrench their emoluments. But they will not tamely submit to be made the subjects of fanciful experiments for every puny statesman to try his 'prentice hand upon ...'

[194] Polson, *Law and Lawyers*, p. 135. The *Law Times*, 1 (1843), p. 15, claimed that the profits of lawyers had been reduced by half 'at least' since 1825.

[195] *The Speech, Delivered in the House of Peers, on Thursday 2 December 1830*, p. 8. Brougham pointed out that the fee of an attorney for attending a trial at assizes could be as much as two guineas a day.

the country as a whole.[196] This case by no means won universal approbation from within the profession; it encountered opposition from start and was effectively blocked for two decades.[197] From the point of view of practitioners in London, there had never been much to recommend the courts of requests with their lay judges, simple procedures and disdain for both legal representation and trial by jury.[198] But it was also their opinion that the proposed new county courts would be no more popular than the courts of requests had been with manufacturers and traders who brought their litigation to London because they wanted proper judges and common law precision. There could be no guarantees about the quality of the judges appointed in local jurisdictions. Furthermore, the creation of a system of local courts would cause the fragmentation of the bar between London and the provinces, thereby undermining one of the greatest strengths of the English system of justice.[199] Although the county court judgeships provided employment for some of its members, the hostility of the bar to the new jurisdictions appears to have continued into the 1890s.[200] Amongst provincial, as opposed to London attorneys, opinion may have been more sympathetic. The first number of the *Jurist*, which appeared in 1837 as a rival to the *Legal Observer and Journal of Jurisprudence*, carried editorial support for Brougham's proposals for the new courts. In 1847 it welcomed the final passage of the act, arguing that the new legislation would at least provide a uniform system of courts for the recovery of small debts, ending the inconvenience for practitioners of having to discover for themselves the particular peculiarities of the numerous different courts of requests.[201]

Despite the profession's mixed feelings, the establishment of the county court system did coincide with a significant increase in the overall number

---

[196] Ibid., p. 23. Though by no means expressing complete hostility to the courts of requests, Brougham noted that they had deficiencies which prevented them from hearing as many cases as they might, and that they were by no means inexpensive. He was also in favour of the establishment of institutionalised arbitration through courts of reconcilement, ibid., pp. 28–29.

[197] The story is told in T. W. Snagge, 'Fifty Years of the English County Courts', *The Nineteenth Century*, 42 (1897), pp. 560–61; and in P. Polden, 'Judicial Selkirks: The County Court Judges and the Press, 1847–80', in Brooks and Lobban, eds, *Communities and Courts*, pp. 245–47.

[198] These were long-standing points of view. See Chapter 3, pp. 42–44, and *Report from the Select Committee on the Recovery of Small Debts*, p. 187.

[199] *Legal Observer and Journal of Jurisprudence*, 1 (1830), p. 104: 'It is a striking and important fact, that public opinion has always been against such courts as are now contemplated. The decent part of the community feel it discreditable to resort to them, and even the very rabble despise them. It is clear that their utility must be much impaired by this state of public feeling'. Ibid., p. 122: Courts of conscience 'are said to be exceedingly unpopular. They do not, generally, try causes by jury, nor proceed according to the course of the common law, which circumstances are at variance with our national predilection'. Ibid., 29 (1845–46), pp. 146, 249: In 1846 the periodical claimed that the bill establishing county courts had been sneaked through the Commons while the lawyer members were away on circuit.

[200] Raymond Cocks, *Foundations of the Modern Bar* (London, 1983), p. 56. Snagg, 'Fifty Years of the English County Courts', pp. 577–78.

[201] *The Jurist*, 1 (1837), pp. 44, 153; 10 (1847), p. 317.

of plaints. The rate of litigation per hundred thousand of population in-creased by some 40 per cent between 1847 and 1871, and there was a steady increase in the total number of plaints over the remainder of the nineteenth century (Figures 4.7 and 4.8, p. 108).

Figure 4.7
Civil Actions Commenced in England and Wales, 1858–1899

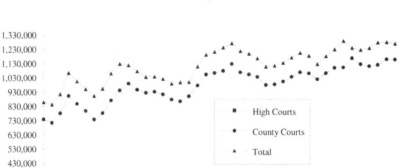

Source: *Civil Judicial Statistics*.

In a celebratory article published in 1897, the county court judge T. W. Snagg commented that the experiment launched by Brougham had turned into a 'judicial steam hammer' which answered the needs of the public. Apart from anything else, the success of the county courts was illustrated by the way in which their business had steadily increased, whereas after 1867 that of the high courts had declined and then stagnated.[202]

It is noteworthy that Snagg cast the success of the new county courts in terms of a 'return to the sounder principles and practice of an earlier age'. He saw the new tribunals as a resurrection of the older 'feudal' jurisdictions, such as the traditional manorial and borough courts, a view which contained an element of truth in formal constitutional terms. Some of the older courts existed by virtue of extensions of jurisdiction either by statute, by grants from the crown to feudal lords, or by charters issued to incorporated boroughs. In this respect they were not unlike the county courts, which had been created in the same way by parliament. Yet the equally important point, which Snagg failed to appreciate, was that many of the traditional courts, especially those associated with manors, were legitimised by little

[202] Snagg, 'Fifty Years of the English County Courts', pp. 569, 573–75.

more than prescription or long usage. Furthermore, nearly all of the older jurisdictions were much more firmly rooted within the local community than those instituted in 1846. Most of the courts which throve between 1500 and 1700 arose directly out of local manorial or borough institutions, and depended heavily on lay participation.[203] In towns, for instance, mayors and aldermen sat as judges; ordinary inhabitants acted as jurors. The town clerks and recorders who assisted and guided them were appointed by borough governments and, up to the middle of the seventeenth century at least, many towns also insisted on regulating the practice of the lawyers who acted in them.[204] Although the courts of requests, which were for the most part established later, were often less accountable to traditional local institutions, they also depended on the services of amateurs willing to sit as commissioners.[205] By contrast, one of the most important features of the new county courts was that the judges were to be appointed, not within the locality, but by the lord chancellor from a pool of candidates provided mainly by the bar. In 1847 contemporaries noted that this amounted to a very significant extension of the patronage of the chancellor, and a golden opportunity for less heavily employed barristers, but they appear to have been genuinely in favour of the principles of centralisation and freedom from local influence. In 1853 the *Jurist* went so far as to argue that, in order to guarantee these expectations, the judges should be required to reside outside the counties in which they acted.[206]

As Patrick Polden has shown, county court judges were rarely advocates of trial by jury. A number of them exercised their offices with a nearly tyrannical disregard for traditional common law principles of due process. They frequently came into conflict with attorneys and other local interest groups, including the provincial press, to such an extent that the bad publicity appears to have been influential in putting a break on the further expansion of the jurisdiction contemplated in the 1870s.[207] Of course, as Polden acknowledges, some judges did their work well, and it is unclear how far the failures of a few detracted from the overall success of the jurisdiction which was claimed for it by apologists such as Snagg. At first sight, the fact that the rate of litigation per 100,000 of population increased dramatically between 1847 and the early 1860s suggests that the new courts

---

[203] Dawson, *History of Lay Judges*, pp. 116ff.

[204] Brooks, *Pettyfoggers and Vipers*, chs 9–10. See also the chapters by Champion, Harrison and Muldrew in Brooks and Lobban, eds, *Communities and Courts*.

[205] See generally, H. W. Arthurs, *'Without the Law': Administrative Justice and Legal Pluralism in Nineteenth-Century England* (Toronto, 1985).

[206] *The Jurist*, 17 (1853), p. 498. 'Let us have *justice*, but not the semblance of it, under the specious pretences of its being cheap, speedy, and convenient. The judges of Westminster Hall are above suspicion; why should we have a class of judges scattered throughout the country, some of whom are lower in public estimation than the "dusty-footed" suitors who come before them.'

[207] Polden, 'Judicial Selkirks', pp. 247–62.

did help to resolve some of the problems of access which had been so frequently complained of earlier in the century (Figure 4.8). On the other hand, there is some convincing contemporary backing for the view that the subsequent increases in county court litigation also owed a good deal to demographic, economic and social factors.

Figure 4.8

Civil Actions in England and Wales per 100,000 of Total Population, 1830–1995

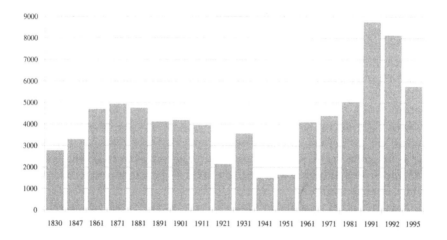

Source: *Civil Judicial Statistics.*

Sir John Macdonell, the distinguished jurist who was editor of the annual 'blue books' of judicial statistics for England and Wales between 1894 and the 1910s, was wary of finding a precise 'law of change' which would explain trends in litigation.[208] Nevertheless, his consideration of the trends between 1858 and 1894 led him to conclude that, while changes in procedure affected the distribution of litigation, they did not alter its rate. Instead, he was

---

[208] Macdonell's contribution to the subject was first identified by McGregor, *Social History and Law Reform*, ch. 4, who gives some biographical details. A Scot, Macdonell (1845–1921) was educated at Aberdeen University and called to the English bar in 1870. The author of works on political economy and the law of master and servant, he was a professor of law at London University and a master of the high court. He edited *Judicial Statistics* between 1894 and 1919, *Dictionary of National Biography*. The Law Amendment Society first demanded the regular collection of statistics in 1857, and Brougham introduced a bill in parliament to that effect. Though this did not become law, the Home Office began from that date to collect data, which can be found in the parliamentary sessions papers. *Judicial Statistics for England and Wales, 1857: Part II, Civil Judicial Statistics* (London, 1858); *Judicial Statistics, England and Wales, 1894: Part II, Civil Judicial Statistics. Statistics Relating to the Judicial Committee of the Privy Council, the House of Lords, the Supreme Court of Judicature, County Courts and Other Civil Courts* (London, 1896), p. 18.

inclined to point towards social and economic explanations for fluctuations in the overall volume.[209] Writing in 1896, he noted that the total number of plaints had increased between 1876 and 1894 in exactly the same proportion as the annual income of the country, a proposition in line with the more optimistic historical accounts of the late Victorian economy.[210] At the same time, he also connected short-term fluctuations with particular economic conditions. He explained the sudden 25 per cent increase in the volume of plaints during the later 1870s as the consequence of a period of economic depression characterised by low wages, pauperism and an associated increase in the debt-collecting business of the county courts.[211] The steady rise in the number of cases in the decade prior to 1903 resulted in contrast from a period of gentle prosperity; while, according to a report sent in from Birmingham, the distinct decline in business observed to have occurred there in 1911 was best explained in terms of a tightening up in the extension of credit by shopkeepers to 'working men'.[212] Finally, although Macdonell did not speculate at any length on their significance, *Judicial Statistics, 1910* contained figures which compared the rate of litigation in England and Wales with those for Australia, France, Germany, New Zealand and Scotland. At 4122 per 100,000, the rate for England was nearly twice that for Scotland, but significantly below that for France and less than half the rate of Germany.[213] To this we might add that, although the proportion of cases which went to the superior courts in England was higher at this date than that in either Germany or France, and although the total rate of litigation was undoubtedly higher in England than it had been for nearly 200 years previously, it was still considerably lower than it had been in the early seventeenth century.[214]

Macdonell's analysis also indicates that nineteenth-century population growth, industrialisation and urbanisation were accompanied by continuities

---

[209] Ibid., pp. 20.

[210] Ibid., p. 19. According to Macdonell both had risen by about 22.5 per cent. He estimated that annual income had risen from £980,000,000 to £1,200,000,000 over the period. For the views of economic historians see, for example, Charles Wilson, 'Economy and Society in Late Victorian Britain', *Economic History Review*, 2nd series, 18 (1965), pp. 183–98; R. Floud, 'Britain, 1860–1914: A Survey', in R. Floud and D. McCloskey, eds, *The Economic History of Britain Since 1700* (3 vols, London, 1984), ii, pp. 1–28.

[211] *Judicial Statistics, 1894*, p. 21. P. Johnson, 'Small Debts and Economic Distress in England and Wales, 1857–1913', *Economic History Review*, 46 (1993), pp. 65–87, draws similar conclusions about economic hardship and increases in debt litigation in the county courts.

[212] *Judicial Statistics, England and Wales, 1903: Part II, Civil Judicial Statistics* (London, 1905), p. 22. *Judicial Statistics, England and Wales, 1911: Part II, Civil Judicial Statistics* (London, 1912–13), p. 18.

[213] *Judicial Statistics, England and Wales, 1910: Part II, Civil Judicial Statistics* (London, 1912–13), p. 12. The rates are as follows: Australia (1909) = 5562/100,000; France (1908) = 4964/100,000; Germany (1909) = 10,372/100,000; New Zealand (1909) = 5561/100,000; Scotland (1909) = 2596/100,000.

[214] See above, pp. 68, 71.

as well as changes in the nature of lawsuits. He took it for granted that the county courts were primarily the places where the personal debts of the less well-off were adjudicated;[215] he certainly noticed that these cases resulted in increasingly large numbers of people being subjected by their creditors to the old common law sanction of imprisonment.[216] By contrast his analysis of cases in the high courts, both in London and on circuit in 1897, indicated that limited companies, as opposed to individuals, constituted about 30 per cent of the litigants.[217] While this undoubtedly amounts to a significant change from earlier periods, when most litigation was carried out in the name of individuals, the same report's quite detailed breakdown of the actions which came before the high courts suggests that, at least in their broad outline, lawsuits were not all that different in content from those brought before King's Bench and Common Pleas in 1750, or indeed earlier. About 70 per cent of them consisted of a long list of actions concerning recovery of money advanced or lent, promissory notes, recovery of rent, breach of promise of marriage and other miscellaneous breaches of agreements.[218] Another 25 per cent included many matters which would have been described under the old common law as trespasses or actions on the case: libel, slander, seduction, nuisance, malicious prosecution, false imprisonment, assault, professional negligence and of course personal injury. The remaining 5 per cent were actions about patents, trade marks, copyrights and other sundries.

While the perennial importance of that most basic of economic relationships, that between debtor and creditor, emerges as the most enduring feature of English litigation over the centuries, there are others worthy of note.[219] One of the few generalisations Macdonell would risk about changes in the pattern of court business was the observation that increases in civil

---

[215] *Judicial Statistics, England and Wales, 1896: Part II, Civil Judicial Statistics* (London, 1897), pp. 45, 71, 79. He also noted a distinct movement of litigation from south to north. In 1845–49 there was little difference as to the number of actions entered between counties south of the line and those north of it; but 1894–96 saw a much greater preponderance of business north of the line.

[216] *Judicial Statistics, England and Wales, 1897: Part II, Civil Judicial Statistics* (London, 1898), p. 31. In 1897 no judgment debtor was imprisoned by order of the high court, but 7729 were imprisoned by the county courts. See also, G. R. Rubin, 'Debtors Creditors, and the County Courts, 1846–1914: Some Source Material', *Journal of Legal History*, 17 (1996), pp. 73–81; and Paul Johnson, 'Class Law in Victorian England', *Past and Present*, 141 (1993), pp. 147–69.

[217] *Judicial Statistics, 1897*, p. 34.

[218] Ibid., pp. 23–38, contains the most complete analysis of any of Macdonell's reports. The average value of verdicts obtained was £393 in London and Middlesex and £195 on circuit (p. 26), but out of a total of 29,580 judgments, 3 per cent were for sums of under £20 and nearly 50 per cent were for sums of between £20 and £50 (p. 30). The amounts recovered in actions of slander were £30 in London and £18 4s. 11d. on circuit. *Judicial Statistics, 1894*, pp. 50–51, notes that the average of costs to plaintiffs after verdicts in the high courts was £133. Fees of counsel amounted to about one quarter of this. The average of all costs in the high courts was £80.

[219] *Judicial Statistics, 1894*, p. 64, indicates that average value of plaints in the county courts in the period 1858–62 was £2 8s. 10d. In 1893–94, it was £3 1s. 0d.

litigation generally followed, if sometimes imperfectly, increases in the level of recorded crime. Although the chronologies so far established for both types of work are still imperfect, this hypothesis would seem to apply reasonably well to the late sixteenth and early seventeenth centuries, and again to the late eighteenth and early nineteenth.[220] At the same time, Macdonell was impressed by the consistently large numbers of actions from both London and the provinces which involved libel and slander (5–7 per cent of the total), a point which suggests that the high rates for the sixteenth and seventeenth centuries may be less exceptional than early modern historians usually assume.[221] Conversely, it seems that (despite the supposedly iron grip of coverture) women were more likely to be involved in high court litigation in the early modern period than during the reign of Victoria. Macdonell found that female litigants made up only 2 per cent of the total during his period, a figure which is considerably lower than those for sixteenth- and seventeenth-century jurisdictions. Perhaps a third of early modern Chancery cases involved women, and it has been estimated that they constituted between 5 and 13 per cent of all litigants in the central common law courts, not to mention the large number of female suitors who appeared before the ecclesiastical courts.[222]

Given the growing number of personal injuries associated with the railways and industry during the nineteenth century, it is likely that the number of tort actions increased, but it is difficult to be certain by how much. Actions concerning wrongs, which might range from slander and professional negligence to assault and unlawful imprisonment, made up about one quarter of the cases brought into King's Bench and Common Pleas before 1750. Trespasses in connection with land, actions seeking remedies for professional incompetence, including medical negligence, and those regarding the

[220] Ibid., p. 20. The point is made with the aid of a comparative chart in *Judicial Statistics, England and Wales, 1903: Part II, Civil Judicial Statistics* (London, 1905), p. 23. For earlier comparisons see Sharpe, *Crime in Early Modern England*, and J. M. Beattie, *Crime and the Courts in England, 1660–1800* (Oxford, 1986).

[221] In *Civil Judicial Statistics, 1894*, p. 47, Macdonell wondered whether there might be a connection between the increase in the number of suits for defamation and a reduction in the number of crimes for violence, an hypothesis which has frequently been discussed in connection with the early modern period. In 1913 he advocated allowing the county courts to hear actions of libel and slander because such cases took up so much of the time of the high court. *Parliamentary Sessional Papers, 1913*, xxxvii, *Minutes of Evidence Taken before the Royal Commission on Delay in the King's Bench Division: With Appendices and Index*, ii (London, 1913), p. 260. 'I find that out of something like 900 cases for trial on circuit in one year, no fewer than 114 were for slander, and in 1911, I find that one-eighth of the total number of cases in London, Middlesex, and on circuit were for libel and slander'.

[222] Brooks, *Pettyfoggers and Vipers*, pp. 281–83. See also Tim Stretton, *Women Waging Law in Elizabethan England* (forthcoming) and Margo Finn, 'Women, Consumption and Coverture in England, 1760–1860', *Historical Journal*, 39 (1996), pp. 703–22. According to Robert Egerton, *Legal Aid* (London, 1945), p. 93, twentieth-century working-class women found having to make a court appearance an extremely difficult experience. Horwitz, *Chancery Equity Records and Proceedings, 1600–1800*, pp. 37–38.

relationship between master and servant (employer and employee) were a well-known part of traditional common law learning.[223] To take an issue which is frequently of concern today, the education of children, and in particular the way they were treated during periods of apprenticeship, made up a significant proportion of the cases in a court like that of the lord mayor of London in the seventeenth century. They also found their way into the common law reports.[224] At the same time, the regulatory regimes of many towns and manors enforced customs and by-laws, frequently involving environmental matters, which provided remedies for nuisances against the community as well as those wrongs which injured the persons or property of individuals.[225]

Unfortunately, given the present state of knowledge, it is difficult to break down statistical evidence about the pre-nineteenth-century numbers of actions of trespass and 'case' into a more precise categories that can be compared effectively with those produced by Macdonell.[226] Nor can we do much more than speculate about how jurisdictional changes and the steadily increasing cost of going to law in the eighteenth century affected the pursuit by individuals of wrongs against them. In 1897 considerably less than 10 per cent of cases in the high court involved personal injuries, probably not an excessive number when it is considered that in the 1870s an average of 1307 persons were killed, and another 4236 injured, in railway accidents alone.[227] Given that mechanised manufacturing was being practised on a significant scale before the end of the eighteenth century, it is notable that the law relating to injuries sustained by employees in such circumstances was not developed to any significant degree before 1840. Although the county courts had from the time of their institution exercised a jurisdiction in tort for the recovery of as much as £50, it has been argued convincingly

---

[223] For a very brief account and further references see Brooks, *Pettyfoggers and Vipers*, pp. 66–71. See also P. Winfield, 'The History of Negligence in the Law of Torts', *Law Quarterly Review*, 42 (1926), pp. 184–99; and M. J. Pritchard, *Scott v. Shepherd (1773) and the Emergence of the Tort of Negligence*, Selden Society Lecture (London, 1976).

[224] Corporation of London Record Office, Lord Mayor's Court, large suits, box 1.11. For the case law see, for example, *The Laws Respecting Women, as They Regard Their Natural Rights, or Their Connections and Conduct* (London, 1777).

[225] The suggestion of Dawson, *History of Lay Judges*, p. 236, that manorial courts were far in advance of the common law courts in enforcing liability in tort remains unexplored, but Lancashire Record Office, Preston, MS DD Pt/46/1, 'Justice Walmesley's Common Place Book', fol. 74, indicates that one of the rights of the lord of the manor of Selby in Yorkshire was that he could take fines as a result of accidents. The examples given are of a faulty board which caused the death of a shipwright and of a horse and cart which ran down and killed a boy. Though Walmesley was an Elizabethan judge, the precedents from Selby date from the 1690s.

[226] Macdonell himself made a point of basing his classifications on the common law forms of action so they might be useful for comparative purposes, *Judicial Statistics, 1894*, p. 17.

[227] A. H. Manchester, *A Modern Legal History of England and Wales, 1750–1950* (London, 1980), p. 283.

that this was not much utilised before the end of the century.[228] Macdonell remarked in 1894 that, in comparison with the number of injuries, relatively few actions entered the courts under the Employers' Liability Act (1880).[229] On the other hand, he noted that the extension of liability under the Workmen's Compensation Act of 1906 was accompanied by a sharp rise in the number of actions from 3330 to 6124.[230]

Although Sir John Macdonell noticed the small drop in the amount of court business which occurred between 1904 and 1905, it so happens that he was thinking about the judicial statistics over a period in which there was usually either a steady rise, or a relatively constant level, in the volume of business. By contrast, what is notable about the remainder of the twentieth century is that it constitutes an era when there have been extremely large fluctuations in the number of plaints and in the rate of litigation per head of population. Indeed, a comparison of the graphic representation of the volume of business in the twentieth century with that for the fifteenth and first half of the sixteenth centuries reveals some striking similarities (Figures 4.2 and 4.9). Given the wild swings, it is perhaps not surprising that the twentieth century has been characterised by both a concern about the inability of ordinary people to use the courts and severe outbreaks of anxiety about excessive litigiousness. At the same time, over the past one hundred years the advent large-scale, state-funded schemes to support some classes of litigants has added an important new dimension to the study of court usage.

As Figure 4.9 makes crystal clear, the greatest drops in the overall level of court business, the trough which opened up in the years between 1914 and 1923, and the even wider chasm which began in 1939 and lasted into the mid 1950s, coincided so directly with the upheavals of war that by comparison even the 'Great Depression' seems to have had little impact, although the growth of tribunals and suspicion of legal procedures have also been identified as contributing to the long mid century decline.[231] Furthermore, there was during each of these periods an intensification in the concern of social and legal observers about the plight of the poorer litigant. The issue had in fact already received some attention in the late nineteenth century, most significantly in 1883 when parliament passed legislation which

---

[228] H. Smith, 'The Resurgent County Court in Victorian Britain', *American Journal of Legal History*, 13 (1969), pp. 130, 133, 136–37. *Cotterell* v. *Stocks* (1840) was evidently the first factory injury case to appear in the press.

[229] *Judicial Statistics, 1894*, p. 66. In 1890, 1206 lives were lost in mines, but there were only 388 actions under the statute. In 1894 there 16,128 deaths referred to as accidents or negligence, but only 533 were sued under the statute.

[230] *Judicial Statistics, England and Wales, 1908: Part II, Civil Judicial Statistics* (London, 1910), p. 19.

[231] B. Abel-Smith and Robert Stevens, *Lawyers and the Courts: A Sociological Study of the English Legal System, 1750–1965* (London, 1969), pp. 258–59; A. Cairncross, *The British Economy Since 1914* (Oxford, 1992), pp. 36–38.

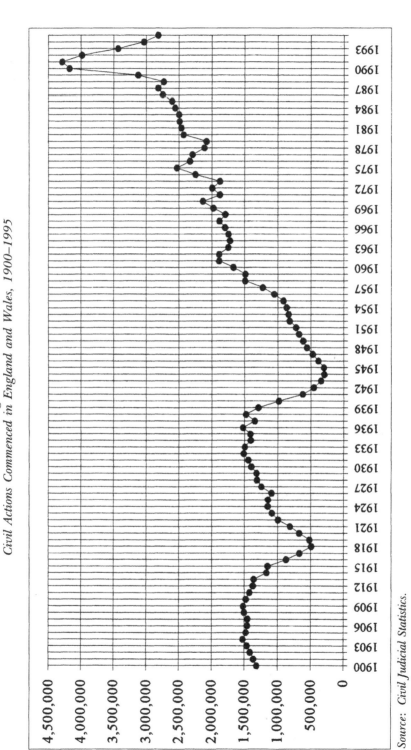

Figure 4.9
Civil Actions Commenced in England and Wales, 1900–1995

Source: Civil Judicial Statistics.

extended the traditional common law remedy for the poor, the capacity to sue *in forma pauperis*, by setting the means test so that those worth less than £25 became eligible.[232] Although the subject clearly remained alive during the 1890s and 1910s,[233] the 1920s were the critical decade for a very significant increase in interest in the problem.[234]

Influences from abroad and changes in ideas about the responsibilities of the state, rather than an awareness of the generally low levels of litigation in the years between 1914 and 1924, appear to have been the most powerful agents of change.[235] Research on the poor and the law was more advanced in the United States than in the United Kingdom, mainly because the difficulties of the rapidly growing immigrant population had led, as early as 1876, to the formation of legal aid organisations in New York City. In addition, there was also a worldwide dimension, the League of Nations publishing a report on *Legal Aid for the Poor* in 1927.[236] British interest was expressed in 1925 when the lord chancellor and home secretary appointed a committee to investigate legal aid, but the reports produced concluded in general that there was no cause for concern about the ability of the poor to go to law.[237] In deciding against the extension of some form of legal aid to county court litigants, Mr Justice Finlay's report of 1928 argued that the number of instances in the lives of ordinary persons 'when legal advice was necessary' should not be exaggerated. The committee was satisfied

> that the cases where the failure to provide legal assistance [in the county courts] amounts to a denial of justice are very few indeed, having regard especially to the assistance given to the poor by Trade Unions, by friends or philanthropic agencies and by solicitors who, if they think that there is a real grievance, are often most generously prepared to take up cases.

[232] The traditional common law ceiling for those eligible was £5 in worldly goods. Robert Egerton, Solicitor of the Supreme Court, with a preface by A. L. Goodhart, Professor of Jurisprudence at Oxford, *Legal Aid* (London, 1945; reprinted with additions January 1946). Published in the series edited by Karl Mannheim, the International Library of Sociology and Social Reconstruction, p. 7. J. M. Maguire, 'Poverty and Civil Litigation', *Harvard Law Review*, 26 (1923), pp. 361ff, provides a very useful historical account of *in forma pauperis*.

[233] Egerton, *Legal Aid*, p. 27. Poor Man's Lawyer Centres first grew up in the 1890s. Egerton, ibid., pp. xv–xvi, also mentions the following works: F. W. Blunt, *Law Hospitals: A Suggestion* (paper read at the eleventh meeting of the Law Society, 1884); J. J. Sprigge, *The Shortcomings of the Machinery for Pauper Litigation* (3rd edn, London, 1893); J. P. Coldstream, 'The Expediency of Uniformity with Regard to Pauper Litigation' (paper read at the Glasgow Conference of the International Law Association).

[234] Maguire, 'Poverty and Civil Litigation', p. 379, suggests that the cheapness of the English county courts may have kept down the number of applications to sue *in forma pauperis*.

[235] Abel-Smith and Stevens, *Lawyers and the Courts*, pp. 102–3, 106, note that there were expressions of concern about the generally high costs of litigation in the late 1920s and early 1930s; and that there was evidence of a growing resort to arbitration in place of litigation.

[236] Egerton, *Legal Aid*, pp. xv, 48, also describes as a classic the American work by Reginald Heber Smith, *Justice and the Poor* (3rd edn, New York, 1924).

[237] E. J. Cohn, 'Legal Aid and the Poor: A Study in Comparative Law and Legal Reform', *Law Quarterly Review*, 49 (1943), p. 250; Egerton, *Legal Aid*, p. xi.

The report rejected the suggestion of one witness that a system of 'legal hospitals' should be established with the memorable remark that 'It is manifestly in the interests of the State that its citizens should be healthy, not that they should be litigious'.[238]

The climate of opinion was, nevertheless, beginning to change. Two members of the Finlay committee drafted a minority report which argued that the need 'for a better provision of free legal advice is urgent and imperative'. During the next decade, the movement towards root and branch reform of legal aid gathered momentum.[239] In a book which he published in 1945 to advance the cause, Robert Egerton was able to point to a considerable body of evidence which had accumulated since the mid 1920s to illustrate how the poor were disadvantaged by their inability to get legal advice or take their grievances before the courts. Most importantly, legal aid was unavailable in the county courts.[240] According to one barrister, there was even an unacknowledged conspiracy by the 'governing class' which favoured maintaining restrictions on access: if the poor 'were really given adequate means for enforcing their rights or defending themselves against injustice, the courts would be choked with a huge volume of additional work'.[241] Sir William Beveridge's report on *Social Insurance and Allied Services* pointed out that one of the disadvantages of the Workmen's Compensation Acts was that they depended ultimately on the threat of litigation, while in reality there was little scope for employees putting themselves in a position to carry it out.[242] No less tellingly, Egerton, like other advocates of the extension of legal aid, took it as axiomatic that if the first, and most ancient, duty of the state was to provide courts where justice might be administered, it followed that the state should also provide the means which would enable those with grievances to get legal advice and pay the costs of using the courts.[243] As E. J. Cohn put it, 'Legal aid is a service which the modern State owes to its citizens as a matter of principle ... To follow the law is the citizen's duty. From that it follows that to be taught the law is his right'.[244]

A practical, if partial, realisation of this viewpoint was the expansion of existing provision as a result of increases in the number of 'Poor Man's Lawyer Centres' (and Citizens Advice Bureaux). This approach, which was pioneered in the 1890s, depended entirely on the voluntary services of the lawyers who conducted surgeries at the centres, taking on the cases which

---

[238] *Parliamentary Papers 1928*, xi, *Committee on Legal Aid for the Poor. Final Report* (London, 1928), especially pp. 250–51.

[239] Ibid., p. 254. The authors of the minority report were Dorothy Jewson and Rhys J. Davies. None of the previous schemes of legal aid had provided for legal advice as opposed to help with the costs of litigation.

[240] Egerton, *Legal Aid*, pp. 20, 23, 73.

[241] Ibid., p. 5. The work quoted was *Justice in England* (1938) by 'Barrister'.

[242] Egerton, *Legal Aid*, p. 4.

[243] Ibid., pp. 1–3.

[244] Cohn, 'Legal Aid and the Poor', pp. 256–57.

ended up going to litigation under the Poor Persons Rules which had been laid down by the superior courts.[245] The supporters of legal aid contended that the centres served a useful function, but they were aware that a disadvantage of the system was that its dependency on the charity of solicitors made the profession as a whole even more reluctant than it might otherwise have been to support further expansion.[246] At the same time, despite his own advocacy of legal aid, E. J. Cohn, writing in 1943, acknowledged that access to the law by the poor had failed to arouse 'more than a casual interest from the political parties', nor was it an issue of great concern to the masses of working people, who frequently depended for help on the trade unions, rather than going to a lawyer.[247]

Despite the idealism of some, it is evident that the prospects for an expansion of legal aid in England and Wales would probably have been remote if it had not been for the existence of another, hitherto unmentioned, factor: the enormous increase during the twentieth century in the number of cases involving the dissolution of marriage. Civil divorce, which permitted estranged partners to marry, was sanctioned by parliament for the first time in 1857, but the social revolution which this legislation made possible took as much as a half century to have an impact on the courts. There were only 547 petitions for divorce in 1894, but Sir John Macdonell noticed a 'remarkable increase' in the ten years up to 1903 when the number stood at 825. One imagines that he would have been even more struck by what was yet to come.[248] By 1938 applications for the dissolution of marriage had risen more than tenfold to 9970.

Divorce is a critical element in the story of the establishment of state-funded legal aid because it is an action which is as likely to be of concern to the poor as to the rich, to women as to men. Furthermore, divorce proceedings constitute a potentially expensive class of litigation since they are in the vast majority of cases sued from the beginning to end rather then following the much more typical pattern of reaching a termination somewhere in the middle. Macdonell noted in 1905 that the costs of petitioning for divorce made it a difficult action for the poor, a consideration evidently

---

[245] *Committee on Legal Aid for the Poor: Final Report*, appendix, contains reports from the Poor Man's Lawyers in Birmingham, Brighton, Bristol, Chesterfield, Halifax, Liverpool, Leeds, Leicester, Manchester, Sheffield, and several in London. Some of the units were founded by the local law society; others, such as that in Leeds, were manned simply by a solicitor and a friend of his. It was also noted that social services students sometimes helped out in order to gain experience. See also J. Mervyn Jones, *Free Legal Advice in England and Wales: A Report on the Organisation, Methods and Future of Poor Man's Lawyers, Prepared for the Executive Committee of Cambridge University Settlement, Camberwell, London* (with a preface by Viscount Maugham, lord chancellor, 1938–39) (Oxford, 1940).

[246] Egerton, *Legal Aid*, p. 17, pointed out that in 1939 the Welsh law societies withdrew from the system until further reforms were instituted.

[247] Cohn, 'Legal Aid and the Poor', p. 252.

[248] *Civil Judicial Statitstics, 1903*, p. 33.

Figure 4.10
*Petitions Filed for Dissolution of Marriage
in England and Wales, 1913–1995*

Year	Number
1913	1267
1918	2689
1923	3213
1928	4232
1933	4975
1938	9970
1943	14,887
1948	37,075
1953	29,854
1958	25,584
1963	36,383
1968	54,036
1973	115,048
1978	162,450
1983	168,428
1988	182,804
1993	184,471
1995	173,966

Source: Civil Judicial Statistics.

influential in the establishment of the 'Poor Persons Rules' in 1914.[249] By 1925 the report of Mr Justice Lawrence concluded that difficulties with the Poor Persons Rules arose solely from the problems involved in finding an adequate number of 'solicitors willing to undertake the conduct of the large number of divorce cases brought by and against poor persons'.[250] The matter became even more acute in the 1930s, and especially in the unsettled wartime conditions of the 1940s, which were accompanied by unprecedented numbers of marriage breakdowns. The Matrimonial Causes Act of 1937 led to immediate increases in the number of petitions: in that year some 47 per cent of all applications for divorce were brought under the Poor Persons Rules.[251] Between 1935 and 1947 the divorce rate increased by more than a factor of ten, from 0.45 to 5.6 per thousand married couples.[252] By 1943 the

[249] Ibid., p. 32. Tanara Goriely, 'Rushcliffe Fifty Years On: The Changing Role of Civil Legal Aid within the Welfare State', *Journal of Law and Society*, 21 (1994), p. 550.
[250] Egerton, *Legal Aid*, p. 15.
[251] Ibid., p. x, preface by A. L. Goodhart.
[252] Goriely, 'Rushcliffe Fifty Years On', p. 550, argues that there was a stress on return to family values in the 1950s and some drop in the rate, which stood at 1.9 in 1958. Since then it has steadily risen to reach 13.5.

Services divorce scheme was nearly at the point of breakdown, and the War Office, the Air Ministry and the Royal Navy had all established legal aid schemes for the personnel in their employ.[253]

There were, of course, voices raised against the expansion of the Poor Persons Rules into a fully state-funded system, at least in part on the grounds the problems which existed would be better addressed by lowering the overall cost of going to law.[254] Nevertheless, changing ideological conceptions of the role of law in society, an awareness that social legislation increasingly created legal problems for ordinary people and, last but hardly least, the crisis in divorce led to the report of the Rushcliffe committee in 1945. This in turn resulted in the passage of the Legal Aid and Advice Act (1949), which introduced a state-funded system administered by Legal Aid committees appointed by the Law Society.[255]

Given the influences which led to its creation, and the limitations on its scope, it is not surprising that modern legal aid has been much more significant in connection with particular classes of legal work than it has been in directly affecting the overall rate of court usage during the second half of the twentieth century.[256] The numbers of petitions for the dissolution of marriage increased steadily during the 1950s and 1960s before another historic take off occurred in the late sixties, by which time as much as 80 per cent of legal aid work was associated with matrimonial causes.[257] As Figures 4.8 and 4.9 indicate, however, during this same period the total volume of litigation increased only gradually. Despite the post-war economic boom, the total number of plaints did not again reach the level of 1939 until 1958. In 1971 the number of actions for each hundred thousand of the population was still lower than it had been in the 1860s, 1870s or 1880s. According to the Cobden Trust report of 1970 on 'Legal Aid as a Social Service':

---

[253] Egerton, *Legal Aid*, p. 34.

[254] For example, Claude Mullins, *In Quest of Justice* (London, 1931), chapter 19, argued vigorously that the Poor Persons Rules of his day were frequently put to vexatious use because successful defendants were unable to recover costs even if they won the case. This also remained an issue after the introduction of the 1949 act, Abel-Smith and Stevens, *Lawyers and the Courts*, p. 340.

[255] 12, 13, & 14 George VI, c. 51. Egerton, *Legal Aid*, ch. 15, for comments on the Rushcliffe Report. See also Seton Pollock, 'The English Legal Aid System', in Cappelletti et al., eds, *Toward Equal Justice*, p. 344. The details of the legislation and its history in the 1950s is dealt with in Abel-Smith and Stevens, *Lawyers and the Courts*, ch. 12.

[256] Most notably the scheme was not extended to the county courts until the later 1950s, and its extension to legal advice made very little progress. Abel-Smith and Stevens credit the distinct upturn in litigation which occurred in 1956 to the extension of legal aid to the county courts, ibid., p. 257. See also G. Dworkin, 'The Progress and Future of Modern Legal Aid in Civil Litigation', *Modern Law Review*, 28 (1965), pp. 432–47.

[257] Alan Paterson, 'Legal Aid as a Social Service', in Cappelletti et al., *Toward Equal Justice*, p. 358.

To the ordinary office or factory worker, the solicitor's office is far more remote and forbidding than the dentist's or doctor's surgery. It is not even open at times he can attend, and if he does get time off work he will be unwelcome without an introduction and prior appointment. If he is seen he will probably be asked for an immediate cash payment and is unlikely to be offered legal aid unless he raises the matter and that particular firm does legal aid work.[258]

Views such as this no doubt explain why the 1970s saw a resurgence of a worldwide access to justice movement.[259] In England legislation early in the decade expanded the scope of legal aid so that by the 1990s it was being used by some 35 per cent of all winning parties, but the percentage of cases involving legal aid differed greatly depending on the type of action. While 92 per cent of medical negligence cases involved legal aid, only 17 per cent of breech of contract cases did so.[260] At the same time, it has been argued plausibly that changes in the political climate over the course of post-war era may have simultaneously altered the propensity of individuals to seek redress for their grievances through the law. If the evolution of the welfare state in the 1950s led to a society in which private businesses were subjected to regulation, and social, medical and educational needs were provided by state-run institutions against which recipients had few rights, the 1980s witnessed a new stress on the 'assertive citizen' who was encouraged to pursue claims in fields such as housing, consumer complaints, education, child and health care through whatever means were available, including the legal system. Thanks to all of these conditions, by the 1990s legal aid was applied so generously that its cost became a concern of governments attempting to balance their otherwise overburdened budgets.[261]

It therefore seems certain that there has been a connection between the widening scope of legal aid in the past thirty years and what has been for the most part a quite gradual increase in the volume of litigation, but the links are not straightforward. The steadily upward trend in court business which characterised the 1950s came to a halt in the 1960s; the overall trajectory of court usage between 1962 and 1979 involved only very modest increases. In 1981, for the first time in the twentieth century, the number of actions per 100,000 of population exceeded those of the 1860s and 1870s. Furthermore, it is clear that short-term economic factors, especially those associated with credit, are also important in determining the picture of court

---

[258] Ibid., p. 354.

[259] McGregor, *Social History and Law Reform*, p. 5, notes the concern expressed by both political parties at the end of the 1960s about the issue of unmet legal need.

[260] *Access to Justice: Final Report by The Right Honourable the Lord Woolf, Master of the Rolls to the Lord Chancellor on the Civil Justice System in England and Wales* (London, 1996), p. 351. Some of the other proportions were as follows: personal injury, 59 per cent; judicial review, 58 per cent; professional negligence, 38 per cent.

[261] Goriely, 'Rushcliffe Fifty Years On', p. 560.

usage that we get from this kind of analysis. The peak in 1975 is attributable to high levels of inflation and the devastating consequences of the oil price embargo of 1973–74.[262] Equally the steady increase in the volume of business in the 1980s coincides remarkably well with the expansion in credit, either in the form of hire-purchase agreements or by the use of credit and store cards. Most strikingly of all, the historic peaks in business which occurred in 1990–91 are the legal reflection of a boom-bust economic cycle, beginning in the late 1980s, which included a large number of defaults on mortgages.[263] This appears from the evidence of litigation to have been unprecedented in more that one hundred years.

A notable feature of court business during this last period has been that a small number of corporate plaintiffs, including banks and credit card issuers, mail order sellers and utilities, dominated proceedings. In 1990 a Summons Production Centre was established to facilitate the delivery of summonses requested via electronic media by major plaintiffs, that is those issuing more than 1000 writs annually. In 1995 it had 135 'customers' who initiated 42 per cent of all the summonses issued by the county courts.[264] This electronic expansion of credit probably should be seen as a phenomenon not dissimilar to that of the late sixteenth and early seventeenth centuries, when verbal and written promises served a similar purpose in a society which was starved of specie.[265] Although they are unlikely to have dominated business to the same degree as their counterparts of today, 'repeat players', often local attorneys acting as agents within wider credit networks, are also known to have been a feature of early modern borough court litigation.[266]

It is perhaps inevitable in this context that the towering peaks of late twentieth-century litigation have been accompanied by simultaneous expressions of concern about access. An editorial in the *Western Daily Press* in August 1987 commented that the British legal system remained 'one of the anachronisms of the Thatcher economic revolution', one which would probably not stand up if it were subjected to the standard of the market place. According to the newspaper, 'Britain is in desperate need of shop-on-the-corner justice, geared to the problems of consumers, employees, and all those who wish to redress a bad deal'.[267] A Civil Justice Review established in the 1980s (to improve the administration of justice by reducing costs, complexity and delays) led to the 1990 Courts and Legal Services Act, which at long last finally abolished most of the jurisdictional distinctions between

---

262 Cairncross, *The British Economy Since 1914*, pp. 38, 182–87.
263 Ibid., ch. 6.
264 *Judicial Statistics England and Wales for the Year 1995* (London, 1996, cmd 3290), p. 37.
265 Muldrew, *The Economy of Obligation*.
266 Muldrew, 'Credit, Market Relations, and Debt Litigation', p. 68; Brooks, Helmholz and Stein, *Notaries Public*, pp. 73–75; Brooks, *Pettyfoggers and Vipers*, pp. 196–97.
267 *Western Daily Press*, 11 August 1987, p. 12.

the high courts and the county courts, a measure which had been pressed for with varying degrees of vigour and success since the nineteenth century.[268] In a public lecture he delivered to describe these reforms, the lord chancellor, Lord Mackay of Clashfern, expressed his own commitment to making it possible for ordinary people better to understand how to use the legal system by announcing the production of illustrated leaflets explaining the procedures of the county courts more fully.[269] Critics nevertheless continued to argue that the system militated against access. Stephen Sedley wrote that a 'policy choice has been made to prioritise commercial and public law at the expense of issues arising from accidents at work, wrongful arrests, contracts of employment' and other issues relevant to individuals.[270] In an article on legal aid published in 1994, Tanara Goreily maintained that there was much evidence that citizens were often 'too ignorant, confused, cowed, isolated, poor, or powerless' to take on the large institutions who were all too frequently likely to be their adversaries.[271] In 1996 another government report, that undertaken by the then master of the rolls, Lord Woolf, listed as one of its major concerns the question of how to 'improve access to justice for individuals and small businesses'.[272]

Throughout the 1980s and 1990s there has also been an increasing amount of academic interest in 'dispute processing' and patterns of litigation. This has included a number of attempts to make comparisons between different national systems both within and beyond the common law tradition.[273] Such studies have generally emphasised the increasing amount of litigation in most developed western countries,[274] but they also showed that the rate of litigation in Britain was considerably lower than that in either the United States or Germany. Whilst fully acknowledging the many pitfalls which beset comparative studies, Professor Markesinis produced figures in 1990 which

---

[268] The early history is discussed in Smith, 'Resurgent County Court'; and some of the disabilities described in Mullins, *In Quest of Justice*.

[269] Lord Mackay of Clashfern, 'Litigation in the 1990s', *Modern Law Review*, 54 (1991), p. 174. According to the lord chancellor, one of the principal findings of the review had been that too many cases of small value or substance were being taken into the high courts. See also Keith Uff, 'The Lord Chancellor's Review of Civil Justice', *Civil Justice Quarterly*, 4 (1985), pp. 193–94.

[270] Stephen Sedley, 'Improving Civil Justice', *Civil Justice Quarterly*, 9 (1990), p. 348. See also Richard Thomas, 'Civil Justice Review; Treating Litigants as Consumers', ibid., pp. 55–57, who notes studies which have shown that around 85 per cent of personal injury victims do not make claims, and that nearly all of the two million debt summonses in the county courts were issued by institutional plaintiffs against individuals. Sir Jack Jacob, *The Fabric of Civil Justice* (London, 1987), discusses the role of nineteenth-century 'reforms'.

[271] Goriely, 'Rushcliffe Fifty Years On', p. 560.

[272] *Access to Justice*, p. 3.

[273] McGregor, *Social History and Law Reform*, p. 12, contains thoughtful reflections on the lack of adequate social and historical analyses of English legal institutions since the mid nineteenth century.

[274] Galanter, 'Reading the Landscape of Disputes', pp. 36–60, warned, however, that recent increases probably did not constitute as great a departure from previous patterns as has sometimes been thought.

indicated that the number of lawsuits in the United States was perhaps five times greater than in England and Wales. He also showed that the differences were particularly striking when tort actions, such as negligence, misfeasance and defamation, were disaggregated from the overall totals. In England the number of tort suits per million of population was only about one-third that in either the United States or Germany.[275]

Even more recently, Gerhard Dannemann calculated that on a per capita basis Germans are twice as likely as English people to seek legal remedies. He concluded that 'Germans are overwhelmingly more litigious than English people [and] that litigation is more accessible to the German public'.[276] Since this observation is based on comparative figures which are in fact remarkably similar in their general import to those published by Sir John Macdonell in 1910, the differences between the two countries must reach back at least a century.[277] Indeed, it is worth noting that some English observers during the eighteenth century commented favourably on radical law reforms undertaken by Frederick the Great in Prussia,[278] and German legal culture was frequently held up as a model for the English during the time of Brougham.[279] Most recently, academic research carried out in connection with Lord Woolf's 1996 report has suggested that one of the reasons why Germany is more litigious than England is that German legal costs are lower and more predictable. The legal profession there operates according to a fixed tariff of fees established by the courts rather than by calculations by the hour of the amount of work involved. The result is evidently that the high volume of business makes up for losses a practitioner might face on any particular case.[280]

Lord Woolf observed that the 'German approach ... presents a challenge to all those responsible for our civil justice system to do better than at present to make justice affordable'.[281] Although there had previously been relatively little systematic research on lawyers' fees, a survey of litigation costs undertaken in connection with the report produced results which confirmed many suspicions, especially in a political climate when there was pressure to reduce government expenditure on legal aid. For example, it was found that in

---

[275] Markesinis, 'Litigation-Mania', p. 240, 147–48.

[276] Gerhard Dannemann, 'Access to Justice: An Anglo-German Comparison', *European Public Law*, 2 (1995), p. 277. He also points out that there are seven times more contested actions in Germany than there are in England.

[277] See above, p. 109.

[278] For example, *Gentleman's Magazine*, 19 (1749), p. 23, contains a favourable account of reforms recently undertaken by the king of Prussia. Attorneys had been abolished and advocates made to do legal work according to 'fixed prices'; the laws themselves had been reduced to a code. Ibid., 20 (1750), pp. 215–17, contains a further discussion of the changes. See also Prest, 'Law Reform in Eighteenth-Century England', p. 122.

[279] See Chapter 6, p. 174, and Michael Lobban, 'Was There a Nineteenth-Century "English School of Jurisprudence"?', *Legal History* 16 (1995), pp. 34–62.

[280] *Access to Justice*, p. 81.

[281] Ibid.

claims in the high court for a value up to £12,500, the legal costs of one of the parties alone exceeded the value of the plaint in 40 per cent of cases. Yet, while Woolf himself stated frequently that high costs were the major impediment to access to the courts, the comparisons with German practices with regard to fees 'occasioned a general outcry from the legal profession'. Consequently, the reforms recommended in the final report stopped far short of a fixed tariff, although they did include proposals that the courts themselves should take more responsibility for managing the course of litigation with a view to keeping excess costs in check. The most novel suggestion was that there should be a 'fast track' for litigation involving claims of less than £10,000, in which there would be a maximum allowable cost of £2500 and fixed fees for advocacy at a trial. At the same time, while Lord Woolf recommended a simplification of legal nomenclature, with a view to making the system easier for lay people to understand, the report also argued that disputes should if at all possible be diverted from the courts to alternative forms of dispute resolution (ADR), namely mediation and arbitration.[282]

In one of the more provocative general remarks in his report, Lord Woolf wrote that 'We have to change from a situation where litigation is being conducted for the benefit of lawyers, to ... it being conducted for the benefit of the litigant'. Yet, to the historian, a striking feature of this observation is that similar expressions might just as easily be found in 1750, or indeed at any number of different points in the centuries before that. In the end, the most straightforward conclusion to arise out of the investigation of the long-term history of civil litigation is that English people have always used courts for remarkably similar purposes. In every age some of them have always been dissatisfied, while the good intentions of reformers have seldom accomplished very dramatic results. Time and again, demographic and economic conditions emerge as the most significant causes of shifts in the overall patterns.

It is none the less evident that there have been from time to time important alterations in the configuration of institutions and significant changes in the legal profession. If we stand back and take a bird's eye view of the first half of the period, that from roughly 1200 to the middle of the sixteenth century, it appears as one in which access to the central courts, often by quite ordinary subjects, became fairly common. At the same time, although developments in the common law may well have put limits on the scope of local jurisdictions, and even given shape to their proceedings and records, the borough court and the manorial court remained the tribunals where most people took their

[282] Ibid., pp. 1–17. Under the headline 'Legal Plans Help Middle Classes', the *Guardian* reported on 15 June 1996 that, in a speech given at All Souls College, Oxford, Lord Chancellor Mackay said that Woolf's proposals would lead to a 'more "mass production" system, replacing the expensive customised system now available "only to the rich or the subsidised"'.

disputes and had the opportunity to state their grievances.[283] As John Baker has reminded us, courts such as those of the manor were probably the earliest forums of any kind in which the inhabitants of a locality were able to meet together and express their ideas and identities as a 'community'.[284]

In manorial courts we encounter plebiscites, by-laws, ancient customs, neighbourliness and common nuisances, as well as transfers of land and actions of debt or trespass. Yet it is not easy for historians to uncover the 'legal culture' of which they were part and how they shaped the ideas about the law which were held by the people who used them.[285] The importance of juries composed of local inhabitants in reaching decisions, and what we imagine as the informality of proceedings which might be held out of doors, at a shop front or in an alehouse, as well as in the moot hall,[286] suggests that such courts may have had more in common with what jurists today would describe as alternative dispute resolution than with litigation as we understand it: that is, they rarely had much to do with legal technicalities and they put a stress on reconciliation rather than an adversarial process where the parties fought it out until one of them was declared the winner. On the other hand, manorial jurisdictions and the county courts of medieval England were open forums, where disputes took place in public, before neighbours, and where the juries did in fact frequently make decisions.[287] Furthermore, manuals explaining how to keep the courts were in circulation by the late thirteenth century; procedures in manorial courts were part of the learning exercises at the fifteenth-century legal inns.[288] Of no less importance in terms of the outlook of the ordinary villager, it is clear from at least the early fourteenth century that tenants of manors took some of their grievances to the common law courts at Westminster. As Figure 4.4 demonstrates, by the early fifteenth century, there were many small farmers and merchants who managed to do their legal business either in the locality or at Westminster, depending on what circumstances demanded.[289]

There is also a distinct possibility that the proportion of lawyers to head of population was greater in the early fifteenth century than it was one hundred years later in the reign of Henry VIII.[290] Yet, while it would be a

---

[283] See above, pp. 69–71, 83–84.

[284] Baker, 'The Changing Concept of a Court', in *The Legal Profession and the Common Law*, p. 165.

[285] See the interesting discussion of these matters in the papers by Lloyd Bonfield and Paul Hyams in Razi and Smith, eds, *Medieval Society and the Manor Court*.

[286] F. J. C. and D. M. Hearnshaw, *Southampton Court Leet Records*, i, pt 3, *1603–1624* (Southampton, 1907), p. 602; Harrison, 'Manor Courts and the Governance of Tudor England', pp. 51–52.

[287] Palmer, *The County Courts of Medieval England*.

[288] See Chapter 7, p. 191.

[289] S. S. Walker, ed., *The Court Rolls of the Manor of Wakefield, 1331–3*, Wakefield Court Rolls Series of the Yorkshire Archaeological Society, 3 (Leeds, 1982), pp. xi–xii. Also, see above, pp. 77.

[290] See above pp. 82–83.

serious mistake either to ignore the implications of this possibility, or to discount the importance of the legal inns as places of learning attended by large numbers of the sons of the gentry and yeomanry,[291] the evidence which points to the late sixteenth and early seventeenth centuries as a watershed in the history of the relationship between the common law and English society seems compelling.[292]

The population of lawyers between 1550 and 1700 was not excessive in historic terms, but it was during this same 150 years that the barristers and the common law attorneys increasingly made their presence felt in the localities as well as in London.[293] Although local court business grew alongside that of the common law courts in this period, it is likely that increasingly large numbers of manorial stewardships, town clerkships and, no less important, town attorneyships came to be held during the course of the period by practitioners who had also spent some time in London.[294] Arguably, this development was associated in the long term with the decline of community involvement in legal institutions, together with the spectre of a law which was beyond the knowledge of the ordinary person. It is, for example, against this background that we should read the demands made by mid seventeenth-century political radicals such as the Levellers that local courts be returned unequivocally to elected lay judges; and that the law itself should be made so simple that any man could use it without recourse to professional advice.[295] On the other hand, although it is perhaps predictable that it took a common lawyer to put a tag on it, the potential for what Matthew Hale called the 'petty tyrannies' of local, communal jurisdictions were also objected to from time to time by laymen.[296] There are numerous recorded occasions when lawyers or litigants expressed their disdain for mayors acting in town courts or the stewards of manorial courts. Occasionally they can be seen throwing their papers down in disgust, and many of them evidently went 'forum shopping' to one of the central courts in hope of a better outcome.[297] At the same time, in the century of religious uncertainty which followed the Reformation, it is clear that professional legal rhetoric provided a mode of political discourse promoted by the monarchy, dispensed in countless speeches given to courts at every level within the localities and frequently taken up by a fair number of the subjects.[298]

---

[291] Thorne and Baker, *Readings and Moots at the Inns of Court.*

[292] See Chapter 2, pp. 10–12 and Chapter 3, pp. 66ff.

[293] Brooks, *Pettyfoggers and Vipers*, chs 3, 6, 9, 10; Prest, *Rise of the Barristers.*

[294] Brooks, *Pettyfoggers and Vipers*, chs 3, 6.

[295] D. Veal, *The Popular Movement for Law Reform, 1640–1660* (Oxford, 1970); N. Matthews, *William Sheppard: Cromwell's Law Reformer* (Cambridge, 1984).

[296] M. Hale, *History of the Common Law*, ed. C. Gray (London, 1971), p. 112.

[297] For a selection, which is by no means exhaustive, see Brooks, *Pettyfoggers and Vipers*, pp. 220. See also T. G. Barnes, 'Star Chamber Litigants and Their Counsel, 1596–1641', in J. H. Baker, ed., *Legal Records and the Historian* (London, 1978), pp. 7–29.

[298] See below, Chapters 8 and 9.

How far all of this may have changed during the early and mid eighteenth century, when the English population appears to have withdrawn itself from courts, is still a matter for investigation. No doubt the printed word, in the form textbooks and newspapers, made up for much by both conveying information to practitioners and informing lay people about what went on in courts.[299] Yet it is hard to avoid the conclusion that the decline of the traditional manorial and borough courts also eventually resulted in a fatal decline in lay participation. In 1598, for example, Peter Graunte, a yeoman farmer of Stanley in Yorkshire deposed in a case before the duchy court of Lancaster that he knew a custom associated with the manor of Wakefield because he had heard it discussed frequently both when he had attended the local court as a boy and, later, when he had served as a juror.[300] By contrast, in the 1830s, the legal publicist Samuel Warren produced a young person's version of Blackstone's *Commentaries*. In his view, since so few schools taught English history, there was a need to supply youth, 'especially intelligent and respectable youth' with a better informed understanding of the laws and constitution under which they lived.[301]

Given the enormous demographic and social changes (from an agricultural to an industrialising society) which separate these two episodes, it is certainly arguable that the some change in the legal regime and in legal culture was inevitable. Nevertheless, despite what many historical and legal writers have taken for granted in the nineteenth and twentieth centuries, the foundation of the new system of county courts in 1846 did not return justice to the localities in the way that it had existed before 1700 or, to be more exact, to some ideal state in which it was thought to have existed in a distant, but imprecise, past.[302] In many respects, therefore, a number of demographic and bureaucratic circumstances in the eighteenth century have contributed much to our own anxiety about the relationship between law and society. For much of the nineteenth century, jurists were at odds about the source of law; but for most of the twentieth century, it has been defined as a legislative authority with little connection to either moral imperatives or communal (as opposed to democratic) sanction.[303] At the same time, for

---

[299] See James Oldham, 'Law Reporting in the London Newspapers, 1756–1786', *American Journal of Legal History*, 31 (1987), pp. 177–208. It is worth noticing, however, that lawyers' briefs and polemical writings do not appear to have had anything like the same public impact in England as they did in eighteenth-century France. See, for example, Sarah Maza, 'Domestic Melodrama as Political Ideology: The Case of the Comte de Sanois', *American Historical Review*, 94 (1989), pp. 1249–64; and David Bell, *Lawyers and Citizens: The Making of A Political Elite in Old Regime France* (Oxford, 1994), esp. ch. 5.

[300] PRO, DL 4, 40/12.

[301] *Select Extracts from Blackstone's Commentaries: Carefully Adapted to the Use of Schools and Young Persons*, ed. S. Warren (London, 1837). The work was favourably reviewed in the *Legal Observer and Journal of Jurisprudence*, 13 (1836–37), p. 116.

[302] See for instance, Mullins, *In Quest of Justice*, p. 283, which is discussed in more detail below.

[303] Lobban, 'Was There a Nineteenth-Century "English School of Jurisprudence"?'; H. L. A. Hart, *The Concept of Law* (Oxford, 1961).

most of the nineteenth and twentieth centuries, England has not been an excessively litigious country in either historical or comparative terms. It is worth putting it forward as an hypothesis that, at almost any point between 1200 and 1700, ordinary people were in court more often, and knew more about 'law' (however defined), than they have at any time subsequently. Furthermore, the significance of this legal 'world we have lost' is as great for the historian as it is for the jurist. In 1931 the barrister Claude Mullins published *In Quest of Justice*, a work espousing law reform that was based on the author's interest in history as well as his own experience as a practitioner.[304] In the chapter on local courts, he noted that one consequence of the changes which had taken place since 1846 was that there had been a practical abolition of the remedy for the poor person who had been libelled and slandered.

> No one who has worked among the poor can be blind to the fact that the spreading of malicious gossip inflicts a very great deal of misery in humble neighbourhoods. It would be well if there were some means whereby poor people could bring promptly to book those who have spread unjustifiable gossip. Several soldiers' wives have come to me in great distress because their husbands have believed malicious gossip which callous neighbours have sent to them. And for this there is no practical remedy.[305]

Actions for libel and slander, especially those brought by ordinary women in the ecclesiastical courts in connection with sex and marriage, are one of the most interesting categories of case in the pre-modern canon of litigation, but perhaps it is not surprising that modern historians find them difficult to interpret. Since such actions are still not covered by legal aid, they have, except in the case of the rich, become even less common since Mullins wrote. In this respect, as in so many others, it is as instructive to investigate the peculiarities of our own times as it is to delve into those of the past.

[304] Mullins, *In Quest of Justice*, pp. ix–xiv.
[305] Ibid., p. 308. According to Mullins, the words were in fact written in 1914–15.

5

The Decline and Rise of the English Legal Profession, 1700–1850

This chapter sets out an overview and interpretation of the professional history of the two principal groups of lawyers in England, the barristers and the attorneys, between the end of the seventeenth and middle of the nineteenth centuries.[1] The general theme is that while professional organisations and values were highly developed amongst English lawyers before 1700, during the eighteenth century there was a decline and what might be described as a phase of deprofessionalisation. Hence it was necessary to recreate many of the institutional elements of professional life during the nineteenth century. Although these were in some respects different from those of earlier periods, it is not clear that they arose out of what might be called a classical agenda of 'professionalisation', or that they created a qualitatively different legal profession.[2] As will become evident, the principal causes of change were fluctuations in the quantity of legal business and consequently in the size of the legal professions. At the same time, there were also important alterations in the place of 'law' in social and political discourse, and in the relationship between London and provincial England, as well as that between the profession and the state, not least in the field of taxation.

I need to begin by describing the pre-modern legal profession as it existed at its apogee between 1550 and about 1700. Thanks to work which has been published within the last ten years, it is arguable that English lawyers were already highly professionalised by the late thirteenth century.[3] The singular

---

[1] An earlier version of this chapter was written in 1994 for delivery at a conference in Lyon on the development of professional organisations in Europe from the eighteenth to the twentieth centuries. It has been published in French as 'Le déclin et la recréation des organisations professionnelles de *barristers* et de *solicitors* aux XVIIIe et XIXe siècle', in *Les structures du barreau et du notariat en Europe de l'Ancien Régime à nos jours*, ed. Jean-Louis Halpérin (Lyon, 1996), pp. 99–112. What appears here is a revised and expanded version of the original.

[2] 'Professionalisation' has been since the 1960s a much discussed concept amongst sociologists and historians. By professional agenda, I mean here the theoretical view that professions aim to create for themselves self-control and a high degree of autonomy from state regulation, mainly by achieving command of the qualifying process. For a useful discussion of recent literature which takes account of a number of national variations, see Hannes Siegrist, 'The Professions, State and Government in Theory and History', in *Governments and Professional Education*, ed. Tony Becher (Buckingham, 1994), pp. 3–20.

[3] See Paul Brand, *The Origins of the English Legal Profession* (Oxford, 1992); and J. H. Baker, *The Third University of England: The Inns of Court and the Common Law Tradition*, Selden Society

importance of the later sixteenth century arises from the fact that it was a period in which there was a remarkable growth in legal business and consequently in the number of practitioners who made themselves available to deal with it.[4] For example, the practising bar, or the upper branch of England's two-tiered legal profession, consisted by 1640 of approximately 500 men, a figure which would not again be reached until the nineteenth century.[5] At the same time, the numbers of attorneys and solicitors rose to nearly 2000, so that the ratio of lawyers to population was in fact not much different from that for the early twentieth century.[6]

Thanks to a number of social, legal and political circumstances, much of the work of these lawyers was concentrated in London. Although the vast majority of them resided in the provinces, increasingly large numbers travelled to London both for their legal training and to do business for their clients when the central courts were sitting.[7] Given these circumstances, the inns of court and inns of chancery in London, the voluntary societies with which the lawyers had been associated since the middle of the fourteenth century, both expanded in size and grew in stature.[8] Subject ultimately to the authority of the royal privy council as well as that of the judiciary, but with governing bodies of their own, the inns provided aural learning exercises, namely moots and lectures (or 'readings'), which were compulsory for those who aimed to practise as advocates. By the end of the sixteenth century, the 'call to the bar' at one of the inns of court was formally recognised as the necessary qualification for achieving the right to appear before the central courts. Granted on proof of continued presence at the inns for a period which usually amounted to seven years, and after the completion of a specified number of learning exercises, the call was not dependent on the successful passage of an examination. Nor should the level of educational provision at the legal inns during this period be exaggerated. Nevertheless, there was sufficient intellectual vitality for the inns to deserve the reputation they enjoyed as the 'Third University' of England.[9]

As always during the period with which we are concerned, the situation within the lower branch of the profession, amongst the attorneys, differed in some important respects from that of the barristers. Attorneys were trained up largely through clerkship to older practitioners, and there was a long history of statutory regulation which specified that they had to be formally

Lecture (London, 1990).

    [4] Chapter 4, pp. 65ff and C. W. Brooks, *Pettyfoggers and Vipers of the Commonwealth: The 'Lower Branch' of the Legal Profession in Early Modern England* (Cambridge, 1986), chs 4–5.

    [5] W. R. Prest, *The Rise of the Barristers: A Social History of the English Bar, 1590–1640* (Oxford, 1986), ch. 3.

    [6] Chapter 7, pp. 182–85.

    [7] Brooks, *Pettyfoggers and Vipers*, chs 3, 6; Prest, *Rise of the Barristers*.

    [8] *Readings and Moots at the Inns of Court in the Fifteenth Century*, ed. S. E. Thorne and J. H. Baker, Selden Society, 105 (London, 1990), pp. xxv–xxxiii; Baker, *The Third University*.

    [9] W. R. Prest, *The Inns of Court under Elizabeth and the Early Stuarts* (London, 1972).

admitted to act in a specific tribunal before being allowed to practice.[10] New recruits to the central courts were administered an oath which laid down principles of professional probity; even those who practised exclusively in the localities were disciplined in the courts before which they worked. Although it had always been subject ultimately to the supervision of the judges, there was also from an early date a certain degree of self-regulation within this sector. Juries of attorneys were frequently appointed to establish rules of practice or to punish those accused of ethical or professional misdemeanours. Even more significantly, for a brief period during the Interregnum of the 1650s, juries of attorneys were formally empowered to examine new aspirants to the profession and to admit them to practice. Finally, throughout the sixteenth and seventeenth centuries, most attorneys joined an inn of chancery in London after their admission, many of them holding chambers for use when they came up to London from their homes elsewhere in the country. Indeed, from the 1630s through to the early eighteenth century, membership was prescribed as a requirement by judicial orders, and the perceived role of the societies was expressed in the following terms by one of them, Barnard's Inn, in the later 1660s. The senior members made rules for the governing of the house 'as well for the initiating of young gents in the knowledge of the common lawes of England as also for the attorneys of the common law', and its members observed 'the rules of the society for the exercising of their profession'.[11]

It is difficult to summarise briefly the quality of professional life which accompanied this organisational regime. There were of course public complaints about unqualified or dishonest practitioners, but it is also evident that the wide availability of work and the critical mass of numbers contributed to intellectual and professional vitality. The centralisation on the legal inns and central courts in London provided a sense of identity which was manifested most visibly in the traditions associated with the taking of meals collectively in commons, as well as in the processions of lawyers of all ranks which celebrated the appointment of the most senior members of the profession below the judiciary, the serjeants at law.[12] Even the morality of practitioners was dictated by regulations at the legal inns which covered, amongst other things, the length of hair, the nature of clothing and sexual rectitude. It is true that most of this supervision (with the exception of the juries of attorneys), like that exercised by other contemporary forms of association such as guilds, was administered in the legal inns by governing bodies whose authority was based on cooptive oligarchy. On the other hand, advancement through the ranks depended largely on professional success.

---

10 See Chapter 4, p. 76.

11 Brooks, *Pettyfoggers and Vipers*, chs 6–8; idem, *The Admissions Registers of Barnard's Inn, 1620–1869*, Selden Society supplementary series, 12 (London, 1995), p. 18.

12 J. H. Baker, *The Order of Serjeants at Law*, Selden Society supplementary series, 5 (London, 1984), ch. 6.

Perhaps more importantly, the social role of the legal profession in this period was validated by the importance humanist thought attached to the place of law as an intellectual discipline and as a vital constituent of social and political life.[13]

Many of the critical elements which constituted these early modern professional structures disintegrated and declined rapidly between about 1680 and 1720. Although the call to the bar at one of the inns of court remained the formal qualification for practice as a barrister in the higher courts, the educational activities at the legal inns atrophied and all but collapsed in the 1670s. At the same time, the attraction of the inns as voluntary associations seems to have diminished. The memberships of all of the societies had contracted so sharply by 1720 that a number of them were in serious financial difficulties. The inns of court largely abandoned their role in professional education and in the maintenance of professional standards. The buildings continued to be used as lawyers' chambers, but membership of the inns themselves was evidently little regarded.[14] If anything, the decline of the inns of chancery was even more catastrophic than that of the inns of court. The governing bodies threatened to lock up the chambers of practitioner tenants who refused to join in the communal activities, but this strategy was unsuccessful. Only a very tiny percentage of eighteenth-century attorneys ever bothered to join a legal inn. The inns of chancery only survived because they transformed themselves into clubs for small groups of practitioners.[15]

There were several reasons for this historically abrupt change in the organisation of English lawyers. First, the teaching exercises at the legal inns never fully recovered from the disruption they suffered during the Civil Wars and Interregnum of the 1640s and 1650s.[16] Secondly, there is a correlation between the decline of the legal inns and the amount of litigation which entered the central courts over this same period from 1680 to 1750. While the number of cases which were being heard by the Westminster and local courts was at an all time high in 1640, by 1750 the numbers of cases in both central and local courts appear to have hit an all time low.[17] The impact on the legal profession of this change in the volume of work was twofold. In the first place, there was a contraction in the number of practitioners. The practising bar may have contracted by nearly 50 per cent.[18] The nature of the evidence makes the size of the 'lower branch', the attorneys and solicitors, much more difficult to calculate accurately for any period before 1731, but between 1735 and 1770 there was a distinct decline in the

---

[13] See below, Chapter 8.

[14] David Lemmings, *Gentlemen and Barristers: The Inns of Court and The English Bar, 1680–1730* (Oxford, 1990), chs 1–2.

[15] Brooks, *Admissions Registers of Barnard's Inn*, pp. 36–54.

[16] See Chapter 6, p. 151.

[17] See Chapter 3, pp. 30–33.

[18] Lemmings, *Gentlemen and Barristers*, ch. 3.

number of new practitioners enrolled, so that by 1770 the total was probably not notably greater than it had been in 1640, despite significant growth in population.[19]

Since there was a drop in the amount of legal business which came from the country to London, from just before the beginning of the eighteenth century local legal practitioners ceased any longer to travel regularly to London, and a very significant division emerged between the attorneys and solicitors who lived and worked in London and those who lived and worked almost exclusively in the provinces.[20] As a result, although judicial orders from as late as 1705 required attorneys and solicitors to join a legal inn, the obligation obviously became an irksome one, with the costs undoubtedly outweighing the benefits when the individual concerned was rarely going to use the facilities in London.[21] In addition, new legislation in the form of the 1729 Attorney Act made the taking out of articles, rather than membership of an inn, the essential qualification for enrolment to practise, so that after that date there was no need at all for such practitioners to join an inn.[22] Consequently, for much of the eighteenth century the education of attorneys and the inculcation of professional ethics, such as they may have been, depended entirely on the quality of training that could be achieved through the apprenticeship of articled clerks to older practitioners, many of whom may have had very little contact with the central courts in London.[23]

In terms of the role of institutions, these changes in the first half of the eighteenth century amounted to something like the deprofessionalisation of the lawyers. Yet the effect on professional values and standards is difficult to measure conclusively. There were complaints about the poor training and ignorance of both branches of the profession; it seems quite probable that the lower branch in particular suffered from uneven standards of practice.[24] On the other hand, the legal profession was not moribund in the early eighteenth century. Nor did it conform to any large degree to the stereotypes that are sometimes used to describe professions before the modern age. If we include the attorneys and solicitors along with the barristers, the social origins of the majority of practitioners in the seventeenth and eighteenth centuries are to be found within the ranks of the affluent and respectable

---

[19] See Chapter 7, p. 184.

[20] See above, Chatper 3, pp. 46–47; Brooks, *Admissions Registers of Barnard's Inn*, p. 36.

[21] Ibid., p. 24–25. PRO, C 106/6, the papers of Joshua Eversden of Cambridgeshire, who joined Barnard's Inn in 1705, indicate that out of a total cost of £9 4s. 6d., which he laid out to become enrolled as an attorney, his admission and 'initiation' at Barnard's Inn cost him £2 0s. 6d.

[22] Brooks, *Admissions Registers of Barnard's Inn*, pp. 45–54.

[23] See Chapter 6, pp. 161–62.

[24] See Chapter 6, pp. 165ff.

middling sort from urban and rural backgrounds, as well as amongst the lesser gentry.[25]

There is also evidence of individual and collective initiative with regard to some of the 'professional' aspects of the occupation. Groups of attorneys sometimes petitioned or lobbied parliament about matters of professional concern. From early on in the period after the Restoration, local practitioners formed clubs both for their entertainment and for self-improvement. At Bristol, the Society of the Rose Garden, which kept a minute book of its meetings from September 1661 to April 1670, was established as a convivial fraternity which shared dinners, but which also adjudicated on accusations of malpractice.[26] Similar clubs, which were formed either for the mutual edification of established practitioners or so that articled clerks could improve their legal training, are known to have existed in London from 1700 onwards.[27] The tendency towards informal association reached a culmination with the foundation in 1737 of the Society of Gentlemen Practisers, the most direct precursor of the modern Law Society. Composed primarily of only one section of the London, as opposed to provincial, practitioners, the early efforts of the society were directed mainly at carrying on a dispute with the rival Scriveners' Company of London over the right to make legal instruments in the City of London. Later on in the eighteenth century it negotiated with court officials over the level of fees, while it also from time to time took steps to have improperly qualified men struck off the rolls of practitioners.[28]

Less is known about the existence of informal societies amongst the barristers, but a letter of advice, dating from 1736, which was addressed by a London practitioner, Nathaniel Cole, to an acquaintance who had asked

[25] Brooks, *Pettyfoggers and Vipers*, ch. 11; Lemmings, *Gentlemen and Barristers*, ch. 3; D. Duman, 'The English Bar in the Georgian Era', in *Lawyers in Early Modern Europe and America*, ed. W. R. Prest (London, 1981), pp. 90–95.

[26] Bristol Central Library, Bristol Collection, 26064, fos 35–43. In 1661 there were fifteen members and ten probationers. At subsequent meetings a barrister who was steward of the Bristol Sheriff's Court, and Gilbert Jones, a civilian, who was chancellor of the diocese, were made honorary members. I am grateful to Jonathan Barry for sharing with me his notes on the society. It is worth pointing out of course that the informal nature of such clubs means that there may have been many more of them than survive in the historical record.

[27] H. Horwitz and L. Bonfield, 'The Lower Branches of the Legal Profession: A London Society of Attorneys and Solicitors of the 1730s and its Moots', *Cambridge Law Journal*, 49 (1990), pp. 461–90; M. Birks, 'John Mander's Book: The Records of an Eighteenth-Century Articled Clerks' Debating Society', *Law Society's Gazette* (December 1958), pp. 763–64. This society, which was formed in 1738, had an elaborate constitution and was limited to fifteen members ('none but persons Studying the Law'), who proposed to meet every Wednesday evening at the Ship in Ship Yard. I am grateful to Henry Horwitz for this reference and for a photocopy of a transcript of the society's rules and regulations, which are in the Law Society Library, Chancery Lane, London.

[28] E. Freshfield, *The Records of the Society of Gentlemen Practisers in the Courts of Law and Equity* (London, 1897); C. W. Brooks, R. Helmholz and P. G. Stein, *Notaries Public in England since the Reformation* (Norwich, 1991), ch. 4.

him about the best way to educate a gentleman of a noble family for the bar, contains a number of fascinating insights and proves that they existed. Cole began by pointing out that learning the law was tedious. He recommended a course of reading and noted that many barristers were 'educated' in the offices of attorneys, but he then went on to say:

> there is another kind of Study, if it may be so called, which will be of great use, and which I have formerly known practised in the Temple, and I suppose is so still, I mean that young Gentlemen, some of the Bar and others intended for it, form themselves into Evening Societies at a Tavern where the first part of the Evening is dedicated to the Law, either by some Gentleman's reporting some resolution of the Courts at Westminster in a Case thought of consequence or else by hearing a discourse or Argument by a gentleman upon a particular Case ... This will give the Gentleman an opportunity to instruct himself in the method of forming an Argument, and will in some measure contribute to introduce him to speak; besides such societies are generally composed of Gentlemen who become Members merely for the better purpose of qualifying themselves for the bar, [and] who have before determined to follow the Practice of the Law. Amongst such Persons a valuable and useful acquaintance may be contracted, and when it comes to his Turn to maintain or defend a Question, if he distinguishes himself even in such a Company as a Person of Ingenuity and Knowledge, it will be spoke abroad to his Advantage.

Establishing a reputation as a 'good lawyer' was a vital building block of professional advantage in a competitive age.[29]

Apart from the significant reminder that success at the bar in the eighteenth century was based more on skill and talent than on birth, Cole's words also indicate that, for the bar, voluntary association coupled with forms of apprenticeship, and not the older institutions, were the keys to professional life during this period. Seen in this light, the history of the legal profession appears to have much in common with other bourgeois institutions, ranging from trade guilds to urban corporations, where older institutional forms were accompanied, or replaced, by informal associations during the course of the eighteenth century.[30] Quite apart from the developments in London, from the 1770s, local attorneys founded at least ten law societies in the provinces, including those in Bristol (1770), Yorkshire (1786), Somerset (1769), Sunderland (1800), Leeds (1805), Devon and Exeter (1808),

---

[29] National Library of Wales, Aberystwyth, MS 9070E, 'Directions for the Study of the Law Written by Nathanial Cole, Basinghall Street, London, to Samuel Buckley, Esq., August 1736'. See also BL, MS Add. 6229, fol. 62, John Ward's 'Adversaria', which notes the existence of a society which met regularly from 1712 to 1742. It was composed of lawyers and divines who read papers and discussed civil law and the 'law of nature and nations'.

[30] See Jonathan Barry and Christopher Brooks, eds, *The Middling Sort of People: Culture, Society and Politics in England, 1550–1800* (Basingstoke, 1994), chs 2–3.

Manchester (1809), Plymouth (1815), Gloucester (1817), and Birmingham, Hull and Kent (1818).[31]

Voluntary association of this kind, which was by its nature piecemeal, did not insulate the late eighteenth-century profession from criticism. During the 1790s in particular, the intellectual problems arising from the common law's notorious lack of coherence, and the informality of legal training, intensified debate (both within and outside the profession) about how improvements might be made. While there is no conclusive proof that the quality of legal practice had declined dramatically, professional literature and the daily press expressed concern about education and standards as the numbers of attorneys began to increase rapidly in the 1780s and 1790s.[32] Although most of the discussion focused on pedagogic rather than institutional questions, in the 1790s a London attorney, Joseph Day, wrote several lengthy pamphlets calling for the establishment by statute of a society or college of attorneys which would be given the power to examine candidates for admission while at the same time serving as a selective society of elite practitioners.[33]

While there is every reason to believe that Day floated this project in the expectation that he personally would benefit professionally and financially from it,[34] the case he had to make was by no means uninformed; indeed, his plan deserves attention precisely because it was so remarkably similar to measures which were eventually adopted in he next century. Observing that 'increases in Manufac[turing] and Commerce, in this populous and flourishing King[dom]' created excellent prospects for lawyers,[35] Day claimed that the low public reputation of the profession was a consequence of the failure of the existing system of articled clerkship to guarantee that men of

[31] David Sugarman, 'Bourgeois Collectivism, Professional Power and the Boundaries of the State. The Private and Public Life of the Law Society, 1825 to 1919', *International Journal of the Legal Profession*, 3 (1996), pp. 81–135. I am very grateful to Professor Sugarman for letting me see an earlier draft of his paper.

[32] See Chapter 6, pp. 164–67.

[33] The draft bill is outlined in *A Plan for Instituting a College for the Better Regulation of Attorneys and the Practice of the Law: Under the Denomination of the Royal College of Attorneys at Law and Solicitors* (London, 1794).

[34] A second-generation London lawyer, Day was articled to his father and admitted to practice in 1781; he lived in in Hatton Gardens, a typical legal address during this period, PRO, KB 170/1; 172/1. Some idea of his life-long 'service' as a projector of minor government reforms can be gleaned from letters which he later wrote to government ministers begging financial reward for his efforts. He left London in the early 1800s and lived until 1811 in Macclesfield, at which point he was experiencing financial difficulties. It is likely that he died in Essex. BL, MSS Add. 38250, fos 191, 260; 38373, fos 218–21, 238–42, 256–67v; 40372, fos 240–40v.

[35] The quotation is from a letter to King George III which Day delivered to Buckingham Palace along with a copy of one of his works. The letter is bound in the British Library copy of Joseph Day, *Thoughts on the Necessity and Utility of the Examination Directed by Several Acts of Parliament, Previous to the Admission of Attorneys at Law and Solicitors: Together with Some Observations on the Constitution and Regulation of the Society of Clerks to His Majesty's Signet in Scotland. The Whole Applying to a Bill Proposed to be Brought into Parliament for the Incorporating and Better-Regulation of Attorneys at Law and Solicitors* (London, 1795).

bad character and inadequate training were excluded from practice. Aware that there was a long history of regulation through rules of court and parliamentary legislation, he was one of the first authors to mount a systematic attack on standards which had been maintained under this regime.[36] Yet, while his was a forerunner of a point of view which informed accounts of professional history well into the twentieth century, it is no less revealing that so much had changed during the course of the eighteenth century that Day had difficulty capturing the substance of professional life as it had been before 1700.[37] He had, for example, little understanding of the historical role of the inns of chancery. Writing exclusively from the point of view of a Londoner, he evidently remained unaware that the memberships and governing bodies of the houses had once consisted largely of country attorneys.[38] Describing the problems of the profession largely in terms of the system of clerkship that had evolved in the wake of the 1729 Attorney Act, but failing to mention the existing provincial law societies, he saw the way forward largely through the beneficial influence which association would have on the character of lawyers.

Providence has beneficently interwoven pride in our nature, and rendered it one of the most powerful springs of action; and there is no mind so utterly depraved and callous as to be wholly insensible on all occasions to its suggestions. If we involuntarily imbibe the sentiments, manners, and even expressions of those with whom we associate; and if the powerful influence of example even in occurrences that are of a triffling nature, be admitted; may we not fairly infer from thence, that if an Association of Persons in any class of life, were to be formed by those belonging to it of known Probity and Respectability, and that the most scrupulous attention should be constantly shewn to exclude all whose want of acknowledged good Character and approved Abilities rendered them undeserving of admission into this universally honoured and esteemed society, can it be doubted, that all those in the same class of life would eagerly use their utmost efforts to become Members; sensible of the Distinction conferred by it, and that their means of Support would alone depend upon the attainment of this Proof of Rectitude and Ability? The influence of these considerations even on the minds of those not naturally well disposed, could not fail to be extremely powerful.[39]

Unfortunately, Day's own extensive writings are the only sources available for measuring professional reactions to his proposals and estimating their

[36] Day, *A Plan for Instituting a College*, pp. A2–5.

[37] Joseph Day, *An Address to the Attorneys at Law and Solicitors, Practising in Great Britain, and to the Public: Upon the Proceedings of a Committee of the London Law Club* (London, 1796), pp. 1–12.

[38] Day, *An Address to the Attorneys at Law and Solicitors*, pp. 46, 131. Day was asked by Justice Buller in September 1794 whether he 'knew what were the constitutions' of the inns of chancery. Day did not then know about judicial rules of 1704 which specified that all attorneys should join one of them or be struck off the roll.

[39] Day, *A Plan for Instituting a College*, p. 6.

chances of success.[40] Reporting on several encouraging conversations which he had with leading legal figures, including Lord Chancellor Loughborough, Lord Kenyon (CJKB), Justice William Ashurst, and attorney-general Sir John Scott (the future Lord Chancellor Eldon), Day may have exaggerated their enthusiasm, but his plans recognised the traditional responsibility of the judiciary for regulating admissions by stipulating that the judges would exercise a general supervisory role over the newly proposed society.[41] While the Royal College of Physicians (which was founded in the reign of Henry VIII) and the more recent incorporation of London surgeons (1745) were the immediate inspiration for his scheme, the idea of looking at the practices of the Society of Clerks to the Signet in Scotland to see whether they might serve as a model had evidently been suggested by the chief justice of the Common Pleas, Sir James Eyre.[42]

There is also some evidence of support for the plan within the profession at large. Day raised money by eliciting subscriptions from some sixty fellow London attorneys.[43] He also entered into discussions with members of the 'Committee' (or governing body) of the Society of Gentlemen Practisers, which was then widely known as the 'Law Society'.[44] It is no doubt significant that Day himself had not joined the society, whose membership at this date was selected by a process that required those who wanted to join gaining a nomination from an existing member before being approved by the whole body.[45] While Day retained this principle of election as the means of determining the professional elite that was to compose the membership of his new college,[46] he eventually accused the 'Law Society' of being more interested

[40] Of the three pamphlets Day wrote on the subject, *An Address to the Attorneys at Law and Solicitors* contains the most thorough description of his dealings with other people. Consisting of 212 pages, and including 'Extracts from a Journal Kept by the Author', it recounts in great detail conversations and meetings with both well-known and lesser-known individuals; it makes fairly interesting reading. There is no evidence that what Day said about other people was ever challenged in court or in print, but it is also worth keeping in mind that his works were privately published and distributed. All three are so rare that they survive only in single copies.

[41] Ibid., pp. 30–74.

[42] Day, *An Address to the Attorneys at Law and Solicitors*, pp. 151. Day relied on an unnamed correspondent in Edinburgh for information. His views on this subject are most fully developed in Day, *Thoughts on the Necessity*.

[43] Day, *An Address to the Attorneys at Law and Solicitors*, pp. 70–73. He gives names and addresses.

[44] Ibid., pp. 39ff. Day's first contact was a conversation in September 1794 with the secretary of the society, from whom he obtained the names of the other committee members.

[45] Ibid., p. 88. One of the members of the society, Mr Manley, remarked that 'he is not a member of the Law Society, he did not know any thing of it; he did not apply to the Law Society; but, notwithstanding, he has taken upon him to lead the whole body of the law'.

[46] Once admitted to practice, any attorney could put himself forward for election by the president, governors and council; all members had to stand for reelection every year. Although he reported that Chief Justice Eyre thought that all attorneys should automatically become members, Day claimed this would 'destroy that distinction between the really respectable attorneys, and those of a different description'. Day, *A Plan for Instituting a College*, pp. 9–11; idem, *An Address to the Attorneys at Law and Solicitors*, p. 142.

in their twice-yearly dinners than in professional improvement.[47] His early approaches to individual members led him to believe that he had their support, but he got nowhere when he put his case before meetings of the committee in early 1795.[48] Without ever putting Day's scheme before the entire membership of the society, or even mentioning it in their minutes, the committee evidently killed the plan dead, apparently with the acquiescence of the judges.[49]

Apart from the suspicions they harboured about his own ambitions, Day's opponents put forward a number of arguments against the plan.[50] The judges were concerned that a statutory body would give the profession too much power; the committee men, on the other hand, were not enthusiastic about the prospect of greater judicial involvement in their affairs.[51] No less significantly, the attorneys suspected that further regulation might lead to higher taxation.[52] It is easy to see why. Even though he protested vehemently against this aspersion, Day admitted having conversations about the plan with secretary of the Treasury George Rose.[53] Later on in life, Day took credit for suggesting ways to apply additional stamp duties to legal instruments in the later 1780s, a period which saw the advent of the hated certificate tax, in effect an annual payment for a licence to

[47] In a letter of September 1794 to Mr White, solicitor to the Treasury, Day wrote 'even if all these gentlemen were to be incorporated, is it not to be feared that to the public eye the corporation would appear deficient of the dignity, authority, and impartiality, which, if constituted as I have proposed, will be its most prominent features'. Later, he called the Law Society a 'tavern society' that in no way represented, or regulated, the profession, ibid., pp. 37, 82, 195. It is true that attendance at the twice-yearly dinners was the main obligation placed on members of the society. In the early 1790s a number of committee meetings were abandoned because of low attendance, though the society did take up with the courts the question of the times available for making writs. The Law Society, Chancery Lane, London, Records of the Society of Gentlemen Practisers, Minutes 1737–1819 (6 vols available on microfilm), iv, pp. 1–71, 74.

[48] In fact, there were already signs of opposition in late 1794; if Day had an ally on the committee of the Law Society it was Thomas Rashleigh, but he eventually turned against the plan. Day, *An Address to the Attorneys at Law and Solicitors*, pp. 39, 50–51, 57, 60–61, 66–68, 76–77, 79–105.

[49] In early 1795 the judges no longer made themselves available to see Day. There is no mention of Day or his proposal in the manuscript minutes of the Society of Gentlemen Practisers. According to Day, it was suggested in December 1794 that he should receive some payment for his pains, and he eventually submitted a bill of costs for £115 14s. 8d. It seems possible that Day eventually earned as much as £200 from the project, all of it from subscriptions. Ibid., pp. 76, 178–79, 182–189, 193.

[50] Ibid., pp. 64, 88, 197. It is worth noting that similar proposals for incorporating attorneys in Ireland also failed at this time because of hostility from the profession. Colum Kenny, *King's Inns and the Kingdom of Ireland: The Irish 'Inn of Court', 1541–1800* (Dublin, 1992), ch. 9.

[51] Day, *An Address to the Attorneys at Law and Solicitors*, pp. 35, 40–41, 44, 60, 87.

[52] Ibid., pp. 80, 83, 99.

[53] Ibid., pp. 47, 49, 80. Day reported that Rose thought the plan a good idea, but that it was not a matter for the government to meddle in.

practise.[54] He may also have had something to do with the introduction in 1797 of high stamp duties on admissions to the inns of court and inns of chancery, a development which almost certainly ruled out any possibility that the latter would ever again have a significant professional function,[55] while launching the Society of Gentlemen Practisers on an unsuccessful campaign for increases in fees which lasted more than a decade.[56] Finally, as far as the regulation of the profession was concerned, the committee thought that the existing legislation and rules of court were sufficient for the purpose,[57] a claim only partially belied by the fact that in January 1797 they began to inspect more carefully than before the termly lists of articled clerks who were standing for admission as attorneys.[58] During the remaining twenty-two years for which their records survive, the society never extended their scrutiny beyond those who were articled in London and in any case rarely entered caveats with the judges against newcomers. On the few occasions when they did do so, the reason was usually some technical insufficiency in the master.[59]

A similar watchfulness on new admissions was no doubt maintained by practitioners in those parts of the country where provincial law societies existed, but, like the London society, they lacked institutional authority and were probably devoted primarily to conviviality.[60] The profession remained

[54] Joseph Day to Lord Liverpool, 28 May 1812, BL, MS Add. 38378, fol. 238. The certificate tax was imposed in 1785 (25 George III, c. 80). For contemporary comment on it, see Anon., *Considerations on the Attorney Tax and Proposals for Altering and Equalising the Same so as to Render it Easy in Operation and Just in Principle* (London, 1786). The long history of professional hostility is outlined in *Legal Observer and Journal of Jurisprudence*, 39 (1849–50), pp. 295–96. Day's proposals were probably connected with stamp duties on legal instruments associated with the probate of wills (28 George III, c. 22).

[55] Day claimed direct responsibility for suggesting that the certificate tax be paid by a specified time each year, BL, MS Add. 38378, fol. 288. 37 George II, c. 90 (1797), which implemented this reform of the certificate tax also put a £4 duty on all admissions to an inn of court or inn of chancery.

[56] In 1797 it was resolved 'That by reason of the various [and] repeated Increases of the Stamp Duties and other heavy Burthens upon the Profession of the Law since the fees allowed to the Practisers thereof were established, & which require a considerable Increase of Capital to enable the Practisers to carry on their Business, it is Considered expedient that it should be Referred to the Committee to Consider whether some and what applications should be made for increasing the fees to Attornies and Solicitors ...' The issue was still being discussed in 1815. Records of the Society of Gentlemen Practisers, iv, pp. 110, 133–34, 137; vi, pp. 5, 20, 38, 59, 140.

[57] Day, *An Address to the Attorneys at Law and Solicitors*, pp. 85–89.

[58] Records of the Society of Gentlemen Practisers, iv, p. 86. The procedure was for the secretary of the society to obtain a list of names of those standing for admission. These were then inspected by the committee.

[59] In 1797, for example, the society entered a caveat against the clerk of John Pugh, a clerk to a master in Chancery, because Pugh had not filed for the certificate tax during the previous five years. Ibid., pp. 96–97, 104.

[60] In 1810 the Liverpool Law Association contacted the Gentlemen Practisers about stopping an admission, ibid., vi, p. 33.

largely unreformed during the fifty-year period from 1780 to 1830, one of the most remarkable phases of numerical growth that it had ever experienced.[61] When major institutional change did come during the later 1820s, it was in response to a general concern about the need for reform throughout the legal system and a reaction to another low point in the public reputation of the profession.[62] It also owed much to wider calls for the establishment of better educational standards for the professions and government officials,[63] demands which frequently divided members of the profession amongst themselves.

Little is known about the exact relationship between the old Society of Gentlemen Practisers and the foundation of a new London Law Society in the mid 1820s; it is most likely that newer society simply superseded the older one in a period when several such associations existed in the metropolis.[64] But, while the last records of the Gentlemen Practisers show it to have been concerned primarily with increasing fees, the leading lights of the new Law Society were keen advocates of improvement in professional education. In addition, while the older body met in taverns in the Strand, the members of the new one subscribed money for the erection of a Greek revival building in Chancery Lane which they named the Law Institute. Furnished with a law library and a room suitable for lectures, it was to be a clubhouse for the relatively small London membership, while (in theory) serving as a place to which country attorneys could resort when they came up to London on business.[65]

Although the proposed provision for provincial practitioners seems a quaint revival of the older role of the legal inns, the new Law Society was in many respects much like its competitors in London and the provinces. What ultimately set it apart was the fact that its membership included wealthy and influential City practitioners who evidently had excellent connections with parliament and the judiciary. Thanks to the influence they were able to wield, when measures were proposed in the 1830s for reforming the admissions process for new practitioners, the society was able to have its members appointed by the judges to act as examiners. Like Joseph Day's proposals over thirty years earlier, the changes were justified by reference to precedents dating from 1654, when similar powers had been granted to juries of attorneys; in a technical sense professional self-regulation was being

---

[61] See Chapter 7, p. 184.

[62] See Chapter 4, pp. 101ff.

[63] See, for example, Richard Lovell Edgeworth, *Essays on Professional Education* (London, 1809).

[64] According to an historical account of the Law Society published in the *Legal Observer and Journal of Jurisprudence*, 35 (1847–48), p. 427, the other societies included the Northern Agents Society and the Metropolitian Law Society.

[65] Sugarman, 'Bourgeois Collectivism and the Boundaries of the State'. Some 170 practitioners subscribed between £250 and £500 each for the erection of the new building, *Legal Observer and Journal of Jurisprudence*, 35 (1847–48), p. 427.

reinvented.[66] By the mid 1830s the Law Society administered a written examination and thereby became the gatekeeper of the profession, a position which eventually enabled it to dominate the provincial societies. In 1843 an Act of Parliament transformed it into the Incorporated Law Society, the present governing body of solicitors.[67]

Far from reflecting the triumphalism so often associated with the rise of the professions, the regeneration of professional organisations within the lower branch was the product of a combination of idealism and anxiety, a state of mind which may well have characterised the lawyers for most of the nineteenth century.[68] In addition to concerns about overcrowding, the interest amongst Londoners in the establishment of stricter qualifying examinations had been stirred in part by the rise of a new breed of practitioner, the conveyancer in chambers.[69] From the 1830s, newly founded periodicals which aimed to create an 'effectual channel of communication [among] professional men throughout the British dominions' provide unprecedented evidence of professional opinion, but they do not reflect self-confidence.[70] Apart from perennial concerns about the consequences of repeated waves of parliamentary law reform, publications from the 1840s and 1850s also reveal a preoccupation with establishing, or maintaining, the 'honourable' and 'gentlemanly' character of the occupation.

Like so much else, this also had its antecedents in the sixteenth and seventeenth centuries, but it is a surprising feature of an age when relatively high apprenticeship premiums and stamp taxes must have been making the profession more, rather than less, socially exclusive than it had been before. In the earlier period the problem of reconciling training through apprenticeship with claims to gentility was to some degree eased by the fact that membership of the inns of chancery, no less than recognition as officials of the courts, entitled practitioners to call themselves gentlemen.[71] In the nineteenth century, publicists aiming to improve the image of the profession stressed a vaguer brand of gentility, but the hallmarks were still certain standards of education, a breadth of outlook and a sense of 'honourable behaviour'. In 1821, for example, the president of the Law Society welcomed special concessions made to aspiring solicitors who had previously studied

---

[66] Sugarman, 'Bourgeois Collectivism, and the Boundaries of the State'; see Chapter 6, pp. 167ff.

[67] Robert Maugham, *The Act 6 & 7 Victoriae: For Consolidating and Amending Several of the Laws Relating to Attorneys and Solicitors Practising in England and Wales. With an Introduction and Analysis of the Act* (London, 1843), pp. 21–22. From 1844 the Law Society was appointed Registrar of Attorneys and Solicitors.

[68] R. Cocks, *Foundations of the Modern Bar* (London, 1983), p. 56, 85–89.

[69] *Parliamentary Papers 1819–20*, i (London, 1820), p. 127. 'A Bill to Prevent Unskilful Persons from Practising as Conveyancers'. I owe this reference to Michael Lobban. See also *Records of the Society of Gentlemen Practisers*, vi, p. 33.

[70] *Legal Observer and Journal of Jurisprudence*, 1 (1830), prospectus.

[71] For the sixteenth and seventeenth centuries, see Brooks, *Pettyfoggers and Vipers*, pp. 178–81.

at the universities of Oxford and Cambridge, because they would help attract to the profession the 'better class' of people who would have come from families wealthy enough to afford such an education.[72] In a series of lectures which he delivered in 1848 to articled clerks at the Law Institute on 'The Moral, Social, and Professional Duties of Attornies and Solicitors', Samuel Warren combined specious rhetorical points about the aims of the profession being identical to those of the public with an exhortation to articled clerks to think of themselves as students rather than mere drudges or office boys. He also stressed that much depended on them behaving as 'gentlemen'. Apart from anything else, their business might bring them into contact with highly refined ladies and gentlemen; any departure from appropriate standards of deportment would produce 'disgust' in such clients.[73]

Because we know so little in detail about provincial legal practice in the nineteenth century, it is difficult to be precise about how far such rhetoric reached out beyond London and the interests of the London profession. It seems likely that in many respects the divide between the London profession, which was dominated in the public arena by agents who acted in the central courts, and provincial practitioners, who were already earning their livings primarily through conveyancing, grew wider. On the other hand, the institution of examinations in 1836 did once again focus attention on a common body of law, and by the late 1840s, the pace of legal reform led the independent London and provincial societies to federate into the Metropolitan and Provincial Law Association.[74] Despite the fact that only a minority of practitioners joined it, for the remainder of the century the Incorporated Law Society undertook defence of the profession's interests, mainly by keeping a watch on any potentially damaging parliamentary legislation. That it performed this task efficiently is attested by the comment of *The Times* in 1893 that it was the 'best organised and most intelligent trade union in the country'.[75]

Yet if self-interest was evident in the success of the Law Society, there was also a genuine commitment to attempting to improve legal education, particularly by encouraging students and putting on public lectures.

[72] *Parliamentary Papers 1821*, iv, *Report from the Select Committee on Admission of Attornies and Solicitors.* (London, 1821), p. 326. Interestingly, this measure was opposed by the Manchester Law Association because they doubted that men from the universities would be willing to undertake the office drudgery which they thought an essential part of the training of attorneys, R. Robson, *The Attorney in Eighteenth-Century England* (Cambridge, 1959), p. 45.

[73] S. Warren, *The Moral, Social and Professional Duties of Attornies and Solicitors* (London, 1848), pp. xii, 2–3, 53–5, 101. A barrister, who was the son of a clergyman, Warren had nonconformist connections and was a well-known legal publicist.

[74] This development is charted extensively in both the *Legal Observer and Journal of Jurisprudence* and its rival the *Law Times*. In 1847 the latter went so far as to call for a union of attorneys and solicitors as well as better efforts to ensure that the interests of the lower branch were more effectively represented in parliament, 9 (1847), p. 114.

[75] Sugarman, 'Bourgeois Collectivism and the Boundaries of the State', pp. 98, 113–15. See also idem, *Brief History of the Law Society* (London, 1995).

Following the lead which was established in the 1830s by its first secretary, Robert Maugham, the Society repeatedly attempted to enlist the support of the older professional organisations, the inns of court and inns of chancery, in this enterprise.[76] During the 1840s and 1850s, parliamentary commissions of inquiry were critical of the quality of the legal education on offer to those who wanted to enter either branch of the profession, especially when comparisons were made with continental Europe or the United States. A number of those who gave evidence, including the representatives of the Law Society and some members of the inns of court, urged that the financial resources (and physical space) of the legal inns should form the basis of a law university, which might also serve as a central institution for the profession.[77] Though never fully realised, this idea continued to find support into the 1880s, while the press, as well as some members of the profession, expressed the (erroneous) opinion that the legal inns had public responsibilities. Referring frequently to the sixteenth- and seventeenth-century histories retailed by writers such as Dugdale, the point stressed was that the inns had been established for the education and regulation of lawyers in much the same way as the universities educated and qualified clergymen.[78] According to one of the leading barrister proponents of reform, Sir Richard Bethell, legal education at the inns had fallen 'into disuse during an age which is to be remarked for its low tone of feeling as to the discharge of public duties, and I am sorry to say that even in the present times we have not hitherto shown a great degree of conscientiousness'.[79]

In reality, the reform of legal education involved so many controversial issues that even its advocates disagreed amongst themselves; it was often difficult to gain the whole-hearted support of either the judiciary or the governing bodies of the legal inns.[80] During the course of the later eighteenth and early nineteenth centuries, the judiciary made a number of decisions which explicitly repudiated the powers which they had previously exercised over the inns of court and chancery. They justified this by describing the inns as voluntary societies which could not be coerced into performing any public functions in connection with either legal education or the management of the profession. At the inns of chancery, whilst some members with antiquarian interests lauded the past glories of their institutions, few seem to have seriously entertained the idea that they might have something to

---

[76] *Legal Observer and Journal of Jurisprudence*, 3 (1831–32), p. 169; 31 (1845–46), pp. 445–46.

[77] *Parliamentary Papers 1846*, x, *Report from the Select Committee on Legal Education* (London, 1846); *Parliamentary Papers, 1854–55*, xviii, *Report of the Commissioners Appointed to Inquire into the Arrangements in the Inns of Court and Inns of Chancery for Promoting the Study of Law and Legal Education* (London, 1855).

[78] See, for example, Brooks, *Admissions Registers of Barnard's Inn*, pp. 69–71.

[79] Thomas Arthur Nash, *The Life of Richard Lord Westbury with Selections from his Correspondence* (2 vols, London, 1888), i, p. 91.

[80] This subject is treated in much greater detail in a forthcoming paper by C. W. Brooks and M. Lobban, 'Apprenticeship or Academy? The Idea of a Law University, 1830–1860'.

contribute to the future of the profession. As their spokesmen made clear to the midcentury parliamentary commissions, one of the reasons for this was their fragile financial positions; but when several of the remaining inns of chancery were sold off in the 1870s and 1880s, the profits were divided between tiny groups of existing members.[81]

Though challenged in the courts, the sales were made on the very plausible grounds that the property of the inns was held by the memberships themselves and had not in most cases been obtained or granted specifically for the purposes of legal education. It was quite true that the legal inns had never been granted charters of incorporation, or any other legal instruments which placed them under enforceable obligations, except those prescribed by the crown and the judiciary. Although there were a number of important figures, including Henry Brougham, the dynamic lawyer and politician, who were advocates of reform, there was also evidently a significant body of opinion (amongst the barristers in particular) that few changes were necessary.[82] There was, therefore, relatively little reform of the organisation of the bar until the 1870s and 1880s.

Throughout the first half of the nineteenth century the only qualification a barrister needed was 'the call to the bar' at one of the inns of court. There was no prescribed method of training or qualifying exam. Although a form of apprenticeship, chamber tuition, had by this time become established as the principal method of acquiring professional knowledge,[83] all that was formally required was attendance at a certain specified number of meals in hall, a point which provided ample ammunition for critics with a satirical turn of mind.[84] At the same time, the governance of the inns of court and vestigial control over professional discipline remained in the hands of the oligarchic benchers who constituted the governing bodies of the inns. In practice this was normally of very little significance, because such regulation of the profession as was achieved occurred at the 'assize messes': meetings over dinner of the barristers who went on circuit all around the country in order to present cases. These were in effect democratic decision-making bodies that ruled on points of etiquette and helped to develop the series of restrictive practices which made the occupation a very lucrative one for those who were successful at it.[85] The bar had always enjoyed a superior social status to that of the lower branch, and there was an assumption that most of those who intended to join it had previously spent time at

81   Brooks, *Admissions Registers of Barnard's Inn*, pp. 62, 66–67, 69–71.

82   Brooks and Lobban, 'Apprenticeship or Academy?'.

83   See Chapter 6, p. 154.

84   See, for examples, Anon., 'Legal Education', *Law Review*, 6 (1847), p. 234. 'It would not be more absurd, more laughable, for the landlord of the Spread Eagle or the Baldfaced Stag to hand the weary traveller a volume or two from his bookshelf, and bid him go to the butchers and bakers for a dinner, than it is for the Inns of Court to give only lodging and entertainment to students eager to learn the law, and bid them go elsewhere for teachers.'

85   Cocks, *Foundations of the Modern Bar*, ch. 1.

university.[86] The need to introduce more organised and 'liberal' education in order to raise prestige was, therefore, evidently less pressing than it had been for the attorneys. While there were those who wanted to reform legal education as a way of reforming the law, traditionalists argued that apprenticeship-type training centred on pupilage in chambers was the method best suited to the occupation. Some went so far as to say that professional success or failure were the only tests of how successfully a junior barrister had learned his trade. The circuit messes arguably provided a satisfactory means of protecting the interests of what remained in the early nineteenth century a relatively small profession, consisting of about 500 active practitioners.[87]

As Daniel Duman has shown, it was only with the coming of the railways and a three- to four-fold increase in the size of the bar that those advocating reforms began to make some progress, though these, too, were frequently frustrated, as had been the case for most of English history, by the heavy representation of the bar in parliament. Some provision for legal education and qualifying examinations were introduced at the inns of court between the 1850s and 1870s, but the loose and autonomous structures remained intact until the 1880s and 1890s when the success of the Law Society in winning work for the solicitors, and the bar's lack of an effective public voice, finally led to a very reluctant transformation. A voluntary organisation, the Bar Committee was established in 1883, to be replaced by the Bar Council in 1894. The Bar Council was and is a democratically constituted representative body of the entire bar, but it did not replace the inns of court in matters relating to the provision of legal education; nor has it yet led to the replacement of the call to the bar at one of the inns as the qualification for practice. In fact a consequence of nineteenth-century developments was that, for most of the twentieth century, it was probably more expensive and difficult to become qualified as a solicitor than as a barrister.[88]

To conclude, the major difference between the professional organisations created in the nineteenth century and those which were in place before 1700 is that the later ones were arguably more democratic in their organisation, insofar as members could choose to join, or not join, a law society and participate in its activities. Secondly, although the rise of organisations like the Law Society, and its successful bid to control admissions to the profession, appears to have coincided with a willingness by the judiciary (and hence the state) to give up the regulation of legal practice which they had exercised

---

[86] Daniel Duman, *The English and Colonial Bars in the Nineteenth Century* (Buckingham, 1983), p. 24, estimates that the percentage of university entrants to the inns of court increased from about 41 per cent in 1785 to 58 per cent in 1835, and 70 per cent in 1885.

[87] Ibid., pp. 6–8. The size of the active bar, as opposed to those who merely received the 'call', is difficult to determine with precision. Duman calculated that in 1835 the number of active practitioners was between 450 and 1010, whereas in 1885 there was a minimum of about 660 and a maximum of 1450. By this calculation the size of the bar in relation to population was dropping.

[88] Ibid., especially ch. 3.

for centuries, the change was in some respects more apparent than real. The organisations of the early nineteenth century were established to confront what appeared to the lawyers to be a deluge of legislative changes in legal practice, which they only rarely felt confident about being able to keep at bay. In this respect, the legal professions differed little from other occupations for which the same three centuries had seen a transition from oligarchic guild organisations to either trade unions or other types of pressure group.

In terms of the *esprit de corps* of the practitioners and the protection offered to the public, there is little to choose between the two phases of professionalisation, the one before 1700 and the other after about 1820. Thanks, for example, to the existence of the notorious court of Star Chamber, it was arguably easier to get relief from incidents of malpractice before 1640 than it was afterwards. It is possible to produce examples of lawyers who were punished for professional misconduct in the pre-modern era. That modern organisations did not prevent it is proven by the fact that a president of the Law Society was prosecuted at the end of the nineteenth century for a fraud involving thousands of pounds.[89]

The path to modern professionalism was hardly clear cut. It was fraught with doubts, idealism, obstinacy, self-interest and controversy. A consequence of the degeneration of the legal inns in the eighteenth century was that these institutions did little to support, and a good deal to hinder, the cause in the nineteenth century. Because of the unique separation of legal education in England from the universities, the decline in the intellectual life of the legal inns in the late seventeenth and eighteenth centuries was particularly deleterious; it had an influence well into the twentieth century. When attempts were made in the mid nineteenth century to reform legal education, the country had gone for well over one hundred years with only a few major contributions from jurisprudence to intellectual, social or political life. It appears to have been much more difficult to argue convincingly in the nineteenth than in the seventeenth century for the value of the academic and theoretical, as opposed to the purely vocational, study of law. Legal science, especially in an age when there were ready competitors in the form of medical and scientific discourse, was not well placed to convince either its practitioners or the public at large that it deserved a special role in society.[90]

---

[89] Sugarman, 'Bourgeois Collectivism, Professional Power and the Boundaries of the State', p. 110.

[90] See Chapter 6, pp. 176ff.

6

Apprenticeship and Legal Training in England, 1700–1850

The history of legal training between roughly 1700 and 1850 is clear enough in its broadest outlines.[1] There was a gradual evolution from apprenticeship, and a low level of institutional provision or regulation, towards more rigorous supervision and, eventually, the creation of more formal 'educational' structures such as lectures and written examinations. The story has often been told to illustrate a progressive 'professionalisation' of the lawyers, in which bad practices were replaced by good ones; in the mid nineteenth century it was already being characterised as part of the transformation of Britain from an ancien régime into a distinctly modern society.[2]

On closer inspection, however, the picture becomes both less simple and a good deal more difficult to interpret. Recent research on the history of lawyers from the high middle ages through to the end of the seventeenth century has shown that legal training was already highly developed before 1700, while it is evident that apprenticeship continued to feature as a persistent element in the process well into the twentieth century. The time is ripe, therefore, for a fresh look at the intervening period. This chapter attempts a provisional reconstruction of the practice of apprenticeship in the eighteenth century, then moves on to examine aspects of the campaign which was mounted against it in the nineteenth. In this light, the eighteenth century emerges as a period of institutional decline and change, while the nineteenth can be seen as one in which there was revival, but also one in which much, most notably apprenticeship, remained the same.

For many centuries before 1700 legal training had revolved around two powerful traditions, one vocational, the other more self-consciously liberal and academic. Clerkship, which amounted to apprenticeship in almost everything but name, had been for centuries the method by which young men trained for and entered the branch of the profession, that of the attorneys

---

[1] This chapter was written originally as a paper for a conference on apprenticeship and skills training which was held in 1994 at King's College, Cambridge.

[2] A. H. Manchester, *A Modern Legal History of England and Wales, 1750–1950* (London, 1980), pp. 50–60, 65–66; Robert Robson, *The Attorney in Eighteenth-Century England* (Cambridge, 1959), pp. 149, 154; Sir George Stephen, *Adventures of an Attorney in Search of Practice* (London, 1839), pp. 192–93; Samuel Warren, *A Popular and Practical Introduction to Law Studies* (London, 1835), p. 10.

and solicitors, which dealt most immediately with clients and specialised in the procedural aspects of litigation.[3] On the other hand, while English common law, as opposed to the civil (Roman) and canon law, was not taught as a degree subject at the universities until the later nineteenth century, the inns of court in London had since the middle ages provided an institutional setting and some formal instruction in the form of lectures and moots for those intending to practise as barristers – the lawyers who pleaded before the royal courts and from whom the judiciary were selected.[4]

The differences in the training undertaken by the two groups of lawyers were accompanied by a species of intellectual and social conflict which will be familiar to any student of apprenticeship. Drawing heavily on classical antecedents and humanist approaches to jurisprudence, the inns of court and the bar claimed that theirs was a scientific subject which involved 'liberal' learning. By contrast, the attorneys were often described as merely 'mechanical' practitioners of a distinctly lower social and political status. One of the main reasons for this was that, while the training of barristers involved academic forms of teaching and private study, the attorneys learned their trade through apprenticeship, the standard preparation for most occupations in the early modern period. Practising attorneys were on these grounds expelled from the inns of court during the second half of the sixteenth century, with the result that between about 1580 and 1680 the 'lower branch' became concentrated in the lesser inns in London, the inns of chancery.[5]

Given this background, eighteenth-century developments in legal education are particularly striking. The teaching and communal functions of the legal inns collapsed. Forms of apprenticeship, articled clerkship and pupilage in barristers' chambers, became paramount in the training of both branches of the profession. These changes had a significant impact on the common law as an intellectual discipline, and, partly for this reason, the tradition of vocational education established by the second half of the eighteenth century made it tenaciously resistant to calls for reform in a more academic direction during the early nineteenth. Today, although legal education is firmly established in the universities, it is arguable that the intellectual content of legal study has changed little since the early nineteenth century when apprenticeship was still supreme.

The critical factors affecting legal education during the first half of the eighteenth century were the atrophy of the learning exercises at the inns

---

[3] C. W. Brooks, *Pettyfoggers and Vipers of the Commonwealth: The 'Lower Branch' of the Legal Profession in Early Modern England* (Cambridge, 1986), ch. 8.

[4] See Paul Brand, *The Origins of the English Legal Profession* (Oxford, 1992); J. H. Baker, *The Third University of England: The Inns of Court and the Common Law Tradition*, Selden Society Lecture (London, 1990); S. E. Thorne and J. H. Baker, eds, *Readings and Moots at the Inns of Court in the Fifteenth Century*, ii, *Moots and Reader's Cases*, Selden Society, 105 (London, 1990); W. R. Prest, *The Inns of Court under Elizabeth and the Early Stuarts* (London, 1972).

[5] Brooks, *Pettyfoggers and Vipers*, chs 6–8; see also, Chapter 5, p. 131.

of court; a severe contraction in the market for legal services which reached a nadir in 1750; and the avariciousness of the British state, which gave shape to new legislation affecting the apprenticeship of attorneys and solicitors.

The reasons for the decline of the learning exercises, which were effectively defunct by the end of the 1670s, were complex but need not detain us for long. A system of training which depended on practising lawyers giving up time to perform teaching functions was perhaps inherently fragile, and the disruptions of the mid seventeenth-century Civil War, followed by years in which a politically manipulated judiciary failed to give a firm lead, dealt blows from which it was never to recover. At the same time, the increasing authority of judicial decision-making, compounded by the wider availability of printed reports, arguably rendered the old oral exercises less useful.[6]

Although study for the bar had always been arduous and largely unsupervised, these changes meant that by the second decade of the eighteenth century there was hardly any formal teaching, nor any prescribed guidelines about what constituted a sufficient level of skill for the call to the bar and hence audience before the courts. The formal requirements were admission to one of the inns of court and the consumption of a specified number of meals.[7] As one author put it in 1804, the legal inns had become 'mere refectories' which no one any longer associated seriously with education.[8] The English bar was becoming the only profession in the western world where the practitioners did not have to undergo any formal training at all.

Nevertheless, although there were contemporary criticisms of the lack of better education for the bar, some alternatives had already emerged by the second third of the eighteenth century. First and most important was independent study. The prospective barrister was supposed to gain an understanding of the ancient foundations of the common law and then follow this up by reading modern reported case law and observing trials in the royal courts. Secondly, it was evidently fairly common for young students to form themselves into 'evening societies' which met in a tavern to have dinner followed by a presentation by one of them of a case recently heard at Westminster Hall.[9] Thirdly, prospective barristers might be placed in the

---

[6] J. H. Baker, 'The Inns of Court and Legal Doctrine', in *Lawyers and Laymen. Studies in the History of Law Presented to Professor Dafydd Jenkins*, ed. T. M. Charles-Edwards, M. E. Owen and D. B. Walters (Cardiff, 1986).

[7] *The Diary of Dudley Ryder, 1715–1716*, ed. William Matthews (London, 1939), pp. 30, 91, 180, 184, 192, 219, and elsewhere, gives a good account of one student's experiences in the early eighteenth century. Ryder eventually became a judge.

[8] Richard Whalley Bridgman, *Reflections on the Study of the Law in Two Parts: Addressed First to the Nobility and Gentry, as the Hereditary and Elective Senators of the Nation, and Secondly to Those Gentlemen who Propose to Study the Law with a View to Professional Practice* (London, 1804), pp. 1–8.

[9] [Joseph Simpson], *Reflections on the Natural and Acquired Endowments Requisite for the Study of the Law by a Barrister at Law* (London, 1764), pp. 48–49, lamented the decline of mooting at the legal inns and recommended that students form themselves into informal groups for private study. Evening societies are known to have been quite popular. See Chapter 5, pp. 134–35.

office of an attorney for a few years; essentially undertaking a kind of apprenticeship. Although this method broke decisively with the traditional Renaissance distinction between mechanical and scientific learning, it gained considerable credibility in the first half of the eighteenth century, not least because Philip Yorke (Lord Chancellor Hardwicke between 1737 and 1756), and several other leading lawyers of the time, had begun their careers in precisely this way.[10] Writing in 1734, for example, the attorney and well-known legal publicist Giles Jacob seems to have summed up conventional wisdom when he lamented the lack of any clear guidance for those studying for the bar. Acknowledging the importance of a smattering of liberal education, perhaps gathered from a couple of years at university, he stressed the value of a clerkship with an attorney for three to five years. Indeed, in his view, some of the older attorneys knew a great deal more about the common law than many a counsellor.[11]

From the point of view of the student, not to mention that of his parents, the emergence of this form of training had a number of practical benefits. Some writers compared clerkship favourably with what they supposed went on in the universities, where freedom from supervision and peer-group pressure might lead the student down the paths of pleasure and dissipation.[12] Clerkship to a seasoned practitioner, on the other hand, kept the student out of trouble. In this respect, it was arguably a better preparation for the 'severe and laborious' study that was necessary in order to master the common law than all the extensive learning of polite literature.[13] At the same time, in a period when legal business, as measured by the amount of litigation in the courts, was declining to less than one-third of the levels of the later seventeenth century, clerkship had professional as well as pedagogic benefits. Even amongst the successful, many eighteenth-century barristers went for long periods without any work. Since it was already common practice for counsel to be briefed by attorneys rather than approached directly by clients, the formation of an early alliance with a practitioner in the lower branch was a potentially astute career move.[14]

Service in the office of an attorney undoubtedly had real advantages as a

[10] John Cooksey, *Essay on the Life and Character of John Lord Somers, Baron of Evesham: Also Sketches of an Essay on the Life and Character of Philip Earl of Hardwicke Proposed to be Inserted in a Compendious History of Worcestershire* (London, 1791), pp. 54, 71. Others mentioned are Lord Chief Baron Parker and Sir John Strange. Another example was Lloyd Kenyon (1732–1802), later lord chief justice, who was articled to a Nantwich solicitor in 1749, see below, p. 160.

[11] Giles Jacob, *The Student's Companion: or The Reason of the Laws of England* (London, 1734), pp. iii–iv.

[12] For the exodus of the gentry from the universities in the century after 1660 see L. Stone, 'The Size and Composition of the Oxford Student Body, 1580–1906', in idem, ed., *The University in Society* (2 vols, Princeton, 1975), i, pp. 6–29.

[13] [Simpson], *Reflections on the Natural and Acquired Endowments*, pp. 18–19.

[14] [Thomas Ruggle], *The Barrister: or Strictures on the Education Proper for the Bar* (2 vols, London, 1792), i, pp. 17–18. This work originally appeared as separate articles in *The World* during 1791.

way of getting to grips with a discipline which was notoriously deficient in abstract principles and which had not received an authoritative general treatment since the days of Sir Edward Coke in the first decades of the seventeenth century.[15] Attorneys were specialists in court procedure, a very technical and particularist body of knowledge, which was undoubtedly more easily mastered by practice and experience than by reading. They were also the lawyers who needed to know which of the different forms of action, the essentially pragmatic set of remedies which formed the essence of common law learning, applied in any given circumstance. Finally, in the first half of the century, their offices were the place to master the art of special pleading. Universally described as arcane, unpleasant and extremely difficult to learn, special pleading involved casting the particular circumstances of a case carefully within the parameters of the law relating to an issue so that as little as possible remained to be decided by the judges. Small slips could result in a non-suit; hence special pleading involved many hours of expert labour and many sheets of incomprehensible paper, all of which, according to contemporary critics, added to the costs and confusion of going to law.[16]

By the middle of the eighteenth century, although critics continued to lament the lack of general principles and effective guidance for students, it is arguable that the common law as a craft and the training of barristers through a form of informal apprenticeship had reached a happily symbiotic relationship. Yet it was at precisely this point that a controversy emerged about the nature of law and legal education which was to continue with greater or lesser degrees of intensity throughout the remainder of the period and beyond. In his famous *Commentaries on the Laws of England*, which had originally been given as the Vinerian lectures at Oxford University in the 1750s, William Blackstone launched a blistering attack on the practice of training barristers in the offices of attorneys. In a work which attempted to describe the common law in terms of comprehensible jurisprudential principles, Blackstone argued that a man so educated could only ever master the practicalities of the law; consequently, it would be nearly impossible for him to achieve a more general understanding. If the student were 'uninstructed in the elements and first principles upon which the rule of practice is founded, the least variation from established precedents will totally distract and bewilder him'. Not surprisingly, he favoured a return to more academic forms of training.[17]

Blackstone effectively joined together questions about legal education with broader issues about the nature of English law; the two remained closely

---

[15] Although it should be noted that there was a significant amount of professional legal publishing in the eighteenth century: see Michael Lobban, 'The English Legal Treatise and English Law in the Eighteenth Century', in *Auctoritates: Law Making and its Authors*, eds, S. Dauchy, J. Monballyu and A. Wijffels (Brussels 1997), pp. 69–88.

[16] For the work of attorneys see Brooks, *Pettyfoggers and Vipers*, chs 2, 3, 9.

[17] William Blackstone, *Commentaries on the Laws of England* (4 vols, Oxford, 1765–69), i, p. 32.

connected in ensuing debates about reform. Although some of his arguments were later supported by the philosopher Jeremy Bentham, they by no means carried the day, especially within the legal profession. In 1783, for example, John Reeves' *History of English Law* countered Blackstone by explicitly denying that the common law was a set of general rules. Instead, he described it as a process for resolving disputes best understood in precisely those terms which were learned though clerkship: the forms of action and procedure.[18] If, as seems likely, it was Reeves rather than Blackstone who more accurately represented opinion within the profession, it is hardly surprising that there was no radical reform of legal education. During the second half of the century, work in an attorney's office came to be replaced, or accompanied by, pupilage in chambers to a barrister or a special pleader. In this respect the bar to some degree avoided its association with the mechanical branch of the profession, but a consequence was that what was universally recognised as the narrowest and most arcane branch of common law learning became entrenched as the cornerstone of legal education. On this basis, the role of apprenticeship had become sufficiently well established for it to be sturdily resistant to demands for change, first in the 1790s and then during most of the first half of the nineteenth century.

Because they were informal, relatively little is known about the detailed arrangements associated with training for the bar in the eighteenth century. We get an impressionistic taste from the 1710s in the well-known story that Philip Yorke, the future lord chancellor, was annoyed at having to do household errands for the wife of his master.[19] By the end of the century, on the other hand, students normally lived out in digs, attending at the offices of their masters between the hours of nine and five. While it is clear that pupilage could be expensive (a fee of between 100 and 300 guineas for three years), some masters were recognised as particularly successful teachers.[20] There is, however, no documentary evidence about the process, because there was no attempt to validate or test the qualifications of students before they were called to the bar. As late as the mid nineteenth century, it was widely held in the profession that examinations or other tests of competence were unnecessary because the market effectively determined whether a barrister was well qualified or not. If he was any good, solicitors would bring him business; if he was not, he did nobody any harm because he would not get any work.[21]

Within the lower branch of the profession, amongst the attorneys and

---

[18] See for this M. Lobban, *The Common Law and English Jurisprudence, 1760–1850* (Oxford, 1991), especially pp. 50–54, 121; John Reeves, *History of English Law from the Time of the Saxons to the End of the Reign of Philip and Mary* (2nd ed., 4 vols, Dublin, 1787).

[19] Cooksey, *Essay on the Life and Character*, p. 71.

[20] [Ruggle], *The Barrister*, ii, p. 99; [John Raithby], *The Study and Practice of the Law Considered in Their Various Relations to Society: In a Series of Letters. By a Member of Lincoln's Inn* (London, 1798), pp. 378–87; *Legal Observer and Journal of Jurisprudence*, 35 (1847–48), pp. 257.

[21] Daniel Duman, *The English and Colonial Bars in the Nineteenth Century* (London, 1983), ch. 3.

solicitors, on the other hand, the early eighteenth century was notable for the passage of legislation concerning the qualifications of those admitted to practice. Although this led to the production of documentary evidence which is of great value to the historian, it seems on balance to have done surprisingly little to change the nature of quality of training. The most important of the statutes concerned, which became law in 1729, reiterated the traditional responsibility of the common law judges for examining the competence of candidates, but introduced a novel requirement that those wishing to enrol as attorneys should present written articles as proof of having served a five-year clerkship.[22] Although this measure has frequently been seen as an innovation, service indistinguishable from articled clerkship had in fact been commonplace in the later sixteenth century, if not long before. Documentary evidence of the written articles themselves, which differ little in form or substance from those in use after 1730, exists from as early as the 1680s; and large numbers of clerks from before 1730 are recorded as having paid the stamp duty on apprenticeship which the government introduced in 1711 to help finance foreign wars.[23]

Judging from the scanty information provided by the parliamentary record, the 1729 Attorney Act was to a degree connected with public concerns about the quality of legal services, but there were also a number of professional and fiscal considerations which in effect meant that the statute had more to do with using formal proof of apprenticeship as a way of collecting government revenue in the form of stamp duties than with reforming legal training. The lawyers themselves were fearful at this time that too many men were chasing too little work, a concern which emerged quite explicitly in 1749, when further legislation along these lines was pending before parliament.[24] No less important, the early eighteenth-century decline in litigation was accompanied by a transformation in the geographical structure of the profession. Country attorneys began the practice of using London agents to transact central court business for them, and consequently ceased coming to London on a regular basis.[25] Admissions to the inns of chancery plummeted, and contemporaries also noticed an increased tendency for practitioners who had not been formally enrolled in the courts to carry out business in them by using the names of those who were. Last, but hardly least, the government was aware that legal practitioners had been avoiding the payment of stamps on the oath administered to attorneys, by using a technical loophole, entering practice by becoming clerks to the prothonotaries of the courts rather than

[22] 2 George II, c. 23, 'An Act for the Better Regulation of Attorneys and Solicitors'.
[23] Brooks, *Pettyfoggers and Vipers*, pp. 137, 139–40, 143–45, 151–58; idem, *The Admissions Registers of Barnard's Inn, 1620–1869*, Selden Society supplementary series, 12 (London, 1995), pp. 37, 43. The tax on apprenticeship premiums was introduced by 8 Anne, c. 9 (1709). The rate was 6d. in the pound for premiums under £50 and 12d. in the pound for those over £50.
[24] For the details, see Chapter 4, p. 96.
[25] Chapter 4, pp. 93–94.

sworn attorneys.[26] Equally, since formal articles of clerkship were not necessary in order to become qualified as an attorney before 1730, many parents and masters undoubtedly neglected to pay the quite considerable stamp taxes which wcrc supposed to due on them.[27]

While many practitioners may well have welcomed those aspects of the act which inhibited increases in the size of the profession, the operation of the 1729 Attorney Act, and the legislation which followed in its wake, was always more concerned with the presentation of fully-taxed articles of clerkship than with a detailed examination of the levels of training provided or the skills achieved; a point underlined by the fact that a flat rate duty of £100 on all articles was introduced in 1794.[28] In the 1730s and 1740s, it was sufficient for the clerk seeking admission to take his articles to a judge in Serjeant's Inn, who would then sign a fiat authorising his admission.[29] Under further legislation passed in 1749, designed to prevent frauds arising from the back-dating of indentures, the contract itself became less important than sworn affidavits, signed by the master, clerk and witnesses, that the articles had indeed been entered into on the date specified.[30] It is true, of

---

[26] There is some discussion of the parliamentary debate in Chapter 3, pp. 44–45. The government and parliament had been concerned about evasions of the stamp taxes by attorneys since the very early years of the century. T. Vardon and T. E. May, *Journals of the House of Commons* (17 vols, London, 1803ff), xiii, pp. 461, 464, 478, 469, bills for 'lessening the number' of attorneys and solicitors; xv, pp. 569, 580, 583, 593, 618, 619, 641, 642, for a draft act 'For Redressing and Preventing Several Frauds and Practices, Relating to Her Majesty's Duties upon Stampt Vellum, Parchment, and Paper, and Reducing the Number of Attorneys and Solicitors Practising in the Courts at Westminster', which was proposed in 1707; xvi, pp. 27, 74, 98, 120, 157, 167, 198, 205, 572, for further unsuccessful efforts to pass the bill in 1711.

[27] Brooks, *Admissions Registers of Barnard's Inn*, pp. 42–49.

[28] 34 George III, c. 14. The anonymous compiler of *A Treatise on the Study of the Law: Containing Directions to Students. Written by those Celebrated Lawyers, Orators and Statesmen, the Lords Mansfield, Ashburton and Thurlow* (1797), pp. v–vi, commented sarcastically that there had been a time when no one could be admitted an attorney without satisfying a judge that he was competent, 'but the way in which it has been lately judged expedient to supersede the necessity of that labourious enquiry, is to call on each individual to shew his fitness for the station he proposes to fill, by paying the revenue £100 ... Making the possession of wealth evidence of sense and virtue, is a policy that will destroy both'. See also Joseph Day, *Thoughts on the Necessity and Utility of the Examination Directed by Several Acts of Parliament, Previous to the Admission of Attorneys at Law and Solicitors: Together with Some Observations on the Constitution and Regulation of the Society of Clerks to His Majesty's Signet in Scotland ... the Whole Applying to a Bill Proposed to be Brought into Parliament for the Incorporating and Better-Regulation of Attorneys at Law and Solicitors* (London, 1795), p. 10.

[29] Articles of clerkship and affidavits relating to their execution which were presented to the Court of Common Pleas survive in disorderly class in PRO, CP 5. However, the PRO has recently published a helpful new class list, and there is an alphabetical index to the clerks whose articles and affidavits survive. Articles of clerkship presented to the court of King's Bench were destroyed in the early twentieth century, but PRO, KB 111/2–4 contains some samples from first half of the nineteenth century which have survived 'by accident'.

[30] 22 George II, c. 46 (1749). Affidavits were to be entered within three months after the execution of the contract. As a result many bundles of PRO, CP 5 for the later eighteenth and early nineteenth centuries contain the affidavits rather than copies of articles themselves.

course, that the judges were responsible for conducting some form of examination, but Joseph Day, a knowledgeable (if prejudiced), writer of the 1790s, plausibly claimed that the judiciary had never had the inclination, let alone the time or expertise, to test the skill of prospective attorneys.[31] While these propositions are not subject to incontrovertible proof, it may be indicative that some of the fiats in the court archives were signed by justices' clerks rather than by the judges themselves. The one known first-person account of an admission, that of William Hickey in 1775, suggests that it was not normally a very rigorous process.[32]

Given the lack of a firm judicial guide in shaping it, the content and experience of articled clerkship in the eighteenth century was probably determined primarily by long-standing customs within the profession, as well as by the particular circumstances of the clerk and master. The articles themselves contain a number of shared provisions which remained very little changed right up until 1850, but there is also variety in some of the detailed arrangements. The formal language and purpose of the indentures indicate that articled clerkship had much in common with the culture of apprenticeship that had evolved in many urban occupations during the course of the early modern period.[33] As an option available for families anxious to provide a young man with the means of establishing an independent livelihood, it encouraged the careful selection of career objectives for individual children. It could also involve the outlay of a considerable capital sum of money in the form of the premium paid to the master, but in return for this the master undertook responsibilities for the training and upkeep of the youth.[34] According to the Anglican writer Thomas Gisborne, who purveyed old- fashioned advice to the new middle classes in the 1790s,

---

[31] Day, *Thoughts on the Necessity*, pp. 6–7. One of Day's points was that the examination of the character of articled clerks was bound to lead to 'indelicacies', which would be much easier for a committee to deal with than for an individual judge, who might find it distasteful.

[32] PRO, CP 5/44/3. Hickey's account is printed in Robson, *The Attorney*, pp. 150–61. Hickey's father had arranged for him to be examined by a friend of his, Justice Yates. Hickey had breakfast with Yates while the judge's clerk dealt with the paperwork. To Hickey's own astonishment, the questioning extended no further than polite inquiries about whether or not he 'liked the law'.

[33] See Christopher Brooks, 'Apprenticeship, Social Mobility and the Middling Sort, 1550–1800', in J. Barry and C. Brooks, eds, *The Middling Sort of People: Culture, Society and Politics in England, 1550–1800* (Basingstoke, 1994), pp. 52–81.

[34] R. Campbell, *The London Tradesman: Being a Compendious View of All Trades, Professions, Arts, Both Liberal and Mechanic ... Calculated for the Information of Parents, and Instruction of Youth in their Choice of Business* (London, 1747), pp. 70–71, 331, suggested that the prospective attorney 'must not be born a Blockhead'. The difficulties of the law meant that it was necessary to possess a clear head, great patience and a prodigious memory. The preparatory education should be 'liberal', not only as a qualification for the profession but to enlarge the mind and give it a bias above 'pettifogging Practice'. Latin was no longer as necessary as it had been before now that legal proceedings were in English. The loving parent should seek out a master of known integrity and good practice. Anywhere from £100 to £1000 was necessary to set up in practice as a master at the end of the term.

attorneys were supposed to use moderation in the amount they charged for premiums and act with 'conscientious attention' in the 'professional instruction' they offered.[35]

Because there was relatively slack demand for entry into the profession in the years between 1730 and 1770,[36] premiums appear to have remained within a range of from £30, for articles with a Staffordshire practitioner, to £250 for those with an 'eminent' Londoner, to as much as £450 for places with the elite sworn clerks in the court of Chancery. These figures matched at the middling level those of other professional occupations, such as that of apothecary or surgeon; but while they were considerably higher than the average for all occupations, they were considerably lower than the premiums fetched by some of the more elite urban wholesaling and retailing trades.[37] Clerks originated from the professional classes, including the clergy, as well as the lesser gentry, yeomanry and more prosperous townsmen.[38] Even so, it is evident that the burden of finding lump sums of money on this scale could amount to a considerable undertaking. To give but one example, in 1711 William Davies's mother agreed to pay £100 in two instalments in order to article him to the Cambridgeshire practitioner Joshua Eversden; when Eversden died, only one year into the five-year term, the boy was extremely anxious to recover the money because, he said, it amounted to his entire inheritance.[39]

It is unclear exactly how far differences in the amount of the premium corresponded to differences in expectation about the potential earning power of the young clerk when he became enrolled and entered into a practice, a correlation which certainly existed in other trades. In law it was probably based more on the type of work associated with the master's practice, whether or not it was based in London, and maybe his reputation or 'eminence' in the profession, than on the anticipation of a partnership or the inheritance of the practice of the master. Nevertheless, while the range of premiums invited and reflected a spectrum of social backgrounds, even if they may in effect have set a ceiling on success, there were other advantages to the process in terms of the flexibility it offered. Trial periods were frequently used to test the compatibility of master and clerk before

[35] Thomas Gisborne, *An Enquiry into the Duties of Men in the Higher and Middle Classes of Society* (Dublin, 1795), pp. 197–98. For Gisborne see *Dictionary of National Biography*.

[36] See Chapter 7, pp. 184–85.

[37] PRO, IR 1, passim. For some comparisions see, Brooks, 'Apprenticeship, Social Mobility and the Middling Sort', pp. 65–69.

[38] PRO, IR 1, and Michael Miles, 'Eminent Attorneys: Some Aspects of West Riding Attorneyship, *c.* 1750–1800' (unpublished Ph.D. thesis, University of Birmingham, 1982), pp. 46–51, describes 61 per cent of entrants from 1709–1792 as being from the 'lesser gentry' with another 34 per cent from the 'middling sort'. There was, of course, much blurring between these two social groups.

[39] PRO, C 104/6, papers of Joshua Eversden. I am grateful to Henry Horwitz for this reference.

articles were signed and premiums handed over.[40] There are also a number of instances where an attorney waived a premium and agreed to articles on the basis of the 'love and affection' he had for the boy concerned or his kin.[41] Although the observation is impressionistic, in the middle of the eighteenth century there appear to have been a large number of instances where sons became articled to their fathers, a trend which is evident in other occupations at the time. Reflecting a general caution in the selection of careers during this period, it may point to a perception that a young man was likely to stand a better chance in an occupation in which his father was already established then in trying out a new and unknown one, where there would in addition be premiums and stamp duties to pay.[42]

Of all the variables revealed in surviving articles, the standard of education was the one that appears in formal terms to have been least open to negotiation. Regardless of the premium involved, nearly all indentures contained a promise from the master which used some or all of the words 'teach', 'instruct' or 'educate' in the 'the profession of the law' or the 'practice of an attorney', although most also specified that the instruction would fall within specific courts or other lines of work, such as conveyancing, normally pursued by the master. More surprisingly, nearly all masters undertook to have the clerk enrolled as an attorney in the court or courts concerned at the end of the term. Only a few expressed the caution found in the articles of Henry Barnes Jr to his father in 1748, where Henry Barnes Sr promised to have his son admitted only if he became 'duly qualified for that purpose and shall desire to do the same'.[43] The reason was probably that this liability was unlikely to have extended further than an obligation on the master to affirm the existence and completion of articles when the time came for their presentation to the courts.[44] While masters could be brought before officials of the courts, or indeed the judges themselves, if they were accused of gross negligence or maltreatment, there was no precise measure of the quality of instruction which could distinguish the incompetent from the mediocre, let alone the good. The only clear-cut test of the sufficiency of the training offered was the crude one of whether or not the master had some work as

[40] [John Fobton], *Friendly Hints to Young Gentlemen Who Are or Intend to be Bound by Articles to Attorneys and Solicitors* (4th edn, London, 1758), pp. A1–2, warned that many 'inconveniencies have been suffered by young Gentlemen bound Clerks' through defective articles and suggested that one of the problems was that trial periods, which were sometimes quite lengthy, were often used to test the compatibility of master and clerk, but unless articles were sealed at the beginning of this period, the time would not count towards qualification.

[41] For example, PRO, CP 5/13/8; CP 5/44/12.

[42] Brooks, 'Apprenticeship, Social Mobility and the Middling Sort', pp. 71–72. Miles, 'Eminent Attorneys', p. 62, notes that almost every West Riding attorney trained one of his sons in the business.

[43] PRO, CP 5/44/4.

[44] This obligation is no doubt related to the fact that one of the traditional complaints by apprentices against masters in all kinds of trades was that they had failed to present them for the 'freedom' of their town or guild at the completion of their terms.

an attorney or solicitor; if he did not, then he clearly could not instruct.[45] There is at least one instance from the mid eighteenth century of a clerk being 'turned over' from one master to another for this reason. It is also worth noting that the stress on practical training effectively ruled out professional teachers.[46]

While the surviving direct evidence about how the obligation to teach and instruct was discussed or carried out in practice is fragmentary, there seems little doubt that clerkship was expected to be arduous. The basic ingredients included the drudgery of copying out documents and running errands, punctuated by time spent reading some of the many printed guides to practice as well as more general works. It was probably common for clerks to keep records of their reading, as well as their practical activities, so that these could be checked by the master.[47] In a letter written in 1750, the future judge Lloyd Kenyon, who began his career as an articled clerk to a Nantwich attorney, envied the amount of leisure which he supposed was enjoyed by one of his cousins, who was at the time an undergraduate at Brasenose College, Oxford. According to Kenyon, clerks in his office did not have

> that servile fear ... which scholars so often are curbed by; but then we can very seldom escape out of this cursed office, Sunday excepted, nor is that always a day of rest ... The law is surely the most irksome and crabbed study of all other ... We are to have another new clerk who is above twenty-two

[45] *English Reports*, xciv, 1 Barnardiston, King's Bench 331 (1730) and 2 Barnardiston, King's Bench 227 (1732) for rules of court which ordered the repayment of premiums after complaints by clerks against their masters, most notably in cases where there had been a collapse of the master's business.

[46] PRO, CP 5/44/28, Robert Randle of Stamford, Lincolnshire, to Thomas Benson in 1759. There was no premium paid, and Randle served Benson except for a period when Benson 'had not full Employment for this Deponent in the Business or Practice of an attorney'. 22 George III, c. 46 (1749) made explicit provisions for clerks who served with masters who had died or fallen out of business and resolved doubts which had apparently arisen about whether clerks could be 'turned over' in such circumstances. W. Freshfield, *The Records of the Society of Gentlemen Practisers* (London, 1897), pp. 11, 17–21, 23, 80–81, 120–21, 129–30, 147–49, 166, 169, 177, 179, 181, 214, 226–28, 329, shows that the London society occasionally took action to prevent clerks from being enrolled, but they invariably did so because of some technical defect in the articles or because of some previous misdemeanour by the practitioner concerned rather than because of any shortcoming in training. It appears from a complicated case of 1798 (*English Reports*, ci: 7 Term Reports 456) that the courts were at that date reluctant to rule against clerks on the basis of technical irregularities.

[47] None of the guide books for would-be practitioners denies the drudgery. Robson, *The Attorney*, pp. 155–58, describes the activities of two Sheffield articled clerks of the early eighteenth century on the basis of their 'day-books', the record they were supposed to keep of work done. Guildhall Library, London, MS 9909, a pocket notebook which records the business done by John Towse during his service to William Hippisley of Fishmonger's Hall between 1759 and 1763, indicates that he normally worked six days a week. He attended clients and escorted them to court; he visited legal offices around London to see that work was going forward; he frequently handled significant sums of money. The business is precisely detailed and written in a neat and careful hand.

years of age; but I think if we were a thousand, our good master would not let us be idle.[48]

The written articles indicate that the kind of regime Kenyon described was usually enforced by a number of specific provisions. Most forbade clerks from undertaking any work for their own profit, but it was not uncommon to allow a 'term fee' of 20s. or so, which rewarded labour and could be used to ensure that the clerk demeaned himself 'diligently in the Service'.[49] Two west country indentures of the 1730s went further than this and anticipated that the young men concerned might practise in local courts before they were enrolled in those at Westminster. Country masters sometimes undertook to provide horses and travelling expenses for clerks who were engaged in business.[50] Most importantly of all, in an age which saw the decentralisation of the lower branch, several provincial indentures from the period before 1750 acknowledged the traditional value of personal attendance at the courts at Westminster by making provision for clerks from the provinces to spend time in London; and some were even 'turned over' for a year to a practitioner in the capital.[51] It is notable, however, that the indenture of Christopher Incledon of Barnstable, which was signed in 1735, specified merely that he could go to London 'if he wished' and 'at his own expense' if he thought it would be useful to furthering his knowledge. Possibly the practice declined during the middle decades of the eighteenth century before making a recovery in the 1780s and 1790s.[52] Hence, the quality of training in the

[48] George T. Kenyon, *The Life of Lloyd, First Lord Kenyon* (London, 1873), p. 12. J. Kendrick's reply began 'It is true, as you observe, that we in college here are not absolutely obliged to pursue our studies, but then there are so many restraints laid upon us, that they almost put it out of our power to avoid it'. He then went on to describe the work he was doing at the university. *Historical Manuscripts Commission*, Fourteenth Report, appendix, part 4, *The Manuscripts of Lord Kenyon* (London, 1894), p. 492.

[49] PRO, CP 5/13/24, 27; CP 5/44/2.

[50] PRO, CP 5/13/26; CP 5/44/6. The extent to which enrolment under the 1729 act affected the right to practise in local courts appears frequently to have been questioned. See, for example, *The Law of Attornies and Solicitors: Containing All the Statutes, Adjudged Cases, Resolutions and Judgments Concerning Them* (London, 1764), pp 59. 22 George II, c. 46 (1749) explicitly limited the right to practise in local courts to those enrolled in the central courts, thus presumably making illegal provisions such as those in the earlier articles.

[51] PRO, CP 5/13/22 (1733), where the master was an attorney of the Palatinate Courts at Durham. CP 5/13/26, articles to an attorney of Somerset, who would allow his clerk to go to London for a year, if the clerk 'shall be desireous and willing to attend his Majestys Court at Westminster'.

[52] PRO, CP 5/44/6. It should be pointed out that this hypothesis is difficult to test thoroughly because many more indentures survive for the earlier than for the later part of the century. The point about the 1790s is suggested by a rule of court from 1791 'That from and after the last day of Michaelmas Term, no person who shall enter into articles with an attorney or attorneys, shall be [at] liberty to serve the agent or agents of such attorney or attroneys, under such articles, for longer time than one year of his clerkship; and that any such service to an agent or agents beyond that time shall not be deemed good service'. Robert Maugham, *A Complete Collection of the Statutes, and Rules and Orders of Court, Relating to Attorneys, Solicitors, and Agents: From the Earliest to the Present Times* (London, 1839), p. 118.

provinces was dependant largely on the abilities of the master and the application of the student. Many clerks may have had little opportunity to sharpen up their expertise by contact with the courts which were actually making the law. By the 1790s the alleged ignorance of country practitioners lent ammunition to those who were critical of professional training.[53]

As was the case with other preindustrial occupations, so too with articled clerks: the settlement of domestic arrangements and the articulation of the master-servant relationship was as important an aspect of the process as technical education. Within the traditional culture of apprenticeship, the development of character and moral qualities were significant considerations. Yet in law, as in other occupations, this may have been precisely the area in which there was greatest change.[54] In London, especially, there was an unmistakable progression during the course of the eighteenth century from the practice of having clerks live within the household of their master to that in which they resided in digs and worked specified office hours.[55] Articles from the 1730s, 1740s and 1750s characteristically lay it down that masters should provide 'meat', 'drink', 'lodging' and 'washing' (sometimes) with the specific proviso that parents should buy clothing and cover medical expenses, presumably because these were the most likely causes of disagreements between the parties. By the end of the century, on the other hand, parents were much more likely to take responsibility for housing and living expenses.[56] This added significantly to the costs of launching a legal career. According to Thomas Gisborne, at least, it was also fraught with moral pitfalls: articled clerks 'placed in lodging houses, and left without control or superintendence as to the employment of their time when out of office' were likely to plunge into every kind of vice.[57]

It is very difficult to say whether the residential clerkship of the early eighteenth century provided more effective moral invigilation and instruction than the less domestic environment of the later period. Living out was probably always more common in London than in the provinces. It may be that individual personalities played a much more significant role than formal regulations or general cultural trends. Compared to indentures for other trades, early eighteenth-century articles are unusual in that they do not normally contain the common formulae which obliged the apprentice to abstain from fornication, marriage or the alehouse.[58] Instead they were more

---

[53] John Fobton's 1758 edition of *Friendly Hints to Young Gentlemen*, p. 4, comments that young attorneys just out of articles rarely had 'a stock of knowledge more than is barely sufficient to entitle them to their admissions'. Unless they added to this by application and experience, they were not likely to be much good.

[54] Brooks, 'Apprenticeship, Social Mobility and the Middling Sort', pp. 73–83.

[55] PRO, CP 5/148/49 is, for example a set of Somerset articles, dated 1808, which specify office hours as 9 a.m. to 2 p.m. and 3 p.m. to 5 p.m.

[56] PRO, CP 5, passim.

[57] Gisborne, *An Enquiry*, pp. 197–98.

[58] Such provisions could, however, be included in individual cases. For example, in PRO, CP

likely to specify that the clerk should undertake not to pass on the secrets, or lose or deface the writings, of his master or of his master's clients. A number of articles required parents to enter into a bond with the master to indemnify against losses of this kind, including embezzlement, while it was more or less standard practice to include a clause which forbade the clerk from leaving his employment without the permission of his master.[59]

Some indentures continued to reflect the patriarchal relationship between master and clerk which characterised traditional forms of apprenticeship. Many clerks promised to behave 'as a good and faithful clerk and apprentice' and to obey the master and live quietly in his family; but it was rare for articles to be as specific as those of a Staffordshire clerk whose relations paid the very low premium of £30, but who was obliged to look after two geldings, serve at table, open the church door and otherwise wait on his master in all respects.[60] Judging from the imperfect evidence of the surviving indentures, there may well have been a decline in the close regulation of the behaviour of clerks by the end of the eighteenth century, but it had by no means died out altogether. A set of articles from Tewkesbury, for example, which were proved in 1808, required 'faithful' service from the clerk and made a point of forbidding him to visit the alehouse.[61] More generally, judging from the printed literature which emerged from the profession, practitioners throughout the period thought of theirs as an occupation which required application and hard work. But Lloyd Kenyon's reflection of this ideal, as it was practised in Nantwich, must also be set alongside a lay tradition which stressed that attorneys were not noted for their honesty or virtue and which detected lewdness and debauchery at the legal inns.[62]

Moving from theory to what little is known of actual practice, embezzlement by articled clerks was certainly a potential danger and one which was sometimes realised.[63] There must also have been many instances where either the incapacity of the master or the disobedience and unruliness of the clerk

5/44/30, John Waugh, the son of a Yorkshire tanner, was bound not to frequent taverns or to contract matrimony. If he was disorderly or 'obstinately refuses to do or willfully leaves undone any reasonable commands' of the master, he was liable to be 'displaced' from the service.

59   For example, PRO, CP 5/44/1, where a Durham attorney required the father to enter into a bond for £1000 to ensure that the articles were kept by his son. By the end of the eighteenth century the parental obligation may well have been taken as implied, regardless of whether it was written down; judicial decisions held then that a person under twenty-one years of age could not bind himself in such a way as to make him liable for an action at law. [James Barry], *The Law Respecting Masters and Servants, Articled Clerks, Apprentices, Manufacturers, Labourers and Journeymen* (London, 1799), p. 21.

60   PRO, CP 5/13/6, 22; CP 5/44/1–2. Unusually, in articles taken out in East Dereham, Norfolk, in 1747, the master extracted a promise that the clerk would never undertake practice in the parish of West Dereham without his 'license and consent', CP 5/44/9.

61   PRO, CP 5/148/46.

62   For example, Campbell, *The London Tradesman*, p. 71.

63   For example *The Times*, 9 January 1795, contains a notice announcing that James Ellis, an articled clerk in London had absconded with £320 in bank notes.

led to a breakdown in the relationship. Some articles made provision for the disposition of the premium when this happened. Indeed, as in other occupations which trained by apprenticeship, the failure rate amongst articled clerks appears to have been high. For example, a study of the West Riding of Yorkshire between 1711 and 1790 shows that, of 272 articles entered into, only 115 of the clerks were later found practising in the region.[64] This may be a reflection of either the difficult conditions for attorneys in the mid eighteenth century or of geographical mobility. It is also possible that there was a significant differential between the success rates of those sent to London and those who stayed in the provinces. But it is also a reminder that any complete understanding of apprenticeship as a social and educational process must consider it in the light of as yet unmade studies of secondary, and even tertiary, occupational mobility and of the psychological and financial costs involved for families.

The prominent place which apprenticeship had achieved in legal education by the end of the eighteenth century is paradoxical insofar as it occurred at precisely the same time as apprenticeship declined in many other occupations, which thereby forfeited the economic security which had been guaranteed by the Statute of Artificers of 1563.[65] In fact the erection of formal qualifications for entry into practice as an attorney made it an important exception to what some claimed was the common law right of every man to employ himself at his pleasure in any lawful trade. Furthermore, clerkship and pupilage even seem to have had the approval of classical economists like Adam Smith and his followers, who were generally hostile to apprenticeship but who tacitly accepted one of its principal features when they argued that the high costs of qualifying as a lawyer or medical man justified the potentially lucrative nature of the occupation.[66]

Despite the persistence of forms of apprenticeship, the years between 1790 and 1850 did see the first steps towards the invention, or reinvention, of academic legal education. In the 1790s, against the background of the intellectual and political turmoil caused by the French Revolution, but with surprisingly little direct reference to it, several authors from within the profession launched criticisms of some of the most vulnerable aspects of the system as it then existed.[67] Writing in 1792, for example, the barrister

---

[64] Miles, 'Eminent Attorneys', pp. 61.

[65] See for example, *Parliamentary Papers, 1812–13*, iv, *Report of Committee on the Several Petitions Respecting the Apprentice Laws of this Kingdom* (London, 1813).

[66] Adam Smith, *The Wealth of Nations Books I-III*, (London, 1970), p. 237. For quite explicit confusion on the subject see John Wade, *History of the Middle and Working Classes: With a Popular Exposition of the Economical and Political Principles Which Have Influenced the Past and Present Condition of the Industrious Orders* (London, 1833), pp. 187–91, 200.

[67] Edmund Burke, the son of a Dublin attorney, and himself a sometime barrister, had of course attributed part of the troubles in France to the significant role played in events there by the new elite, which consisted of attorneys and other 'lower lawyers', who aimed to establish a

Thomas Ruggle noted that success in the upper branch had been difficult in the immediately preceding decades because of the lack of work, but he also thought that this uncertainty was compounded by the absence of any supervision of students for the bar. Within the lower branch, on the other hand, he suggested the atrophy of the business of provincial attorneys, coupled with their lack of first-hand contact with the central courts, had apparently 'superseded all necessity of an intimate knowledge of the law amongst country practisers'.

> There was a time when the country Attorney was nearly as much to be depended on for advice, especially in titles and conveyances, as the Barrister; when Coke's Littleton was at their finger's ends; and wise axioms, together with black lettered lore, distilled from their lips, as honey from those of the Maeonian bard; but that race of men is nearly extinct; a kind of Lawfactor has succeeded in their stead; and the London Agent has superseded all necessity of an intimate knowledge ...[68]

No less important, between 1793 and 1795, a number of well-publicised cases of malpractice undermined the public esteem of attorneys and raised questions about the efficacy of the qualifying procedures. Giving judgment to strike one of the guilty practitioners off the roll in 1795, the former articled clerk, now Lord Chief Justice Kenyon, remarked that, if he had been tried by a jury, the culprit would have been sent to Botany Bay.[69] Writing within this same climate of opinion, Joseph Day supported his proposal for the creation of a statutory college of attorneys by arguing that the 'whole of Society' had reason to be deeply interested in ensuring that attorneys demonstrated 'competent professional knowledge and Integrity'.[70] Although Day did not want to abandon articled clerkship as a way of teaching the law, he claimed that bad masters spread incompetence.[71]

'litigious constitution'. Edmund Burke, *Reflections on the Revolution in France* (New York, 1961; originally published 1790), pp. 54–55, 57, 212.

[68] Ruggle, *The Barrister: or Strictures*, i, pp. 4, 18, 28, 30–33.

[69] The majority of the cases concerned various forms of malpractice such as acting in another practitioner's name in order to extort money through legal processes or perjury, but in one of them it emerged that an enrolled attorney had never served a clerkship and that another one had been practising in the Common Pleas for some years after having been struck off. *The Times*, 29 January 1795, 31 January 1795, 10 February 1795 (for Kenyon's remarks), 13 May 1795. Only one of the cases was remotely political. It involved an attorney called Martin who had acted in order to recover from a lunatic asylum the goods of Thomas Hardy, who was subsequently tried for high treason after claiming that he had been sent by God to rid the world of all crowned heads of state. Martin claimed that he knew nothing of Hardy's religious and political views. When his case was finally heard, after he had spent eight months in the Tower, the judges evidently believed his story. He was not struck off the roll (ibid., 12 February 1795). Interestingly, in another case of the same period the earl of Abingdon was fined £100 for unjustly slandering an attorney (ibid., 13 February 1795).

[70] Day, *Thoughts on the Necessity and Utility*. For more on Day and this proposal, see also Chapter 5, pp. 136–40.

[71] Day, *Thoughts on the Necessity*, p. 10.

He was also implicitly critical of the judges' failure to carry out examinations of new entrants in accordance with their statutory duties. He attributed this in part to their lack of time as well as their lack of expertise in the attorneys' craft, but he also thought the judiciary shared some of the commonplace contemporary assumptions which made them reluctant to play a more active role. The payment of a premium and the performance of the prescribed service earned a 'right' to admission. It was wrong to make a clerk suffer if he had the misfortune to be articled to a dishonest or incompetent master. Examinations of young men were unlikely to prove anything about their moral character or their potential competence as practitioners.[72]

Other writers of the 1790s began to emphasise that there was a fundamental difference between a liberal education and a vocational one. This led to a reprise of sixteenth-century debates about the capacity of apprenticeship to permit the pursuit of a more elevated 'scientific' knowledge. Thomas Ruggle, for instance, argued that, since judges were selected from the practising bar, training for the bar should be capable of producing men who were not 'mere lawyers', but men of literature, learned in other subjects such as philosophy and history.[73] He deprecated the example set by Lord Chancellor Hardwicke in encouraging barristers to train in the offices of attorneys. The influx of men who had not received the education of a scholar and a gentleman should give 'real concern to all who have a regard for the profession'. Unlike most earlier commentators, he praised the universities as seats of learning, admired the establishment of the Vinerian Chair of English Law at Oxford, and thought that the inns of court should require entrants to have bachelor's degrees, while resurrecting their old orders against admitting attorneys.[74]

Like many others who argued in the same vein, Ruggle was influenced by writers such as Blackstone and Bentham who advocated a more theoretical legal science rather than the narrow legal craft which the common law had arguably become. Changes in education were in many respects a mere epiphenomenon of this programme. Even amongst those who did not go as far as this, it would seem that the tide was turning against training barristers through service in the offices of attorneys. In a freshly penned handbook for prospective law students, notable for its insistence on the pursuit of excellence, the barrister John Raithby assumed that future counsellors would have completed two years at university, and that they would have studied history and religion as well as law. Yet he was also aware that clerkship and pupilage in chambers were the only available forms of training. He observed that 'our frugal and industrious ancestors prepared their

---

[72] Ibid., pp. 5–9, 11–12, 19, 24–29.

[73] A similar impulse lay behind the anonymous collection *A Treatise on the Study of the Law: Containing Directions to Students: Written by Those Celebrated Lawyers, Orators and Statesmen, the Lords Mansfield, Ashburton and Thurlow* (London, 1797).

[74] Ruggle, *The Barrister*, i, pp. xi, 12, 28, 36, 38, 50, 53, 60.

children for common avocations by a seven year term of apprenticeship'; in fact advocates had in the past been called apprentices. Although he was firmly in favour of discipline and hard work, Raithby completed this line of thought with the ambiguous, but revealing, comment that apprenticeship had 'in these polished days' become a 'disgusting epithet'. He was clear that clerkship with an attorney could result only in an education in 'tricks and finesse', the 'quirks and quibbles' that cunning and unprincipled men have from time to time invented. If the student was young, he ran the risk of contracting 'low and ungentlemanlike habits'. He was liable to encounter persons, who, 'however honourable they may be for diligence and integrity, are accustomed to manners and to dialect which are the too natural consequences of a confined education, and this is no unimportant danger'.[75]

In retrospect, the polemical criticisms of legal education in the 1790s are more significant as markers of changes in attitudes than as successful calls for action. Joseph Day's scheme for a law society and public examinations for the lower branch was not realised. Although several individuals undertook to reintroduce the practice of lecturing at the inns of court in the 1790s, they did not enjoy much support from the benchers and the experiments collapsed.[76] As late as the 1830s, many future barristers still performed their 'noviciate' in an attorney's office.[77] On the basis of its decisions in matters relating to the inns of court and chancery, it seems the judiciary also became less rather than more inclined to get further involved in formal legal

---

[75] [Raithby], *The Study and Practice of the Law Considered*, pp. 1–3, 6, 33, 35, 74, 367–72. The work was dedicated to the Scottish lord chancellor of the day, Alexander Lord Loughborough. The potential significance of practices in Scotland, where legal training was better integrated into university education than in England, is suggested by the importance of figures such as Mansfield and Loughborough in the eighteenth century and of Henry Brougham in the nineteenth. See also Chapter 5, p. 138.

[76] In fact Danby Pickering, a prodigious legal publicist and barrister of Gray's Inn, gave lectures there in the 1760s, *Dictionary of National Biography*; *The Pension Book of Gray's Inn: Records of the Honourable Society. 1569–1800*, ed. R. J. Fletcher (2 vols, London, 1901). I owe this reference to Professor Wilfrid Prest. The efforts of Michael Nolan and Sir James Mackintosh to revive lectures in the mid 1790s are described in *Legal Observer and Journal of Jurisprudence*, 31 (1845–46), pp. 496–97. The benchers of Lincoln's Inn were evidently not receptive to the suggestion that Mackintosh, a Scot, who was suspected of being the author of *Vindiciae Gallicae* (London, 1791), should use their hall for lectures on the law of nations, but nevertheless granted permission at the urging of the prime minister, William Pitt the Younger. Nolan lectured on municipal institutions. According to the same source, Joseph Chitty delivered lectures on pleading at Lincoln's Inn in the 1820s but these were not well attended, largely because the subject matter was not appropriate to that form of instruction.

[77] Richard Lovell Edgeworth, *Essays on Professional Education* (London, 1809), pp. 312–15: 'The Time of apprenticeship to attorneys, solicitors, and special pleaders, is now postponed till after the student has been at college'. Warren, *A Popular and Practical Introduction*, p. 89, remarked that 'Those who come to the bar, after a noviciate performed in an attorney's office, are not inconsiderable in numbers; and, if possessed of several peculiar advantages, have also certainly to contend with some disadvantages ...'

education.[78] Nevertheless, as litigation and the numbers of legal practitioners began to grow quickly in the nineteenth century, both the courts and the legal professions were the targets of reformers including some, like Henry Brougham, who aimed both to simplify procedure and to make the common law more comprehensible as a set of ideas.[79] Meanwhile the movement for self-improvement within the lower branch of the profession reached a new stage in the 1820s with the foundation of the London Law Society, a body which soon afterwards became a catalyst for major changes in legal education.[80]

Judging from the position adopted by its first secretary, the long-serving Robert Maugham, the Law Society from at least as early as 1830 was calling for the reinvigoration of legal education.[81] In Hilary Term 1836, the judges of the high courts with characteristic caution followed a precedent of 1654, and issued a set of orders which effectively transferred their powers of examining candidates for admission to committees of practitioners who were henceforth to be nominated by the society. Since the presentation of duly stamped articles remained a major prerequisite for admission as an attorney, the new measures in some important respects departed very little from previous practice. But the judges also specified that the articles should be accompanied by answers to a series of questions about the service and conduct of the clerk, and the society printed these up on a form which had to be filled in and signed by the clerk and master.[82] The candidate was required to state whether he had served the full term, whether he had engaged in any profession other than that of a clerk, and whether he had been absent without permission – points that had frequently been covered in the traditional indentures. The attorney with whom he served had to confirm, deny or qualify the answers and respond to a further query about whether the clerk had been 'faithfully and diligently' employed in professional business. The surviving forms show that straightforward yes or no answers were regularly recorded; while these were evidently sufficient in most cases, the examiners were authorised to put further questions to the candidate if they thought them necessary.[83]

Although accompanied by the novelty of a form to fill out and the domination of the process by a committee of London practitioners rather

---

[78] *English Reports*, xcix, civ, cxi, 1 Douglas 354 (1780), *King v. Benchers of Gray's Inn*; 4 Barnewall and Cresswell 855 (1825), *King v. Benchers of Lincoln's Inn*; 5 Adolphus and Ellis 17 (1836), *King v. Principal and Antients of Barnard's Inn*.

[79] See above Chapter 4, pp. 102–104. Lobban, *Common Law and English Jurisprudence*, pp. 189, 191. See also *Parliamentary Papers, 1831–32*, xxv, *Fourth Report of the Commissioners on the Practice and Proceedings of the Superior Courts of Common Law with a Supplement and Appendix: Part I* (London, 1832).

[80] See Chapter 5, pp. 141–42.

[81] Maugham's views are expressed in *Legal Observer and Journal of Jurisprudence*, 3 (1830–31), p. 169.

[82] Maugham, *A Complete Collection of the Statutes ... Relating to Attorneys*, pp. 123–45.

[83] PRO, KB 111/2 contains many examples of filled in forms.

than court officials, all of these aspects of the new procedures reflected the traditional culture of apprenticeship. Much more innovative was the creation of a day-long written examination to be administered in the hall of the Law Institute in Chancery Lane (the home of the Law Society) in order to test competence. This consisted of a preliminary paper followed by five additional ones covering common law, statute law and the practice of the courts; conveyancing; equity; bankruptcy practice; and criminal law, including proceedings before justices of the peace.[84] In addition, the society at the same time began supporting three courses of twelve lectures each given in London by notable authorities, but these could not be compulsory because they were open only to clerks whose masters were members of the society and who paid a £2 fee for each course.[85]

Despite the changes, service in offices remained central to the training process. No doubt for this reason, Robert Maugham took pains to preface a collection of examination questions which he published in 1841 with remarks which explained their relevance to active practitioners. Acknowledging that many lawyers thought 'that the examination has thrown additional duties and obligations on the practitioner in regard to the instruction of his articled clerk', he accepted that the primary duty of the attorney consisted in 'devoting the best power of his mind to the interests of his clients'. He also reminded his readers of the traditional terms of articles, which obliged the master by 'the best ways and means in his power, and to the utmost of his skill and knowledge, to teach and instruct his clerk in the practice or profession of an attorney and solicitor'. Maugham stressed the importance of information communicated 'in the course of real business', and pointed out that the advantage of the questions he had put into print was that they would help the busy lawyer who was short on time to organise exercises that the clerk could perform and then present for oral discussion with his master. In his view, the utility of questioning was obvious because all sciences tested students by this means. Catechising was a learning method so appropriate to the law that it was 'singular' that it had not been adopted in the past.[86]

Since the 1500 examination questions that Maugham printed in his *Digest* had been produced over a five-year period by traditionally trained members

---

[84] Maugham, *A Complete Collection of the Statutes ... Relating to Attorneys*, pp. 125–45.

[85] These are described briefly in *Parliamentary Papers 1846*, x, *Report from the Select Committee on Legal Education* (London, 1846), p. xv.

[86] Robert Maugham, *A Digest of the Examination Questions in Common Law, Conveyancing, Equity, Bankruptcy and Criminal Law: With a Collection of Questions Founded as Well on Blackstone's Commentaries and Other Text-Books; as on Recent Statutes and Decisions* (London, 1841), preface. In fact a work published in 1831 had already experimented with the method of using questions as a pedagogic technique. Francis Hobler, Jr, *Familiar Exercises between an Attorney and his Articled Clerk on the General Principles of the Laws of Real Property: Being the First Book of Coke upon Littleton Reduced to the Form of Questions* (London, 1831). In one of his few surviving letters Maugham told the historian Stacey Grimaldi in January 1839 that his 'boys' had been 'highly interested in your Synopsis of English History, and are examining the whole family out of it', BL, MS Add. 34189, fol. 169.

of the examination committees, there is a need for caution in dismissing the amount of law which could be learned through articled clerkship. It is clear, moreover, that there was considerable doubt within both branches of the profession about how far newer methods of training, most notably lectures, could replace traditional ones. In a work which generally lamented the lack of a systematic and uniform method of tuition for the bar, for example, the well-known barrister, publicist and novelist Samuel Warren nevertheless argued vigorously against the pedagogic value of lectures. He encouraged those reading for the bar to supplement their legal learning with more liberal studies, quoting with approval the remarks of the Scottish-born judge, Lord Kames, who had said that 'without regarding substance, law, instead of a rational science, becomes a heap of subterfuges and inconveniences, which tend, sensibly, to corrupt the Morals of those who make the law their profession'. However, Warren also accepted the arguments against lectures which were made by Edward Coppleston, bishop of Llandaff, who was a staunch defender of tutorial teaching at the universities and an advocate of the close moral supervision of students. In addition, he drew comparisons with medicine in order to emphasise the importance of the practical element in legal training. Medical students were not shunted off into a room and told to read a treatise, nor did they attend lectures. Only after they had attained manual and technical dexterity could they begin to feel interested in the reasons and principles of the science. Much the same was true of law. In any case (according to Warren) the 'promiscuous intercourse of students', which accompanied attendance at lectures, could only lead to the temptations of idleness and irregularity. 'Chamber tuition' with an attentive lawyer who allowed plenty of time for reading was the best course for the intending barrister.[87]

By the 1840s, Warren was himself more favourably disposed towards lectures but, while professional 'improvers' like he and Maugham were both advocates of a legal profession which was well trained and which adhered to high standards of moral behaviour and public service, both also assumed that forms of apprenticeship, with modifications, would remain an important part of the process for both branches of the profession.[88] Indeed, in many respects the eighteenth-century culture of apprenticeship can be said to have served well in the transition to the changed conditions of the early

[87] Warren, *A Popular and Practical Introduction to Law Studies*, pp. 4–5, 8–10, 18, 34, 69–69, 73, 82–85, 88–89, 120ff, 165ff, 231–32, 253–54, 257. Amongst his other achievements, Warren published an extremely popular novel, *Ten Thousand a Year* (London, 1841), the plot of which centred around the dishonest practices of two attorneys who helped to falsify an inheritance. There is also an interesting discussion of the value of lectures in *A Manual for Articled Clerks* (London, 1837), which was composed by a group of barristers and attorneys in order to help students pass the new examination, pp. 186–191. For some evidence on chamber tuition, see *Report from the Select Committee on Legal Education*, p. 7.

[88] In April 1846 the *Legal Observer and Journal of Jurisprudence*, 31 (1846), p. 496, assured readers that recently proposed lectures at the inns of court were intended not to replace, but to be an auxiliary to, the 'well-tried and advantageous system of tuition in chambers'.

nineteenth. The explicit obligations which formal articles put on the master to teach and the pupil to learn were matched by late Georgian and early Victorian reminders to clerks that they should work as diligently at their tasks as Lloyd Kenyon had done in 1750.[89] The moral exhortations that Samuel Warren addressed to articled clerks in a series of lectures which he delivered at the Law Institute in 1848 can be found in printed works published a century earlier.[90] Even the introduction of written examinations was an extension of the very ancient rules that required attorneys to demonstrate professional competence in some way. Since it led to demands from students that they should receive more systematic instruction, this last change ultimately had profound consequences; but, if the method of testing qualifications was new, the principles which lay behind it were not, and the programme of training for the vast majority of articled clerks remained unchanged.[91] In 1847 it was said that, although there were over 2000 articled clerks in London, only 200 of them attended lectures at the Law Institute.[92] As late as the 1850s the examinations were often criticised for being too easy, and it is certainly the case that 95 per cent of students passed them.[93] Since many of those who did not pass were in fact referred to the consideration of the judges because of technical questions about their articles, the success rate was probably not much different from that which had pertained under the unreformed system.

Even so, the move towards examinations and lectures first taken by the attorneys in 1836 was part of a process from which not even the barristers were able to remain immune. Although pupilage in chambers, and even service in the offices of attorneys, remained entrenched as the primary methods of instruction, Samuel Warren noted that 'the attorney's clerk of 1835, is, or ought to be, a very different person from the attorney's clerk of 1753'; he thought that the quality of teaching in chambers had improved

---

[89] There was a minor literary tradition: Jacob Phillips (of the Inner Temple, formerly an articled clerk), *A Letter from a Grandfather to his Grandson, an Articled Clerk: Pointing Out the Right Course of his Studies and Conduct during his Clerkship, in Order to his Successful Establishment in his Profession* (London, 1818); A. C. Buckland, *Letters to an Attorney's Clerk: Containing Directions for his Studies and General Conduct* (London, 1824); Hobler, *Familiar Exercises between an Attorney and his Articled Clerk*.

[90] Samuel Warren, *The Moral, Social and Professional Duties of Attornies and Solicitors* (London, 1848). By way of comparison see, for example, *Observations on the Duty of an Attorney and Solicitor Submitted to the Public Consideration: But Addressed More Especially to Young Practisers of the Law* (London, 1759).

[91] See, for example, the *Law Students' Magazine*, 1 (1844), pp. 1–3, 127; 2 (1845–46), p. 202.

[92] *Report from the Select Committee on Legal Education* (1846), p. 199.

[93] The *Law Students' Magazine*, 1 (1844), p. 6, noted that 'only' seventy-one of seventy-five candidates passed in Trinity Term 1844. The *Legal Observer and Journal of Jurisprudence*, 28 (1844), p. 131, reported that in the past year 359 had passed the examination, and eleven had not. Ibid., 34 (1847), p. 265, acknowledges that the examination might be made more difficult, but remarks that 'the judges do not wish that the examination should be conducted otherwise than it is'.

in recent years.[94] In 1840, the legal biographer Archer Polson repeated the well-known criticisms of Hardwicke and Kenyon: they lacked classical educations; the chief disadvantage of service with an attorney of the kind they had undertaken was that it did not sit well with time spent at the universities, something which was essential if the bar was to be graced, as it should be, with men of liberal learning. To this end the Inner Temple had since 1828 been examining entrants on either Greek or Latin, as well as history and general literature.[95] Nevertheless, Polson was still convinced that forms of service were essential parts of legal education. In his opinion 'The most industrious study would never teach the surgeon how to amputate a limb, or even bandage a fracture. As substitutes for either study or pupilage, it would be absurd to recommend law lectures; but, as auxiliaries to these, we believe them to be beneficial'.[96] In late 1845 the benchers of the inns of court entered into discussions which eventually led to the foundation of a series of lectures and a voluntary examination, but these were by no means accepted as constituting a substitute for the older methods of learning.[97]

During the course of the first half of the nineteenth century, therefore, apprenticeship evidently continued to provide a method of education which was broadly acceptable to both branches of the profession. It lay at the heart of an occupational culture which put a premium on application and hard work, as well as the responsibility of both masters and students to participate in the business of professional training. It had even led to a number of gradual changes, including the introduction of written examinations for the lower branch. However, if this cautious revision is allowed to replace the generally hostile verdicts of historians about the nature of the 'unreformed' legal education, then the findings of the select committee which was appointed by parliament in 1846 to investigate the state of legal education seem difficult to explain.[98] Quite rightly identified as the catalyst which precipitated major changes in the direction of institutional legal education during the second half of the nineteenth century, the committee's report, which argued for the establishment of compulsory examinations and lectures for students of the bar, was highly critical of the existing state of affairs, a view which was evidently shared to some degree by the national

---

[94] Warren, *A Popular and Practical Introduction*, pp. 5, 89, 231–32, 501.

[95] A[rcher] Polson, *Law and Lawyers: or Sketches and Illustrations of Legal History and Biography* (2 vols, London, 1840), i, pp. 6, 8, 16, 27–28, 30–31.

[96] Ibid., i, pp. 27–28.

[97] *Legal Observer and Journal of Jurisprudence*, 31 (1845–46), pp. 253–54, 264, 372, 445. Gray's Inn was to fund lectures on real property and conveyancing, the Inner Temple on common law, Lincoln's Inn on equity and the Middle Temple on civil law and jurisprudence. This subject is treated more fully in a forthcoming paper by C. W. Brooks and M. Lobban, 'Apprenticeship or Academy? The Idea of a Law University, 1830–1860'.

[98] Manchester, *Modern Legal History*, pp. 54–55; B. Abel-Smith and Robert Stevens, *Lawyers and the Courts: A Sociological Study of the English Legal System, 1750–1965* (London, 1970), pp. 64ff.

press.[99] It found that students for the bar were still left entirely to their own devices in learning the law. If anything, attorneys and solicitors had even less of a chance of education: they were treated as mechanical agents for carrying out practical processes. 'As the future chemist and apothecary is bound an apprentice, so is the future solicitor articled as a clerk, for the purpose of learning what has been too much considered in both cases as a matter of mere manual dexterity.'[100]

While these propositions were arguably true, they simplify things considerably.[101] Furthermore, a closer inspection of the select committee, and the witnesses called before it, suggests that it was never likely to come to any other conclusion.[102] The quality of existing professional legal training was not extensively investigated; in fact in many respects it was not even the central issue under consideration. The principal remit of the committee was an assessment not just of professional education but of the quality of legal education for the community at large, a population which was usually more narrowly defined as the sons of country squires who might eventually find themselves sitting as justices of the peace; or those who were destined to serve as administrators or judges in more distant parts of the empire. Much of the focus was therefore on the universities, and several of those giving evidence were professors of Roman and common law at Oxford, Cambridge and University College, London. Since the common law was not a degree subject at Oxford and Cambridge, whose schools were engaged primarily in the production of clergymen, these men reported a generally sorry state of affairs.[103] For example, only thirty-eight people heard the Vinerian lectures at Oxford in 1846. The more professionally oriented lectures in London were not doing much better. No more than a handful of students in the early 1830s attended what subsequently became the famous lectures on

99 For example, *The Times* in September 1847 dismissed the proposals of the inns for introducing lectures and voluntary examinations as doing little 'to encourage the industrious pupil, and nothing at all to prevent the idle and ignorant from attaining the rank of barrister … The public interest requires some guarantee of qualification …' Quoted in *Legal Observer and Journal of Jurisprudence*, 32 (1847), p. 494.

100 *Report from the Select Committee on Legal Education*, pp. iii–xlviii.

101 For example a review in the *Legal Observer and Journal of Jurisprudence*, 13 (1836–37), p. 501, of John Gray's *The Country Solicitor's Practice* (London, 1837), argued that many country practitioners lacked sufficient legal knowledge.

102 The select committee was formed on the initiative of Sir Thomas Wyse, MP for Waterford, who had initially seen it as a device for investigating ways to improve legal education in Ireland. The extension of the investigation to England was evidently the product of a suggestion in the House by Henry Warburton, a non-lawyer, who was an early supporter of the foundation of the University of London. T. C. Hansard, *The Parliamentary Debates from the Year 1803 to the Present Time*, 85, p. 677 (7 April 1846); *The Times*, 9 August 1846. I owe this information to Michael Lobban. *The Legal Observer and Journal of Jurisprudence*, 32 (1847), pp. 120–22, noted Wyse's emphasis on the point that the general importance of the legal profession made its education of importance to the community. A school or college of law would introduce a 'more philosophical spirit' into the study of a practical subject.

103 *Report from the Select Committee on Legal Education*, pp. iii–xlviii.

jurisprudence given by John Austin. One of his successors as professor at University College, J. T. Greaves, testified that he had resigned his post because of the very small interest expressed by students in his subject.[104]

Not surprisingly, the academic evidence tended to support the conclusions of the committee's report, which made unfavourable comparisons between England and other countries, most notably Germany, where legal education was an important component of university degree courses; where there was thought to be a philosophical basis to the discipline which raised it to the status of a science; and where there were publicists and professors who both taught the young and communicated to a wider public.[105] While most of those who appeared favoured examinations as a way of testing competence, many were sceptical about lectures. It is apparent that there was confusion about the exact relationship between training, developing general public knowledge and the encouragement of moral rectitude. For instance, Edward Creasy, a barrister and Professor of Ancient and Modern History at University College, lamented the ignorance amongst the educated of the legal and constitutional history of the country. Although he thought that the inns of court should resurrect their ancient role in legal education, and although he acknowledged the usefulness of lectures, he was also worried that lectures usually led to cramming, and so favoured the habits of habitual study which accompanied pupilage with special pleaders, a practice he hoped would not be abandoned. Creasy was convinced that examinations, similar to those administered by the Law Society, should be instituted for the bar because 'the test of education, if you want to have men of honourable and right mind, is the best that you can employ'. Yet he was not, he claimed, saying that it was any more possible to make a lawyer by giving lectures than it was to make a skilful physician by examining him upon works on the subject of diseases. In addition, he did not think the new examinations should be made too difficult or 'too competitive', because this would discourage those country gentlemen who joined the inns in order to gain a mere smattering of the law.[106]

How far these thoughts reflected wider opinion within the judiciary or the profession is difficult to measure, at least in part because the select committee made very little effort to find out. Not a single pupil in chambers was questioned, and it is likely that the very cautious steps taken by the inns of court in the late 1840s to introduce lectures and voluntary examinations only dimly reflected the vigorous calls for reform voiced by the most influential lawyers to be heard by the select committee, Lords Brougham and Campbell and Sir Richard Bethell.[107] Both Brougham and Campbell attacked

[104] Ibid., pp. xv, 56–61, 199.
[105] Ibid., pp. xvi, xxix, xxxiv.
[106] Ibid., pp. 25–38.
[107] Bethell made a motion for the establishment of a lecturer at the Middle Temple in November 1845, *Law Times*, 6 (1846), p. 331. For his career, see Thomas Arthur Nash, *The Life of Richard Lord Westbury with Selections from his Correspondence* (2 vols, London, 1888).

the absence of a regular course of study leading to the call to the bar, and they pointed out some of the adverse consequences which arose from the prevailing methods of training. They produced, for example, the unacceptable situation in which inadequately prepared barristers, who were failures in practice at home, found employment as judges in the colonies. They also repeated the Benthamite call for a more theoretical and scientific approach to English law which they thought would be a positive consequence of the introduction of more systematic teaching at the inns of court.

The evidence taken by the select committee from the lower branch included that given by Robert Maugham, as well as the testimony of the leader of the recently formed Articled Clerk's Society in London, Edward Turner Payne, who made personal representations to the chairman of the committee, Sir Thomas Wyse, so that the voice of the articled clerks might be heard.[108] Payne complained about the lack of opportunities for articled clerks to extend their studies and pointed out that the facilities of the Law Institute in Chancery Lane were only open to the clerks of members of the Incorporated Law Society. His proposal was that a new law institute or society should be established which would enable articled clerks to attend classes and lectures given by noted professors. Although there is evidence that there was significant support amongst articled clerks, who increasingly referred to themselves as law students, in the provinces as well as London, Payne's proposal had its critics amongst his fellows. In any case the geographical dispersal of the lower branch of the profession made the establishment of a central institution problematic. Although the select committee noted some of the shortcomings to which Payne pointed, it generally praised the efforts of the Law Society since the introduction of written examinations in 1836; while at the same time explicitly leaving attorneys and solicitors outside the scope of the law university it advocated. The argument was that, given the traditional divisions between the two branches, such a measure would not be acceptable to the bar.[109]

The evidence of Payne and Maugham was to some degree overshadowed by the other major source of professional input from the attorneys and solicitors, the testimony of Sir George Stephen. Son of the legal official (and brother-in-law of Wilberforce) James Stephen, and uncle of the well-known Victorian judge and publicist, Sir James Fitzjames Stephen, Sir George was as vigorous an advocate of raising the intellectual and moral calibre of the lower branch as one might expect of a man with such a background.[110] But

---

108 *Law Students' Magazine*, 2 (1845–46), pp. 202, 584.

109 *Report from the Select Committee on Legal Education*, pp. xv, 161–66, 195–99.

110 See *Dictionary of National Biography*. Stephen was also the author of a popular novel, *Adventures of an Attorney in Search of Practice* (London, 1839), which is primarily a collective portrait of eccentric and unusual clients, but which also suggested that there had been improvement in the profession. For example, Stephen wrote (ibid., p. 192) that, forty or fifty years before, the attorneys' claim to be ranked amongst the middle classes was equivocal: 'Mr Latitat was the rogue in every farce'.

he was doubtful about the adequacy of examinations for such purposes, nor was he impressed by those administered by the Law Society. These, he said, tested for little more than complete incompetence, a point he supported by telling the story of an articled clerk of his who was completely negligent and unsuitable for practice, but who passed the examinations and then went on to a successful career as a crammer. Stephen's prescriptions for change, moreover, appear to have been based on what can only be described as a profound sense of social snobbery. He said that the range of business for which solicitors were responsible made it necessary for them to come to the profession with a broad, gentlemanly education, by which he meant the study of the classics. Since he also held what can only be described as the manifestly absurd opinion that attorneys came from the inferior sections of society, he was in favour of raising the tone by instituting qualifying exams in classics and other 'liberal' subjects before students entered into articles.[111] This proposition was criticised vigorously in written evidence submitted to the committee by Robert Maugham, who pointed out that if higher educational attainments were demanded of those aiming to become articled clerks, this would raise the age at which articles might be entered into and would also increase the cost of legal education and hence create an expectation that 'professional advantages should be enhanced in proportion'.[112] Nevertheless, discussion of the introduction of such qualifying examinations appears to have become more lively in the 1850s than it had been in the 1840s, at least partly because reductions in the stamp duty and the annual certificate tax evidently made the question of how the profession could maintain its gentlemanly respectability (and limit the number of newcomers) even more acute than it had been in the past.[113]

Reform along the lines suggested by the 1846 select committee gradually came into place over the next half century. The subsequent chapters in the slow-moving story of the institutionalisation of legal education saw the introduction of compulsory examinations at the inns of court and, eventually, the establishment of degrees in the common law at the universities. Yet the centrality of pupilage in the training of barristers persisted for at least another two decades after 1850; articled clerkship remained important for the lower branch into the mid twentieth century. The tensions between the vocational and craft versus the academic and liberal ideals also continue to persist, particularly in the relationship between academic lawyers and practitioners. The subject matter of university degree courses, and many of the examination questions, are not radically different in kind from those compiled by Robert Maugham at the end of the age of simple apprenticeship.

[111] *Report from the Select Committee on Legal Education*, pp. 144–56.
[112] Ibid., pp. 368–69. Maugham indicated that the cost of becoming articled ranged between £200 and £400, plus the £120 stamp duty.
[113] *Legal Observer and Journal of Jurisprudence*, 47 (1853–54), pp. 83, 106, 141, 389

More significantly in the light of the objectives of the Benthamite reformers, the common law has remained relatively impervious to general principles and simplicity of form. Modern courses on jurisprudence or legal history are marginal in a menu which consists largely of technical subjects.[114]

The movement first towards and then away from apprenticeship as a mode of legal training in the two and a half centuries since 1700 was influenced at different times by fluctuations in the amounts of legal business, by government taxation policies and by ideology. Commentators in the nineteenth century frequently pointed to the role played by legal inns before 1700 (in the age of the 'Third University') as a model for reform, but it was of course eighteenth-century conditions, and not the ancient institutions, which did the most to shape it.[115] From one perspective, the changes which gradually occurred during the course of the nineteenth century were simply a necessary consequence of the rapid growth of the profession, which in turn created a need for more effective ways of processing larger numbers of students while at the same time demonstrating to the public that the practitioners possessed a minimum degree of competence. These same problems had arisen in the other great age of growth, the later sixteenth century. Similarly, many of the well-intentioned Victorian reformers who attacked the eighteenth-century process were driven by a mixture of assumptions about respectability, gentlemanly conduct and liberal learning which had much in common with Renaissance distinctions between 'mechanical' versus 'scientific' knowledge.

While the introduction of written examinations gradually created a demand from students that they should have better teaching, it also seems likely that the cost of legal education rose during the nineteenth century, and that the practice of the law became more socially exclusive than it had been in the eighteenth century and earlier.[116] As traditionalists predicted, the newer methods of training did produce 'crammers' both at the time and in different forms thereafter. Modern British law students learn the basics of their craft, and are examined at college or university, after a total of a year and a half of full-time study; and they then proceed to a period of practical service which lasts another three. By contrast, articled clerks and pupils for the bar before 1850 spent anywhere from four to seven years

---

[114] The subsequent history is briefly summarised in *Report of the Royal Commission on Legal Services* (London, 1979), ch. 38. Stafan Collini, *Public Moralists: Political Thought and Intellectual Life in Britain, 1850–1930* (Oxford, 1991), ch. 7, provides a perceptive account of the predicament of professional law teachers in the second half of the nineteenth century.

[115] See also Chapter 5, p. 144.

[116] Warren, *A Popular and Practical Introduction*, p. 6, noted that it cost about £150 in the 1830s to join a legal inn. In addition pupilage cost 100 guineas a year for three years, and then there were books and lodgings to be paid for. It then required an income of £150 a year to enter the profession. Duman, *The English and Colonial Bars*, p. 19, notes that while fewer sons of the gentry went to the bar in the nineteenth century, it was hardly an avenue of upward social mobility, since increasingly large numbers of barristers came from families already numbered amongst the professional or urban business classes.

achieving the same ends. Indeed, it is arguable that the wider liberal learning which late eighteenth- and early nineteenth-century commentators thought was essential for the lawyer in general, and most particularly, for the barrister, has become rarer rather than more common as the content of courses has become more specialised.

7

Law, Lawyers and the Social History of England, 1500–1800

Since the early 1970s the history of crime and the criminal law and the history of those who serviced legal institutions – lawyers (excluding judges), jurymen and constables – have occupied a great deal of scholarly attention. While much has been achieved, there are also grounds for concern about the apparent failure of these branches of what might be described as socio-legal history either to communicate much with each other or to make a significant impact on the general social and political history of England between 1500 and 1800.[1] In most textbook accounts of early modern history, lawyers appear primarily as a species of social actors who enjoyed special access to the escalators of upward social mobility, not as groups of people through whom we can learn much about the nature of social and political developments in the past. Even more surprisingly, lawyers figure very little in recent accounts of the role of law in English society. Historians of crime have in this respect been much more influential than those of the legal profession, but many of the works which have followed in the wake of the pioneering *Albion's Fatal Tree* have concentrated primarily on processes: on the analysis of statistical facts about indictments, convictions and executions.[2] Insofar as the attitudes and assumptions of those involved are concerned, there has been more work on juries and constables than on magistrates or the legal profession.

The root of the problem is that we still lack an analytical perspective capable of doing justice to the complex and multi-faceted role of law in society. Most commonly, the law is depicted as the creature of the state, a monster descending downwards and outwards to conflict with and confront the values of 'the community'. Even in *An Ungovernable People?*, where John Brewer and John Styles emphasised the role of law as a common political and social language, the main analytical thrust was to examine the ways in which the law empowered the state and the elite.[3] More remarkably, in her

[1] This chapter is a revised and expanded version of a paper presented for discussion at a one day conference on 'Law, Legal Sources and the Social Historian', sponsored by the Economic and Social Research Council and held at the University of Essex in March 1992

[2] D. Hay, P. Linebaugh et al., *Albion's Fatal Tree: Crime and Society in Eighteenth-Century England* (London, 1975).

[3] *An Ungovernable People? The English and Their Law in the Seventeenth and Eighteenth Centuries*, ed. John Brewer and John Styles (London, 1980), introduction.

book *The Common Peace*, Cynthia Herrup gives an account of the criminal
legal process in the sixteenth and seventeenth centuries which self-consciously ignores the law as a formal set of values or a genre of discourse.[4]
While these fine works, and a number of others as well, have taught us
much, there is still confusion and a lack of purchase in our perception of
the place of legal culture in early modern history more generally. For
example, in *Revel, Riot and Rebellion*, David Underdown states within the
space of a few pages that, on the one hand, the common people had a view
of national issues which reflected their underlying concern for law, custom
and good rule; but that, on the other, their notions about such issues differed
from those of the elite. In any case, he adds, given the hierarchical structure
of early modern society, the gentry could expect their hegemony to be
upheld by a deep fund of deference. Maybe it is not surprising that his
examination of the relationship between popular culture and politics in the
period concentrates more on cricket and stoolball than on a serious analysis
of his somewhat paradoxical characterisation of the place of the law.[5]
    To some extent, the lack of communication between the sub-branches of
socio-legal history can be explained by chronological accident. The seminal
works on crime and the criminal law appeared between 1975 and the mid
1980s.[6] Work on lawyers (and constables and jurors) has only been published
in significant quantities since the mid 1980s, a little too early perhaps for
it fully to have assimilated the studies of crime – and certainly too late for
much feedback to have worked in the other direction.[7] There have also been
different intellectual agendas. Students of the criminal law have interested
themselves in the impact of authority on the weakest members of society.
Those looking at lawyers have used mass-biographical techniques to pursue
questions about social origins and mobility. Nor have they entirely overcome

    [4] Cynthia B. Herrup, *The Common Peace: Participation and the Criminal Law in Seventeenth-
Century England* (Cambridge, 1987), esp. chs 1, 6.
    [5] David Underdown, *Revel, Riot and Rebellion: Popular Politics and Culture in England,
1603–1660* (Oxford, 1985), pp. 119–25.
    [6] Hay, Linebaugh et al., *Albion's Fatal Tree*; E. P. Thompson, *Whigs and Hunters: The Origin of
the Black Act* (London, 1975); *Crime in England, 1550–1800*, ed. J. S. Cockburn (London, 1975);
J. A. Sharpe, *Crime in Seventeenth-Century England: A County Study* (Cambridge, 1983); idem, *Crime
in Early Modern England, 1550–1750* (1984); J. M. Beattie, *Crime and the Courts in England,
1660–1800* (Oxford, 1986).
    [7] D. Duman, *The Judicial Bench in England, 1727–1875* (London, 1982), and idem, *The English
and Colonial Bars in the Nineteenth Century* (London, 1983); M. Miles, 'Eminent Practitioners: The
New Visage of Country Attorneys, c. 1750–1800', in *Law, Economy and Society: Essays in the History
of English Law, 1750–1914*, eds G. R. Rubin and David Sugarman (London, 1984); Wilfrid
R. Prest, *The Rise of the Barristers: A Social History of the English Bar, 1590–1640* (Oxford, 1986);
idem, ed., *Lawyers in Early Modern Europe and America* (London, 1981); C. W. Brooks, *Pettyfoggers
and Vipers of the Commonwealth: The 'Lower Branch' of the Legal Profession in Early Modern England*
(Cambridge, 1986); Joan R. Kent, *The English Village Constable, 1580–1642* (Oxford, 1986);
J. S. Cockburn and Thomas Green, eds, *Twelve Good Men and True: The Criminal Trial Jury in
England, 1200–1800*, (Princeton, 1988); David Lemmings, *Gentlemen and Barristers: The Inns of
Court and the English Bar, 1680–1730* (Oxford, 1990).

the propensity of the history of professions to become obsessed with the details of structure, organisation and demarcation. Yet, if the study of professionalisation has been an obvious concern of those interested in lawyers, assumptions about professionalisation in fact lie at the heart of the failure of either group of scholars to exploit fully the law as a set of institutions and discourses with much to teach us about social and political relationships in the past. It is time to set down what we have learned in the name of professionalisation but to discard it as a guideline for future research.

In social theory, professionalisation acts as one of the benchmarks of modernity itself. Harold Perkin has depicted the last one hundred years of English history as 'the rise of professional society'.[8] In his attempts to redefine a distinctive modernity, Anthony Giddens emphasises the importance of risk-taking by individuals dependent on the guidance of professional cadres who control universalising knowledge.[9] By implication, the association of professionalisation with modernity has always led to the view that pre-modern professions (those before 1800) were different. Their numbers were smaller; they lacked effective organisation and standards of practice; they were primarily the servants of the aristocracy and gentry and, consequently, wholly preoccupied with the defence of landed property.[10] Significantly, this view of the professions meshes well with our predilections for distinctions between elite and popular cultures, and our assumptions that, in pre-modern times, overarching discourses (such as law or religion) were only of interest to and shaped by the ruling elite.[11] For the rest of the population they were at best irrelevancies or at worst oppressive mystifications.

There is much that rings true in the detailed analysis of writers like Giddens and Perkin of the role of professions in modern society. It is also easy to see ways in which the history of legal institutions and the legal professions contributed to the nineteenth-century evolution of the concept of professionalisation. The years from roughly 1820 to 1880 were clearly some kind of watershed. Although local communities had been losing control of the constable since at least 1600, police forces were professionalised in the nineteenth century. At the same time advocates were permitted a much greater role in criminal trials.[12] Turning from the criminal to the civil law, the high courts were reorganised, office-holding was rationalised and new local jurisdictions were created. Professional organisations were founded in

[8] Harold Perkin, *The Rise of Professional Society: England since 1880* (London, 1989).

[9] Anthony Giddens, *The Consequences of Modernity* (Stanford, 1990), ch. 3.

[10] W. R. Prest, 'Why the History of Professions is Not Written', in *Law, Economy and Society, 1750–1914*, eds Rubin and Sugarman, pp. 300–20.

[11] See G. Strauss, 'The Dilemma of Popular History', *Past and Present*, 132 (1991), pp. 130–49, for some interesting thoughts on this issue.

[12] The significance of this last development in the long history of the legal profession clearly warrants a great deal of thought and further research. See J. M. Beattie, 'Scales of Justice: Defense Counsel and the English Criminal Trial in the Eighteenth and Nineteenth Centuries', *Law and History Review*, 9 (1991).

order to vet those who wanted to become lawyers and to eliminate those
accused of malpractice. Eventually, the study of the common law became
part of the curriculum of the universities.[13]

These developments, which were accompanied by many volumes of parliamentary reports and thousands of words of depositions, have attracted
much less attention than they deserve from historians interested in one of
the major transformations of the industrial age. They constitute a potentially
rich subject for future study. If there is one thing that recent research on
early modern lawyers has demonstrated, however, it is that the unique
association of professions with modernity is mistaken.[14] Between 1500 and
the present day the trajectory of professional change has, if anything, been
circular rather than linear. It is a point that can be demonstrated in quantitative as well as qualitative terms.

There is no foolproof way in which to count the number of legal practitioners in England at any one time in the past, but if we concentrate on
those who practised in, or registered their qualifications with, the central
courts, there would appear to have been a dramatic and unprecedented
growth during the course of the sixteenth century. Since then fluctuations
have been much more moderate. Between 1480 and 1640 there was something like a seven- to tenfold increase, as the numbers of barristers rose
from perhaps 100 to more than 400. Attorneys enrolled in the central
common law courts multiplied from no more than 200 to at least 1750.[15]
Thereafter, although the pace of increase abated somewhat, it may have
continued up to around 1690; after which there appears to have been, first,
a period of stagnation; and then one of contraction, as an overcrowded
profession adjusted to the decline of litigation during the first half of the
eighteenth century. Admissions to the inns of court were as a much as a
third lower in the period 1688–1714 than they had been in the early
seventeenth century.[16] The number of calls to the bar, and the number of
practising barristers, dropped gradually during the four decades following
1700 before reaching a low point in the 1760s.[17] According to the most

[13] For some of these changes, see above, Chapters 4, 5, 6.

[14] Although Professor P. Corfield's interesting recent book, *Power and the Professions in Britain,
1700–1850* (London, 1995), avoids associating the importance of lawyers with a 'modern'
professionalising agenda, it seems to this reader to take insufficient account of developments
before its starting dates and thereby fails to make a case for the particular significance of the
period it covers.

[15] For the barristers, see Prest, *Rise of the Barristers*, pp. 79, 331. For the attorneys, see Chapter
2, p. 20, and Brooks, *Pettyfoggers and Vipers*, pp. 112–13. It should be stressed that in 1640 there
were still many attorneys, perhaps as many as 500, who practised exclusively in the localities and
who therefore are not included in these counts. For the numbers of practitioners before 1480,
see Chapter 4, pp. 76, 83.

[16] Lemmings, *Gentlemen and Barristers*, p. 6 and 123ff; D. Duman, 'The English Bar in the
Georgian Era', in *Lawyers in Early Modern Europe*, ed. Prest, p. 88.

[17] The distinction between the number called to the bar and the number practising is
important. In the eighteenth century, as in the sixteenth and seventeenth, significantly more

recent researches of Dr David Lemmings, by 1770 there were only 255 barristers practising in the central courts, nearly 50 per cent less than the highest numbers recorded for the seventeenth century.[18]

Although the evidence is not easy to interpret decisively, a similar pattern of change appears to have taken place amongst the more numerous attorneys and solicitors. If taken at face value, enumerations made within the courts of King's Bench and Common Pleas in 1673 and 1698 indicate that numbers were declining (see Figure 7.1); there is even a note attached to the latter list which suggests that it is inflated by the names of a number of dead men.[19] On the other hand, admissions to the inns of chancery, in which many such practitioners enrolled, appear to have remained high through the 1680s, and even into the 1690s, after which a rapid decline set in.[20] Furthermore, from the 1690s, when stamp duties were first introduced on legal proceedings,[21] it was alleged that there were many men who practised as attorneys in the central courts without taking the oath of office and becoming enrolled, mainly because they wanted to avoid paying the duties.[22] According to a inquiry conducted by a committee of the House of Commons in 1708, there were as many as 3000 attorneys of the Common Pleas who were not properly enrolled.[23] This seems likely to have been an exaggeration, but the figure is in line with counts made of the names listed in the comprehensive enrolment of practitioners which took place in conjunction with the 1729 Attorney Act, when 4121 were recorded for King's Bench and Common Pleas.[24] This figure is, however, almost certainly inflated by large numbers of articled clerks who took advantage of the opportunity which the legislation offered to become enrolled on relatively easy terms.[25] Consequently, since the nature of the evidence means that the seventeenth-century figures are almost certainly too low and those for 1730

men became technically qualified to practise in the courts than actually did so.

[18] I am grateful to David Lemmings for sharing with me the statistical evidence for calls to the bar and practising lawyers which he has gleaned from the registers of the legal inns and the records of the central courts. The material will be presented in full in his forthcoming book on the eighteenth-century bar.

[19] *Historical Manuscripts Commission, new series, iii, The Manuscripts of the House of Lords, 1697–99* (London, 1905), pp. 82–87.

[20] C. W. Brooks, *The Admissions Registers of Barnard's Inn, 1620–1869*, Selden Society supplementary series, 12 (1995), pp. 25, 46–47.

[21] E. Hughes, 'The English Stamp Duties, 1664–1764', *English Historical Review*, 56 (1941), pp. 234–44.

[22] This is discussed in more detail in Brooks, *Admissions Registers of Barnard's Inn*, p. 46. Some of the practitioners were alleged to have practised simply by having themselves accepted as clerks by the prothonotaries of the Common Pleas.

[23] *Journals of the House of Commons* (London, 1803ff), xv, p. 619. The committee claimed to have this information from the keeper of the rolls of attorneys of the Common Pleas.

[24] This is discussed extensively in Chapter 6, p. 155, and in Brooks, *Admissions Registers of Barnard's Inn*, p. 47–48.

[25] Ibid.

Figure 7.1
Heads of (Total) Population per Attorney/Solicitor, 1560–1989

Date	Population	Attorneys/Solicitors	Population/Attorney
1560 [a]	3,010,000	200	15,050
1606	4,100,000	1050	3905
1640	5,220,000	2000	2610
1673 [b]	4,980,000	2103	2368
1698 [c]	5,050,000	1625	3107
1731 [d]	5,350,000	4121	1298
1777 [e]	6,440,000	2356	2733
1801 [f]	8,892,536	5270	1687
1821	12,000,236	8702	1379
1841	15,914,148	10,073	1580
1861	20,066,224	10,229	1962
1881	25,974,439	12,688	2047
1901	32,527,843	16,265	2000
1921	37,886,699	14,623	2591
1939	41,460,000	17,102	2424
1951	43,757,888	17,396	2515
1961	46,104,548	19,438	2372
1971	48,749,575	25,366	1922
1977	49,154,687	32,812	1498
1989 [g]	49,000,000	50,337	973

Sources: Note that all of the figures up to and including 1731 are counts of King's Bench and Common Pleas attorneys only. The inclusion of the regional councils and the palatinate courts might certainly inflate the numbers by as much as 500. In addition, none of the figures before 1731 include practitioners who may have worked exclusively in the provinces, mainly in incorporated towns, or in manorial jurisdictions. The number is difficult to calculate, it but probably declined from 1560 onwards (see Brooks, *Pettyfoggers and Vipers*, chs 3, 6).

[a] Figures for 1550–1640 are from Brooks, *Pettyfoggers and Vipers*, p. 113.

[b] House of Lords Record Office, London, Main Papers, 14 February 1673.

[c] *Historical Manuscripts Commission*, new series, iii, *The Manuscripts of the House of Lords, 1697–99* (London, 1905), pp. 82–87.

[d] *Lists of Attorneis and Solicitors Admitted in Persuance of the Late Act for the Better Regulation of Attornies and Solicitors: Presented to the House of Commons* (London, 1729); *Additional Lists of Attornies and Solicitors* (London, 1731).

[e] J. Browne, *Browne's General Law List* (London, 1777).

[f] Figures for 1802 to 1977 are from D. Podmore, *Solicitors and the Wider Community* (London, 1980), p. 14.

[g] B.S. Markesinis, 'Litigation-Mania in England, Germany and the USA: Are We So Very Different?', *Cambridge Law Journal*, 49 (1990), p. 244.

too high, the period from about 1690 to 1730 should be described as one of at best relative stability. It is more certainly the case that the numbers enrolled declined between 1735 and 1765.[26] While recent eighteenth-century social historians may not be mistaken in describing the importance of figures such as local attorneys in the social and political life of early Georgian towns, they are not justified in claiming that it was novel.[27] Attorneys and barristers were already well-established figures in urban life before 1640, and the greater centralisation of the eighteenth-century bar around London probably means that barristers would have been rather less prominent in provincial towns during the eighteenth century than they had been previously.[28]

Predictably, increases in the number of lawyers began again in the 1770s, 1780s and especially the 1790s, as the population of England began to grow and legal business entered into another period of upturn. There were probably twice as many practitioners in 1801 as there had been in 1770. During the first four decades of the nineteenth century both branches underwent very dramatic increases in numbers, but this slowed down thereafter.[29] If we consider it solely in terms of the attorneys and solicitors, the general practitioners of the law, then the century and a quarter from the 1880s to the 1960s was one in which number in relation to total population was relatively low, although there has been an increase of historic proportions since the mid 1970s.

The history of the professional organisation and education of lawyers follows the same contours as that of their numbers. The sixteenth-century increase was accompanied by what might be described as centralisation and a relatively high degree of organisation based on the courts and the inns of court and inns of chancery in London. In contrast by 1700, and certainly by 1750, so many of the features of this regime had collapsed that it is legitimate to speak of the deprofessionalisation of the legal profession. In the early eighteenth century the membership of the legal inns dropped off to such an extent that several of the houses were nearly bankrupt; and institutional legal education became a thing of the past. Finally, and perhaps most importantly, by the early eighteenth century country attorneys had abandoned the earlier practice whereby men from the shires come up to London each term to attend the courts. Instead, they hired London agents to do the work for them and were

[26] Ibid., p. 49. Whereas 202 enrolled in 1735, only 146 did so in 1765.

[27] G. Holmes, *Augustan England: Professions, State and Society, 1680–1730* (London, 1982), ch. 4; P. Borsay, *The English Urban Renaissance: Culture and Society in the Provincial Town, 1660–1760* (Oxford, 1989), pp. 19–20, 37, 200–11, 231.

[28] Brooks, *Pettyfoggers and Vipers*, chs 6, 9, 10; Prest, *Rise of the Barristers*, ch. 8; Duman, 'The English Bar in the Georgian Era', in Prest, *Lawyers in Early Modern Europe and America*, p. 97, noted that while circuit work was important for Georgian barristers, not a single provincial barrister was included on the 1785 *Law List*; and in 1793 there were only three listed as resident in provincial towns. This changed significantly in the nineteenth century.

[29] Duman, *The English and Colonial Bars*, p. 8, estimates that by 1835 the practising bar had grown in numbers to between 450 and 1010.

no longer in a position to observe in person the activities of the courts or to participate in a broader, national, professional culture. Viewed against the history of the previous four centuries, therefore, the creation of national professional organisations by the solicitors and the belated introduction of academic training for lawyers in the middle and late nineteenth century, like the increase in the numbers of practitioners, looks more like the reinvention of the wheel than the creation of a new social form.[30]

Exorcising professionalisation is liberating. The revised history of the legal profession tracks quite closely that of mercantile and craft guilds and thereby invites the study of lawyers and their forms of organisation alongside those of other occupational groups.[31] Indeed, 'professionalisation' may well be an optical illusion created as much by the eighteenth- and nineteenth-century decline of the older forms as by the 'rise of the professions'. We are also faced with intriguing questions about why the size and organisation of the legal profession have both fluctuated over time. Why, for example, do the seventeenth and nineteenth centuries, otherwise so dissimilar, appear to have a common preoccupation with lawyers, courts and legal procedures. Is it that absolutist states, whether monarchical or parliamentary, naturally find much of their legitimacy in terms of the ideal of the rule of law? Alternatively, it is worth considering why older professional ideologies, such as religion and law, have in the modern period been challenged by newer ones centred on medicine or the social sciences.[32]

While there is still plenty of room for more work on professional structures and activities, and for collective biographies of practitioners (especially in the periods prior to 1450 and after 1660), the important point is that there have been periods in the past, most notably the sixteenth and seventeenth centuries, when lawyers have been every bit as significant a feature of the social structure as they are today. Rejecting professionalisation as a characterisation of the way the present differs from the past opens the door to a consideration of lawyers for what they were: a diverse group of people who were at the centre of the creation and exchange of one of the major social discourses of the day: the set of norms, practices and ideologies known collectively as 'the law'.[33]

---

[30] See above, Chapter 5.

[31] For some examples, see Chapter 9, pp. 236–37.

[32] See, for instance, Donald Kelley, *The Human Measure: Social Thought in the Western Legal Tradition* (Cambridge, MA, 1990).

[33] I wish to acknowledge four works, two of them perhaps at first sight unlikely, which have helped me to shape the views I put forward in the remainder of this essay: Robert W. Gordon, 'Critical Legal Histories', *Stanford Law Review*, 36 (1984), pp. 57–125; Sally Humphreys, 'Law as Discourse', *History and Anthropology*, 1 (1985); Jurgen Habermas, *The Structural Transformation of the Public Sphere: An Inquiry into a Category of Bourgeois Society*, trans. Thomas Burger with assistance of Frederick Lawrence (Cambridge, MA, 1989); R. Chartier, *Cultural History: Between Practices and Representations* (Oxford, 1988).

This proposition may seem novel when applied to lawyers, but it has after all long been a commonplace in the study of the clerical profession and theology. Furthermore, while it is certainly necessary to accept that the discourse of law was heavily influenced by the state, the elite and (not least) the interests of lawyers themselves, the next phase in our studies must surely take account of another fact which has emerged from recent work. Whether we are considering criminal trial jurors or the legal professionals, the social groups we encounter most frequently when investigating those who service legal institutions are not the elite, but that 70 per cent of the population which constituted neither the very rich nor the very poor: the middling sort. No less important, between 1550 and 1700, this same collection of social groups comprised at least 70 per cent of the litigants in the courts; they were the principal source of customers for early modern lawyers.[34]

These findings raise a fundamental question, and they open up possibilities for fresh approaches to social history. Can we any longer assume that the law was solely the property of the state or the elite, or that the middling sort were merely the conduit through which elite ideology was channelled to the rest of society, rather than a dynamic force in shaping legal ideas and values in the first place?[35] Equally, if we move our focus away from crime and the criminal law to consider the civil lawsuits of a very litigious society, and the decisions which resulted from them, we enrich the body of material from which we can learn about social and economic relationships and about the way they changed over time.

The sources available for the kinds of work I want to advocate are mainly those produced by lawyers, but they need not be exclusively so. If taken literally, as it certainly should be, the list of those who serviced legal institutions would include constables and jurymen as well as members of the gentry who acted as justices of the peace or members of parliament. Although there have been many studies of quarter sessions records, it is still a nice question whether JPs thought of themselves as servants of the law or protectors of their own private honour or class interests.[36] At the same time, since the rule of law was such an important element in early modern conceptions of the state, discussion of it can be found in sermons (including those addressed to meetings of quarter sessions and assizes), as well as in the ruminations of country squires like Sir Edward Rodney of Somerset or Sir John Newdigate of Warwickshire, both of whom for one reason or another thought a great

---

[34] Herrup, *Common Peace*, ch. 5; Cockburn and Green, *Twelve Good Men*; Kent, *English Village Constable*; Brooks, *Pettyfoggers and Vipers*, chs 4, 5, 11. See also Chapter 4, p. 73.

[35] I hope this is not too crude a summary of the subtle statement of the case for 'descending' influence in K. Wrightson, *English Society, 1580–1680* (London, 1982), 'Conclusion'. I have tried to tackle the problem of the 'middling sort' and professional values in Chapter 9.

[36] For the latter view see A. Fletcher, 'Honour, Reputation and Local Officeholding in Elizabethan and Early Stuart England', in A. Fletcher and John Stevenson, eds, *Order and Disorder in Early Modern England* (Cambridge, 1985).

deal about the subject.[37] Plebeian attitudes are admittedly more difficult to trace, but they emerge in places such as guild ordinances, in the written depositions taken in Star Chamber or Chancery cases and in the nature of lawsuits themselves.[38]

There is also much unexploited lawyerly material. Although mostly in manuscript, written in barbarous law French, and sometimes diabolically obscure, readings or law lectures at the inns of court have hardly been touched, but a little digging can produce some gems. For instance, a fifteenth-century lecture, which uses Magna Carta as a vehicle for explaining the criminal law, proves that lawyers did after all have some interest in the subject. In the Elizabethan period, the puritan James Morice gave a reading on the royal prerogative which postulates a contractual basis for royal authority. In 1617 Serjeant Francis Ashley, starting with chapter 29 of Magna Carta, gave a lecture on the liberty of the subject, which is less interesting for its views on royal authority than for what it says about the relationship between the individual, the community and the state.[39] This list of material could be expanded to include printed law texts, speeches in parliament or at state trials, unpublished treatises, and the addresses which were regularly used to preface charges delivered to quarter sessions and assizes – public utterances which often dilated on the role of law in society.[40] Sources such as these enable us to broaden the scope of legal ideology beyond the rather narrow and precedent ridden 'common law mind' formulated by Professor Pocock.[41] They illustrate the ways in which it was exchanged with the wider public. They offer the prospect of a history of generalised legal ideas about the state and society which can be traced over time and compared with that of other strands of thought.

If there are two kinds of source which, more than others, cry out for more exploitation than they have hitherto received from social historians, they must be the records of the civil, as opposed to the criminal, courts; and the case law of the sixteenth, seventeenth and eighteenth centuries, some of which remains in manuscript, but the vast bulk of which is in fact readily available in printed reports. Many social historians will have used such sources at one point or another in their studies, either to establish what the law was

---

[37] Sir Edward Rodney's papers are in BL, MSS Add. 34239–40; those of Newdigate are in the Warwickshire County Record Office. See also Richard Cust, ed., *The Papers of Sir Richard Grosvenor, 1st Bart (1585–1645)*, Record Society of Lancashire and Cheshire, 134 (1996).

[38] For interesting qualitative analyses of the written depositions given in criminal cases, see Malcolm Gaskill, 'Attitudes to Crime in Early Modern England: With Special Reference to Witchcraft, Coining and Murder' (unpublished Ph.D. thesis, University of Cambridge, 1994).

[39] BL, MS Harleian 1210, fos 144 ff; MS Add. 36081, fos 229ff; MS Harleian 4841.

[40] See, for example, George Lamoine, ed., *Charges to the Grand Jury, 1689–1803*, Camden Society, 4th series, 43 (London, 1992).

[41] J. G. A. Pocock, *The Ancient Constitution and the Feudal Law: A Study of English Historical Thought in the Seventeenth Century. A Reissue with a Retrospect* (Cambridge, 1987). I have explored some of these issues in Chapter 8.

with regard to the subject in which they are interested or to mine for material about social and economic practices.[42] In contrast, there are very few examples of systematic study of case law to establish what it might have to tell us about whole categories of social relationships: economic transactions; husband and wife; landlord and tenant; judge and defendant; urban oligarch and freeman; community and person. The reason for this neglect must be the received orthodoxy that the law was exclusively concerned with rights to property to land and therefore of interest only to the elite. These assumptions are in fact false, and there is much to learn from trying to unravel the intellectual, social and political ingredients which went into judicial reasoning, particularly in the sixteenth and seventeenth centuries when judges were making decisions which became the law enshrined in the black-letter tradition. Until it is proved otherwise, it is a mistake to assume that judicial thought diverged significantly from other contemporary values.[43] Even if judges should (at least at different points in time) be seen as servants of the state,[44] the lawyers who argued cases before them worked for individuals rather than institutions. In this respect the arguments that failed are as interesting as those that succeeded.[45] At the same time, the use of court records to monitor the frequency of various types of case, and to point to cross-cutting sources of the sort which are familiar to the social historian, can stop the study of legal decisions from degenerating into the pursuit of doctrinal genealogies, a tendency which has contributed in the past to the intellectual isolation of legal history. The great thing about lawsuits is that, while they tell us about norms, they also show how people exploited, challenged or sought to alter them. As Sally Humphreys has put it, legal discourse always includes assumptions about the nature of the person, social relations and knowledge.[46] These are all subjects of interest to the social historian.

It is of course easier to propose programmes of research than to carry them out or to demonstrate that they will produce significant results. Yet there are some encouraging signs. Amy Erickson's successful utilisation of Chancery records and legal treatises to demonstrate that married women's property rights were better protected than has been previously thought is an

[42] For a recent work that discusses the documents and illustrates some of the possibilities, see Henry Horwitz, *Chancery Equity Records and Proceedings, 1600–1800: A Guide to Documents in the Public Record Office* (London, 1995).

[43] This point is developed in a very suggestive way in Lawrence Rosen, *The Anthropology of Justice: Law as Culture in Islamic Society* (Cambridge, 1989).

[44] Even if this is the case, of course, those who have positions in the 'state' frequently have different views. See, for example, some of the insights about the political history of the Elizabethan regime which emerge from *Reports from the Lost Notebooks of Sir James Dyer*, ed. J. H. Baker, Selden Society, 109–10 (2 vols, London, 1993–94), i, 'Introduction'.

[45] For an interesting use of this approach see Sarah Hanley, 'Engendering the State: Family Formation and State Building in Early Modern France', *French Historical Studies*, 16 (1989).

[46] Humphreys, 'Law as Discourse', p. 252.

encouraging example of what can be accomplished; so, too, is Lawrence Stone's pursuit on the action of criminal conversation as a milestone on *The Road to Divorce*.[47] Michael Sonescher's work on eighteenth-century French artisans is a striking example of how a move away from the criminal law (and professional history) towards an understanding of civil litigation can reveal much about social relationships and the part legal language played in conceptualising them; the key to his approach is to marry a deep awareness of social realities with a careful reading of legal discourse.[48] Unfortunately, similar studies relating to early modern England are very rare. More than a quarter of a century has passed since Christopher Hill fired a brief debate on the 'economic liberalism' of Sir Edward Coke, but, despite their resonances with late twentieth-century concerns, the sort of questions he raised have not been followed up.[49] I have interpreted my own findings that many lawsuits before 1700 were based on conditional bonds as indicative that economic relationships between ordinary people may have been based on the Hobbesian concern about the crucial role of the state in ensuring that promises were kept. In his impressive study of the court of pleas at King's Lynn, Craig Muldrew has drawn a picture of market and credit relationships which were also infused with notions of equity and Christian charity.[50] More generally, it could be hypothesised that early modern lawyers had complex, maybe even contradictory, views which attempted to balance the public interest against their promises to protect private property. For instance, the author of an early seventeenth-century proposal to prevent fraud in the Newcastle sea-coal trade found it necessary to argue around the fact that chapter 29 of Magna Carta could be used to protect a man's goods as well as his person.[51] On the other hand, Coke approved of the use of guilds as a means of maintaining consumer protection;[52] and it seems likely that judges left many details of business dealings and 'industrial relations' to juries.[53]

So much work remains to be done on these and related issues that they constitute virtually new fields of study for early modern scholars. Lawyers'

[47] A. L. Erickson, 'Common Law Versus Common Practice: The Use of Marriage Settlements in Early Modern England', *Economic History Review*, 2nd series, 43 (1990), pp. 21–39; idem, *Women and Property in Early Modern England* (London, 1993); L. Stone, *Road to Divorce: England, 1530–1987* (Oxford, 1990); see also, W. R. Prest, 'Law and Women's Rights in Early Modern England', *The Seventeenth Century*, 6 (1991), pp. 169–87.

[48] Michael Sonescher, *Work and Wages: Natural Law, Politics and the Eighteenh-Century French Trades* (Cambridge 1989), esp. p. 46.

[49] C. Hill, *Intellectual Origins of the English Revolution* (Oxford, 1965), pp. 225–65; B. Malament, 'The "Economic Liberalism" of Sir Edward Coke', *Yale Law Review*, 76 (1967), pp. 1321–58.

[50] See Chapter 4, pp. 86–89. Craig Muldrew, 'The Culture of Reconciliation: Community and the Settlement of Economic Disputes in Early Modern England', *Historical Journal*, 39 (1996).

[51] Inner Temple Library, London, MS Petyt 538(43), fos 155–62.

[52] *English Reports*, lxxvii, 11 Coke 53, *Case of Merchant Tailors of Ipswich*.

[53] This observation is based mainly on the mid eighteenth-century trial notes of Sir Dudley Ryder. Unfortunately, material of the same quality has not come to light for earlier periods. See Chapter 3, pp. 55–57, for more detail.

law can also make a contribution to areas that have already gained a place in the secondary literature, namely the relationship between law and the community and that between class power, discretion and deference. In modern writing, the first of these issues has perhaps been put most clearly on the agenda as a result of a seminal article by Keith Wrightson. This focused on the constable as a way of depicting a conflict in the early seventeenth century between the law of the elite (and of the state) and the more easygoing neighbourly relations typical of the customary life of villages.[54] There is much that is convincing in this formulation, but it has always seemed to me that one serious weakness is that it does not confront the question of when, if ever, lawyers and the law were not so intimately involved in village life that social relations might be discussed without reference to them. In this connection, the critical institution was the manorial court, a jurisdiction whose existence and activities have been woefully neglected by sixteenth-century social historians.[55] It is true that the presentment of offences at courts leet and courts baron, and much of the responsibility for judging them, rested with local inhabitants. It also seems to be the case that, until the late sixteenth century, the stewards who convened them were more likely to have been amateur than professional lawyers.[56] Many parliamentary statutes were, nevertheless, enforceable in the manorial courts. Practice in them was a subject of study at the fifteenth-century legal inns, and a published manual (the *Modus tenendi curiam baronum*) listing matters to be dealt with in manorial courts covers many regulatory issues ranging from the brewing of faulty ale to illicit games, the erection of cottages, environmental issues and scolding women.[57] Even a casual glance at the records themselves reveals village life to have been anything but ideally peaceful and devoid of contention.

The significance of the manorial courts is that they throw into bold relief, indeed problematise, an issue which is perennially important to those who consider court usage. It is one which has been particularly prominent in historical thinking of recent times about the relationship between law and society: the relationship between custom and the generalised values of local

[54] K. Wrightson, 'Two Concepts of Order: Justices, Constables and Jurymen in Seventeenth-Century England', in Brewer and Styles, *An Ungovernable People?*

[55] Honourable exceptions are F. J. C. Hearnshaw, *Leet Jurisdiction in England* (Southampton, 1908); J. P. Dawson, *A History of Lay Judges* (Cambridge, MA, 1960); M. K. McIntosh, *Autonomy and Community: The Royal Manor of Havering, 1200–1500* (Cambridge, 1986); and its sequel *A Community Transformed: The Manor and Liberty of Havering, 1500–1620* (Cambridge, 1991). See also C. Harrison, 'Manor Courts and the Governance of Tudor England', in C. W. Brooks and M. Lobban, eds, *Communities and Courts in Britain, 1150–1900* (London, 1997), and Chapter 4, pp. 69–71, 84.

[56] See Chapter 4, p. 83.

[57] Brooks, *Pettyfoggers and Vipers*, chs 6 and 9; *Modus tenendi curiam baronum cum visu franci plegii* (Wynkyn de Worde, London, 1506); M. J. Ingram, '"Scolding Women Cucked or Washed": A Crisis of Gender Relations in Early Modern England?', in Jenny Kermode and Garthine Walker, eds, *Women, Crime and the Courts in Early Modern England* (London 1994).

communities versus the formal legal ideas and processes, such as those which
were enshrined in parliamentary statues or enforced by the courts (a classic
example of our obsession with the distinction between elite and popular
culture).[58] Knowing something about manorial courts does not solve the
difficulty of defining a 'popular concept' of justice and order. Very often
the only records they have left behind are highly formal ones; and, of course,
such courts were held by lords of manors at least partly for the pursuit of
profit. Yet they are intriguing because they were institutions in which a great
deal of community autonomy met with a considerable amount of formal
law. Local inhabitants made presentments and acted as jurors to settle
disputes according to local custom, but they were not completely insulated
from the law of Westminster Hall. Finally, manorial court evidence certainly
shows that social change within traditional communities, or nothing more
than two people who did not like each other, could break out into anomie,
litigation and (very often) physical violence. Instead of communities where
Christian charity, neighbourliness and informal means of resolving disputes
were the predominant feature of popular attitudes to order, we can just as
easily insert one in which people were regularly in court and where the
more prosperous members of the community used the institution of manorial
justice to resolve disputes and regulate behaviour.[59]

The gradual, but by no means complete, decline of manorial courts during
the seventeenth century, and a transferral of much of their jurisdiction,
including the appointment of constables, to quarter sessions and the central
courts was an extremely important development. Judicial decisions no less
than legislative policy undoubtedly played their part in helping it to take
place.[60] On the other hand, the law reports also suggest that much of the
pressure for reducing the powers of such courts came from individuals who
(with the help of lawyers) brought actions which they hoped would free them
from acting as constables or paying fines for breaches of communal regulations.[61] It is therefore as likely that communal regulation collapsed from
within as much as under pressure from outside. In any case, given the wide
range of issues for which the manorial court had traditionally been responsible, the shift in jurisdiction makes it plausible to argue that by 1600 there
had already been a significant reduction in the powers of the community at
large to interfere in the affairs of individual inhabitants. The case law shows
that early seventeenth-century judges were defining manorial jurisdictions,
as opposed to that of the common law, as the only venue where offences

---

[58] See the interesting recent discussion of 'custom' by Tim Stretton, 'Women, Custom and
Equity in the Court of Requests', in Kermode and Walker, eds, *Women, Crime and the Courts*.

[59] These issues will be explored more thoroughly in my forthcoming book about law, society
and politics in early modern England.

[60] Kent, *English Village Constable*, p. 19. See also Sir Francis Bacon, 'The Answers to Questions
Propounded by Sir Alexander Hay, Knight, Touching the Office of Constable, AD 1608', in
Works, ed. J. Spedding et al. (14 vols, London, 1857–74), vi, pp. 749–54.

[61] *English Reports*, lxxvii–lxxviii, 8 Coke 38, *Griesley's Case*; Croke Eliz., 698, *Steverton v. Scroggs.*

against the 'community', including environmental matters, such as the fouling of watercourses or the damage caused by wandering animals, could be heard.[62]

The differences between the communal justice of the manor and the law dealt in by lawyers and administered by judges or the gentry acting as justices of the peace demands further investigation. At the same time, taking account of the existence, activities and decline of the manorial jurisdiction may lead us to shift the focus of our attention away from the relationship between the law and the community towards a consideration of the place of the individual person in the face of both the community and the authority of state law. Here again legal thought and lawyers' law can offer new perspectives.

In their public rhetoric, especially during the sixteenth century, lawyers argued for the advantages of their view of the social and political world largely in terms of self-interest. Political allegiance, for instance, might well be divinely ordained, but it also offered the practical benefit of the rule of law; and the rule of law guaranteed the protection of the property and person of the individual. Justice was also supposed to be no respecter of persons, including the rich and powerful, and there was in fact a strong strain within early modern legal thought which was openly hostile to the overmighty. The remedy was the foundation of a state and the rule of law which would protect the weak from the strong.[63]

If equality before the law was the basis of rational obedience to political authority, judicial discretion was bound to be problematic. On the one hand, legal thought advocated the importance of mercy and discretion in the carrying out of the criminal law. A short essay in the papers of Lord Chancellor Ellesmere, for instance, referred to a wide range of classical and biblical sources in the course of arguing that there should be an 'abatement of severity' in magistrates. 'There should be a Sweet temper always used, not the harsh rigidness which is found in some that know not how to shew mercy unto any.'[64] On the other hand, there was also an awareness that discretion threatened the rule of law. Hence another early seventeenth-century writer criticised the use of discretion by inferior magistrates as a usurpation of monarchical power. 'It is Easy to him that knoweth no lawe or Justice to rule as he Lysteth.' The conclusion was that judges should be restricted to governing according to law.[65] There are in fact many instances, particularly from Star Chamber cases, where justices of the peace were prosecuted for exceeding their powers.[66] Furthermore, surviving manuscript

---

[62] *English Reports*, lxxvii–lxxix, 5 Coke 73, *William's Case*. Croke Eliz., 415, *Evington v. Brimston*; Croke Jac., 382, *Pratt v. Stearn*.

[63] See Chapters 8 and 9, pp. 206–7 and 243–44, for specific examples.

[64] Henry E. Huntington Library, San Marino, California, MS Ellesmere 1163.

[65] BL, MS Cotton Vespasian C, xiv, vol. ii, fos 176ff–77v, 'Therefoare it maye seeme they Rather seeme to desyre to be kynges then to rule the people under the kynge who will not admynestere Justyce by law but by their owne willes'.

[66] For example, W. P. Baildon, ed., *Les reportes del cases in Camera Stellata, 1593–1609* (London, 1894), p. 234; *English Reports*, lxxvii, 5 Coke, 100, *Rooke's Case*.

reports of cases tried at assizes, which are lamentably rare but which nevertheless have been seriously neglected by students of both the criminal and
the civil law, leave little doubt that judges instructed juries and played an
important role in either downgrading or upgrading charges in line with
their interpretation of the technical questions.[67] For example, in Holloway's
Case, which eventually produced an authoritative and widely-reported decision, the jury was apparently undecided on how to deal with an incident
in which a woodward so brutally maltreated a boy who was stealing wood
from the park of the earl of Denbigh that the lad eventually died. The
partial verdict hinged on the question of whether this was murder or
manslaughter. The judges at Newgate determined that it was murder and
the woodward was hanged.[68] Both the initial indecision of the jury and the
eventual resolution of the judges raise interesting questions about the extent
to which there was toleration of the use of arbitrary force in defence of the
property rights of the powerful.[69]

If juristic thought offered the rule of law in return for political obedience,
it is also true that the exchange was to some extent non-negotiable. People
who criticised the exercise of legitimate authority were subject to prosecution.
Sir Edward Coke for one argued that all libels of magistrates which touched
on the performance of their duties should be 'severely punished'.[70] Yet, on
closer inspection, the number of libels which came before the courts in the
early seventeenth century is striking, as is the fact that many verbal and
written attacks on magistrates at all levels were made by lawyers, such as,
for instance, a local attorney who was sued in Star Chamber for publishing
the view that the sheriff of Lancashire 'vexed poor ... people'.[71] These may,
moreover, have been related to two further characteristics of the legal life
of the period. First, by the early seventeenth century lawyers were clearly
involved in the defence of cases which came before urban courts and quarter
sessions.[72] Secondly, while it may have been difficult to make public criticism
of officials, it was certainly becoming fairly common practise to sue them.
The examples of this range from the use of actions of trespass against
constables who distrained property in connection with the raising of Ship
Money, to suits in Star Chamber or common law actions of unlawful

[67] The best examples I have found are BL, MS Hargrave 44; and Exeter College, Oxford MS
168.

[68] *English Reports*, lxxxii, Jones 198 for Holloway's Case.

[69] James Cockburn has always argued for the importance of the judiciary in understanding
the operation of the criminal law. For a restatement which takes account of recent work showing
that juries were unlikely to have been self-informing, see his review of Herrup, *Common Peace* in
Law and History Review 9 (1991), pp. 173–79.

[70] *English Reports*, lxxvii, 5 Coke 125, *De libellis famosis*.

[71] Inner Temple, MS Add. 19, Star Chamber Reports 1630–33, fol. 16; BL, MS Hargrave 46,
Justice Hutton's Reports, fol. 171, where Sir Robert Hitcham brings action on the case against
an attorney for defaming him in connection with his duties as justice of the peace.

[72] Brooks, *Pettyfoggers and Vipers*, pp. 190–91.

imprisonment against justices of the peace or town officials who threw people in gaol for uttering opprobrious words.[73] It would take more work than has yet been done in the central court records to establish the exact number and nature of such cases, but that they were not uncommon is attested by the passage of a statute in 1609 which was designed to make it more difficult to prosecute contentious suits against justices of the peace and other officials.[74] When this class of litigation is put alongside the large numbers of known cases in which copyhold tenants sued and won actions in defence of their tenures and 'reasonable' rents, a new picture of the role of law in society begins to emerge.[75] Rather than seeing it as the unbending defender of authority and the class interests of the aristocracy and gentry, it appears as a potentially powerful solvent on the deferential posture of ordinary people which the elite undoubtedly expected, which modern historians frequently take for granted but which may not in reality have been accepted all that supinely by contemporaries.

No less important, it is worthwhile to investigate those strains in early modern legal thought which promised protection against the oppression of the individual by the authority of urban oligarchs, justices of the peace and, maybe, acts of parliament or the community itself. For instance, one of commonplaces of early modern social history is that everyone had the right to know everyone else's business; but from the lawyer's perspective it is actually far from clear that this was in any simple sense the case.[76] Eavesdropping (or listening under the windows of a neighbour's house) was one of the standard offences that were supposed to be investigated by manorial court juries, and actions of slander were regularly brought and won against those who retailed malicious rumours about their neighbours.[77] In a similar vein, Sir Edward Coke on more than one occasion pronounced the maxim that 'the House of every one is to him as his Castle and Fortress, as well for his Defence against Injury and Violence, as for his repose'.[78] There are

---

[73] *English Reports*, lxxvii, 5 Coke 152, *Clark's Case*; 11 Coke 93, *James Bagg's Case*.

[74] 7 James I, c. 5; continued and enlarged in 21 James I, c. 12.

[75] *English Reports*, lxxvii, 4 Coke, pp. 21ff.

[76] A strong case for a lack of privacy is made in K. V. Thomas, *Religion and the Decline of Magic: Studies in Popular Beliefs in Sixteenth and Seventeenth Century England* (London, 1973), pp. 628ff. For earlier doubts see M. Ingram, *Church Courts, Sex and Marriage in England, 1570–1640* (Cambridge, 1987), p. 30.

[77] *Modus tenendi*; Brooks, *Pettyfoggers and Vipers*, pp. 107–11, 279; Kent, *Village Constables*, pp. 246, 261; R. H. Helmholz and T. A. Green, *Juries, Libel, and Justice: The Role of English Juries in Seventeenth- and Eighteenth-Century Trials for Libel and Slander* (Los Angeles, CA, 1984).

[78] *English Reports*, lxxvii, 5 Coke 91, *Semayne's Case*. It was noted that there was no penalty for murder in defence of the house. However, the point of law resolved was that while a sheriff could break into the house of a defendant when the king was a party, the sheriff should explain the reasons for his coming and make a request to open the doors. After discussion it was also concluded that the sheriff could not break into a house to serve civil process. Coke did not invent the dictum: it apparently dates from at least the time of Henry VII. See J. H. Baker, *The Reports of Sir John Spelman*, ii, Selden Society, 94 (London, 1978), p. 316 n. 2.

any number of cases in the law reports which were brought to court on actions of trespass by people who claimed that their rights had been unjustly infringed by constables or who took direct action against officials for entering their houses. In the reign of Charles I, Justice Jones ruled at assizes that a constable could commit to prison anyone who broke the peace or offered to break it in his presence, and that it was lawful to arrest a nightwalker for the prevention of malfeasance. But he also said that it was unlawful to arrest a 'good householder' who had business at night; one of the lawyers present at the trial noted that Chief Justice Popham had given a similar judgment some years earlier in London in a case which involved a woman who was visiting her husband at the Inner Temple.[79] In another case, the judges directed the jury to find not guilty on a charge of murder brought against a man who had killed a sergeant, who was trying to serve him a writ of adultery out of high commission, because the writ itself was judged to be illegal.[80] Finally, although the argument was ultimately unsuccessful, it is worth noting that there was a legal case to be made against the summary jurisdiction of houses of correction such as the London Bridewell, institutions established from the later sixteenth century onwards to round up vagrants and to punish petty crime and vice. According to a late Elizabethan treatise, the Bridewell's commission was 'repugnant' to the principles of due process laid down in Magna Carta because hearings were held in secret rather than in open court, and the accused were tried at the discretion of magistrates rather than by juries.[81]

On the other hand, the late sixteenth and early seventeenth centuries did see a spate of (largely unsuccessful) bills proposed in parliament for the regulation of personal conduct.[82] In 1601, Coke acting as attorney general, drew up a set of instructions for constables which, amongst other things, ordered them to report 'unlawful games, drunkenness, etc. in private families'.[83] The famous Elizabethan author of guide books for justices of the peace, William Lambarde, appears to have toyed with the idea of casting the charge for the commissioners of the peace under the headings of the Ten Commandments.[84] Apart from anything else, these campaigns for moral reformation raise inevitable and important questions about the relationship

---

[79] Exeter College, Oxford, MS 168, fol. 117v.

[80] Inner Temple Library, MS Miscellaneous 20, fol. 57

[81] Cambridge University Library, MS Ee. 2.30, fos 1–8. Attributed to both Francis Bacon and William Fleetwood, the tract is reprinted in Spedding et al., eds, *Life and Letters of Bacon*, vii, p. 509. For the attribution see J. H. Baker and J. S. Ringrose, *A Catalogue of English Legal Manuscripts in Cambridge University Library* (Woodbridge, 1996), p. 183.

[82] Joan R. Kent, 'Attitudes of Members of the House of Commons to the Regulation of "Personal Conduct" in Late Elizabethan and Early Stuart England', *Bulletin of Institute Historical Research*, 46 (1973), pp. 41–71.

[83] R. Lemon and M. A. E. Green, eds, *Calendar of State Papers, Domestic Series, of the Reigns of Edward VI, Mary, Elizabeth, James I, 1547–1625* (12 vols, London, 1856–72), v, p. 519.

[84] BL, MS Egerton 3676. Lambarde did not put the idea into print.

between law and religion, a subject which has certainly figured in the historiography but which has not received a systematic treatment on anything like the scale it deserves. The topics which would repay investigation range from, at the highest level, a comparison of the philosophical and political outlooks of the two disciplines, to study of the conflict between the ecclesiastical and temporal jurisdictions (the dispute over prohibitions), down to the speeches used by hanging judges when they were passing sentence.[85] For instance, one consequence of the passage of moral legislation was that the jurisdiction for the matters concerned shifted from the ecclesiastical to the common law courts; the church court officials subsequently claimed that their jurisdiction was likely to collapse as a result of common law actions which were brought to block its judgments and officials.[86]

Just as there were differences of opinion in the House of Commons about the passage of moral legislation, so also there were clearly differences of opinion amongst lawyers and judges, and these were fully tested by litigants. Much of the evidence we have of puritan attempts to control morality comes from lawsuits in which their activities were being challenged in the courts.[87] Furthermore, the basis of judicial ambivalence about such issues may be explained partly by the fact that activities such as the haunting of alehouses or gambling were statutory rather than common law offences.[88] Although some judges, such as Sir John Dodderidge, were campaigners against the evils of the alehouse, it is notable that both Dodderidge and Sir Francis Bacon made a point of telling grand jurors that Englishmen were lucky that they lived in a country where there were no moral censors.[89] Other judges appear to have been doubtful about the usefulness of excessive zeal in dealing with personal conduct, and there were certainly litigants who were willing to challenge attempts to control their drinking habits. Take, for example, a case from Banbury in the late 1620s in which a man called Weston brought a highly technical action of unlawful imprisonment against constables who apprehended him for drinking after hours. The fact that he was willing to bring an action to defend himself against an offence which carried a fine of 3s. 4d. is in itself interesting. No less so were the remarks of the presiding

[85] Some of these issues are touched upon in Chapter 9.

[86] Inner Temple Library, MSS Petyt 538(38), fos 260, 286; 518, fol. 62v. However, it seems that such claims were unduly alarmist. See Chapter 4, p. 71.

[87] For example, although it was ultimately unsuccessful, a man called Philip Haines brought a case in Star Chamber in 1628 against Ignatius Jordan, the then mayor of Exeter, because Jordan had used his secular authority to imprison and whip Haines for committing adultery and fornication. Jordan was one of the leading lights behind the successful passage of the draconian Adultery Act of 1650, BL, MS Lansdowne 620, fol. 47v; K. V. Thomas, 'The Puritans and Adultery: The Act of 1650 Reconsidered', K. V. Thomas and D. Pennington, eds, *Puritans and Revolutionaries* (Oxford, 1978), pp. 257–82.

[88] *English Reports*, lxxiii, lxxvii, 3 Dyer 255, *Bell* v. *Bishop of Norwich*; 11 Coke 85, *Darcy* v. *Allen* (Case of Monopolies).

[89] BL, MS Harleian 583, fos 1v, 17v–18v; Cambridge University Library, MS Gg. III. 26, fol. 136, 'Sir Francis Bacon's Charge at a Verge Court'.

judge, Jones, who commented that local authorities could more profitably spend their time searching out seditious preachers than harassing respectable men who were enjoying a drink.[90]

The preceding observations are obviously intended to be suggestive rather than conclusive. I have tried to show how a consideration of lawyers' law in a highly litigious age might lead to a rethinking of established orthodoxies and provide a new, and largely untapped, body of source material about social and economic relationships. Studies of crime and the criminal legal process, like the statistical analysis of civil litigation, and the mass biographical approach to the history of the legal profession, have provided two strong pillars on which to base an understanding of the role of law in society. Until we cap this with investigation of juristic ideas and the development of the substantive law, the edifice will however lack the arch which can give it shape. If we could better appreciate the role of due process of law in the relationship between a justice of the peace and a seventeenth-century villager, we might be better placed to talk about the place of legal ideology in the origins of the English Civil War. David Sabean has suggested that the formation of historical consciousness takes place somewhere between the assertion of authority and the means by which authority was legitimated.[91] There are no social groups who have historically been more actively engaged in this dialectic than judges and lawyers. If we now know that the legal profession has had a complex history over the past six hundred years (and before), the study of legal discourse and the way it related to social practice may offer a rewarding tool for conceptualising the past on its own terms and charting change over time.

[90] BL, MS Hargrave 44, fol. 27v.

[91] David Warren Sabean, *Power in the Blood: Popular Culture and Village Discourse in Early Modern Germany* (Cambridge, 1984), p. 25.

8

The Place of Magna Carta and the 'Ancient Constitution' in Sixteenth-Century English Legal Thought

Legal thought and questions about the relationship between legal ideas and other strains of political and social theory are important and interesting aspects of sixteenth- and seventeenth-century English history, but they are subjects which have suffered in recent years both from scholarly neglect and from misunderstanding. The neglect can be explained partly by reference to the sociology of knowledge. British universities, which were founded and flourished for much of their history as training grounds for clerics, have recently been much more successful in producing students of ecclesiastical history and religious ideas than of legal history and juristic thought. At the same time much recent writing on the political and social history of the period, such as the so-called revisionist reinterpretations of the causes of the civil wars of the mid seventeenth century, has tended to discount the role of ideas of any kind, much less legal ideology, in the general history of the period.[1]

This neglect is also one of the primary reasons for the misunderstandings of English legal thought which have accumulated over the years. In particular, it accounts for a failure to investigate or reinterpret a category of analysis which has for too long exercised a paradigmatic influence on our conception of the nature of legal ideas about politics and society: the notion of the common law mind. This concept became an orthodoxy in modern scholarship with the publication in 1957 of Professor J. G. A. Pocock's magisterial study of English historical thought, *The Ancient Constitution and the Feudal Law*. Concerned mainly with the attitudes of lawyers to the past, and basing his thesis largely on the works of Sir Edward Coke and his contemporary Sir John Davies, Pocock postulated a typical common law view of politics and society which was essentially a forerunner of that made famous by Edmund Burke in *His Reflections on the Revolution in France* (1790). According to Pocock, the key to the common law mind was the assumption that English law had no history, that it had been virtually unchanged by any of the major or minor upheavals in the history of England either before or after the Norman Conquest. English lawyers thought that English laws were the best laws because they represented the product of immemorial custom, a kind

---

[1] For one of many possible examples, see J. S. Morrill, *The Revolt of the Provinces: Conservatives and Radicals in the English Civil War, 1630–1650* (London, 1976).

of mystical process by which the common law had proven itself to be satisfactory to the English through constant usage from a time beyond the written records or memories of men. In addition, the common lawyers completely denied that the civil law had ever had any influence in their country. They were also extremely insular in their refusal to consider jurisprudential ideas which were contained within the civil law tradition; or to wake up to the advances in historical scholarship which were being made by continental humanist legal scholars such as Budé, Cujas and Hotman.

Although his own study concentrated on the history of historical thought, Pocock also believed that the 'common law mind' had a wider application to the political history of the early seventeenth century, and this is a position which he has amplified in a restatement of the thesis. Coke and Coke's ideas were part of a mentality which had an important place in the controversies between the early Stuarts and their parliaments. The lawyers' idea of an unchanging legal tradition provided a standard, an 'ancient constitution', which could be used as a defence by the subject against the encroachments of the crown.[2]

There is no doubt that parts of this picture demand assent. Pocock's interpretation of Coke's thought is accurate, and 'ancient constitutionalism' was put to effective use by lawyers during some of the early Stuart parliaments, perhaps most notably in 1628. What is in doubt, however, is whether 'ancient constitutionalism' had always been the major constituent of English legal thought; and whether it was part of a longer tradition within English law. So much of the debate to date has been about legal attitudes towards history that we tend to lose sight of more general legal attitudes towards the law, politics and society. Consequently, it is far from clear how significant the ancient constitution was within the nexus of thought and practice which made up the intellectual environment of the legal profession and which was transmitted by the lawyers to the wider public.

Integral to both questions is the problem of what it was that might have made up the legal mentality of both lawyers and laymen (of different social groups) during the early modern period, and the ways in which these mentalities may have changed over time. The object of this chapter is to approach this problem by looking first at the structure of legal thought in general during the sixteenth century. Then it attempts to find a place for the history of that greatest of documents of the 'ancient constitution', Magna Carta, within it. In general, the picture that emerges is quite different from that of the common law mentality we have known for so long. In the first place, English legal thought in this period is best seen as part of the broader

---

[2] J. G. A. Pocock, *The Ancient Constitution and the Feudal Law: A Study of English Historical Thought in the Seventeenth Century* (Cambridge, 1957). The new formulation and a very accurate account of the debate which the original interpretation engendered can be found in J. G. A. Pocock, *The Ancient Constitution and The Feudal Law: A Study of English Historical Thought in the Seventeenth Century. A Reissue with a Retrospect* (Cambridge, 1987).

European tradition of Renaissance jurisprudence rather than *sui generis*. For that reason I have perhaps gone overboard in avoiding the term 'common law mind'. Secondly, but perhaps not surprisingly when it is considered that the Tudor state frequently presented itself as an absolute monarchy, sixteenth-century lawyers were as often concerned with order, and indeed the basic problem of political obligation, obedience, as with questions concerning the liberty of the subject. For both of these reasons, neither ancient constitutionalism or Magna Carta, at least until the 1590s, was very significant feature of legal thought. There was a distinctive legal mentality during this period, but it contained many branches. Ancient constitutionalism was only one of them, and a relative latecomer at that. Finally, the chapter offers an account of the particular circumstances in the late sixteenth century and first decade of the seventeenth which led Coke to express for the first time an elaborate ancient constitutionalist account of English law and government. I conclude with some brief remarks on the broader significance of early modern legal thought in the Anglo-American political tradition.

The sixteenth century was a great age for the English legal profession. From the 1530s, but especially from about 1560, there was a spectacular increase in the amount of litigation which came before the central courts, so that by 1600 the rate of litigation was considerably higher than it is today. At the same time, the legal profession centred on the Westminster courts grew from a relatively small band of lawyers to a social group with a profile relative to the size of the population as a whole that was little different from that of the early twentieth century. It is not surprising, therefore, that much Tudor social and political thought, and not just that produced by lawyers, was articulated in legalistic terms.[3]

In spite of this, an attempt to identify the most basic attitudes of English lawyers toward their law and its place in society does have to confront problems of evidence. The English legal profession and English legal education had an overwhelmingly vocational orientation. Lawyers learned their craft at the inns of court in London rather than in the universities. The inns had a teaching function and some teaching exercises. Indeed, the sixteenth century can be said to have marked a high point in the history of the inns as intellectual centres, and this is important in considering the role of legal ideology in this period. Nevertheless, there were limits on the extent to which English lawyers were free to speculate about jurisprudential matters. The senior members of the inns were primarily active practitioners; no English lawyer earned his living exclusively from teaching or writing about the law.[4] Hence, unlike the continental university schools of law, the inns of court and the English legal profession produced few general works, even

---

[3] See Chapters 4 and 7, pp. 70–71, 182–84.

[4] W. R. Prest, *The Inns of Court under Elizabeth I and the Early Stuarts, 1590–1640* (London, 1972).

fewer which laid out with clarity the theoretical and philosophical foundations of the common law. The legal thought of the period must be pieced together from the examination of the odd textbook, one-off tracts, lectures delivered to students at the inns of court and speeches made at meetings of courts such as quarter sessions and assize.

English jurisprudence was not highly articulate, but it did consist of a number of identifiable assumptions and ideas. These can be most easily introduced by looking initially at *De laudibus legum Angliae*, a classic work written by Chief Justice Sir John Fortescue in the 1470s. Fortescue is frequently cited, with Sir Edward Coke, as a writer who exemplified the English legal tradition, and *De laudibus* does contain a number of points which fit well with the stereotype of the 'common law mind'. Fortescue compared foreign, especially French, legal institutions unfavourably with those of the English. He did not like the civil law doctrine, 'What pleases the prince has the force of law'. He also held that, since English kings ruled both politically and regally, no English monarch could introduce new laws without the consent of the people.

These aspects of Fortescue's thought are important, but the fact that they are familiar should not lead to the conclusion that he was writing in exactly the same mode as Coke was to do over one hundred years later. In most respects their approaches were quite dissimilar. Coke filled his works with constant references to the landmarks of the common law past, such as the laws of Edward the Confessor, Magna Carta and Littleton's Tenures. By contrast, the writer to whom Fortescue refers most frequently is Aristotle. *De laudibus* is in essence an Aristotelian account of the place of law in society filtered through the interpretations of the medieval schoolmen. According to Fortescue, the grounds of English law were the divine laws which permeate throughout the universe; natural law; and human laws in the form of statute and custom. Divine law and natural law were ideally discovered either by revelation or by a kind of divine light which illuminated the intuitions of man. For obvious reasons, man's knowledge of these sources of law was bound to be imperfect. Consequently, although human (or positive) laws were supposed to conform to the higher laws of God and nature, there were inevitably going to be some areas in which such guidance was unclear. In these circumstances, Fortescue thought that the maxims of the human law (in England the maxims of the common law) should be used as the basis for judicial decision-making. However, human laws contrary to the laws of nature were invalid and, if necessary, there was no reason why human laws should not be amendable in order to bring them into line with the higher laws.[5]

Many similar opinions, although much more skilfully elaborated, can be found in another work which became a classic in the canon of sixteenth-

---

[5] Sir John Fortescue, *De laudibus legum Angliae*, ed. S. B. Chrimes (Cambridge, 1942), pp. lxxix, 25, 37–41.

century legal thought, Christopher St German's *Doctor and Student*. First published in Latin in 1523, the main purpose of this treatise was to lay down a set of rules about the circumstances in which men should be allowed to seek remedies in cases of conscience from the court of Chancery: it is the fundamental early modern statement about the grounds for equitable relief within the English legal system. Although the objectives of the tract were in this sense fairly technical, the realisation of them involved the use of sophisticated philosophical arguments about the nature of law. While much of Fortescue's scholastic learning was culled from a fifteenth-century compendium of quotations, St German enjoyed a reputation as a thinker with expertise in the common, civil and canon laws, as well as in philosophy and the liberal arts. His concept of equity was drawn largely from the work of the fourteenth-century Parisian conciliarist Jean Gerson.

Doctor and Student, which is in the form of a dialogue, begins with a doctor of divinity asking a student of the common law about the grounds on which the law of England is based. The reply is that there are six grounds: the laws of God; the laws of nature (which in England are called the laws of reason); diverse general customs of the realm; maxims of the common law; diverse particular customs; and, finally, statutes. A discussion then follows about the relationship among God's law, natural law and the positive laws of men. In general the conclusions are that human laws should agree with the laws of God and the law of nature as far as possible, but that in fact many laws, including some canon laws, are appointed purely for the sake of 'political rule', and therefore cannot be shown to be entirely valid according to the higher laws. For example, the student points out that in England the law of property is based only on the authority of a custom of the realm which is not contained in any writing or statute. He even wonders whether such a custom can be considered a sufficient authority for any law. The reply of the doctor is that a law grounded on custom is the most certain law, but it must nevertheless be understood that such a custom cannot be allowed if it is contrary to the law of reason or the law of God.[6]

Between the publication of *Doctor and Student* and the early seventeenth century there was no English law book which set out so systematically an overview of the nature of law. Nevertheless, there is little doubt that the kind of scholastic thought which both Fortescue and St German espoused survived largely intact into the reign of Elizabeth, which began in 1558. Quite apart from the fact that there were frequent references to both writers, Aristotelian teaching was an important part of the syllabus of the universities. During this age of rapidly rising admissions, many more common lawyers than ever before prefaced their legal educations with a period of scholastic

6 C. St. German, *Doctor and Student*, ed. T. F. T. Plucknett and J. L. Barton, Selden Society, 91 (London, 1974), pp. 15–17; Zofia Rueger, 'Gerson's Concept of Equity and Christopher St German', *History of Political Thought*, 3 (1982), pp. 1–30. See also J. Guy, *Christopher St German on Chancery and Statute*. Selden Society supplementary series, 6 (London, 1985).

study at Oxford and Cambridge. Sir Thomas Egerton, the future Lord Chancellor Ellesmere, undertook extensive study of Aristotle at Brasenose College, Oxford, in the 1550s; while Sir Edward Coke's library at Holkham was well-stocked with the works of the Greek philosopher. In addition, Ellesmere and Elizabeth's chief counsellor, Lord Treasurer Burghley, were patrons of the leading late Elizabethan Aristotelian, Dr John Case, whose *Sphaera civitatis*, a commentary on the *Politics*, became a basic university textbook in the 1590s.[7]

The survival of scholastic jurisprudence can also be illustrated by examples drawn from everyday legal practice. The notion that law had to conform to the English version of the law of nature, right reason, remained fundamental. The decision-making process of the judiciary was discussed in these terms. In an age in which printed law reports were still anything but comprehensive, there was as yet no clearly established principle that past precedents should bind current decisions.[8] Furthermore, right reason served as a basic principle for justifying the making of new statute law. For example, *A Treatise Concerning Statutes or Acts of Parliament* referred to *Doctor and Student* frequently in the course of developing an argument that existing laws which were not conformable to the laws of reason should be corrected by statute. In short, the anonymous author of this tract presents a justification for the mass of Elizabethan parliamentary legislation which is perfectly compatible with the views of Fortescue or St German, but very far from vaunting the perfection of immemorial common law in the manner of Coke.[9]

If scholastic Aristotelianism and a fundamental outlook which stressed natural law theory were aspects of English legal thinking which may be said to have been inherited from the medieval past, there were also newer influences, or at least changes in emphasis, which arose out of the specific conditions of the sixteenth century itself. As is well known, the Elizabethan age in particular seems to have been obsessed with general fears of social and political chaos which were reflected in common law thought by a quite striking emphasis on obedience and law enforcement. To a large extent this was a product of the quite real threats posed to the realm by religious heterodoxy and the possibility of invasion by the most powerful ruler in Europe, Philip II of Spain; and by the dislocation characteristic of a society in which the number of people was rapidly outpacing the capacity of the

---

[7] L. A. Knafla, *Law and Politics in Jacobean England: The Tracts of Lord Chancellor Ellesmere* (Cambridge, 1977), p. 40; W. O. Hassall, *A Catalogue of the Library of Sir Edward Coke*, Yale Law Library Publications, 12 (New Haven, CT, 1950); C. B. Schmitt, *John Case and Aristotelianism in Renaissance England*, McGill-Queen's Studies in the History of Ideas, 5 (Kingston and Montreal, 1983), pp. 6–9, 43, 87, 104, 136–37.

[8] Edmund Plowden, *Commentaries or Reports of Edmund Plowden, of the Middle-Temple, Esq., an Apprentice of the Common Law* (London, 1761), pp. 9, 13, 27.

[9] Sir Christopher Hatton [?], *A Treatise Concerning Statutes or Acts of Parliament and the Exposition Thereof* (London, 1677).

economy to employ them. Yet this new strand in legal thinking also had identifiable roots in the intellectual inheritance of the English Renaissance.

In England, as elsewhere in Europe, the key to the Renaissance was the humanist movement, and humanism can be defined accurately, if rather generally, as simply a revival of interest in the classical literature of ancient Rome. Surprisingly perhaps, this classical revival had a considerable influence on the legal profession. Whereas in his *De laudibus* Fortescue identified lawyers with priests, during the 1520s and 1530s a new image began to emerge.[10] The first evidence of this appears in one of the most important works of the English humanist movement, Sir Thomas Elyot's *The Boke Named the Governour*. Elyot was the son of a judge, a member of the Middle Temple and an associate of both Thomas More and Thomas Cromwell. Like some other English humanists, he found the Law French of the common law barbarous in comparison with the classical Latin that was his ideal. The other notable feature of his work was the advocacy of a legal profession which modelled itself on the *prudentes* of classical Rome. Elyot wanted a profession in which law and rhetoric were combined to produce men who did not simply grovel for fees, but who combined a knowledge of law with oratorical and rhetorical skills in order to serve their country effectively as governors as well as lawyers. His models were the historian Tacitus, the famous politician and jurisconsult Servius Sulpicius and, of course, Cicero.[11]

The ideal proposed by Elyot seems to have been largely adopted by the English profession. It lay behind the evolution of the idea that barristers should be paid by *honoraria* or gratuities rather than set fees, and it is perhaps most convincingly exemplified by the fact that even Sir Edward Coke garnished his works with quotations from Cicero. Indeed, in the preface to the *First Part of the Institutes*, Coke pointed out to his readers that the fifteenth-century English lawyer Littleton had a coat of arms which contained 'escalop shells, which the honourable Senators of Rome wore in bracelets'.[12]

English lawyers absorbed jurisprudential ideals from their ancient models. In this respect they shared an outlook which had much in common with continental legal thought. In his excellent book on *Natural Rights Theories*, Richard Tuck has suggested that, from about the middle of the sixteenth century, the humanist lawyers of continental Europe were much more interested in humanly constructed law, the law positive (or *jus gentium*) and civil remedies than in abstract discussions of natural law. According to Tuck, the central characteristic of their attitudes towards law was a contrast between

---

[10] Fortescue, *De laudibus*, pp. 20–22.

[11] Sir Thomas Elyot, *The Boke Named the Gouernour (1531)*, ed. H. H. S. Croft (2 vols, London 1880), i, pp. 154–55, 157.

[12] W. R. Prest, *The Rise of the Barristers: A Social History of the English Bar, 1590–1640* (Oxford, 1986), pp. 315–18; Edward Coke, *The First Part of the Institutes of the Lawes of England* (London, 1628), preface.

civilisation and the rude and barbaric life of precivilised peoples. Moreover, the *locus classicus* of this view was contained in the first few pages of Cicero's *De inventione*, in which he gave an account of the origins of eloquence by comparing a time when men wandered the fields aimlessly, and in danger of oppression, with the time when a great man had formed them together into a civilised society. In general, eloquence and law came to be seen as the means whereby men moved from a naturally brutish life to one of civility.[13]

In England these links, connecting law, rhetoric and the civilising process, were similarly emphasised by early Tudor humanists. Thomas Starkey, one of the leading members of Thomas Cromwell's circle of intellectuals and propagandists, expressly embraced the ideal that law was one of the principal means by which rude nature was transformed.[14] Elyot's *Governour* devotes many thousands of words to the task of trying to convince the aristocracy and gentry that they should give up their ignorant and warlike ways, acquire some book-learning and take their proper place in the state as inferior magistrates.[15]

Among the lawyers, this notion that positive law was the prime defender of civilised life and a bulwark against its disintegration into a brutish state of nature was also a constantly reiterated theme. For example, the preface of the 1572 edition of John Rastell's important legal textbook, *An Exposition of Certaine Difficult and Obscure Wordes*, begins with the general remark.

> Like as the universall worlde can never have his continuance but only by the order and lawe of nature which compellethe every thing to doe his kinde: so there is no multitude of people in no realme that can continue in unitie and peace without they be thereto compelled by some good order and law.[16]

At times, the very expressions used echo quite clearly the words of Cicero. English lawyers were particularly addicted to the formula found in *De legibus* which postulated that without government and law the household, the city, the nation and the human race could not survive. An early example occurs in a manuscript treatise written in the 1540s by the humanist, lawyer and sometime reformer John Hales, entitled 'An Oration in Commendation of the Laws'. According to Hales:

> If law be gone farewell love, farewell shame, farewell honestie, farewell truthe, farewell faith and all vertue. And in with deceipte, crafte, subtiltie, periurye, malice, envie, discorde, debate, murder, manslaughter, tyrannye, sedition, burnyng of houses, pullinge downe of cyties and townes, ravishing of virgins, violation of widowes ...

[13] R. Tuck, *Natural Rights Theories: Their Origin and Development* (Cambridge, 1979), pp. 33–34.
[14] Thomas Starkey, *A Dialogue between Cardinal Pole and Thomas Lupset, Lecturer in Rhetoric at Oxford*, ed. J. M. Cowper, Early English Text Society, extra series, 32 (London, 1878), pp. 50–53.
[15] Elyot, *The Governour*.
[16] J. Rastell, *An Exposition of Certaine Difficult and Obscure Wordes* (London, 1572), sig. Aii.

By contrast, law 'reteynethe justice, justice causeth love, love contynueth peace, peace causeth quyet, quyet causeth men to applie their industrie and fall to labour'.[17] It is a litany which soon becomes familiar to any reader of Elizabethan law books.

For many English lawyers, the ideal of the rule of law was reified to almost totemistic proportions. In 1589, for instance, Sir Christopher Yelverton told an audience at Gray's Inn, which was assembled to mark his promotion to serjeant at law, that:

> I cannot sufficiently, nor amply enough magnifie the majestie and dignitie of the lawe, for it is the devine gifte and invention of god, and the profound determination of wise men, the most strong synewe of a common wealth and the soule without which the magistrate cannot stand ... The necessitie of lawe is such that as in some nacons, where all learning is forbidden, yet the houses of law be suffred, that thereby the people may the sooner be induced to civilitie and the better provoked to the performance of their duty ... to live without government is hellish and to governe without Lawe is brutish ... the Law (saith Tully) containeth all wisdome, and all the rules of philosophie, and let them all (saith he) say what they will, if a man would search the originall and very groundes of the Lawes, they seeme for weight of authoritie, strength of reason, and plenty of profit to excell all the philosophers' Libraries.[18]

Roman texts became a mine of aphoristic truths.[19] Furthermore, many English barristers appear to have been quite familiar with works of continental juristic humanism which shared their own assumptions about the importance of law to civilised life, and which promoted the idea that jurisprudence was the queen of all sciences. For example, Sir John Dodderidge, William Lambarde, and Sir Christopher Yelverton were all familiar with the work of Joachim Hopperus, a Flemish civilian who enjoyed a successful career under Philip II of Spain. They, like many others, knew the works of Jean Bodin.[20] Henry Finch's *Nomotexnia* (*The Art of Law*), which was composed in the 1580s, followed continental examples in attempting to apply Ramist logical techniques to English law.[21] Late in the reign of Elizabeth, Dodderidge, who later became a judge, produced a list of books relevant to a treatise on the royal prerogative which he planned to dedicate

[17] BL, MS Harleian 4990, fos 8–8v.

[18] BL, MS Add. 48109, fos 12v–13v.

[19] The Elizabethan lord keeper Sir Nicholas Bacon decorated his country house with quotations from Cicero and Seneca, Elizabeth McCutcheon, *Sir Nicholas Bacon's Great House Sententiae*, English Literary Renaissance Supplements, 3 (Claremont, CA, 1977).

[20] Lambarde's copy of *Tractatus de iuris arte, duorum clarissimorum iurisconsul Ioannis Corassii et Ioachim Hopperi* (Cologne, 1582) was purchased in 1583; it is copiously annotated, BL, Department of Printed Books, shelf mark 516. a. 55.

[21] For a discussion of Finch see T. K. Shaller, 'English Law and the Renaissance: The Common Law and Humanism in the Sixteenth Century' (unpublished Ph.D. thesis, Harvard University, 1979), pp. 310–15.

to Thomas Sackville, Lord Buckhurst, a major figure in Elizabethan government, who appears to have been at the centre of a legal circle which also
included Coke, William Fleetwood and Thomas Norton, the translator of
the *Institutes* of John Calvin into English.[22] Dodderidge's work was to be
based on the records and constitutions of the common law, but he also
intended to draw on works of divinity, philosophy and the law of nations:

> Imitatinge heerin a Learned Searjaunt and afterward in the tyme of Kyng
> Edward the fourth a learned Judge who very well said that 'when newe matter
> was considered whearof no former Lawe is extant, we do, as the Sorbonists
> and Civilians, resorte to the Lawe of Nature which is the Grownde of all
> Lawes and thene drawing that which is most conformable for the Common
> Wealthe do adjudge hit for Lawe'.

The proposed references range from the Bible and Thomas Aquinas, to
Plato and Aristotle (as well as Aristotle's ancient and modern interpreters).
Then there are Machiavelli, Justus Lipsius and a number of French lawyers,
including Bodin and François Hotman.[23]

No less important, English lawyers also shared general humanist principles
about the way in which law should be administered in any society. First, as
John Hales put it in the 1540s,

> if lawe be a rule whereunto every man shoulde reduce his lyvinge me thinketh
> it veraie necessarie, to put it in writinge to the intente the People might
> knowe what they oughte to doe and not hange in one man or in fewe learned
> mens heades.[24]

Although many writers did not go this far in calling for the codification of
the law, there is no doubt that the advisability of making the law known to
the population at large was a question frequently debated during the course
of the later sixteenth century. On the whole the argument was won decisively
by the publicists.[25]

Secondly, lawyers argued that law was of value to society only if it was a
source of justice. Hence they tended to see the rule of law as a system of
authority before which all men were equal, and which disregarded the more
traditional and informal bonds that existed in early modern society, such
as those between magnate and retainer, those between neighbours, and those

---

[22] For Coke, see BL, MS Harleian 443, fol. 1; for Fleetwood BL, Stowe 423, fol. 107, and BL,
MS Harleian 6234, fol. 10v. Norton and Sackville collaborated on *The Tragedie of Gorboduc:
Whereof Three Actes Were Wrytten by Thomas Nortone, and the Two Laste by Thomas Sackvyle* (London,
1565). See also *Dictionary of National Biography*.

[23] BL, MS Harleian 5220, fos 3–21. See also BL, MS Stowe 423, fos 106ff, Historical Discourse
by William Fleetwood, Recorder of London.

[24] BL, MS Harleian 4990, fol. 16.

[25] See, for example, Ferdinando Pulton, *De Pace Regis et Regni viz A Treatise Declaring Which
be the Great and General Offences of the Realme and the Chiefe Impediments of the Peace of the King and
Kingdome* (London, 1609), preface.

of kinship. Since jurists held that political society was founded to protect the weak from the strong, it followed (and this idea was also found in Cicero) that in theory at least lawyers should be no friends of magnate retinues and that they should emphasise equality before the law.[26] According to John Hales, one of the chief virtues of justice was that it had 'noe respecte to nature, kynrede, affynitie, frendshippe, envie, malice' or hatred. Similarly, William Lambarde reminded Kentish grand jurymen that they should not let their ties in the local community prevent them from doing their lawful duty in presenting malefactors at quarter sessions. Most lawyers appear at the least to have paid lip service to Sir Edward Coke's declaration at the Norfolk assizes in 1606 that if 'Justice [were] withheld only the poorer sort are those that smart for it'.[27] As one anonymous seventeenth-century writer put it:

> If we would perfectly execute justice wee must make no difference betweene men for their frendship, parentage, riches, povertye, or dignitye. Cicero sayth that wee must leave our pleasures and particular profits to embrace the publick good.[28]

The ideal of the rule of law and its corollaries became commonplaces for lawyers, and the notion that law was necessary for the maintenance of society in general was doubtless accepted by many laymen as well. The wider political implications of these general truths were, however, subject to a variety of interpretations. On the one hand, the rule of law could become a weapon in the art of statecraft and a principal justification for demanding absolute obedience to the prince. In the 1530s, for instance, Richard Morrison, a propaganda writer for Thomas Cromwell, who has been identified by Felix Raab as an early English Machiavellian, drew up a set of proposals for reforming the laws of England. One part of the scheme suggested that summer holidays, which had traditionally been used by the common people to celebrate Robin Hood and 'disobedience also to [the king's] officers', should be made instead into occasions which attacked the bishop of Rome and showed the people 'the obedience that your subiectes by Goddes and mans Lawes owe unto your majestie'.[29]

Morrison's project was apparently rejected, but a manuscript called 'A Book of Things Inquirable at Inferior Courts', which dates from the later 1530s, possibly 1538, may well have been concocted for the use of lawyers acting as stewards in town courts, sheriff's tourns and manorial courts. It

---

[26] See, for example, Anon., *A Collection of the Lawes and Statutes of this Realme Concerning Liueries of Companies and Reteynours* (Richard Tottel, London, 1571). William Lambarde owned a copy.

[27] Conyers Read, ed., *William Lambarde and Local Government: His 'Ephemeris' and Twenty-Nine Charges to Juries and Commissions* (Ithaca, NY, 1962), pp. 70, 73, 89; E. Coke, *The Lord Coke His Speeche and Charge* (London, 1607), sig. Civ. Many other examples could be given.

[28] BL, MS Add. 12515, fol. 42.

[29] F. Raab, *The English Face of Machiavelli* (London, 1964), p. 34; BL, MS Cotton Faust. C. II., 'A Discours Touching the Reformation of the Lawes of England', fos 18–18v.

explains that in the past only matters within the jurisdiction of such local courts had been given in the charge addressed to the jurors, but now the king was intent that the unlearned and ignorant people should 'better knowen and due their dewtie first to God, then to his highness as Godes vicar'. In addition to its use in local courts, the charge was also supposed to be read at least four times a year in the parish church. Among a long list of matters dealing with both the administration of justice and the defence of the Henrician Reformation, there was a clear statement that the king had been appointed by God to rule over the commonwealth; any disobedience to the monarch was a violation of holy ordinances.[30]

In the Elizabethan period, the necessity of the rule of law was also often linked to calls for obedience to established authority. Some legal publicists, and even councillors in the queen's government, began to argue that the maintenance of the rule of law was in itself a sufficient foundation for the obedience a subject owed to his prince. The key precept in this line of thinking was that some government was better than no government. The rule of law protected property and the person. It was a way of keeping the animal passions of men, which coloured life in the state of nature, at bay. Consequently, it offered an incentive for accepting the existing government on the grounds of self-interest, even if one had doubts about the issue as a matter of conscience. This was essentially the basis of the accommodation which Elizabethan government offered to English Catholics. For example, in a piece of propaganda addressed to those involved in the 1569 rebellion, Thomas Norton, the translator of Calvin, member of parliament and man of business to Lord Treasurer Burghley, wrote:

> The common weale is the ship we sayle in, no one can be safe if the whole do perish. To God, and then to the realme, the crown, to the law and government ... we all do owe our selves and all that we have.[31]

Some lawyers extended the connection between the value of the rule of law and the necessity for obedience into a conventional theory of divine right monarchy. For example, in 1587 Richard Crompton, one of the more important Elizabethan legal thinkers, published *A Short Declaration of the End of Traytors*, a pamphlet which contained the substance of a speech he had given before a meeting of the Staffordshire quarter sessions earlier that year. The setting is significant because such orations, or 'charges', appear to have been a normal part of the procedures which surrounded the opening cere-monies of most local courts during the period. They were probably the main avenue through which the ideology of the lawyers was professed openly to a public which reached at least as far down the social scale as the lesser gentlemen and yeomen farmers who served on petty and grand juries.

---

[30] BL, MS Add. 48047, fos 59–61v. The dating is based on internal evidence.

[31] Thomas Norton, *To the Quenes Maiesties Poore Deceyued Subiectes of the Northe Countrey Drawen into Rebellion by the Earles of Northumberland and Westmerland* (London, 1569), sig. Gi.

According to Crompton's preface to the printed version, his aims on this particular occasion had been to show the people the good they received by the law; to explain their duty to obey the prince; and to illustrate the fate of traitors. He wanted to warn them about the dangers of treason on the grounds of conscience and to set out a legal justification for the execution of Mary Queen of Scots. Like many other tracts of the same vintage and purpose, *The Declaration* was filled with cautions about the dangers of the times (the Spanish Armada would soon set sail) and stressed the advantages which England was enjoying under the beneficent leadership of Queen Elizabeth, especially in comparison with the bloody murders and discords which were taking place on the Continent.[32]

Although hardly systematic, Crompton's call for obedience to Queen Elizabeth was a classic piece of absolutist humanist jurisprudence. His conception of the foundations of political society was a conflation of pagan ideas about a state of nature ruled by the law of nature; and an interpretation of the scriptures which placed the foundation of human society after the 'universall flodde', when God had appointed kings and magistrates to rule over the people. In addition, he incorporated two fairly straightforward quotations from Cicero's *De legibus*. Law is the highest reason granted in nature: it commands what things are to be done and forbids those which are not. According to Crompton, it followed from this that there was a need for preeminence and superiority in government: for without government no house, no city could stand. Kings were ordained by God to govern, and their subjects were commanded to obey. Even in the face of injustice or tyranny, subjects had no right to rebel against the prince. Even the Turks (whose government Englishmen always associated with the worst form of oppressive regime) had no right to overthrow the ruler God had put on the throne to govern them. The laws of God, the laws of nature and the laws of the realm all demanded absolute obedience.[33]

Richard Crompton certainly expressed views which would have pleased the queen's government. It is much less certain how far they can be described as typical. Only a tiny minority of the thousands of charges which must have been delivered have survived.[34] Much of what Crompton said in Staffordshire was conventional and commonplace, but other writers may have altered the emphasis. For example, William Lambarde's account of the origins of political life sounds very much like that found in the most popular work of Cicero in England, *De officiis*. In the beginning the only political society was

---

[32] Richard Crompton, *A Short Declaration of the Ende of Traytors and False Conspirators against the State, and the Duetie of Subjectes to Theyr Soueraigne Gouernour* (London, 1587).

[33] Ibid. Similar views are also expressed in his *The Mansion of Magnanimitie: Wherein is Shewed the Most High and Honorable Acts of Sundrie English Kings, Princes, Dukes, Earles, Lords, Knights and Gentlemen* (London, 1599).

[34] I have not been able to identify more than a dozen in manuscript for the period from roughly 1550 to 1640.

the family governed by the patriarch; but, as population grew, the weak and helpless began to be oppressed by the strong. Consequently, the people went to the man who was most distinguished for his virtue and established him as their king. He protected the weak and set up an equitable system of government which united the highest and lowest in equal rights. Lambarde developed this view of the origins of political society further by adding that once the rulers who had been established by the people became corrupted, 'then were Lawes and rules of Justice devised, within the which as within certaine Limits, the power of governors should from henceforth be bounded to establish laws by which both governors and governed could be ruled'.[35]

A more detailed insight into an Elizabethan lawyer's attitudes towards government is revealed in a series of 'readings', or lectures, on the royal prerogative which were given at the Middle Temple in 1579 by James Morice, a man who was on close business terms with Lord Treasurer Burghley, and who was also associated with the Elizabethan presbyterian movement.[36]

Morice started his discourse by explaining that he had selected his subject because he wanted to come to a better understanding of the authority of princes and the duty incumbent on subjects to obey them.[37] He also pointed out that there had long been debate about which was the best form of government: monarchy, aristocracy or democracy. Each form had its defects. Democracy tended to anarchy; oligarchy, or the rule of the few, to faction. Even though history, particularly Roman history, taught that monarchy was the most effective, monarchy was inclined to slip into tyranny and oppression. Therefore another form of government, whereby the prince governed by law, had been established.

> And for that good kynges and Prynces are nither by Nature Imortale, nor of them selves being Men, Imutable. An other State of kyngdome and better kynde of Monarchie hathe byne by common Assent ordayned and establyshed,

---

[35] William Lambarde, *Archion: or A Commentary upon the High Courts of Justice in England* (first published London, 1635, but the preface is dated 1591, and there are earlier manuscript copies), pp. 1–5.

[36] Edmund Lodge, *Illustrations of British History, Biography and Manners, in the Reigns of Henry VIII, Edward VI, Mary, Elizabeth and James I* (2nd edn, 3 vols, London, 1838), ii, pp. 443–46; J. E. Neale, *Elizabeth I and Her Parliaments, 1584–1601* (London, 1957), pp. 267–79.

[37] The reading survives in two versions, BL, MS Add. 36081, fos 229ff, and BL, MS Egerton 3376, a contemporary fair copy with a dedication to Lord Treasurer Burghley. The statutory text on which Morice chose to read was chapter 49 of the Statute of Westminster I, essentially a short saving clause, in which the king stated that none of the previous provisions of the statute should result in prejudice to himself, *Statutes of the Realm*, ed. A. Luders, T. E. Tomlins, J. Raith (11 vols, London 1810–28), i, p. 39, c. 50. In the course of apologising for selecting this ancient, short and rather general clause, Morice explained that he did so largely because it enabled him to discuss more generally questions about the power of the monarch, BL, MS Add. 36081, fos 230–30v.

wherein the Prince (not by Lycentious will and Imoderate Assertions but by the Law, That is by the prudent Rules and Preceptes of Reason agreed vppon and made the Covenant of the Comon Wealth) may Justly governe and commande, and the People in due obedience saeflie lyve and quyetly enioye their owne.[38]

Morice then considered the etymology of the word 'prerogative' in such a way as to be able to make the point that among 'The Romaynes the Consent of the people was requysite to the Establishment of their Lawes'. He argued that while it was sovereign kings who actually made laws, this was always done through consultation with the people. Such a system worked because 'what cawse agayne haue the Comons to murmor or rebell agaynst the Lawes and Statues by which they are governed syns they them selves are of Counsell and consent to the makinge of the same'. Finally, he came to the question of whether the king be above or below the law. The answer was formulated as follows:

It is a comon Sayinge amonge many that the Kinge by his Prerogatyve is above his laws which rightly understode is not amisse spoken ... But to say that the Kinge is so a Emperor over his Lawes and Actes of Parliament (bycawse he hath power to make them), as that he is not bounde to governe by the same but at his will and pleasure, is an Oppinyon altogeather repugnant to the wise and politicke State of government established in this Realme, which placeth the Royall Majestie of the kynge as the Leiutenant of Almightie God in the Reverent Throne of Justice and true Iudgment. [It is] Contrarye to the Rule of Equytie and common reason which sayeth [that laws] beinge made by so grave a Counsell, uppon so greate deliberacion and by the Common Consent of all [should be followed by the king.][39]

The detailed survival of this reading is exceptional; so too, perhaps, was James Morice's attachment to the radical puritan cause. Yet the fact that the queen's principal adviser, Burghley, requested that Morice send him a copy of the text may suggest that the ideas it expressed were not outrageously unconventional.[40] It seems safe to conclude that most Elizabethan lawyers would have been aware of Aristotle's classification of the different varieties of constitution; many of them may have supported Morice's defence of mixed monarchy. Thus an anonymous paper delivered to the Society of Antiquaries in the late 1590s or early 1600s stressed that the court of parliament had a double power. One involved consultation by way of deliberation for the good government of the commonwealth, so it is *consilium*, not *curia*. The other power came from parliament's role in the administration of

---

[38] Ibid., fol. 231.

[39] Ibid., fos 235, 243v–44v.

[40] BL, MS Egerton 3376, fol. 1. See also P. Collinson, 'The Monarchical Republic of Queen Elizabeth', *Bulletin of the John Rylands University Library*, 69 (1987).

justice.[41] For some this conclusion may have arisen from a consideration of the nature of the origins of the state along the lines laid out by Lambarde. For others it may have been a natural corollary of the kind of legal realism imbibed from writers such as Bodin. For example, in the late 1590s the speaker of the House of Commons, Sir Christopher Yelverton, informed the House that there were many forms of government, but monarchy was the best; the English polity was particularly good because there were practical advantages in allowing the people themselves to be the framers of their own laws.[42]

These views amount to contemporary refutations of Sir Geoffrey Elton's depiction of the Elizabethan parliament as a court which had no significant political or advisory function.[43] Yet it is at the same time important to recognise that much of Elizabethan legal thought also bears a close resemblance to what continental historians describe as political neostoicism.[44] The rule of law was the greatest benefit of government, one which could be maintained only through absolute obedience to the monarch. However, political obligation was not based entirely on divine injunctions that the subject accept the will of the prince. It also involved a calculation of self-interest. The king was supposed to rule for the good of his people and govern according to law. Hence there was a clear perception of the difference between good government and bad government, between just rule and tyranny. Few lawyers went so far as to share the suspicion of the royal use of the law which is expressed in the poetry of the aristocrat Fulke Greville:

> For though perhaps at first sight laws appear
> Like prisons unto tyrants' soveraign might,
> Yet are they secrets, which Pow'r should hold dear
> Since envyless they make her infinite;
>   And set so fair a gloss upon her will,
>   As under this veil Pow'r cannot do ill.[45]

---

[41] BL, MS Add. 48102, 'The Severall Opinions of Sundarie Antiquaries Touching the Antiquitie Power, Order, Estate, Persons, Manner and Proceeding of the High Court of Parliament', fol. 12.

[42] BL, MS Add. 48109, Speeches and letters of Sir Christopher Yelverton, JKB (1535–1612). In his speech at the beginning of the session in 1597 he said that political society had been founded when 'pollicie, springinge of ... necessitie did force men to submitte theire libertie to the frame of others soveraignty' (fos 18–19). In his closing speech he argued that 'the people' were most likely to be ruled by the law when they 'be agents in framing them' (fol. 22). Bodin wrote 'When edicts are ratified by Estates or Parlements, it is for the purpose of securing obedience to them, and not because otherwise a sovereign prince could not validly make law', *Six Books of the Commonwealth by Jean Bodin*, ed. M. J. Tooley (Oxford, 1967), p. 32.

[43] G. R. Elton, *The Parliament of England, 1559–1581* (Cambridge, 1986).

[44] Gerhard Oestreich, *Neostoicism and the Early Modern State* (Cambridge, 1982). See also *Two Bookes of Constancie Written in Latine by Iustus Lipsius, Englished by Sir John Stradling*, ed. Rudolf Kirk and C. M. Hall (New Brunswick, NJ, 1939), pp. 3–34, for an account of English neostoicism.

[45] *The Works in Verse and Prose of Fulke Greville Lord Brooke*, ed. A. B. Grosart (4 vols, London, 1868), i, pp. 94–95.

But many of them did have a clear perception of the potential danger of tyranny. In a speech to quarter sessions dating from the late 1560s or early 1570s, Sir Christopher Yelverton reminded his listeners 'How easilie may the haughtie raigne of the unskillful prince slide into Tirranie'.[46] More cautiously, but nonetheless clearly, the anonymous author of *The Laudable Customs of London* (1584), noted that:

> We find it necessarie in all common wealthes, for subiects to live under the direction of Lawes, constitutions, or customs, publickly knowen and received, and not to depende only upon the commandment and pleasure of the governor, be the same never so iust or sincere in life and conversation. For that the Law once enacted and established, extendeth his execution towards al men alike without favour or affection: Whereas if the word of a Prince were a lawe, the same being a mortall man must needes bee possessed with those passions, and inclinations of favour or disfavour that other men be: and sometimes decline from the constant and unremoveable levell of indifferrencie, to respect the man besides the matter, if not to regard the person more than the cause. Wherefore it was wel agreed by the wisest Philosophers and greatest politicks, that a dumme lawes direction is to be preferred before the sole disposition of any living Prince, both for the cause afore touched, and for other reasons which I will here omit.[47]

Although Elizabethan legal writers were well aware of the potential conflicts between the power of princes and the liberty of the subjects, and although they were perfectly capable of discussing such matters in very general theoretical terms, they normally avoided drawing the precise lines between the two. In the light of wartime dangers to political stability which they perceived, it is hardly surprising that the monarch was frequently given the benefit of the doubt. This important characteristic of the interrelationship between legal theory and political reality is perhaps best summed up in the anonymous *Collection of the Lawes and Statutes of this Realme Concerning Liueries of Companies and Reteynours* (1571). Its author was quite open about the abuses of kings such as Henry I, Richard II and Richard III, but he also took pains to point out that 'the Whole body of our law books' show that at no period in history had questions concerning princes been as often referred to the determination of the law as during the reign of Queen Elizabeth.[48]

As should already have become evident from the previous discussion, neither ancient constitutionalism of the sort associated with Coke or Magna Carta, was particularly prominent in sixteenth-century legal thought. Nor by now

---

[46] BL, MS Add. 48109, fol. 37.

[47] *A Breefe Discourse, Declaring and Approuing the Necessarie and Inviolable Maintenance of the Laudable Customes of London: Namely of That One Whereby a Reasonable Partition of the Goods of Husbands Among Their Wiues and Children is Provided* (London, 1584), pp. 3–4.

[48] *A Collection of the Lawes and Statutes of this Realme Concerning Liveries of Companies and Reteynours* (London, 1571), fos 13v–14v.

should the reasons for this be surprising. It is true that the common law was perceived as a set of rules and procedures which had accumulated over time in the year books, law reports and registers of writs; but within the jurisprudential framework laid down by, for example, *Doctor and Student*, customary practices were valid only so long as they adhered to the laws of God and reason. The essence of English law lay not so much in particular precedents or customs as in maxims which enshrined its reason. There was no systematically thought out view that customs were valid simply because long usage had proved their utility and justness. In fact, one of the major characteristics of legal development under Elizabeth and the early Stuarts was the regular testing of the reasonableness of such customs against the common law or equity. Most common lawyers, including Sir Edward Coke, were active during this period in subordinating local custom to their notion of the law as administered through the royal jurisdictions at Westminster.[49] Indeed, in the wake of the attack on tradition which accompanied the Reformation, customs themselves were seen to have no intrinsic value. In 1569, for instance, Thomas Norton warned the participants in the Northern Rebellion not to be misled into thinking that they were defending ancient liberties and customs:

> Are all customes, without respect of good or bad, to be restored; are not rather the bad to be reformed: and so is it true libertie to be delivered from them, and not remayne thrall and bounde unto them?[50]

Within this world view, legal history was certainly of interest, but it was not of vital importance in interpreting the law. Hence an Elizabethan recorder of London, William Fleetwood, was fascinated by antiquities but had read enough of writers like Bodin to be sceptical of his sources.[51] The first printed edition of Bracton (1569) warned the reader to take into consideration changes in the common and statute law since the middle ages.[52] Authors such as Crompton and Dodderidge found no difficulty in accepting that the Norman Conquest had changed English institutions.[53]

---

[49] C. W. Brooks, *Pettyfoggers and Vipers of the Commonwealth: The 'Lower Branch' of the Legal Profession in Early Modern England* (Cambridge, 1986), pp. 198–99.

[50] Norton, *To the Quenes Maiesties Poor Deceyued Subiectes*, sig. Eiiiv–iv.

[51] BL, MS Stowe 423, fol. 133, for Fleetwood's references to Bodin's *Methodus ad facilem historiarum cognitionem*. There were editions in 1566, 1572 and 1583.

[52] D. E. C. Yale, '"Of No Mean Authority": Some Later Uses of Bracton', in *On the Laws and Customs of England: Essays in Honor of Samuel E. Thorne*, ed. M. S. Arnold, T. A. Green, S. A. Scully and S. D. White (Chapel Hill, NC, 1981), p. 386. As Yale suggests, it seems quite likely that the preface to this edition was written by Thomas Norton, although there is no definitive proof. Also, though it is not a point that has been developed here, there is much evidence that Bracton's popularity in the later sixteenth century was connected with the 'Romanising movement' which characterised the legal thought of the period.

[53] Crompton, *Mansion of Magnanimitie*, sig. [B]. Dodderidge believed that William the Bastard and William Rufus had ruled by their swords, BL, MS Add. 48102A, fol. 6v. See also, C. Brooks and K. Sharpe, 'History, English Law and the Renaissance: A Comment', *Past and Present*, 72 (1976).

There was no reason why these past events should necessarily determine the validity or invalidity of present laws and governmental arrangements.

Against this background, Magna Carta found its place in legal thought, not so much as a charter of customary liberties but as a statute, albeit the first of the collection known as the *statuta antiqua*.[54] Consequently, the most detailed discussions of it are found in connection with the readings, or lectures, which senior members of the inns of court gave for students, and which were always based on a statute. Even in this context, Magna Carta does not figure so frequently as to suggest that it was considered of extraordinary importance. But it was often employed as a vehicle for describing or discussing major areas of the law of the land, both civil and criminal.[55]

On the whole, and in the pre-Reformation period in particular, the readings contained little of politics or of political controversy. Authors took it for granted that the Charter was a statute which corrected defects in the common law at the time of its enactment. For example, a mid fifteenth-century reading, which, unusually, survives in English, begins:

> Before the makyng of this statuet, that is to seie the great chartoure, there was certein lawes used, by the whiche men hade profit and also mouche harme. And therefore the kyng, seyng this mischief, ordeyned the greet charter, wherein is contened alle the fruyt of lawes bifore used turnyng to the people profit and al other put away. Yet notwithstondyng that it is called a chartere, it is a positif lawe ...[56]

Similarly, a sixteenth-century reading, which must date from just after the break from Rome in the 1530s, starts with the assertion that before the Charter only the common law was used.[57] Both lectures point out specific chapters which had altered the existing common law.

Comprehensive treatments of the entire Charter appear to have been comparatively rare. In most cases the reader chose to expound on no more than a single chapter. For instance, a late fifteenth-century lecture on chapter 17 ('Nullus vicecomes, constabularius') involved a consideration of the methods of appointment of local officials, their functions, and a discussion of various headings of the criminal law such as murder, manslaughter, burglary, and so on.[58] On the other hand, lectures on chapter 1 ('Quod

---

[54] Faith Thompson, *Magna Carta: Its Role in the Making of the English Constitution, 1300–1629* (Minneapolis, MIN, 1948), p. 38.

[55] I am very grateful to Professor J. H. Baker for helping me to locate manuscript readings on Magna Carta. In the discussion that follows, I have referred to chapters of the 1225 version of Magna Carta.

[56] G. O. Sayles, 'A Fifteenth-Century Law Reading in English', *Law Quarterly Review*, 96 (1980), p. 571.

[57] Cambridge University Library, MS Hh. II. 6, fos 1–27. Early sixteenth-century hand, but states that the grants to the church in chapter 1 were 'voide'.

[58] BL, MS Harleian 1210, fol. 144. Robert Brook used the Charter for a similar purpose in the mid sixteenth century, Cambridge University Library, MS Gg. V. 9, fos 56–97.

Anglicana ecclesia libera sit') were frequently used to lay out the law of sanctuary; chapters 1–8 were often read in order to explain aspects of the land law such as wardship or the rights of widows.[59] Even chapter 29 ('Nullus liber homo capiatur') was put to work on relatively technical matters. In an early sixteenth-century reading it was employed to argue against the practice of using the writ of capias, or arrest, as a leading process in civil cases.[60] In 1580 Robert Snagge selected it as a text for a lecture concerned primarily with uses, a form of trust frequently employed by landowners.[61]

Not surprisingly, some parts of the Charter did become more controversial during the course of the English Reformation. Both Robert Aske, the lawyer leader of the Pilgrimage of Grace of 1536, and Sir Thomas More, common lawyer and sometime lord chancellor of England, based part of their resistance to the religious policies of Henry VIII on an interpretation of chapter 1, which took literally the king's promise to protect the liberties of the English church.[62] On the other hand, in 1534, chapter 29 of Magna Carta, along with subsequent statutes on due process of law, were cited in support of a parliamentary attack on an early fifteenth-century statute which gave the English church powers to repress heretical preaching.[63] Similarly, an anonymous reading on chapter 1,[64] which appears to have been given at one of the inns of court either in the 1530s or early in the reign of Elizabeth, posits royal, rather than papal, supremacy over the English church and cleverly limits the discussion of the 'liberties' of the church to a consideration of particular privileges of ecclesiastical personnel, the nature of sanctuary and the jurisdiction of the church courts.[65]

This reading is also prefaced by some general remarks on the nature of law and the origins of the Charter which illustrate the kinds of polemical use to which Charter history, like the law itself, was put in the Tudor era.

---

[59] Sayles, 'A Fifteenth-Century Law Reading'; Cambridge University Library, MS Hh. II. 6, fos 2–27; BL, MS Hargrave 87, fos 195–218.

[60] Cambridge University Library, MS Hh. II. 6, fol. 23v. This was also the drift of Cambridge University Library, MS Ee. V. 22, fol. 18.

[61] BL, MS Add. 16169, fol. 245.

[62] Thompson, *Magna Carta*, pp. 140–41.

[63] PRO, SP 1/82, fos 55–58; J. P. Cooper, 'The Supplication against the Ordinaries Reconsidered', *English Historical Review*, 72 (1957), pp. 636–38; S. Lehmberg, *The Reformation Parliament, 1529–1536* (Cambridge, 1970), pp. 186–87. I am grateful to Professor John Guy for bringing this incident to my attention. Magna Carta was used again to attack procedures in the ecclesiastical courts during the reign of Elizabeth, see below, pp. 220–21.

[64] BL, MS Harleian 4990, fos 154v and following. Thompson, *Magna Carta*, p. 192, suggests, on the basis of some internal evidence, a date early in the reign of Elizabeth, but the reading consistently refers to the 'king' and also appears to assume the existence of priors and abbots. There is an additional peculiarity in that the preface is in English whilst the remainder of the reading is in the more usual Law French.

[65] Ibid., fol. 163v, for the intriguing statement that an argument at the commencement of 'this vacation' had demonstrated that the king, not the pope, had always been held supreme governor of the spirituality by the common law.

The reader reminded his audience that the laws of the land had continued in long use before the making of the Charter, and that some of these laws had been made by Lucius, some by Edward the Confessor and some by William the Conqueror. But these remarks were distinctly secondary to the force of the preface in general which harps primarily on the familiar theme of the necessity of the rule of law for the maintenance of peace and prosperity within the commonwealth. Echoing Fortescue, the author described law as the means by which the 'body politique' was bound together. He went on to explain that a body without law was a dead body which could not 'move or stirr'. This point, he claimed, could be demonstrated from the histories of many foreign countries, but it was not necessary to consider those. The history 'of our own country', and of the making of the Charter, proved it well enough.

> And for your better understandinge therein I have thought good to shewe unto you what disorder doth growe by the lacke of lawe and dewe execution of the same. And howe that for lacke of good lawes, great warres and discentions did growe within this realme betwext the kinge and his subiectes, which was the onelie cause of the making of the forsaid statute, and therefore as concerninge the lacke of lawes in the Comonaltie yt cannot be denyed but that contrie or Commonwealth that is not ruled by certayne lawes and provisions can never contynewe any tyme in peace and order but shall alwaise remayne from tyme to tyme in disorder and discention ... If Law be taken from the Prince, what tormoyle is like to grow amonst the subjects.[66]

The fact that chapter 1 had become controversial must have made it particularly difficult for some time after the break from Rome to see the Charter as a whole as a statement of immemorial law still in force. For example, another reading of chapter 1, which dates from the reign of the Protestant successor to Henry VIII, King Edward VI, states that grants of liberty to God and the English church were void because God and the church were not the sort of legal entities capable of receiving such grants.[67]

Magna Carta was, none the less, the first of the ancient statutes; it clearly contained within it many of the major principles of the practice of the common law. Its position between 1530 and 1570 is perhaps best summed up by George Ferrers in the preface to his English translation. His purpose in undertaking the work, like that of so much Tudor legal publishing, was to make the laws of the realm more widely known to the public. Ferrers thought that this was particularly necessary in the case of Magna Carta, because 'many of the termes aswell frenche as latyn be so fer out of use by reason of theyr antiqyte, that scarcely those that be best studyed in the lawes can understand them ...' But for Ferrers, the translation also had more than merely antiquarian interest. In these old laws, if 'they be well

---

[66] BL, MS Harleian 4990, fos 154–56v.
[67] BL, MS Lansdowne 1138, fol. 1.

sought, is conteyned a great part of the pryncipples and olde groundys of the lawes. For by searching the great extremites of the common lawes before the makynge of statutes, and the remedyes provyded by them, a good student shall soone attayne a perfect judgement'.[68]

By comparison with this evidence of the interest in the Charter which existed in the first half of the sixteenth century, that which survives for most of the Elizabethan period is relatively meagre. Magna Carta seems to have figured only infrequently in lectures at the inns of court or, if Faith Thompson is an accurate guide, in the everyday practices of judicial decision-making. As we have seen already, the thrust of Elizabethan juristic thought depended little on ancient constitutionalism. There is surprisingly little mention of Magna Carta in the systematic works which were addressed by the legal profession to the public at large.

There are from the 1580s and 1590s several exceptions to this generalisation which must be pursued in some detail. First, in the 1590s, two men sympathetic to the Elizabethan puritan movement, James Morice and Robert Beale, referred to Magna Carta in the course of their attacks on the legality of the infamous oath *ex officio* which was administered by the ecclesiastical court of High Commission. The point at issue, in what became a raging controversy, was whether people accused of religious nonconformity could be forced to swear that they would truthfully answer questions even though no specific charges had been laid against them.[69] In his *A Brief Treatise of Oathes*, for example, Morice cites chapter 29 in his efforts to prove that the use of such oaths was contrary to the common law. What is more interesting is that Morice's position in fact depends very little on either the Charter or on a more general ancient constitutionalist argument. His treatise proceeds primarily by way of an account of the use of oaths in both the canon and civil law as well as at common law. The main thrust of the case is that the oath *ex officio* is contrary to the laws of God and reason. Morice quotes Christopher St German for the view that laws against the laws of God are void ('neither righteous or obligatorie'). Magna Carta is referred to briefly in a section of the work which examines the common law position on the oath, but chapter 29 is not vital to the case as a whole; it is not put forward by Morice as if it were. His mode of argument is quite consistent with the kind of thought which we have seen already in his reading on the royal prerogative in 1579, which was typical of scholastic and humanistic legal discourse rather than ancient constitutionalism.[70]

Robert Beale, on the other hand, did appeal more often to the 'law of

---

[68] [George Ferrers], *The Great Charter Called in Latyn Magna Carta: With Divers Olde Statutes Whose Titles Appere in the Next Leafe* (London, 1542), 'To the Reader'.

[69] Participants in the Elizabethan controversy referred to that of the Henrician period which has been mentioned above, p. 218.

[70] James Morice, *A Brief Treatise of Oathes, Exacted by Ordinaries and Ecclesiastical Judges* (London, c. 1592), pp. 33–34, 47.

laws' in his contribution to the argument. But his use of the charter and other early statutes appears more like the lawyerly citation of legislative authority than a fully developed view that such 'olde Lawes' established an inviolable 'ancient constitution'.[71] In this respect, it is useful to compare Beale's approach with that of another puritan lawyer, Nicholas Fuller, whose attack on the oath *ex officio* was published in 1607, some time after the appearance of the first of Sir Edward Coke's influential *Reports*. Fuller clearly expresses the classic ancient constitutionalist view that the authority of laws like Magna Carta rested precisely on the fact that they were old. Thus the king and subjects of England were guided by laws, 'which ... by long continuance of time and good indeavor of many wise men, are so fitted to this people, and this people to them, as it doth make a sweete harmony in government'.[72]

No less interesting are references to Magna Carta by two other lawyers whose writings have already been examined in some detail, Richard Crompton and William Lambarde. Crompton's *Short Declaration of the End of Traitors*, it will be remembered, was in the main a glorification of the ideal of the rule of law and a call for absolute obedience to the monarchy. However, Crompton concluded this tract, which includes quotations from Cicero, Aristotle and Marsilius of Padua, with a note that the English were particularly blessed because they had the law of 9 Henry III (he does not mention Magna Carta by name) which laid it down that no man shall be taken or imprisoned, nor disseised of his freehold, nor put out of his liberties or free customs, but by the judgement of his peers. In addition, he remarked that although she was above 'her lawes' in some respects, the queen was pleased to be ordered by the same 'as other her noble progenitors have doone ...'[73]

Magna Carta and the rights which it epitomised were therefore important for Crompton. They provided the basis for the comparisons he made in this and other works between the 'blessed' state of the English and the tyrannies suffered by those who lived in other European countries, a theme which both echoes Fortescue in *De laudibus legum Angliae* and which was to be continued in the political speculations of some seventeenth-century parliament men. Even so, although Crompton saw the Charter as a source of exemplary laws, he does not appear to have been discussing political obligation or the nature of the English state in terms of an ancient constitution. The liberties of Englishmen in his scheme of things were simply a *quid pro quo* of obedience.

William Lambarde's public remarks on the Charter occur in a charge he delivered at the Michaelmas meeting of the Kentish sessions of the peace in 1586. It is important to stress that Lambarde's utterance on this occasion

[71] Thompson, *Magna Carta*, pp. 216–22.
[72] *The Argument of Master Nicholas Fuller in the Case of Thomas Lad and Richard Maunsell* ([London], 1607), pp. 13–14.
[73] Crompton, *A Short Declaration of the Ende of Traytors*, E4v-F.

was even less than Crompton's a statement of any kind of systematic political theory. His primary aim was to convince the grand jurors to whom he was speaking that they should participate actively in what Lambarde saw as the essential purposes of quarter sessions: the encouragement of public virtue and the punishment of vice. Nevertheless, his analysis of the origins of Magna Carta makes interesting reading:

> The times hath been when the nobility and commons of this realm have (with all humility and heart's desire) begged at the hands of their princes the continuation of their country laws and customs; and not prevailing so, they have armed themselves and have sought by force and with the adventure of their honors, goods, and lives to extort it from them. But we (God's name be blessed for it) do live in such a time and under such a prince as we need not to make suit, much less to move war, for our country laws and liberties. We have no cause to strive so much and so long about Magna Charta, the Great Charter of England, as it was called. For our prince hath therein already prevented us, so that not only the parts of the Great Charter but also many other laws and statutes no less fit and profitable for us than they are freely yielded unto us.[74]

In many respects, this speech certainly sails very close to ancient constitutionalism. Such an interpretation may seem all the more justified when it is recalled that Lambarde was a leading Elizabethan antiquarian who published a Latin translation of Anglo-Saxon laws.[75] Nevertheless, he should not be stereotyped too rashly. His heavily annotated copy of *Tractatus de iuris arte duorum clarissimorum iurisconsul Ioannis Corassii et Ioachimi Hopperi*, purchased just one year after it was published, shows that he was in fact a follower of continental legal science of the non-historical variety.[76] As we have seen, he had a general theory about the origins of political society which appears to have presupposed a degree of popular participation in the framing of government.[77] Furthermore, Lambarde was well aware that important changes had taken place in the nature of English legal institutions since the Conquest, not to mention before it. He believed that William I had ruled as a conqueror, and that parliament was for a short time discontinued as a consequence of the Norman invasion. In his textbook for justices of the peace, *Eirenarcha*, he equates the creation of royally appointed justices of the peace by Edward III with the time when 'the election of the simple Conservators or Wardens of the Peace, was first taken from the people, and translated to the assignment of the king'.[78] At the point at which his historical

---

[74] Read, ed., *William Lambarde and Local Government*, pp. 79–80.

[75] W. Lambard, *Archaionomia: sive de priscis Anglorum legibus libri ... G. Lambardo interprete* (London, 1568).

[76] See n. 20 above.

[77] Lambarde, *Archion*, pp. 20, 108–10.

[78] William Lambarde, *Eirenarcha: or Of the Office of the Justices of Peace in Two Bookes* (London, 1581), pp. 20–21.

and his legal thought met, Lambarde was seeking in the past for an ideal constitution which embodied a large degree of participation at both the national and the local level, and as near a perfect expression of justice as possible. He was not necessarily arguing for particular laws or institutions simply because they had a long history.

All qualifications notwithstanding, these references to the Charter remain intriguing. In one sense, they undoubtedly reflect a legal and political chauvinism which can be traced back at least as far as Fortescue. In another, they illustrate the way in which the classically inspired ideal of the rule of law paved the way for a notion that such rule should be based on traditional practices and procedures, the native law of the realm. This idea was likely to have been particularly appealing to writers such as Lambarde, Morice and Beale who would have been well aware of simultaneous scholarly efforts to prove that, in spite of papal usurpation, royal supremacy over the English church dated back to the days of primitive Christianity. In any case, it was a fairly common precept of juristic humanism that laws should be well suited to the people they governed.[79] Magna Carta and other ancient statutes had long been used to illustrate due process of law within the English system. For this reason, if no other, it was bound to be of fundamental interest to English lawyers.

The references by Crompton and Lambarde to Magna Carta and the ancient customs of the English were made in speeches delivered to lesser gentry and yeoman farmers (the men who served as jurors at quarter sessions). Were they adopting such reference points because they felt they would have a particularly convincing impact on their audiences? This introduces the problem of how the Charter was perceived at the popular level, not an easy matter to resolve. If reissues of the Charter were read aloud in the county courts of the thirteenth century,[80] it enjoyed no comparable exposure in the sixteenth. On the other hand, the idea that there was a prescriptive process by which customs became law as a result of usage beyond the memory of men may have been relatively well known in the world of truly unwritten law which surrounded the activities of manorial courts. In this sense, the notion that there was an ancient constitution which had proved itself over time may well have been grasped easily by ordinary people. The difficulty is that there is not much evidence that this was in fact the case. Faith Thompson found that, throughout the sixteenth and the early seventeenth centuries, Magna Carta was much more frequently referred to by lawyers than by laymen.[81] As we have seen, although lawyers thought a good deal about law and government, ancient constitutionalism was not in the

[79] *The Six Bookes of A Common-Weale: Written by I. Bodin, a Famous Lawyer, and a Man of Great Experience in Matters of State. Out of the French and Latine Copies, Done into English by Richard Knolles* (London, 1606), pp. 469–70.
[80] J. C. Holt, *Magna Carta* (Cambridge, 1965), p. 288.
[81] Thompson, *Magna Carta*, p. 279.

sixteenth century a major component of the ideology which they exchanged with the public. Instead, they advocated the rule of law and justice, usually being willing to allow that any statute, including Magna Carta, could be changed by parliament to bring English law into line with the laws of reason and the laws of God. Nor did they need to believe in immemorial laws in order to define a tyrant.

If ancient constitutionalism and Magna Carta were relatively insignificant in the sixteenth century, the task remains of trying to explain, briefly, why they became more important in the seventeenth. At this point it is necessary to offer an interpretation of how their leading proponent, Sir Edward Coke, came to employ the concept of 'immemorial usage' as a way of discovering the 'reason' which Cicero had claimed was inherent in all laws.

Much depended on a set of circumstances which made older modes of common law thought vulnerable at about the time James I came south from Scotland to the throne of England in 1603. On the one hand, lawyers were facing serious public criticisms because they seemed unable to solve the administrative and professional problems associated with the sixteenth-century increase in litigation; and because their system of judge-made law was extremely susceptible to the charge that it was uncertain.[82] 'Right reason' as a basis of decision-making raised suspicions that the law was nothing more than what a particular judge willed it to be at any given moment.[83] The writings of many of the leading figures of the first fifteen years of the seventeenth century – Bacon, Coke, Davies, Ellesmere, Selden, for example – display a great defensiveness about the common law and its practitioners.[84]

No less important, lawyers also had to come to terms with the accession of James I. The new king brought with him a sophisticated and clearly articulated argument in favour of an absolute monarchy which upheld, but which was essentially unbounded by, law.[85] Even more disturbingly, one of his major political ambitions was the creation of a union between the kingdoms of England and Scotland.[86] While nearly all Englishmen seem to

---

[82] Brooks, *Pettyfoggers and Vipers of the Commonwealth*, ch. 7.

[83] See, for example, D. E. C. Yale, ed., *Epieikeia: A Dialogue on Equity in Three Parts*, Yale Law Library Publications, 13 (New Haven, CT, 1953), p. 25; and BL, MS Add. 41613, fol. 81vff, 'The Course of the Lawes of England and the Abuses of the Ministers Thereof Laid open'.

[84] Knafla, *Law and Politics in Jacobean England*, p. 274; F. Bacon, 'Maxims of the Law', *Works*, ed. J. Spedding (14 vols, London, 1857–74), vii, pp. 315–19; Sir John Davies, 'Discourse of the Common Law' (1615), in *The Complete Works of Sir John Davies*, ed. A. B. Grosart (3 vols, London, 1869–76), ii, pp. 263–72; J. Selden, 'Notes on Sir John Fortescue, *De laudibus legum Angliae*', *Opera omnia* (3 vols, London, 1726), iii, p. 1183.

[85] 'The Trew Law of Free Monarchies: or The Reciprock and Mutuall Duetie Betwixt a Free King and his Natural Subjects', *The Political Works of James I*, ed. C. H. McIlwain (Cambridge, MA, 1918), esp. pp. 61–64.

[86] Bruce Galloway, *The Union of England and Scotland, 1603–1608* (Edinburgh, 1986).

have hated this prospect on purely racial grounds, many also realised that a 'perfect' union of the two kingdoms would require a union of laws. Hence a defence of the uniqueness of the common law became a politic means of opposing the union. At the same time, the possibility of such an amalgamation of laws led some lawyers to contemplate the relationship between systems of laws and the societies in which they worked. For example, Sir John Dodderidge's 'A Brief Consideracon of the Unyon of Two Kingedomes in the Handes of One Kinge' noted:

> By the unyon of kingedomes, a totall alteracon of lawes of those nacons, or at least of one of them is introduced. But lawes were never in any kingedome totallie altered without great danger to the whole State. And therefore it is well said by the Interpreters of Aristotle, that lawes are not to be chaunged but with ... cautions and circumspectons ... no Nacon willinglie doth alter theire lawes to the which they have bene borne, and brought upp, as the provinces of Netherland maye well witnes ...[87]

The gradual emergence of Coke's view of the ancient constitution in his published *Reports* was influenced by these same factors, although there was yet another, a controversy with the English Jesuit Robert Parsons, which also played a vital part.

The prefaces of the first two of Coke's *Reports*, published in 1600 and 1602 respectively, offer much in the way of praise for English law, being primarily concerned with the need to maintain its certainty by establishing better law reporting.[88] But in the *Fourth Reports*, which was published in 1604, Coke began to address the issues which arose in the wake of James I's accession one year earlier. His basic message was that changes in the law were dangerous. Furthermore, he explained clearly his view on the relationship between the law and monarchy:

> The King is under no man, but only God and the law; for the law makes the King: therefore let the King attribute that to the law, which from the law he hath received, to wit, power and dominion; for where will and not law, doth sway, there is no king.[89]

Similarly, in the *Fifth Reports* (1605), Coke expressed a sentiment which was particularly appropriate in the context of the Anglo-Scottish Union: the common law is our birthright and the best inheritance that the subject has.[90] Somewhat incidentally, in his discussion of Cowdrey's Case, he also claimed that the Protestant church in England had existed since the beginning of

---

[87] BL, MS Sloane 3479, fos 60–61.

[88] *Les reports de Edward Coke, l'attorney generall le roigne* (London, 1600), 'To the Reader'. The preface is headed by a quotation from Cicero: 'Lex est certa ratio'; E. Coke, *Le second parte des reportes* (London, 1602).

[89] *Le quart part des reportes del Edward Coke* (London, 1604), sig. [B5].

[90] *Quinta pars relationum ... The Fift Part* (London, 1604), 'To the Reader'.

Christianity. It was this assertion which brought forth a published attack on
the *Fifth Reports* by Parsons, whose main point was that he did not see how
Coke could justify this claim, since there was little evidence about the law
before the Conquest. Parsons argued instead that the common law had been
brought in by William of Normandy. If it was the birthright of any, it
benefited very few.[91]

In the sixth of his *Reports* (1607), Coke made a point of saying that he
was not going to bother to answer the criticisms made by Parsons. But in
fact his most strenuous efforts to prove the antiquity of the common laws
and to nullify the consequences of the Norman Conquest began at this
point.[92] The *Seventh Reports* (1608) provided a brief interlude from the
historical theme, but in the *Eighth* (1611) he returned to criticisms that had
been raised against his claim for the antiquity of English law, and joined
issue with unnamed historiographers who wanted to see more of his evidence.[93] By the time of the publication of the *Ninth Reports* in 1613, Sir
Edward had found that the 'light touch' he had given his recent publications
by including history in them had been successful with readers, so he churned
up some more exhibits 'which I am persuaded will add to their satisfaction
and solace therein, who do reverence and love (as all men ought) the national
laws of their native country'.[94]

Ancient constitutionalism as formulated by Sir Edward Coke was a response to a particular set of political, religious and legal conditions. It was
not the product of a deep rooted mentality, even though it is easy to see
how the idea of the singular importance of the rule of law, even political
neostoicism itself, could lead to a view that government in England was
defined by a set of ancient legal practices which had proved themselves over
time. It was a handy way to argue for the rule of law without having to
make commitments about the nature of political obligation. Nevertheless,
ancient constitutionalism had so few clear antecedents in sixteenth-century
English thought that it is tempting to suggest that its systematic formulation
may have owed something to the importation of foreign ideas. In its hatred
of popery and in its insistence on the existence of ancient liberties, which
could be proved by the study of the past, English ancient constitutionalism
bears a number of resemblances to the work of the French Protestant
François Hotman, in particular to his *Francogallia*. Hotman's political radi-
calism, his disparagement of Coke's hero, Littleton, and his paradoxical
hatred of lawyers undoubtedly made his name one with which Coke would

[91] [Robert Parsons], *An Answere to the Fifth Part of Reports, Lately Set Forth by Syr Edward Cooke, Knight, the Kings Attorney Generall, Concerning the Ancient and Moderne Muncipall Lawes of England Which Do Apperteyne to Spiritual Power and Iurisdiction. By a Catholic Divine* ([St Omer], 1606), preface, pp. 12–16.

[92] *Le size part des reports* (London, 1607), 'To the Reader'.

[93] *La huictme part des reports* (London, 1611), 'To the Reader'.

[94] *La neufme part des reports* (London, 1613), 'To the Reader'.

not like to have been associated.[95] Yet Hotman's works were certainly known in late sixteenth-century England. As we have seen already, John Dodderidge, a member of the legal circle connected with Thomas Sackville, Lord Buckhurst, and which also included Coke, ranked Hotman among the most important of authors to be consulted in connection with a treatise on the royal prerogative. Furthermore, Hotman's son and literary executor, Jean, resided in England for a lengthy period during the 1580s. He became a friend of the courtier Sir Philip Sidney, and secretary to the queen's favourite, the earl of Leicester, during the latter's military campaign in the Netherlands in 1586.[96]

To reapply a phrase from F. W. Maitland, a Roman reception in sixteenth-century England did lead to something of a Gothic revival in the seventeenth. What must also be stressed, however, is that many aspects of sixteenth-century legal thought survived into the seventeenth century as well. Any analysis of the relationship between law and politics in the early Stuart period which depends exclusively on a common law mind whose main component is ancient constitutionalism is doomed to failure.

To argue this is not to deny the importance of the common law mind, but to enrich it. As Professor Judson found some years ago, the ideal of the rule of law was as much a commonplace in the seventeenth century as it was in the sixteenth.[97] As in the sixteenth, the political significance of this commonplace could be elaborated by both lawyers and laymen alike in a number of different ways. For those with a puritan cast of mind, the idea that human law should conform to the law of God led to calls that the laws of England should be remodelled in accordance with Mosaic law. For many the logic of the fight against social and political chaos led mainly to an acceptance of the necessity for obedience to the established monarch. For others, it was associated with a state ruled by laws made jointly by king and parliament.[98] This latter view may in fact have been the one which was most often supplanted in the seventeenth century by the ancient constitutionalist argument. The fact that lawyers found it necessary to employ history in order to secure the liberties of Englishmen is a testimony both to the success of the early Stuarts in promoting divine right monarchy and to the fact that by the early seventeenth century contractual arguments had been seriously tainted by popery.[99]

---

[95] *Francogallia by Francois Hotman*, ed. and translated by R. E. Giesey and J. H. M. Salmon (Cambridge, 1972), pp. 497–513, for Hotman on lawyers; E. Coke, *La dixme part* (London, 1614), preface, for Coke on Hotman.

[96] *Francogallia*, ed. Giesey and Salmon, pp. 109–10.

[97] M. A. Jusdon, *The Crisis of the Constitution: An Essay in Constitutional and Political Thought in England, 1603–1645* (New Brunswick, NJ, 1949).

[98] I hope to deal elsewhere with the relationship between legal and political thought in the early seventeenth century.

[99] J. P. Sommerville, *Politics and Ideology in England, 1603–1640* (London, 1986).

The ideal of the rule of law also had a logic of its own which arguably made a significant contribution to the political and social culture of the period. This is not to deny that the idea in some form already had a long history in 1500,[100] but to observe that during the sixteenth century it was quite regularly promoted by a large legal profession, and at times by the state itself, to levels of the population which reached down to the tenants of manorial courts. There were significant differences between the lawyers' idea of a society, in which order was maintained through equality before the law, and other strands of early modern political thought, such as those which emphasised hierarchy and those which prescribed deferential obedience based on a patriarchal concept of authority. In this respect legal ideology has been unduly neglected in recent historiography as a factor in shaping the mentalities of governors and governed between the Reformation and the outbreak of the Civil War in 1642.

Legal thought did not stress that England was a society of orders – ideally law was no respecter of persons. Nor did it very often see political society as a body politic in which all the parts were assigned their proper place and function, just as head and feet have their proper roles in the human body. Lawyers certainly advocated obedience to established authority, but they usually argued the case in terms of the self-interest of the individual and rarely in the sixteenth century utilised patriarchal arguments in which the duty to obey the prince or local justice of the peace was derived from the Fifth Commandment (the injunction that children should obey their parents).[101] It is true that the necessity for order was frequently stressed, but this order was an alternative to a Hobbesian state of nature, not the maintenance of any particular social order. Conflict between the civil society of equals before the law (as advocated in legal thinking) and other notions about an ordered society can indeed be seen clearly in connection with reactions to the enormous increase in the number of lawsuits during the second half of the sixteenth century. Among many lay, patrician social critics, litigation was regarded as a dangerous phenomenon which threatened to allow tenants to vex their landlords and promised generally to upset the social order. Amongst legal thinkers, on the other hand, although there were critics of vexatious litigation, it was argued simply that lawsuits enabled men to redress the wrongs they thought had been committed against them.[102]

---

[100] I have been struck by Professor Holt's emphasis in *Magna Carta* on the extent of an awareness of justice and the rule of law in the county communities of the twelfth and thirteenth centuries.

[101] Many early modern historians see patriarchalism as the dominant social and political mentality of the late sixteenth and early seventeenth centuries. For an account, see Gordon J. Schochet, *Patriarchalism in Political Thought: The Authoritarian Family and Political Speculation and Attitudes Especially in Seventeenth-Century England* (Oxford, 1975).

[102] Brooks, *Pettyfoggers and Vipers of the Commonwealth*, pp. 132–36.

Magna Carta and ancient constitutionalism might have been significant in promoting such ideas, but the evidence suggests that for much of the sixteenth century they were not. Indeed, the importance of both in the seventeenth century depended largely on the existence of classically inspired attitudes towards law. Insofar as the concept of a civil society ruled by law became an important part of Anglo-American political discourse, perhaps even of the Anglo-American mentality, part of the story lies in the Renaissance jurisprudence of the sixteenth century.

9

Professions, Ideology and the 'Middling Sort of People', 1550–1650

There is a long tradition in social theory and historical writing which makes a connection between 'the rise of the professions', the evolution of the middle classes and the making of the modern industrial world. Consequently, it is often taken for granted that before 1750 the professions were numerically insignificant and tied largely to the interests of the aristocracy and gentry. Yet recent research on doctors, lawyers and clergymen is opening new perspectives which suggest that it is time to reconsider some of our preconceptions about the long-term history of the professions. Most notably, viewed from the sixteenth and seventeenth centuries, the social and numerical prominence of groups such as doctors and lawyers in the nineteenth and twentieth centuries appears much less singular than was previously imagined.[1]

Nor were the professions mere adjuncts of the elite. Between 1500 and 1700, 70 per cent of the most numerous medical practitioners, the apothecaries and surgeons, came from social backgrounds outside the landed gentry, and a third of those who did claim gentry parentage were in fact the children of the 'lesser' or parish gentry rather than the greater gentry (those who sat on commissions of the peace).[2] Well into the eighteenth century, apothecaries and surgeons were trained primarily by apprenticeship and were organised into guilds with institutional histories closely resembling those of other occupations.[3] Although they were educated mainly in the universities, the

---

[1] See above, Chapter 7, p. 184.

[2] C. Brooks, 'Apprenticeship, Social Mobility and the Middling Sort, 1550–1800', in J. Barry and C. Brooks, eds, *The Middling Sort of People: Culture, Society and Politics in England, 1550–1800* (Basingstoke, 1994), pp. 56–59.

[3] S. R. Roberts, 'The Personnel and Practice of Medicine in Tudor and Stuart England. Part I. The Provinces', *Medical History*, 6 (1962), pp. 363–82; M. Pelling and C. Webster, 'Medical Practitioners', in *Health, Medicine, and Mortality in the Sixteenth Century*, ed. C. Webster (Cambridge, 1979), pp. 166–67, 183, 225; M. Pelling, 'Appearance and Reality: Barber-Surgeons, the Body and Disease', in *London, 1500–1700: The Making of the Metropolis*, ed. A. L. Beier and Roger Finlay (London, 1986), pp. 82–112; E. Shelton-Jones, 'The Barber-Surgeons Company of London and Medical Education, 1540–1660' (unpublished M. Phil thesis, University of London, 1981); T. D. Whittet, 'The Apothecary in Provincial Guilds', *Medical History*, 8 (1964), pp. 245–73; C. Wall, H. C. Cameron and E. A. Underwood, *A History of the Worshipful Society of Apothecaries of London* (2 vols, Oxford, 1963), i, ch. 2; S. R. Roberts, 'The London Apothecaries and Medical Practice in Tudor and Stuart England' (unpublished London University Ph.D. thesis, 1964), pp. 201ff; G. Holmes, *Augustan England: Professions, State and*

social profile of the membership of the small and elitist Royal College of Physicians in London during the Tudor and Stuart period was much the same, and so too was that of the early seventeenth-century parish clergy, between two-thirds and three-quarters of whom were of non-gentry origins.[4] Even the lawyers conform to this pattern. Before 1640, the practising bar was drawn just about equally from gentry and non-gentry backgrounds. The much more numerous 'lower branch of the legal profession', the attorneys and solicitors, were recruited from the same social groups which supplied entrants to the more elite retail and mercantile trades. Clerkship, apprenticeship in everything but name, was the standard mode of training.[5]

Equally, although the rapacity and wealth of lawyers, in particular, were legendary, the prosperity of most professional men in the early modern period is best described as solid rather than spectacular. While some judges, barristers and crown law officers did achieve great riches, marry into the aristocracy, and obtain titles on their own account, the law was a high-risk career. Many barristers failed to establish large practices, although there is no doubt that some of them found their way into the gentry. Most attorneys lived in towns, where their social standing in the community was very likely to depend on the competition. In large, prosperous cities such as London, Bristol and Norwich, even a wealthy attorney would not have been as rich as the most successful merchant and would have wielded much less political power. By contrast, in smaller county towns, even shire towns which were administrative centres, such as Warwick or Stafford, attorneys had by 1640 emerged as part of the local elite. Much the same is true of medical practitioners.[6]

These findings, which derive mainly from mass-biographical studies, locate professional occupations within the social world of the merchant, the artisan and the yeoman farmer, as much as within that of the nobleman or greater country squire. In this chapter, they are the starting point for an attempt to explore further the relationship between the professions and the middling sort by looking at words rather than individuals. Concentrating mainly on lawyers and clergymen, it considers the professions as groups of men who produced and interpreted social and political ideology. It tries to probe the relationship between professional discourse and the urban and rural social groups between the gentry and the poor.

Society, 1680–1730 (London, 1982), pp. 191–92; D. Embleton, 'The Incorporated Company of Barber-Surgeons and Wax and Tallow Chandlers of Newcastle-upon-Tyne', *Archaeologia Aeliana*, 15 (1892), pp. 228–69; M. C. Barnet, 'The Barber-Surgeons of York', *Medical History*, 12 (1968), pp. 19–30.

    4 William Birken, 'The Social Problem of the English Physicians in the Early Seventeenth Century', *Medical History*, 31 (1987), pp. 9, 216; L. Stone, 'Social Mobility in England, 1500–1700', *Past and Present*, 33 (1966), p. 48.

    5 W. R. Prest, *The Rise of the Barristers: A Social History of the English Bar, 1590–1640* (Oxford, 1986), pp. 87–95; C. W. Brooks, *Pettyfoggers and Vipers of the Commonwealth: The 'Lower Branch' of the Legal Profession in Early Modern England* (Cambridge, 1986), pp. 242–47.

    6 Prest, *Barristers*, ch. 5; Brooks, *Pettyfoggers and Vipers*, pp. 272–78.

Religious, medical and legal rhetoric were important constituents of the early modern mental world. Clergymen, doctors and lawyers dealt with the state of men's souls, their bodies, and their relationship to the broader community. Their sermons, speeches, legal decisions and technical writings helped set the agenda and determine the content of public discourse in an age which was well aware of the importance of ideas in shaping consciousness, and hence as a source of power. To give but one example, although medical rhetoric is explored much less thoroughly in this chapter than it deserves to be, it was commonplace to diagnose problems in the body politic in terms of illnesses within the human body, and hence to draw on a language where harmony and balance were contrasted with distemper and corruption.[7]

Apart from notable exceptions in connection with theology and religion, there has been relatively little study of the making, propagation and reception of ideology in the sixteenth and seventeenth centuries.[8] Much recent work has been influenced by an inclination of historians of many different outlooks to draw their conclusions in terms of a dichotomy between supposed realms of elite versus 'popular' culture. Some deny that learned or professional discourse had much impact on the reality of political and economic relationships dominated by the power and interests of the ruling elite.[9] Others have argued that law and religion were hegemonic ideologies controlled by the state and the elite, which were imposed upon, and came into conflict with, traditional community values arising from family, neighbourhood or civic relationships.[10]

---

[7] For some concise comments on the political use of images of the body, see Kevin Sharpe, *Politics and Ideas in Early Stuart England: Essays and Studies* (London, 1989), pp. 61–63. Lack of space and the inadequate knowledge of the present author are the reasons why the politics of the body have not been pursued further in this essay, but for some perceptive and suggestive work, see R. Porter, ed., *Patients and Practitioners: Lay Perceptions of Medicine in Pre-Industrial Society* (Cambridge, 1985).

[8] Sharpe, *Politics and Ideas*, pp. 3–9, usefully explains some of the reasons for the failure of recent early modern historians to pursue the connection between 'ideas and events'.

[9] Extreme statements of what is now commonly described as the 'revisionist' view of seventeenth-century political history are, for example, A. Everitt, *The Community of Kent and the Great Rebellion* (London, 1966); and J. S. Morrill, *The Revolt of the Provinces* (London, 1976). Religion is now, however, widely accepted as a crucial determinate of political allegiance. See, for example, J. S. Morrill, 'The Religious Context of the English Civil War', *Transactions of the Royal Historical Society*, 5th series, 34 (1984), pp. 155–78; a number of the writers in Richard Cust and Ann Hughes, eds, *Conflict in Early Stuart England* (London, 1989) make strong cases for the importance of ideological conflict. None of these works looks at the sections of the population who dwelt beyond the studies of the learned or the social milieu of the gentry.

[10] This case is put in K. Wrightson, 'Two Concepts of Order: Justices, Constables, and Jurymen in Seventeenth-Century England', in *An Ungovernable People: The English and Their Law in the Seventeenth and Eighteenth Centuries*, ed. J. Brewer and J. Styles (London, 1980), pp. 21–46. See also C. B. Herrup, *The Common Peace: Participation and the Criminal Law in Seventeenth Century England* (Cambridge, 1987), ch. 1. However, there have been dissenting voices. See, for example, James Sharpe, 'The People and the Law', in *Popular Culture in Seventeenth-Century England*, ed. Barry Reay (London, 1985), pp. 244–70, and Eamon Duffy, 'The Godly and the Multitude in Stuart England', *The Seventeenth Century*, 1 (1986), pp. 31–55.

The middling sort rarely emerge from such studies as anything other than conduits for and absorbers of world views which they derived largely from other sources.[11] If they often seem to have been written out of the general political and social history of the period, that must be at least in part because they are assumed to have had little influence in determining the terms on which important issues were discussed. A failure to investigate the political and social idioms available to the social groups that composed the middling sort partly explains the confused and inconclusive state of recent writing about the relationship between social structure and politics in the Tudor and Stuart periods.[12]

The value of an examination of professional discourse in this connection is that its articulation in sermons, public speeches, private speculations and published tracts provides an insight into the ways in which a broad range of social and economic interests were mediated and expressed. Lawyers and clerics operated within broader ideologies to a degree manipulated and shaped by the Tudor and Stuart monarchs, as well as by the aristocracy and gentry. But professional ideology was also influenced by the self-perceptions and interests of practitioners and by the fact that the middling sort comprised their largest single source of clients and the audience for many of their public pronouncements.

The complexity of the social space occupied by the professions resulted in the persistent tensions which characterised legal and clerical thought throughout the period from the Reformation to the Civil War. There was a conflict between the professional desire to maintain a monopoly over specialised fields of knowledge and the belief that these were too important to society at large for them to be withheld. The assertion of authority was counterbalanced by a tendency both to proselytise and to find a language of persuasion which would strike chords within a wider population. Despite the connections between them and the political and social elite, the dependence of the professions on a broader constituency meant that the ideologies they articulated, and hence the general political language of the day, was much less monolithic than is sometimes assumed. Although the term 'middling sort' does not appear all that often by name, the 'people' outside the ruling elite emerge as an important contemporary category of analysis, one that had a significant impact, for example, on the way in which legal and religious language was mobilised by propagandists for both the royalist and parliamentarian causes during the Civil War. At the same time, by the later 1640s one of the most powerful popular onslaughts in English history had been mounted on the professional monopolies and practices of clergymen, doctors and lawyers.

---

[11] For a subtle statement of this view, which does nevertheless acknowledge the importance of the middling sort, see K. Wrightson, *English Society, 1580–1680* (London, 1982), 'Conclusion'.

[12] This issue is put in historiographical context by Cust and Hughes, *Conflict*, pp. 33–38.

To say that the Tudor and Stuart monarchy and the learned professions were mutually supportive is hardly an exaggeration. The crown and its servants had considerable sources of patronage, including the power to appoint bishops and judges. Equally, given the limited coercive powers available to the state, it was widely appreciated that rhetoric was an important weapon in securing the compliance of the subject.[13] In this respect the professions, like the middling ranks more generally, supplied loyal subjects of the crown. The famous Elizabethan *Homily on Obedience* was backed up by numerous sermons which put forward powerful arguments for the obedience that subjects owed to the monarchy: kings had been appointed by God to rule and their subjects were obliged by this divine authority to obey.[14] Similarly, in the wake of the break from Rome in the 1530s, Henry VIII's government issued a set of general statements about the nature of political obligation which were designed to be used by stewards in the charges they addressed to juries of town courts, sheriff's tourns and manorial courts. Apart from a defence of the new royal supremacy over the church, the principal objectives were to remind subjects all over the realm that the king had been appointed by God to rule over the commonwealth, and that any disobedience was a violation of holy ordinances.[15] During the remainder of the period, speeches made primarily, though not exclusively, by lawyers on the nature of law and political authority became common features of the meetings of all local courts, from those of the manor to those presided over by the royal justices riding the assize circuits. Most of them undoubtedly promoted both royal authority and the existing social order.[16] As Sir Edward Coke, the most famous lawyer of the age, once put it, law and religion were twin pillars supporting the king's throne.[17]

There were also many strong links between the aristocracy, the gentry and at least the upper ranks of the professions. Clergymen depended on gentry patronage.[18] Bishops and judges sat in the House of Lords. Very few barristers made it as far as that in one lifetime, but many established places for themselves in the gentry and worked alongside other squires as justices of the peace, or sat as MPs in the House of Commons.[19] Furthermore, learning of the sort associated with the professions became an important element in a calculus of social differentiation which united the professions

[13] Stephen Greenblatt, 'Murdering Peasants: Status, Genre, and the Representation of Rebellion', in idem, ed., *Representing the English Renaissance* (Berkeley, CA, 1988), pp. 18–19, 29.

[14] J. Griffiths, ed., *Homilies Appointed to be Read in Churches in the Time of Queen Elizabeth* (London, 1857), pp. 95–99; Patrick Collinson, *The Religion of Protestants: The Church in English Society, 1559–1625* (Oxford, 1982), ch. 4.

[15] BL, MS Add. 48047, fos 59–61v.

[16] See, Chapter 8, pp. 210–11, for a quarter sessions charge by Sir Richard Crompton in 1587.

[17] *English Reports*, lxxvii, 11 Coke 70. Coke's Reports were originally published in separate volumes in Law French between 1600 and 1615 (see Chapter 8, pp. 225–27).

[18] See for example, Everitt, *Community of Kent*, pp. 33–55.

[19] Prest, *Rise of the Barristers*, ch. 5.

and the gentry. Professional occupations successfully claimed a special status because of their education and learning. Physicians and barristers were regularly described as esquires. Attorneys are difficult to identify in contemporary records because they invariably have 'gent' written after their names, and as such are indistinguishable from minor country squires and the upper reaches of the urban elite. At the same time, it became fashionable in the second half of the sixteenth century for the sons of the gentry to attend the universities of Oxford and Cambridge, and the inns of court and inns of chancery in London, places which were essentially academies for the professions.[20] While there is good reason to question exactly how much such 'students' learned, one of the most striking features of the early Stuart era was the apparent keenness of squires, and sometimes their wives, to sit down in the wainscoted studies of their country houses to work out their views on law, government and religion, or to add to the store of family medical knowledge.[21]

Despite all this, professional practitioners also had much in common with the middling sort, as well as an identity which was to a large extent based on their own view of themselves. As has already been observed, many professional occupations recruited from the prosperous townsmen and yeomen who made up local elites.[22] Based as it was on apprenticeship, the training of apothecaries, surgeons and attorneys was little different from that of other moderately affluent urban and rural social groups. Indeed, in an age when the culture of guilds was theoretically based on the possession of a specialised skill mastered through a long period of training, contemporaries did not draw distinctions between professions and other occupations as easily as we do today.[23] It was the type of learning which professionals possessed, rather than social status or institutional forms of

---

[20] L. Stone, 'The Education Revolution in England, 1500–1640', *Past and Present*, 28 (1964), pp. 41–80.

[21] For a telling contemporary observation, see *Wiltshire: The Topographical Collections of John Aubrey*, ed. John Edward Jackson (Devizes, 1862), p. 16. For examples, see V. M. Larminie, *The Godly Magistrate: The Private Philosophy and Public Life of Sir John Newdigate, 1571–1610*, Dugdale Society Occasional Papers, 28 (Oxford, 1982); BL, MS Add. 34239, Rodney of Stoke Rodney papers, fos 15, 21–27, 52ff; and Sir Edward Dering's concern for the education his sons were getting at Cambridge in the 1630s, P. A. Salt, 'The Origins of Sir Edward Dering's Attack on the Ecclesiastical Hierarchy, *c.* 1625–1640', *Historical Journal*, 30 (1987), p. 41. Elizabeth Brereton owned a copy of Ferdinando Pulton, *De Pace Regis et Regni viz A Treatise Declaring Which be the Great and Generall Offences of the Realme and the Chiefe Impediments of the Peace of the King and the Kingdome* (London, 1609), Bodleian Law Library, Oxford, shelf mark 35 e. 26. See also W. R. Prest, 'Law and Women's Rights in Early Modern England', *The Seventeenth Century*, 6 (1991), pp. 169–87. There are thought-provoking analyses of the significance of gentry education in M. E. James, *Family, Lineage and Civil Society: A Study of Society, Politics and Mentality in the Durham Region, 1500–1640* (Oxford, 1974), pp. 177–98; and idem, *Society, Politics and Culture: Studies in Early Modern England* (Cambridge, 1986), pp. 375–413.

[22] Wrightson, *English Society*, ch. 1.

[23] Brooks, *Pettyfoggers and Vipers*, pp. 270–72.

organisation, which set them apart from other groups, and which also added an independent dynamic to their thought.

According to the influential Cambridge theologian William Perkins, the callings of lawyer, schoolmaster, physician and minister of the word occupied the first place amongst all occupations because they alone required academic learning and judgment.[24] Some clergymen and lawyers went so far as to define their own importance in terms of their disciplines. In 1632, for instance, the Leicestershire clergyman Thomas Prestell was accused of claiming that the calling of a minister was higher than that of a king because, while the king had power only over the bodies of men, the minister had power over both the soul and the body.[25] If anything, lawyers were even more inclined than the clergy to promote their own self-esteem in terms of what they saw as the centrality of the institutions and ideas within which they worked. Thus, in a speech given at Grays Inn in 1589, Sir Christopher Yelverton began by saying that he could not 'sufficiently, nor amply enough magnifie the majestie and dignitie of the law'.[26]

If learning and knowledge united the professions, they were also the single most important sources of internal dissension within the various groups of doctors, lawyers and clergymen, and a cause of conflict with those whom they aimed to exclude from practice. The division which exists today within the English legal profession between the barrristers, who specialise in pleading in court, and solicitors, who traditionally have been associated with the practical side of legal work, has a history which stretches back into the middle ages, but it was strengthened during the early modern period largely because the inns of court, where barristers received their education, excluded the attorneys, who were trained by apprenticeship, from their membership.[27] Quarrels between the apothecaries and surgeons, who dealt in drugs or in the 'mechanical' or 'pragmatic' side of medical work, and the physicians, who were trained either at the universities or through the Royal College of Physicians, were a constant feature of medical history throughout the period from 1500–1730.[28] Furthermore, if plebeian tin-tub preachers and self-styled theologians were a thorn in the side of the clerics, there can be no doubt that any thorough consideration of the 'legal profession', and especially the medical men, would have to include the numerous practitioners who were in a formal sense imperfectly qualified.[29]

While controversies between the qualified and outsiders were often about

24 W. Perkins, 'A Treatise of the Vocations or Callings of Men', in *The Works of W. Perkins* (Cambridge, 1605), p. 915.
25 Henry E. Huntington Library, San Marino, CA, MSS Hastings, legal box 5/8.
26 BL, MS Additional 48,109, fos 12v–13v. For the remainder of the quotation see, Chapter 8, p. 207.
27 Brooks, *Pettyfoggers and Vipers*, pp. 173–81.
28 Wall, Cameron. Ashworth and Underwood, *Worshipful Society of Apothecaries*, i, pp. 82–192.
29 Brooks, *Pettyfoggers and Vipers*, ch. 3, pp. 141–45; Pelling and Webster, 'Medical Practitioners', in *Health, Medicine and Mortality*, pp. 165–235.

little more than the maintenance of social status and restrictive practices, in the minds of contemporaries they also involved attempts to maintain standards of professional service. In 1633, for example, Alice Mays, 'a doctoress or Doctor Woman', was tried for murder, the charge being that she had caused the death of patients she had treated in the vicinity of the town of King's Lynn. Although she claimed that she was qualified to dispense internal medicines by virtue of having studied 'learned physic' with eminent doctors in Cambridge and York, Alice's skills are perhaps best described as those of a 'cunning woman', an amateur herbalist who might also practise some magic. Despite several attempts by the authorities to try her, local juries refused to convict on the grounds that no one could convincingly establish that her prescriptions had killed. Thus it was left to the assize judge, Sir Robert Heath, to stop her from prescribing medicines to be taken internally. It was, he said, impossible that a 'silly [unlearned] woman' should have the skill to administer 'inward physic', but for 'outward applications' she might happen to have some knowledge.[30]

In a period when the skill of empirics, especially in the medical field, was often likely to have been as effective for the patient as the Galenic learning of physicians, distinctions between theoretical or scientific knowledge, which could be obtained from books, and empirical knowledge, which was accumulated through practice and observation, very often amounted to little more than a weapon in the struggle to maintain professional (and gender) hegemony, especially when it is clear that many empirics were hardly ignorant.[31] Although the evidence is ambiguous, those concerned with the case of Alice Mays were, after all, convinced that her cures were murderous. Another dimension of professional attitudes towards knowledge encouraged campaigns to improve standards of practice in the interest of the public, and to propagandise for the acceptance within society at large of the professionals' way of looking at the world.[32]

Inspired by the influence of humanist thought on education, and facilitated by the development of the printing trade, the first half of the sixteenth century was notable for the production of a large number of books which

---

[30] Norfolk Record Office, King's Lynn Borough Records, Book of Francis Parlett, recorder, fos 69vff; John Cotta, *A Short Discoverie of the Un-Observed Dangers of Severall Sorts of Ignorant and Unconsiderate Practisers of Physicke in Englande Profitable Not Onely for the Deceived Multitude, and Easie for Their Meane Capacitites, but Raising Reformed and More Advised Thoughts in the Best Understandings* (London, 1612), pp. 25–30, expresses the mutual suspicion which apparently characterised the relationship between physicians and women.

[31] The London Barber Surgeon's company carried out public dissections and the Apothecaries tested entrants to the company on their ability to read Latin. See Shelton-Jones, 'Barber-Surgeons of London', pp. 25–55, 64–68, 92, 97, 173–91; Guildhall Library, London, MS 8200/1, p. 209. For attorneys, see Brooks, *Pettyfoggers and Vipers*, pp. 173–81.

[32] See, for example, Cotta, *A Short Discoverie*, esp. pp. A3, 10, 21, 25; Wylliam Clowes, *A Prooved Practise for All Young Chirurgians* (London, 1588), p. 1, praises a Derbyshire attorney who had an allegedly unskilful surgeon banished from the county.

aimed to propagate knowledge both within the professions and to the wider public. The phenomenon can be illustrated in a nutshell by the publishing career of the Oxford educated physician and lawyer Thomas Phaer (1510–60). He translated Vergil's *Aeneid*, Englished a French work on childhood health and diseases, *The Regiment of Life* (1545), and edited a compilation of legal instruments, *The New Book of Presidents* (1543). Like many other Protestant 'commonwealth men' of his time, Phaer's inspiration was the conviction that the information he possessed was potentially useful for all ranks of society, a belief that it was wrong to keep 'the people in ignorance' by locking up the 'treasure' of knowledge in untranslated Latin works.[33] His example was followed during the course of the sixteenth century by large numbers of works written and published with the specific intention of making them available to the literate middling ranks of the population.[34] Amongst the more 'pragmatic' professions, especially, the power of the written word was perceived as a powerful tool for breaking through traditional ignorance.[35]

Alongside this enthusiasm for publishing, however, there was controversy about whether there should be limits on the dissemination of knowledge. Lawyers wanted to convince people of the benefits which would accrue to them by adhering to the rule of law. A powerful element in the vocational self-image of post-Reformation clergy was the idea that the objective of a Protestant preaching ministry was to guide their parishioners in the joint project of reading and interpreting the scriptures. But self-interest inevitably produced contrary arguments which reinforced professional claims to an authoritative monopoly over their fields of expertise. No less importantly, many contemporaries, lay and professional alike, were convinced that wider access to certain kinds of knowledge might threaten the political and social status quo.

The paradigmatic issue in both respects was the debate which began in the reign of Henry VIII about whether the Bible should be translated into English; who should read it; and how far the Protestant notion of a 'priesthood of all believers' entitled any man or woman, armed with the scriptures, to make their own interpretation of their relationship to God and the church.[36] There was a parallel debate about whether the law, which was written primarily in barbarous forms of Latin and Norman French, should be translated entirely into English and perhaps even

---

[33] Thomas Phaer, *The Regiment of Life: Wherunto is Added a Treatise of the Pestilence, with The Boke of Children, New Corrected and Enlarged* (London, 1545), sig. Aii-Aiii. For a fuller account, see C. W. Brooks, R. H. Helmholz and P. G. Stein, *Notaries Public in England since the Reformation* (Norwich, 1991), pp. 85–88.

[34] L. B. Wright, *Middle-Class Culture in Elizabethan England* (London, 1935), pp. 160ff.

[35] Clowes, *A Prooved Practise*, sig. A3.

[36] Measures to make the English Bible available in the 1530s were followed by a statute of 1542 which restricted its readership, 34 and 35 Henry VIII, c. 1. The Act for the Advancement of True Religion and for Abolishing False Doctrines was repealed under Edward VI.

codified.[37] For many lawyers, the example of the scriptures was, at the very least, a strong argument for wider publication. In his *Advancement of Learning*, for example, the polymath lawyer Sir Francis Bacon wrote: 'to say that a blind custom of obedience should be a surer obligation than duty taught and understood ... is to affirm that a blind man may tread surer by a guide than a seeing man can by light'.[38] Nevertheless, Bacon was contesting the notion that widening the availability of knowledge would undermine reverence for laws and government; indeed, after the first decade of the seventeenth century, although the publication of English legal manuals continued, calls for reforms in the language and structure of the law largely disappeared, not to resurface again until the 1640s.[39] In short, an impulse which stressed the importance of understanding and conscience in human behaviour conflicted with social, political and professional imperatives which stressed unqualified obedience and the expediency for the elite of keeping those over whom they ruled in ignorance. To take an economic and social illustration, at the same time as a steward in Lancashire practised the archaic Aristotelian technique of using songs to help manorial tenants remember their rights at law, another lawyer, William Barlee, protested to Lord Treasurer Burghley that some members of his profession opposed making the law of copyholds openly available in print because this would enable 'the common sort of people' to vex lords of manors.[40]

These debates about access to learned discourse were of more than theoretical interest. They had a practical significance because, throughout the Elizabethan and early Stuart periods, professional success depended very largely on the cultivation of work for people from a surprisingly broad social range, not least those who composed the middling sort. Work for the lesser gentry, the yeomanry, urban merchants and artisans constituted the bread and butter of barristers and attorneys, as indeed it also did for the medical practitioners.[41]

[37] Chapter 8, p. 208. It is also worth noticing Margaret Spufford's observation that the need to understand legal documents, such as bills and bonds, must have been as powerful an incentive for ordinary people to learn to read as Protestant emphasis on knowledge of the Bible, M. Spufford, 'The Limitations of the Probate Inventory', in John Chartres and David Hey, eds, *English Rural Society, 1500–1800: Essays in Honour of Joan Thirsk* (Cambridge, 1990), p. 173. See also, H. J. Graham, '"Our Tong Maternall Marvellously Amendyed and Augmented": The First Englishing and Printing of the Medieval Statutes at Large, 1530–33', *UCLA Law Review*, 13 (1965), pp. 58–98.

[38] *The Two Bookes of Francis Bacon: Of the Proficience and Advancement of Learning, Divine and Humane* (London, 1605), pp. 10–11. See also Margo Todd, *Christian Humanism and the Puritan Social Order* (Cambridge, 1987), ch. 6.

[39] See below, p. 257, although it is notable that in 1609 James I advocated making the law available in more systematic English works. C. H. McIlwain, ed., *The Political Works of James I Reprinted from the Edition of 1616* (Cambridge, MA, 1918), pp. 307, 311.

[40] Brooks, *Pettyfoggers and Vipers*, pp. 135, 200. See above, Chapter 2, pp. 24–25.

[41] See Chapters 2 and 4, pp. 14–16, 74–75. M. Pelling, 'Child Health as a Social Value in Early

Lawyers and clergymen, like apothecaries and surgeons, could not therefore avoid being aware of the interests of the population beyond the monarch, the aristocracy and the gentry. The important question is how far this fact can be said to have determined the character of social and political life during the period or to have influenced the content of professional ideology. For instance, while historians quite naturally accept that the rule of the gentry in the localities was based both on the deferential posture of their social inferiors and the control over legal processes which their positions as justices of the peace enabled them to exercise, the picture may not have seemed so clear-cut to contemporaries. Recent work on the criminal legal processes, on local officials such as constables, and the composition of juries at quarter sessions and assizes, has uncovered an important participatory role for members of the rural middling sort.[42] Equally, one of the most common criticisms of the increase in the number of lawyers during the period was that they encouraged ordinary people to go to law in the pursuit of their interests.[43] As one clergyman put it in the 1630s, the problem with the lawyer was that he 'flatteringly sheweth every man a fairer face how illfavoured soever he be. Thus can he persuade the simple swaine that his matter will bear a strong action' no matter how weak it really was.[44]

Since a large amount of public professional rhetoric was addressed to middling urban and rural social groups, it could not afford to be too far out of tune with their perceptions. An unusually intriguing illustration of this was the admission of the long-serving minister of Blackfriars, William Gouge, that the women in his congregation disagreed with his interpretation of the biblical duty of wives to subordinate themselves to their husbands.[45] Most clergymen regularly preached to congregations composed of ordinary people of moderate status. Consequently, many of the commonplaces of clerical thought were perfectly compatible with traditional urban and rural values. William Perkins' view of vocations, which stressed the importance of each man contentedly fulfilling his role in life, was little more than a theological gloss on a style of life which was familiar in urban guild culture.[46] The puritan stress on sobriety and self-control had a counterpart in the more secular notion of 'honesty', a set of values summarised by the life-sized statues depicting the civic virtues, Discipline, Justice, Fortitude, and Temperance,

Modern England', *Social History of Medicine*, 1 (1988), pp. 135–64.

42   Joan R. Kent, *The English Village Constable, 1580–1642: A Social and Administrative Study* (Oxford, 1986). Herrup, *The Common Peace*.

43   See Chapter 4, pp. 86–87.

44   National Library of Wales, Aberystwyth, MS 5932A, anonymous notebook of sermons written about 1635. No pagination.

45   *The Workes of William Gouge in Two Volumes: The First Domesticall Duties; The Second the Whole Armour of God* (London, 1627), epistle, sig. A3.

46   Perkins, 'A Treatise of the Vocations or Callings of Men', pp. 747–50; P. Seaver, 'The Puritan Work Ethic Revisited', *Journal of British Studies*, 19 (1980), pp. 35–53; and idem, *Wallington's World: A Puritan Artisan in Seventeenth-Century London* (Stanford, CA, 1985).

which adorned the entrance of the London's medieval Guildhall.[47] Even the patriarchal turn of much clerical thought was tailored to the concerns of merchants and artisans, not to mention apothecaries and barristers, who managed large households of servants and apprentices; men who also found it necessary to define their position with regard to other potential claimants to authority, their wives.[48]

It is true that the lawyers' vision of social relations in certain respects contrasted with, even though it did not necessarily oppose, some traditional rural values based on neighbourliness, or urban ones which stressed the non-contentious settlement of disputes in the search for 'charity' and 'love'.[49] But it is also notable that legal thought had little time for paternalism, deference or a hierarchical society unified by a great chain of being.[50] The rhetoric of the legal profession, moreover, consistently relied on persuasion as much as it did on authoritarian pronouncement. Speeches delivered to rural grand juries, whose ranks were filled by husbandmen, yeomen and the lesser gentry, or to urban corporations, frequently described the divine origins of monarchical authority, but the lawyers who made them were also quick to add that there was a practical inducement to obedience, one which was based on self-interest. Authority made possible the rule of law, and the rule of law prevented social and political chaos and protected the persons and property of the subjects from arbitrary power. In his address to the Shropshire grand jury in 1588 (which was later published), Richard Crompton stressed that in England loyalty was compensated for by traditional liberties such as the fact that the subjects were not liable to 'taxes or tallages' without their consent.[51] According to Sir Francis Ashley, who delivered a series of lectures on Magna Carta at the Middle Temple in 1616, the law enshrined not just franchises and special privileges, but 'liberties' and indeed 'freedoms' inheritable by all the freemen of England. These included the right to due process of law, trial by one's peers and protection against the

---

[47] John Stow, *A Survey of London*, ed. C. L. Kingsford (2 vols, Oxford, 1971), i, p. 272.

[48] For clerical patriarchalism, see Gordon J. Schochet, *Patriarchalism in Political Thought: The Authoritarian Family and Political Speculation and Attitudes Especially in Seventeenth-Century England* (Oxford, 1975); D. E. Underdown, 'The Taming of the Scold: The Enforcement of Patriarchal Authority in Early Modern England', in *Order and Disorder in Early Modern England*, ed. Anthony Fletcher and John Stevenson (Cambridge, 1985), pp. 116–36; Prest, *Rise of the Barristers*, pp. 123–26.

[49] Wrightson, *English Society*, pp. 51–57, 61–65. However, institutionalised forms of conflict resolution were also traditional features of both urban and rural communities. Steve Rappaport, *Worlds within Worlds: Structures of Life in Sixteenth-Century London* (Cambridge, 1989), pp. 201–14; Brooks, *Pettyfoggers and Vipers*, pp. 33–36.

[50] As David Underdown, *Revel, Riot and Rebellion: Popular Politics and Culture in England, 1603–1660* (Oxford, 1985), pp. 63, 66, reminds us, many popular customs were supported by the elite precisely because they were associated with hierarchy and deference.

[51] Richard Crompton, *A Short Declaration of the End of Traytors and False Conspirators against the State and the Duetie of Subjectes to Theyr Soveraigne Governour* (London, 1587), sigs E4v-F; see also Chapter 8, pp. 210–11, 221.

'oppressions' of landlords, justices of the peace and the ruling bodies of urban corporations. Like many other leading lawyers of the Jacobean period, he was clear that the royal grants of monopolies, which lined the pockets of courtiers at the expense of ordinary tradesmen, were against the law of the land.[52]

There was also a well-documented line in professional discourse which was openly hostile to abuses of power by the economically or socially over-mighty. It was an often-repeated tenant of Christian humanism that the powerful should not use their strength to oppress the weak.[53] In legal thought this precept found a number of practical expressions in ideas about the foundation of political societies, on the history of England, and in the notions of lawyers about the application of the rule of law itself. In his treatise on the *Origins of Cities*, an early seventeenth-century town clerk of Winchester, Henry Trussell, developed a perfectly conventional theme in his explanation of the reasons why government according to law was first instituted:

> When the distinction of property by *meum* and *tuum* had found out sufficient Combustible stuff to set Ambition on fire, and by the reflection thereof gave Avarice [means] to see how to increase its profit, as the other to extend its power, then the weakest went to the wall, And those that were simply modest were either enforced to serve others, or starve themselves, loosing either property, or liberty (nay often life) to the stronger ...[54]

If one of the purposes of political society was to protect the weak, and indeed the moderately well off, from the overmighty, a natural corollary was that abuses of power by the great magnates were an evil. As Sir Christopher Yelverton explained in a charge to an Elizabethan meeting of quarter sessions in Northamptonshire, the disobedience and oppressions of the great were a major source of danger to the state. If there were no laws to bridle them, neither could the people live quietly nor the prince rule safely.[55] In fact, apart from limited privileges accorded the titled nobility, the common law, as opposed to some parliamentary legislation, took little account of social status, as opposed to age or gender, as a criterion for decision-making.[56] In the words of an early seventeenth-century recorder of London, Sir Anthony Benn, the value of the rule of law was that it allowed '*every man*' (my italics) to go his own way and accumulate wealth.[57]

---

[52] BL, MS Harleian 4841.

[53] Todd, *Christian Humanism*, pp. 196ff; Fritz Caspari, *Humanism and the Social Order in Tudor England* (Chicago, 1954).

[54] Hampshire Record Office, Winchester, MS 107 M88/W23.

[55] BL, MS Add. 48109, fos 37–38, 42.

[56] Apart from sitting in the House of Lords, the most significant privileges of the nobility were probably exemption from torture, imprisonment and jury service for debt, *English Reports*, lxxvii, 12 Coke 96.

[57] Bedfordshire Record Office, Bedford, MS L28/49, 'God before All and All After the King by Sir Anthony Benn, Knight, Recorder of London' (*c.* 1610), [fol. 2].

Expressions such as these articulated a justification for political allegiance, and indeed the existing social order, in terms which took into account the interests of a 'people' outside the ruling elite.[58] Nor is there any doubt that in this context 'the people' included the middling sort. The Elizabethan legal writer William Lambarde made it plain that at least one of the many charges he delivered to Kentish grand juries was aimed specifically towards the 'middle sort' of small farmers.[59] A seventeenth-century treatise of knighthood refers to the 'yeomanry or common people', a group which was allegedly richer and more numerous in England than elsewhere.[60] Furthermore, since lawyers and clergymen, like other learned men of the period, drew their principal categories of political analysis from Aristotle, they would have been aware of the theoretical connection between the economic interests of various social groups and the ways in which these might find expression in the constitutional arrangements of particular states.[61] Apart from anything else, references to the alternative forms of government described by Aristotle frequently appeared in the speeches made at the opening of sessions of parliament by the lawyers appointed by the monarch to serve as speakers of the House of Commons.[62]

Given the potential significance of these simple equations about the relationship between social structure and the constitutions of states, it is hardly surprising that 'the people' was also a contested category. The legal notion that there was little technical difference between those below the rank of knight was important because it cut across other outlooks, which stressed social distinctions based on birth, status, education or the holding of office, while at the same time enabling 'the people' to be an expansive term in political discourse which could include the gentry as well as the

---

[58] According to the Gloucestershire clergyman John Corbet, many of these same values characterised those of the middling sort who supported the parliamentary cause in the 1640s, David Rollison, 'The Bourgeois Soul of John Smyth of Nibley', *Social History*, 12 (1987), pp. 325–26.

[59] Conyers Read, ed., *William Lambarde and Local Government: His 'Ephemeris' and Twenty-Nine Charges to Juries and Commissions* (Ithaca, NY, 1962), p. 167 (I am grateful to Keith Wrightson for this reference).

[60] Hertfordshire Record Office, Hertford, MS Gorhambury VIII. B. 108, 'A Treatise of Knighthood' (no pagination). This reference to yeoman farmers appears to be in the tradition of the well-known fifteenth-century judge, Sir John Fortescue, *De laudibus legum Angliae*, ed. S. B. Chrimes (Cambridge, 1942), p. 67–71, who stressed the unique character of England because there were large numbers of men of modest landed wealth who constituted juries.

[61] G. E. M. De Sainte Croix, *The Class Struggle in the Ancient Greek World* (London, 1981), pp. 70–76; *The Politics of Aristotle*, ed. Ernest Barker (Oxford, 1958), books IV-V; see above, Chapter 8, pp. 202–5.

[62] Folger Shakespeare Library, Washington, DC, MS Va 197, fol. 59v, where the speaker in 1575 is described as having given a lengthy account of sundry kinds of government; BL, MS Add. 48109, fos 18v–20, Sir Christopher Yelverton, 1597; E. S. Cope and W. H. Coates. eds, *Proceedings of the Short Parliament of 1640*, Camden Fourth Series, 19 (London, 1977), p. 127 (John Glanvill, 15 April 1640).

middling sort.[63] On the other hand, public descriptions of the forms of government inevitably came to the conclusion that monarchy was the most effective by far, while hierarchical ideas about the social and political order had a wide currency. Judges and justices of the peace, the holders of commissions from the king, certainly regarded themselves as the political superiors of the juries with whom they dealt at quarter sessions and assizes. In 1619, the judge Sir John Dodderidge was even the butt of a satire because he had apparently complained about the social quality of a Huntingdonshire jury.[64] In towns oligarchic progression, from disenfranchised apprentice to freeman, to common councillor, alderman and mayor, contributed to a distinction between rulers and ruled. While this boundary was in fact frequently challenged in the early seventeenth century, especially in connection with election disputes where freemen householders challenged oligarchic ruling bodies, there were limits. It was entirely natural for the puritan lawyer William Prynne to argue in the Tewkesbury election case of 1640 that the granting of the parliamentary vote to every inhabitant, including servants, women and almsmen, would enable the 'very scum of the people' to overrule the 'better sort'.[65] Since professional men, like the middling sort more generally, included individuals who might at any given point be either rulers or ruled, professional opinion about the political significance of the people altered over time and according to individual dispositions and circumstances.[66]

Some lawyers, like James Morice or William Lambarde in the Elizabethan period and John Selden in the early seventeenth century, envisaged the origins of political society emerging from a contract between ruler and the people.[67] Yet even if one concluded, as most probably did, that monarchical government was God-given rather than the product of human agency, it was a commonplace of humanist jurisprudence that laws worked best as a means of governing a society if the people had a hand in formulating them through a representative institution.[68] On the other hand, especially during

---

[63] Hertfordshire Record Office, Hertford, MS Gorhambury VIII. B. 108.

[64] 'A True List of the Jury Impanneled at Huntingdon Assizes before Judge Dodderidge', in W. Oldys and T. Park, eds, *The Harleian Miscellany: A Collection of Scarce, Curious and Entertaining Tracts* (10 vols, London, 1803–13), iii, p. 396.

[65] Northamptonshire Record Office, Northampton, MS Finch-Hatton 3467, opinions concerning the Higham election to the Short Parliament; Inner Temple Library, London, MS Petyt 511(23), fol. 1.

[66] For example, unless they held local offices, urban attorneys were not likely to be amongst the ruling councillors or aldermen, Brooks, *Pettyfoggers and Vipers*, pp. 209–17.

[67] See Chapter 8, pp. 211–14. John Selden, *Titles of Honour* (London, 1614), pp. 1–15. Although later editions of this work place less emphasis on the popular origins of government, it seems unlikely that Selden fundamentally changed his opinions. J. P. Sommerville, 'John Selden, the Law of Nature and the Origins of Government', *Historical Journal*, 27 (1984), pp. 437–48; D. S. Berkowitz, *John Selden's Formative Years: Politics and Society in Early Seventeenth-Century England* (Washington, DC, 1988), pp. 294–95.

[68] Chapter 8, p. 214.

the early seventeenth century, lawyers who were themselves amongst the rulers frequently detected too much interest by the people in matters which were above their station. Sir Anthony Benn observed that 'as into the ark of the highest misteries every Tinker will in these days be peeping, and not satisfied will also be prating, so there are in government and state affaires certain Eavesdroppers and wise fellows that will not only let and hinder this chariot ... but others there are that will be ever reforming the reins'. Elsewhere, in an unpublished essay, he revealingly associated popular disquiet about James I's financial difficulties with the puritan emphasis on the personal interpretation of the Bible. The one might lead to chaos in the state, just as the other produced the religious confusion of anabaptism.[69]

As for the clergy, while many surviving sermons emphasise the importance of obedience to established authority, they also show that the political role of the people was widely canvassed in controversial works designed to discredit the allegedly 'popular' political theories of the papists. Sermons delivered in the first two decades of the seventeenth century at meetings of local courts, such as quarter sessions and assizes, relentlessly describe and then reject Catholic monarchomach theories based on the principle of popular sovereignty. Bartholomew Parsons, a chaplain to the Bishop of Salisbury, explained to the Wiltshire assize court in 1614 the subversive doctrines of Cardinal Bellarmine, who allegedly held that all government depended on the 'consent of the multitude'.[70] Intriguingly, such sermons also frequently suggest that other members of the profession might not have been following the same line, and that even that 'the people' themselves might have opinions of their own. For instance, at the Warwick assizes in 1619, Samuel Burton pointed out that since the beginning of Christianity there had been foolish apostles who had mistakenly extended the idea of Christian liberty in order to argue that men were free from subjection and tribute. He claimed that the current age was addicted to speaking ill of rulers and criticised those 'zealous Preachers, which seem so dearly to tender the instruction of the people', but who spent all their time attacking maypoles rather than pressing 'the point of Obedience more closely to the Consciences of the People'.[71]

It is hardly surprising that sermons delivered before judges, lawyers and justices of the peace should emphasise the authority of the rulers, especially if, as seems the case, they evidently thought themselves under threat. But

---

[69] Bedfordshire Record Office, Bedford, MS L28/46, 'Essays of Sir Anthony Benn, Knight, Recorder of London', fos 44v–45; MS L28/49, 'God Before All and All After the King'.

[70] Bartholomew Parsons, *The Magistrates Charter Examined: or His Duty and Dignity Opened in a Sermon Preached at an Assizes Held at Sarum in the County of Wiltes on the Ninth Day of March, Last Past, 1614* (London, 1616), pp. 8–20. The work was dedicated to the judges Sir Henry Hobart and Laurence Tanfield, who had apparently approved of the sermon when they heard it delivered.

[71] Samuel Burton, *A Sermon Preached at the Generall Assises in Warwicke, The Third of March, Being the First Friday in Lent, 1619* (London 1620), pp. 1–20.

it is no less important to stress that in this period vigorous support for the
divinely appointed nature of authority could also be cast in language which
was designed to appeal to the merchants, tradesmen and professional men
who composed the urban elites. At King's Lynn in 1634, the recorder, Francis
Parlett, skilfully drew on the stock of traditional urban rhetoric about harmony and love in order to elaborate a patriarchal account of the authority
of governors and government. He told the mayor on his installation that
'The government you are to enter into is over a town consisting of divers
families, not by a natural necessity, but by a civil subordinate delegation
from him that is the supreme natural parent'. The metaphors which appear
most frequently in Parlett's numerous speeches to grand juries, and on
occasions of civic ceremonial, were ones based on love, community and
subordination. 'Love the town and it will love you. The oath of office is the
vow of matrimony. The mayor is the civil husband of a civil wife.'[72] On a
more practical level, this rhetorical support for the urban governors was
backed up by legal decisions which reinforced their grip on power. In a
famous opinion of 1598, the royal judges asserted that even in towns where
charters prescribed that mayors, aldermen and other officials were elected
by the commonalty (all the freemen), more recent ordinances limiting the
franchise to selected members were agreeable to the law because they
prevented popular disorder and confusion.[73]

If judicial decisions in general favoured the interests of richer urban
oligarchs, the law also formed the most effective means for townsmen outside
the ruling circles to express their grievances and concerns. Attorneys were
frequently to be found in the midst of the many challenges to local authorities
which were based on differing interpretations of charters or customary
practices.[74] A wide range of social relations arising out of apprenticeship
and trade practices were tested in the courts, and in London and provincial
towns it was common by the early seventeenth century for both individuals
and guilds to employ legal advisers.[75] It is an error to say that the judiciary
was completely hostile to guild control of economic activity, but prescriptive
corporate powers did tend to be narrowly interpreted.[76] In the famous case

[72] Norfolk Record Office, Norwich, 'Book of Francis Parlett', fos 6v–8, 11v, 72, 99–100. This
kind of political rhetoric was also characteristic of the Caroline court. See Kevin Sharpe, *Criticism
and Compliment: The Politics of Literature in the England of Charles I* (Cambridge, 1987), ch. 6.

[73] *English Reports*, lxxvi, 4 Coke 77b–78a.

[74] A number of examples are given in Brooks, *Pettyfoggers and Vipers*, pp. 220–23.

[75] Goldsmith's Company, Goldsmith's Hall, London, MS Court Minute Book N, part 1,
pp. 109–10: Attorney General Coke requests severe penalties against two men for making false
plate, 1597; Minute Book Q, part 1, pp. 57, 80: consultations with John Selden, William Noy
and Sir Edward Coke about the threat of the establishment of a new Royal Exchange, 1627–28.
Guildhall Library, London, MS 8200/1, pp. 283–4: two apothecaries represented by counsel in
a dispute concerning precedence within the Apothecaries Company, 1631.

[76] *English Reports*, lxxvi-lxxvii, 5 Coke 62b, *Chamberlain of London's Case* (1590); 8 Coke 113b,
Dr Bonham's Case (1610); 8 Coke 121b, *Case of the City of London* (1610), where the usefulness of
guilds for establishing 'good order and rule' is acknowledged.

of the Merchant Tailors of Ipswich (1615), the judges decided that, within limits, the common law right of every man to earn his own living outweighed the claims of corporate privilege.[77]

This last case, like a number of others brought by individuals, revealed the tensions which existed in legal thought between the imperatives of order and the rights an Englishman might reasonably expect to enjoy. In 1616, for instance, James Bagg, a burgess of Plymouth, brought a suit in the court of King's Bench to have himself reinstated as a freeman after he had been disenfranchised for criticising the mayor for carrying out his office 'foolishly', calling for the support of the other burgesses to throw him out of office and elect another.[78] The judges declared the disenfranchisement illegal because, in the words of Sir Edward Coke, such a course of action would force a man to close his shop and consequently ruin his trade, credit and means of earning a living. The freedom belonged to Bagg as his freehold for life and could not arbitrarily be taken from him. Lord Chancellor Ellesmere, on the other hand, criticised Coke's claim in this case that the King's Bench had the authority to apply considerations of due process of law in order to prevent alleged misgovernment which tended to oppress or wrong the subject. Perhaps facetiously, Coke's own published report of the case reminds his readers to note that much was said at the trial 'to exort Citizens and Burgesses to yield obedience and Reverence to the Chief Magistrates in their Cities and Boroughs, because they derive their authority from the King'.[79]

Neither the common law nor the Protestant religion were simply hegemonic ideologies which descended from London outwards and downwards to the rest of the population. Common access to the scriptures and notions of spiritual equality promised the literate middling sort some control over their religious lives, just as the ideal of the rule of law in theory guaranteed a certain degree of protection from arbitrary power in social and economic relationships. At the very least the public expressions of lawyers, like the sermons of the clergy, ensured that a generalised discourse about the nature of political life, and the place of the individual person in society, penetrated surprisingly deeply into the localities.[80] At the same time it is clear that the

---

[77] *English Reports*, lxxvii, 11 Coke 53a.

[78] This James Bagg seems to have been the father of the James Bagg, a client of the duke of Buckingham, who warned Buckingham that it was dangerous for Sir John Elyot's petition against the forced loan of 1626 to be circulated amongst the many-headed people. H. E. Hulme, *The Life of Sir John Eliot* (London, 1957), pp. 43, 62, 97, 170. Bagg Sr had served as a mayor of the town and had refused to contribute to the 'free gift' to the king in 1615, R. N. Wroth, *Calendar of the Plymouth Municipal Records* (Plymouth, 1893), pp. 21, 148. Nevertheless, he had friends in London to whom he complained about the injustices done to him by the mayor of Plymouth, *Acts of the Privy Council of England*, xxxiii, p. 411.

[79] *English Reports*, lxxvii, 11 Coke 93b.

[80] Brooks, Helmholz, and Stein, *Notaries Public*, pp. 82–91; see also Chapters 4 and 7, pp. 126–27, 191–92.

more general political impact of professional ideologies was hardly straight-forward. Although the common law, and puritan religious convictions, have frequently been depicted as the enemies of early Stuart government, as part of the ideological armoury which was employed against the king on the 'high road' to Civil Wars, this oversimplifies highly complex cultural con-structs.[81] As Patrick Collinson has argued, there was as much in puritan thought which coincided with conventional values as there was to challenge them.[82] The participatory characteristics which meant that the common law represented the interests of those outside the political elite also meant that those same social groups could find much that was satisfactory in existing social and political arrangements. If the king was the fountain of justice, the protector of social order and the property of the subjects, then the logic of the case that obedience to the monarchy was a practical as well as a moral duty could be compelling.[83]

It is no less misleading to reduce professional discourses to unifying or integrative ideologies which inevitably led to, or reflected, consensus within the wider population.[84] The Reformation and religious controversy during the sixteenth century meant that questions about political as well as moral authority were much more widely ventilated than they are today. The range of social interests and intellectual positions which influenced professional thought provided a potentially rich diversity of opinion. In times of political tension, such as the 1620s and 1630s, when unpopular royal policies in connection with war, taxation and religion produced expressions of discon-tent, arguments for both the crown and its critics were articulated in legal and religious rhetoric which had multivalent resonances, but which reveals distinctive views about the nature of politics and society.

Within the church, conflict emerged between the Arminian and puritan

---

[81] There is a long tradition, of which J. G. A. Pocock, *The Ancient Constitution and the Feudal Law: A Study of English Historical Thought in the Seventeenth Century. A Reissue with a Retrospect* (Cambridge, 1987; 1st edn 1957), has probably been the most influential in modern times. J. P. Sommerville, *Politics and Ideology in England, 1603–1640* (London, 1986), ch. 3, discusses some formal aspects of common law thought and refines Pocock. While he achieves a great deal in systematising legal thought, he oversimplifies its political impact. The works of Christopher Hill, especially *Puritanism and Revolution: Studies in Interpretation of the English Revolution of the Seventeenth Century* (London, 1958) and *Society and Puritanism in Pre-Revolutionary England* (London, 1964), make the case for religion. See also G. Burgess, *The Politics of the Ancient Constitution: An Introduction to English Political Thought, 1603–1642* (London, 1992).

[82] Collinson, *The Religion of Protestants*, ch. 4.

[83] John Rushworth, *Historical Collections: The Third Part in Two Volumes. Containing the Principal Matters Which Happened from the Meeting of the Parliament, November the 3rd 1640 to the End of the Year 1644* (London, 1692), i, pp. 294. Lord Keeper Coventry remined the judges, as they were about to go on circuit in June 1635, that one of the purposes of assizes was to give the 'People a better knowledge of Justice ... that they may bless God and the King for the same'.

[84] For references and criticisms of the relevant historiography, see Cust and Hughes, 'Introduction' in *Conflict in Early Stuart England*, pp. 4–6. For a sophisticated argument in favour of a more consensual view see, Sharpe, *Politics and Ideas*, pp. 3–75.

factions of the clergy. The former advocated the suppression of debate about contentious theological issues, increased episcopal control over the clergy and a return to more ritualistic forms of worship. The latter, by contrast, maintained their adherence to a preaching ministry, Calvinist theological doctrine and, according to their enemies, a greater say for ordinary laymen in the conduct of their spiritual lives.[85] A range of political opinion also existed within the legal profession. In both fields a general acceptance of the value of authority, and an ambivalent attitude towards the people, may well have provided common ground for the majority of practitioners. During the reigns of both James I and Charles I there were, however, a number of telling conflicts between some lawyers and some members of the Arminian faction of the clergy. These reflect the political impact of 'the people' outside the ruling elite on professional perceptions of politics.

In 1637, for example, just after the judges had delivered their decision in the famous case to determine the legality of Ship Money, a Northamptonshire clergyman called Thomas Harrison walked into the court of Common Pleas at Westminster and accused Sir Richard Hutton, one of the judges who had dissented from the majority decision in favour of the king, of treason and moving 'the people' to sedition.[86] Hutton eventually won an action of slander against Harrison, but this incident, along with others, appears to have stuck in the minds of members of the legal profession. In February 1640 the Northamptonshire lawyer Edward Bagshaw alluded to the case in the opening remarks of a lecture he gave at the Middle Temple on the relationship between the civil and ecclesiastical jurisdictions. In his view, both the ancient and honourable common law, as well as the lawyers, had recently been 'traduced in Pamphlets, jeered and derided in plays, and play books, and openly ridiculed and slandered at Bars at Law' by clergymen. In the event, Bagshaw's own lecture, which argued for limitations on the temporal authority of the churchmen, was suppressed by Charles I and Archbishop Laud; a rebuff which did not prevent the lawyer from riding out of London accompanied by fifty or sixty fellow members of the inns of court.[87]

While these and similar incidents reflect a professional animosity between the lawyers and the clergy which dated back at least as far as the break from Rome in the 1530s,[88] in the 1620s and 1630s broader issues were at stake. Thomas Harrison claimed that it was the opinion of all the 'Orthodox divines

---

[85] N. Tyacke, *Anti-Calvinists: The Rise of English Arminianism, c. 1590–1640* (Oxford, 1987).

[86] *Cobbett's Complete Collection of State Trials and Proceedings for High Treason and Other Crimes and Misdemeanors from the Earliest Period to the Present Time* (42 vols, London, 1809–98), iii, pp. 1369–76. See also W. R. Prest, ed., *The Diary of Sir Richard Hutton*, Selden Society supplementary series, 9 (London, 1991).

[87] BL, MS Hargrave 206, fol. 2v; MS Harleian 1222, fos 108–9; *A Just Vindication of the Questioned Part of the Reading of Edward Bagshaw* (London, 1660), pp. 1–7, explains his eventual disillusionment with the parliamentary cause. See also the comments Justice Croke made about the political ideas of the clergy during the Ship Money trial, *State Trials*, iii, p. 1186.

[88] J. Guy, *Tudor England* (Oxford, 1986), p. 372; Sommerville, *Politics and Ideology*, pp. 118–19.

in this Kingdom' that it was unlawful to refuse to pay Ship Money. From the 1620s, if not before, clergymen of an Arminian persuasion were turning arguments about the divine ordination of government into reminders of the dangers of popular rule, the necessity for obedience to the monarchy, and the right of kings to make levies against the property of their subjects.[89]

By contrast, one of the most persuasive elements in traditional legal ideology was the proposition that the law protected the lands and goods of the subjects, hence legal arguments in defence of property rights formed the basis for much of the criticism directed against royal policies between 1625 and the autumn of 1641. Whether or not an individual happened to accept theories about the divine ordination of government, it was a commonplace of juristic thought that there was an important distinction to be drawn between what was a described as a royal or lawful monarchy, where the king ruled according to the law of nature and protected the property of his subjects, and a seigniorial or lordly monarchy, where the king was lord of the goods and persons of his subjects, and where he ruled as the father of a family ruled over his slaves.[90] This connection between seigniorial monarchy and the absence of a clear right to property, or freedom of the person, lies behind much of the rhetoric of bondage, villeinage and slavery used by MPs critical of royal policies in both the later 1620s and during the early 1640s. In the parliament of 1628, for example, Francis Alford referred to the need to maintain a legal and royal monarchy. On the same occasion, Sir Dudley Digges said that a king not tied to laws was a king of slaves, and Sir Edward Coke pointed out that a lord might tax his villeins 'high and low, but this is against the franchise of the land for freeman'.[91]

These defences in parliament of rights to property clearly reflected the interests of the gentry as much as those of the middling sort. Yet, as the quotation from Coke suggests, what is particularly interesting is that they were couched in legal language associated with copyholders, that quintessential group of small farmers whose rights had undergone a significant transition during the Tudor period. Before the mid sixteenth century, copyholders were largely denied access to the common law courts. The judges held that copyhold was a form of base tenure, analogous to the bond tenure or villeinage which was associated in the middle ages with serfdom.[92]

---

[89] Ibid., chs 1, 4, 6. See also P. Lake, *Anglicans and Puritans? Presbyterianism and English Conformist Thought from Whitgift to Hooker* (London, 1988), esp. pp. 245–46.

[90] The critical source of this view was a work of continental jurisprudence which was widely known to English lawyers, Jean Bodin *The Six Bookes of a Commonweale: A Facsimile Reprint of the English Translation of 1606 Corrected and Supplemented in the Light of a New Comparison with the French and Latin Texts*, ed. Kenneth D. McRae (Cambridge, MA, 1962), esp. pp. 199–201, 210–12, but many also found it implicit in the thought of the thirteenth-century judge, Henry de Bracton. See also, Chapter 8, pp. 213–14, and Sommerville, *Politics and Ideology*, pp. 145–51.

[91] M. F. Keeler, M. J. Cole, and W. B. Bidwell, eds, *Proceedings in Parliament 1628* (6 vols, New Haven and London, 1984), ii, pp. 64, 66, 358; iii, p. 494.

[92] Brooks, *Pettyfoggers and Vipers*, pp. 86, 89.

The change came during the reign of Elizabeth, when the courts entertained the cases of copyholders and ruled against the claims of lords of manors to exact arbitrary or excessive entry fines from them. In 1600 Coke himself argued that 'if the lords might assess excessive fines at their pleasures', this would destroy copyholders and thereby ruin a 'great part of the realm'.[93] In his reading on Magna Carta in 1616, Sir Francis Ashley said that when a lord exacted excessive and unreasonable fines, this amounted to oppression contrary to the liberties of Englishmen.[94] In short, copyholders had become freemen of England, not bondmen subservient to a feudal lord who could make arbitrary claims on their property.

By 1628 the rights of all landholders, large and small, with respect to the most powerful lord in the realm, the king, were therefore being defended in a language which arose partly from professional jurisprudence and partly from the conflicts between small farmers and their landlords. There is no better single example of the influence of a group within the middling sort on professional discourse and, indeed, political ideology more generally. The message was also broadcast to a public outside parliament;[95] and, from the reign of James I, there was a consistent line of hostile reaction which explicitly associated lawyers with a dangerous brand of populism. The king was irritated by the 'sharpe edge and vaine popular humour of Lawyers that think they are not eloquent and bold spirited enough except they meddle with the king's prerogative'.[96] In a bitter attack on Sir Edward Coke, Lord Chancellor Ellesmere warned Coke's successor as chief justice of England, Sir Henry Montague, that 'it is dangerous in a Monarchy for a man holding a high and eminent place, to be ambitiously popular'.[97] A correspondent writing in 1634 about the death of attorney general William Noy noted that he had once been held in high esteem amongst the people for his extraordinary ability in the law and his courage in pleading the 'subjects' cause though against the King' in the 1620s. Since Noy had joined the king's service and been the architect of several notably unpopular fiscal policies, however, opinion had changed. 'Divers sorts of men now strike not

---

[93] *English Reports*, lxxvi-lxxvii, 4 Coke 27b, *Hobart v. Hammond*. See also 4 Coke 36b, 46; 11 Coke 42; 13 Coke, 1.

[94] BL, MS Harleian 4841, p. 50.

[95] An anonymous quarter sessions charge, which probably dates from the 1620s, declared 'Had we not this Guardian Angell of the Law to protect us we should be exposed to every Insulting and uncontrolled power ... our goods ... Ravished and snatched from us by violent exactions', Cambridge University Library, MS Dd. XIV. 3, fol. 213. Interestingly, in June 1632, Richard Neile, archbishop of York, expressed the concern of the privy council that clergymen ill-disposed towards the government were allowed to give assize sermons. *Historical Manuscripts Commission*, Fourteenth Report, appendix, part 4, *The Manuscripts of Lord Kenyon* (London, 1849) p. 49.

[96] BL, MS Hargrave 132, fol. 68v. The words are attributed to James I.

[97] Printed in *Cases collect and report per Sir Francis Moore, chivaler, serjeant del ley* (London, 1663), p. 827. There are several surviving manuscript copies.

to express a gladness that he is gone.'[98] Finally, one of Thomas Harrison's charges against Justice Hutton was that the judge had broadcast his dissenting opinion about Ship Money in speeches which he delivered on circuit. The alleged consequence was that all of Harrison's Northamptonshire parishioners were debating the validity of the levy. It is worth noting that there are a number of known instances where grievances against royal policy in the 1630s were expressed through the medium of the grand jury.[99]

There was, as always amongst lawyers and the clergy, an opposing line of thought which identified 'popularity' with a threat to the professions as well as to the king and the existing social order. Not surprisingly, given his background as a loyal servant to King Charles, the judge Sir Robert Heath in the 1630s spied a dangerous time when witchcraft and popular sedition shared a common disregard for divine authority. Attempts to promote a popular belief that laws, liberties and the privileges of parliament were at stake were little different from the faith in charms employed by the superstitious.[100] In a sermon which he delivered at Lincoln assizes in March 1637, a royal chaplain, Thomas Hurste, hit with comprehensive clarity on the issues which united the professions with the divine authority of the monarchy.[101] Speaking a few months after the judgment in the Ship Money case, Hurste quipped that some might think a discussion of 'the power of one man over another' either 'Apocryphall' or an 'Exchequer-chamber [the court where Ship Money was tried] case'. He justification for pursuing the question contained a dark warning:

> Some (especially inferiors) think that one should be as good as another: that as we were at our births, and shall be at our deaths, so in our lives we should be equal. Being Christian brethren in Divinity, and partaking the same Sacraments, so (Anabaptistically) we should bee in Politics; and the perching of one man over another is but human invention and commanding policy.

Hurste went on to point out that insurrection and rebellion always began with 'noise' for the 'liberties' or privileges of the people, but only became particularly dangerous when the bonds of conscience which were upheld by religion came under attack. Predictably, his response to this dangerous state of affairs was to assert the view that the authority of 'emperors' stands 'not only upon the crutches or stilts of human power, but upon the firm basis of divine institution that some should ride on horse-back, while others walk on foot'. He also warned his audience not to encourage the people by

---

[98] Somerset Record Office, Taunton, MS DD/PH 212/12. For an account of Noy's career see W. J. Jones, '"The Great Gamaliel of the Law": Mr Attorney Noye', *Huntington Library Quarterly*, 40 (1977), pp. 197–226.

[99] *State Trials*, iii, p. 1374. For examples of grand jury presentments, see E. S. Cope, *Politics without Parliaments, 1629–1640* (London, 1987), pp. 101–6, 150–51, 185–86, 194–95.

[100] BL, MS Egerton 2982, fos 81–83.

[101] For more detail on Hurste's career, see Clive Holmes, *Seventeenth-Century Lincolnshire* (Lincoln, 1980), pp. 112, 195.

throwing 'dirt' at the king's government. Aware that he was addressing a gathering of judges (including, incidentally, Sir Richard Hutton), lawyers and county magistrates, he also took particular care to point out how necessary it was for those who acted in the names of law and religion to maintain a solidarity with each other. 'The people' would neglect both callings if their practitioners did not substitute mutual support for mutual recrimination. '*Theologia* [and] *Ius* must *fraternizare*.'[102]

While it is a commonplace of early modern historiography that contemporaries lacked the vocabulary to make a class analysis of society and politics, the evidence presented in this chapter suggests that the proposition is only half true. The intellectual tools available to the learned professions, as well as pressure from their congregations and clients, meant that social groups between the poor and the elite were a constant preoccupation. Sometimes referred to specifically as the middling sort, but more often described simply as 'the people', they had been appealed to ever since the break from Rome in campaigns to publicise professional ways of looking at the world. Particularly during the 1620s and 1630s, a kind of populist politics was identified as a threat to authority, both monarchical and professional. In the hands of a writer like Thomas Hurste, the expression of this problem provides a penetrating contemporary guide to the fate of both political authority and the learned professions themselves during the calamitous years of civil war in the 1640s and 1650s.

During the Short Parliament, and in the first year of the Long Parliament, lawyers and laymen alike attacked royal policies and criticised the clergy for telling people that they had no rights to their liberty or property.[103] As many historians have observed, the critical question about the outbreak of the Civil War is how the king eventually gathered a party which would fight in his defence, and in this connection attacks on the established church and the traditional balance of the constitution played a major role.[104] As Thomas Hurste predicted in 1637, hostility to clerical politics and Arminian religious policies led to a profound questioning of both the episcopal structure of the English church and the control of the clergy over their profession as ministers of God. In January 1641 the Root and Branch petition, which called for the abolition of bishops, was presented to parliament accompanied by 30,000 signatures. It ushered in more than two decades of deeply divisive controversy

---

[102] Thomas Hurste, *The Descent of Authoritie: or The Magistrates Patent from Heaven. Manifested in a Sermon Preached at Lincoln Assizes, March 13, 1636* (London, 1637), pp. 1–3, 5, 26, 32.

[103] Cope and Coates, eds, *Proceedings of the Short Parliament of 1640*, pp. 136, 141, 153–54, 172, 178; Wallace Notestein, ed., *The Journal of Sir Simonds D'Ewes from the Beginning of the Long Parliament to the Opening of the Trial of the Earl of Strafford* (New Haven, CT, 1923), pp. 6, 7, 8–11. For the period generally, see Anthony Fletcher, *The Outbreak of the English Civil War* (London, 1981).

[104] S. R. Gardiner, *History of England from the Accession of James I to the Outbreak of the Civil War, 1603–1642* (10 vols, London, 1884), x, pp. 10–12, 59; Morrill, *Revolt of the Provinces*, p. 13.

about the degree to which the English people were entitled to select their own path to salvation rather than accept the one which was purveyed to them by the authority of the bishops, the established clergy and the Book of Common Prayer. Some of the sects which eventually emerged even went so far as to allow women into the pulpit.[105]

At the same time, a backlash of support for episcopacy was the principal cause around which a Royalist party began to coalesce in the autumn of 1641.[106] Although ostensibly religious matters, questions about the structure of the church were also professional problems. Seeing them as such can help us to understand that they involved the same fundamental questions about authority which had been at issue for more than a century. Royalist rhetoric was quick to draw the familiar analogy between a breakdown in the authority of the church and the collapse of civil authority more generally. For example, a petition from Cheshire criticised the use of pamphlets and pulpits to spread ideas 'dangerously exciting a disobedience to the established form of Government'. Stirring up the 'Common people' would lead to 'an Anarchy, which we have just cause to pray against, as fearing the consequence would prove the utter loss of learning and laws, which must necessarily produce an extermination of nobility, gentry, and order, if not religion'.[107]

Parliamentary propaganda, not surprisingly, exploited the more populist strand within professional thought. Writers, like the sometime barrister of Lincoln's Inn Henry Parker, aimed to show that since (as nearly everyone agreed) government was supposed to serve the people, it was logical to support parliament, the institution which claimed its authority in the name of the people. In addition, Parker in particular frequently buttressed his position by drawing on analogies from everyday legal practice. For instance, he explained that the right of the king to the property of his subjects was not the same as the property the king had in his horse. Instead, the king held his subjects' property in trust and, as everyone knew, a trustee who held to the use of another was responsible for protecting the property of the beneficiary, not laying it to waste. Although the king might be said to rule his subjects in the same way as a husband ruled his wife, both relationships

[105] K. V. Thomas, 'Women and the Civil War Sects', in *Crisis in Europe 1560–1600*, ed. Trevor Aston (New York, 1967), pp. 332–57.

[106] W. H. Coates, ed., *The Journal of Sir Simonds D'Ewes from the First Recess of the Long Parliament to the Withdrawal of King Charles from London* (New Haven, CT, 1942), pp. 14–15, 21, 24, 30, 44, 51, 112, 117, 133, 150–51, 165, 183, 187, 290, 327, 337.

[107] *A Collection of Sundry Petitions Presented to the Kings Most Excellent Majestie as also to the Two Most Honourable Houses, Now Assembled in Parliament: And Others. Already Signed, by Most the Gentry, Ministers, and Free-Holders of Severall Counties, in Behalfe of Episcopacie, Liturgie, and Supportation of Church-Revenues, and Suppression of Schismaticks. Collected by a Faithfull Lover of the Church, for the Comfort of the Dejected Clergy, and All Moderately Affected Protestants. Published by his Majesties Speciall Command* (London, 1642), pp. 2–3. *His Majesties Answer to the XIX Propositions of Both Houses of Parliament* (London 1642), pp. 11, 18, 22.

were in fact subject to the intervention of the law. Another author justified rebellion by arguing that since 'the People may be legally assembled to aprehend Robbers, nay to deliver a possession forceably detained against the sentence of some inferior court' it followed that they ought to 'bistirr themselves to keep in being and preserve that Government which maintains them in possession of their liberty and property'.[108]

As Conrad Russell has reminded us, the king, no less than parliament, had by 1642 adopted a stance which enabled him to claim that he was fighting for the rule of law and the maintenance of true religion. Yet to argue, as Russell does, from these facts to the conclusion that there were no significant expressions of ideological differences between the two sides is to ignore the evidence, which we have seen throughout the sixteenth and seventeenth centuries, of religious, legal and political discourse polarising around notions which stressed authority versus those which advocated openness and a greater or lesser degree of popular legitimisation.[109] An understanding of the political allegiance of the rich Dorsetshire squire, Sir John Strangeways, who had opposed royal policies in the 1620s but who became a royalist in 1640–41, may be found less in his views on the rule of law than in the fact that he was the patron of the English translator of a Spanish work which explicitly warned that popular forms of government took no account of the wealthy or virtuous and inclined towards the worst forms of tyranny. Strangeways was to gain first-hand experience of the threat. He complained, in November 1641, to the House of Commons that he had been intimidated outside Parliament by armed citizens of London demanding that he vote against the bishops.[110]

We have also seen that the language of authority, no less than that of popularity, had a wide currency and could strike chords amongst the many different constituencies within the middling sort. We should not dismiss the appeal of patriarchal arguments (which linked anarchy in the state with anarchy in the family, the disobedience of wives and an attack on property) to householders who wanted to hang onto their landholdings or maintain their position within the oligarchic, but fluid, course of life followed by urban merchants and artisans. Amongst the lawyers, as amongst the clergy, the choice of sides seems to have been a difficult one. As far as we can tell,

---

[108] [Henry Parker], *Some Few Observations upon his Majesties Late Answer to the Declaration or Remonstance of the Lords and Commons of the 19 of May 1642* (London, 1642), pp. 7, 8, 12, 15; Northamptonshire Record Office, Northampton, MS Finch Hatton 4132. Anonymous, undated, and unpaginated.

[109] Conrad Russell, *The Causes of the English Civil War* (Oxford, 1990), esp. ch. 6.

[110] Ibid., pp. 131–33. Juan de Santa Maria, *Policie Unveiled: Wherein May be Learned the Order of True Policy in Kingdomes and Commonwealths* (London, 1634), was translated by the sometime fellow of Magdalen College, Oxford, James Mabbe, who lived in Strangeways' house from 1627 until his death in 1642. See also *Dictionary of National Biography*; Coates, ed., *The Journal of Sir Simonds D'Ewes from the First Recess of the Long Parliament to the Withdrawal of King Charles from London*, p. 214.

while a scant majority supported the parliamentary cause, there were many waverers and defectors.[111]

For many in the professions, the course of events bore out the worst prognostications of royalist propaganda. As Thomas Hurste had forecast in 1637, challenges to the authority of the king and the bishops led first to impeachments of Caroline judges deemed to have betrayed the liberty of the subject,[112] and eventually to demands for the root and branch reform of the law and the legal profession.[113] Just as the abolition of bishops and the clerical monopoly over the ministry of the word was advocated in the name of religion, so too change in the legal system was demanded in terms of ideas about justice which had long been part of the populist vocabulary of legal discourse. For example, the Leveller John Warr based his case for radical reform on the principle that the primary function of the law was to protect the poor against the rich and to keep the rulers within the bounds of just and righteous government. Although based on different premises, many of his propositions could have come from the mouth of the likes of Sir Edward Coke three or four decades earlier.[114]

On the other hand, a common denominator of most calls for reform was hostility to the professional monopoly of the lawyers, accompanied by a desire to open up their secrets to all the people. For many, the translation of legal proceedings into English, which was accomplished (temporarily) in 1654, was the essential first step. In addition, there were proposals for making justice available in local courts where there would be few technicalities, where professional advice would be unnecessary, and where local freeholders would serve as the judges.[115] The radical ideal was that the resolution of disputes should be handed back to the community, and that everyman should be able to act as his own lawyer. The values of the rule of law, which the lawyers themselves had done so much to promote, were accepted, but corrupt human agency, which depended on an unjust monopoly over a valuable field of knowledge, was attacked. In this respect, calls for law reform had much in common with similar proposals for opening up all arts and sciences, from that of medicine to that of ordinary trades, to wider public access.[116]

It is typical of the relationship between the professions and society in this period that many of these proposals failed because they evidently failed to

111 Prest, *Rise of the Barristers*, pp. 276–80; Brooks, *Pettyfoggers and Vipers*, pp. 223–24.

112 W. J. Jones, *Politics and the Bench: The Judges and the Origins of the English Civil War* (London, 1971), pp. 137–48, 209–15.

113 See generally D. Veall, *The Popular Movement for Law Reform, 1640–1660* (Oxford, 1970).

114 John Warr, 'The Corruption and Deficiency of the Laws of England, Soberly Discovered: or Liberty Working up to its Just Height' (1649), *Harleian Miscellany*, iii, pp. 240–49.

115 Veall, *Popular Movement*. For the 1650s, see N. L. Matthews, *William Sheppard: Cromwell's Law Reformer* (Cambridge, 1984).

116 C. Webster, *The Great Instauration: Science, Medicine and Reform, 1626–1660* (London, 1975), pp. 131, 180, 256–61, 285.

generate sufficient support amongst the middling sort.[117] The Interregnum assault on the professions is final testimony to the influence of professional discourse in shaping the social and political values of the period. Despite the elements of self-interest which led professionals to maintain occupational closure or to ally themselves with the ruling elite, many elements of professional thought also expressed the aspirations and values of 'the people'. Although these were generally monarchical, they were not unself-interested. At the same time, different aspects of professional thought also reflect the fear of 'the people' by the elite and by professionals themselves. What we now need are more studies of how this complex relationship between the professions, professional thought and society at large changed and developed between 1650 and 1800.

[117] Brian Manning, *The English People and the English Revolution* (London, 1978), pp. 331, 339.

Index

—, comparisons of seventeenth-
and eighteenth-century calls for,
92
—, eighteenth-century calls for,
44–45, 47, 61–62, 95
—, in court of requests of City of
London, 99–101
—, Leveller demands for, 126
—, nineteenth-century, 101–8, 143,
168
—, twentieth-century, 121–22, 124
—, *see also* legal aid
Reformation, Protestant, 6, 126, 210,
216, 217–18, 235, 248, 249; *see also*
religion
regulation, moral and social, 89, 90, 191,
196, 197
religion, 5, 7, 246, 248, 255, 256; *see also*
Arminianism; Church of England;
clergy; oath *ex officio*; puritanism; Reformation; sermons
Renaissance, 205–7, 229
replevin, action of, 69
reports, law, 151, 188, 192, 194, 224–27
restrictive practices, *see* professions
retaining, 208–9, 215
Robin Hood, 209
Rodney, Sir Edward, 187
Roman history, 212, 213
Roman law, 200, 202, 227
Root and Branch Petition, 254
Rose, George, 139
Royal College of Physicians, *see* medical
practitioners
Ruggle, Thomas, 165, 166
Russell, C., 256
Ryder, Sir Dudley, 55–57

Sabean, D., 198
Sackville, Thomas, Lord Buckhurst, 208,
227
St German, Christopher, 203, 204
Santa Maria, Juan de, 256n
Scotland, Clerks to the Signet in, 138
—, rates of litigation in, 109
—, *see also* union, Anglo-Scottish
Scott, Sir John, Lord Eldon, 138
Sedley, Stephen, 122
Selden, John, 224, 245, 247n

self-interest, 189, 193, 195, 214, 242,
258
serjeants at law, 76, 96
sermons, 233, 234
—, at quarter sessions, 246
—, political attitudes expressed in,
235, 246, 253
sexual continence, 71; *see also* ecclesiastical courts; regulation
Sharpe, J. A., 27
Sheffield, 93, 160n
Ship Money, 194, 251, 252–53
Shrewsbury, 70, 72, 92
Shropshire, 242
Sidney, Sir Philip, 227
slander, 74, 127
—, in ecclesiastical courts, 71
—, in seventeenth century, 89, 90,
195, 250
—, in eighteenth century, 55–57,
—, in nineteenth century, 110–11,
123
—, in twentieth century, 128
Smith, Adam, 58, 164
Smith, John of Nibley, 17
Snagg, T. W., 106, 107
Snagge, Robert, 218
social change, *see* litigation
social hierarchy, 242, 245–46
social history, study of, 5, 189
social relations, 189
social structure and politics, 234–35, 254
societies, 142, 146–47, 151, 167
—, Articled Clerks', 175
—, Metropolitan and Provincial
Law, 143
—, of the Rose Garden, Bristol, 134
—, proposal for a college of
attorneys, 136–40
—, provincial law societies, 135–36,
137, 140
—, *see also* Law Society; Society of
Gentlemen Practisers
Society of Antiquaries, 213
Society of Gentlemen Practisers, 104,
134, 138–40, 141, 160n
Somerset, 21, 88, 105, 135, 187
Sonescher, M., 190
special pleading, 95, 153

Lightning Source UK Ltd.
Milton Keynes UK
UKOW06n2331100315

247601UK00010B/178/P